T0377689

SUSTAINABLE VALUE CREATION IN THE EUROPEAN UNION

The Treaty on European Union after Lisbon emphasises the overarching objectives of sustainable development and a highly competitive social market economy, aiming at full employment, high levels of environmental protection and social progress. Yet, in 2022, it is clear that these ambitions have not been fully achieved. The ongoing pandemic, the continuing fall-out from Brexit and the resulting economic damage, a Grexit avoided and potential other exits from the EU have come to undermine the political consensus of the idea of a European Union. Amidst these challenges, the debates on how to achieve the United Nations Sustainable Development Goals have turned towards demanding more sustainable economic policies, financial investments and business actions. This book provides a much-needed space for in-depth discussion of the concept of sustainable value creation and how it can be achieved within the ecological limits of our planet through the prism of an interdisciplinary concept of sustainability.

Beate Sjåfjell is Professor of Law at the University of Oslo and Visiting Professor at College of Europe.

Georgina Tsagas is Senior Lecturer in Private and Commercial Law, Brunel University London. She is a practising solicitor in England and Wales and a UK accredited mediator.

Charlotte Villiers is Professor of Company Law and Corporate Governance at the University of Bristol Law School.

Sustainable Value Creation in the European Union

TOWARDS PATHWAYS TO A SUSTAINABLE FUTURE THROUGH CRISES

Edited by

BEATE SJÅFJELL
University of Oslo

GEORGINA TSAGAS
Brunel University London

CHARLOTTE VILLIERS
University of Bristol

CAMBRIDGE UNIVERSITY PRESS

CAMBRIDGE
UNIVERSITY PRESS

University Printing House, Cambridge CB2 8BS, United Kingdom

One Liberty Plaza, 20th Floor, New York, NY 10006, USA

477 Williamstown Road, Port Melbourne, VIC 3207, Australia

314–321, 3rd Floor, Plot 3, Splendor Forum, Jasola District Centre, New Delhi – 110025, India

103 Penang Road, #05–06/07, Visioncrest Commercial, Singapore 238467

Cambridge University Press is part of the University of Cambridge.

It furthers the University's mission by disseminating knowledge in the pursuit of education, learning, and research at the highest international levels of excellence.

www.cambridge.org
Information on this title: www.cambridge.org/9781009243896
DOI: 10.1017/9781009243841

First published 2023

A catalogue record for this publication is available from the British Library.

A Cataloging-in-Publication data record for this book is available from the Library of Congress

ISBN 978-1-009-24389-6 Hardback

To the people of Greece, for their incredible kindness and hospitality (φιλοξενία) and their unwavering courage in difficult times

And to our families, past, present and future generations, especially:

my dearest daughter, Katarina, and my always supportive partner, Steinar (Beate Sjåfjell)

my mother, Julie, and in the loving memory of my father, Gregory (Georgina Tsagas)

my children, Amelia and Laurie, and my nephews, Joe and Alex, all young adults who provide me with much hope for the future of our beautiful planet and its people (Charlotte Villiers)

πῶς οὐκ τὴν εἰρήνην ποιητέον ἡμῖν;
'Why should it not be our duty to secure peace?'

Andocides. Minor Attic Orators in two
volumes 1, Antiphon Andocides

Contents

Figures

Tables

Contributors

Aikaterini Argyrou is an assistant professor at Nyenrode Business University and an external research affiliate at the Utrecht Centre for Water, Oceans and Sustainability Law. Her research focuses on the examination of normative frameworks that deliver substance to the concept of sustainability in entrepreneurship and company law with focus on social entrepreneurship. She obtained her PhD in 2018 from the Faculty of Law at Utrecht University. Her PhD dissertation was entitled 'Social Enterprises in the EU: Law Promoting Stakeholder Participation in Social Enterprises'. She is a qualified attorney in Greece and has been a member of the Athens Bar Association since 2012. Prior to her PhD studies (2011–13), she was involved in many corporate social responsibility (CSR) research projects in the Hague, the Netherlands.

Robert Jan Blomme is Associate Dean of Degree Programs and Faculty and Full Professor of Organization Behaviour at the Nyenrode Business University, Full Professor of Management and Organization at the Open University Netherlands and a visiting professor at different universities including Leiden University and the Hotelschool The Hague. In addition, he serves as an (associate) editor and reviewer for the international academic community, including the position of editor-in-chief for *Tijdschrift voor Management en Organisatie*. He mostly researches psychological, sociological, humanistic and institutional aspects of organisational behaviour and organisational development, and has published a variety of books, including *Alignment: A Study in Organizing Processes and Alignment between Individual and Organizational Competencies* and *Another State of Mind: Perspectives from Wisdom Traditions on Management and Business* (Gopher, 2003), a diversity of book chapters, management articles and peer-reviewed articles in a variety of journals.

Michael James Boland is a researcher and tutor at University College Cork and an Irish Research Council Government of Ireland scholar. His research is in corporate law, where he is considering the impact of corporate action on stakeholders such as employees and society at large, trying to show how most corporate law frameworks expect a stakeholder-orientated or entity approach to be taken in decision-making. He holds an LLM from University College Cork.

Roberta Consiglio was formerly a research associate at the Appui au Developpement Autonome (ADA) Chair in Financial Law and Inclusive Finance at the University of Luxembourg and works now in business development at the Luxembourg Finance Labelling Agency. Previously she has worked on small and medium-size enterprise financing at October Italia, project finance at Crédit Agricole Italy and mergers and acquisitions at NOAH Advisors Ltd in Berlin and JESA Investment and Management in Shanghai.

Jay Cullen is a professor at Edge Hill University and an adjunct research professor at the University of Oslo. where he co-ordinates research on sustainable finance. He is also a research fellow at the Global Institute for Sustainable Prosperity and an associate of the Association for the Promotion of Political Economy and the Law. Previously he was a professor of financial regulation and director of research at the University of York, and he has worked at the University of Sheffield as a reader in law and at Liverpool John Moores University as a senior lecturer in law. He has internationally recognised knowledge of financial regulation and has published widely in the field and presented at venues including the Bank of England, the European Commission, the European Parliament and leading universities, including Oxford, Cambridge and Cornell.

Andrew Johnston is Professor of Company Law and Corporate Governance at the School of Law at the University of Warwick. Prior to this he was Professor of Company Law and Corporate Governance at the University of Sheffield, and he has taught at the universities of Cambridge, Queensland and Warsaw. He has been a research team member for the SMART project and holds multiple external positions, including as a research associate at the University of Cambridge Centre for Business Research and the Centre de Gestion Scientifique at Mines ParisTECH, a member of the GOODCORP Research Network, a research fellow at the Bankruptcy Research Centre of Renmin University, China, and a partner of the Modern Corporation and the Purpose of the Corporation projects.

Henk Kievit is director of the Nyenrode Faculty Center for Entrepreneurship, Governance & Stewardship and the modular executive MBA programmes for Food & Innovation, Business & Technology, Public & Private Organizations. He teaches on (social) entrepreneurship and (social) venture capital at

Nyenrode Business University. He is also Professor of Conducive Organizations at the Christian Applied University Ede. He obtained his PhD with his dissertation entitled 'Social Venturing Entrepreneurship – a Positioning' (2011) and received his master's degree in agricultural economics at Wageningen University (1994). His research focuses on social venturing entrepreneurship activities, the new form of entrepreneurship for sustainability in society. Prior to joining Nyenrode, he worked in the international business of information technology, family philanthropy and impact investments.

Voula Kratimenou received her BA degree from the University of Patras and her MA and PhD degrees from the University of Peloponnese. Her PhD dissertation (2018) was entitled 'Four Essays in Greece's Economic Adjustment Programs'. She has participated in many conferences and has written a number of papers in the area of EU and Greek fiscal policy.

Alexandros Kyriakidis is a postdoctoral research fellow at the Hellenic Foundation for European and Foreign Policy, and Head of Operations and Research at the Center for Research on Democracy and Law of the Department of International and European Studies of the University of Macedonia. He holds a PhD with distinction from the Department of International and European Studies of the University of Macedonia (2021). His doctoral dissertation was entitled 'The Effect of EU Integration on the EU Democratic Deficit'. He also holds an MPhil in politics from the University of Sheffield, an MSc in global politics, and a BA in political science from the College of Woosteu. He has published a number of journal articles and chapters in edited volumes, and given multiple university lectures on EU politics and European constitutional law, European integration and political economy, among other subjects.

Tineke Lambooy is Professor of Corporate Law at Nyenrode Business University. As a faculty member of the Research Center for Entrepreneurship, Governance and Stewardship, she conducts various multidisciplinary studies with a focus on sustainable business models, governance and international supply chains, business and human rights, and private investment in ecosystems. She is a research fellow with the Utrecht Centre for Water, Oceans and Sustainability Law at the University of Utrecht, where she also lectures on CSR, corporate law, and mergers and acquisitions. Her areas of interests include social entrepreneurship and the available legal forms, as well as the interaction between business, society and ecosystem services.

Panagiotis Liargovas received his BA degree from the University of Athens and his MA and PhD degrees in economics from Clark University, Worcester.

He has been a Fulbright scholar, a Bakalas Foundation scholar, a teaching assistant scholar (Clark University) and a European Commission trainee (Brussels). He has taught in many universities including Clark University, Bologna University, and the universities of Athens, Patras and Crete. He has served as economic advisor to the Greek Ministry of Finance, the Greek Ministry of Foreign Affairs and the Municipality of Athens on many occasions. For the period 2013–18 he was the head of the Parliamentary Budget Office at the Hellenic Parliament. He is currently a professor at the Department of Economics at the University of Peloponnese, where he has the Sustainable Development and Entrepreneurship Laboratory. He is also the Director of the Jean Monnet Centre of Excellence at the University of Peloponnese.

Irene Lynch Fannon is head of Knowledge Management at Matheson. Previously she was a professor of law at the School of Law at University College Cork, where she was also head of the Department of Law, dean of the Faculty of Law and head of the College of Business and Law. In addition, she is currently a ministerial appointee to the Company Law Review Group, and has been a ministerial appointee to the Audit Review Group, the Business Regulation Forum and the High Level Group on Business Regulation. She has published extensively on corporate Insolvency and rescue law, corporate governance and corporate law theory. Her publications include *Corporate Insolvency and Rescue* (co-authored with Gerard Murphy, Bloomsbury Professional, 2012) and *Working Within Two Kinds of Capitalism* (Hart Publications, 2003). She has also received funding for multiple projects, the most recent being the now concluded Judicial Cooperation in Economic Recovery in Europe (JCOERE) project funded by the EU Commission.

Jukka Mähönen is a professor of law at the University of Oslo Faculty of Law and a professor of co-operative law at the University of Helsinki School of Law. He is deputy head of the Oslo Research Group Companies, Markets and Sustainability, he was a member of the SMART project research team and he is currently leader of the research project Futuring Sustainable Nordic Business Models (2019–23). He holds LLM, MSc, LLLic and LLD degrees. Before coming to Oslo in 2015, he was a professor of civil law and dean at the University of Turku. His research interests are in company and co-operative law, accounting and auditing law, tax law and economic analysis of law, all in the context of sustainability.

Trevor Pugh has been a financial markets practitioner for over twenty-five years. For most of that time he has been involved in the trading of government bonds and the management of trading desks in investment banks. He joined

BZW (Barclays) in 1995, eventually becoming managing director and head of gilt trading and in 2014 he joined HSBC as managing director and head of sterling rates trading. Since 2019 he has been involved in financial markets as a consultant to various companies, which has included acting as chief operations officer to hedge funds, chief financial officer for an emerging markets data company and writer and presenter for a financial video learning platform for professionals in the industry. Trevor has an MA in law from Cambridge and an MBS (Financial Services) from University College Dublin's Smurfit Graduate Business School. He was previously an advanced visiting fellow at the University of Sheffield.

Heidi Rapp Nilsen is an associate professor at the Department of Industrial Economics and Technology Management at the Norwegian University of Science and Technology (NTNU). Prior to this she held a position as postdoctoral researcher at NTNU Oceans at the Faculty of Humanities and the pilot programme HAVANSVAR. She has a background from the research institute Norut, which is now part of NORCE, and has worked with sustainability, applied ethics, corporate social responsibility and other management-related subjects in two United Nations (UN) organisations: the Food and Agriculture Organization and the UN Industrial Development Organization. Her overall research theme is sustainability applied in different spheres: ethics, investments, circular economics, CSR and project management. She holds a master's degree in economics from the University of Bergen and a PhD in ecological economics and ethics from the University Nord in Boda, Norway.

Roseanne Russell is a senior lecturer in law at the University of Bristol. Her research interests lie in corporate governance, labour law and feminist legal theory. She is particularly interested in women's treatment, progression and representation within the corporate workplace. Before moving to academia, she was a solicitor in Scottish and City private practices, and also worked in-house at the UK's former Equal Opportunities Commission. She is a member of the Law Society of England and Wales's Employment Law Committee and co-convenor of the Society of Legal Scholars Company Law Stream. She is a co-editor of the *Common Law World Review* and sits on the editorial board of the UK Employment Lawyers Association Briefing.

Beate Sjåfjell is Professor of Law at the University of Oslo, Faculty of Law and Visiting Professor at College of Europe, European Legal Studies Department. Professor Sjåfjell is head of the Faculty's Research Group Companies, Markets and Sustainability as well as several international projects and networks, including the EU-funded SMART project (2016–20) and Daughters of Themis: International Network of Female Business Scholars (2015–). Sjåfjell publishes extensively on EU law, company law and sustainability. Her publications include *The Cambridge Handbook of Corporate Law, Corporate Governance and Sustainability* (co-edited with Christopher M. Bruner; Cambridge University Press, 2019), *Creating Corporate Sustainability: Gender as an Agent of Change* (co-edited with Irene Lynch Fannon; Cambridge University Press, 2018), and *Company Law and Sustainability: Legal Barriers and Opportunities* (co-edited with Benjamin J. Richardson; Cambridge University Press, 2015).

Georgina Tsagas is a senior lecturer in private and commercial law at Brunel University London. She is also a solicitor, qualified in England and Wales. She holds a PhD from Queen Mary University of London. She has formerly held posts at the University of Bristol Law School, the London School of Economics, Department of Law and at University College London, Faculty of Laws. Her research interests include corporate law, mergers and acquisitions, securities regulation and corporate governance. Selected publications include: 'Section 172 of the Companies Act 2006: Desperate Times Call for Soft Law Measures', in Nina Boerger and Charlotte Villiers (eds.) *Shaping the Corporate Landscape* (Hart Publications, 2018); 'A Long-Term Vision for UK Firms? Reconsidering Target Directors' Advisory Role Post the Takeover of Cadbury's plc', *Journal of Corporate Law Studies*.

Charlotte Villiers is a solicitor and professor of company law at the University of Bristol Law School. She has written several books and articles on various aspects of corporate governance, including *Company Law and Corporate Reporting* (Cambridge University Press, 2006). She was a member of the research team on the SMART project, for which she wrote papers on the issue of accounting and integrated reporting. She is co-editor, with Nina Boeger, of the volume *Shaping the Corporate Landscape: Towards Corporate Reform and Enterprise Diversity* (Hart Publishing, 2018). Other selected publications include: 'Corporate Governance, Responsibility and Compassion: Why we Should Care', in Nina Boeger and Charlotte Villiers (eds.), *Shaping the Corporate Landscape: Towards Corporate Reform and Enterprise Diversity* (Hart Publishing, 2017) and 'Gender Justice in Financial Markets', in Lisa Herzog (ed.), *Just Financial Markets?: Finance in a Just Society* (Oxford University Press, 2017).

Olivera Vuletic graduated from Utrecht University in 2016. She completed the bachelor of laws and the legal research master. Currently she is part of the employment and benefits team at the law firm Loyens & Loeff in the Netherlands.

Dirk Andreas Zetzsche is a professor of financial law, holds the ADA (Appui au Developpement Autonome) Chair for Financial Law (inclusive finance) and heads the House of Sustainable Governance and Markets at the University of Luxembourg. He also functions as a director of the Center for Business and Corporate Law at the University of Düsseldorf and is Visiting Professorial Fellow (2021–24) at the University of New South Wales. His more than 300 academic publications deal with fintech, collective investment schemes and asset management, corporate governance, international financial regulation as well as sustainable and inclusive finance. Since 2019, he has been listed by the Social Science Research Network as among the top ten legal scholars worldwide by downloads in the last twelve months. He has served as adviser to and participated in expert working groups initiated by public institutions, such as the European Commission, the European Parliament, the European Securities & Markets Authority, the European Banking Authority, the Bank of International Settlement, as well as various governments and supervisory authorities throughout Europe and Asia. He has also worked in the private sector, as a lawyer licensed under German law and board member of regulated entities.

Foreword

This is a worthy and thought-provoking collection of essays that seeks to critique the European Union (EU)'s model of value creation and calls for greater emphasis on sustainability. The concept of value creation is discussed in the light of two overarching principles: first, the aim of the EU to achieve 'a highly competitive social market economy' (Article 3(3) TEU), a noble but elusive goal that allows for different understandings of the role of the state in the economy and can accommodate varied integration paradigms; secondly, environmental protection and the promotion of sustainable development, which are transversal EU objectives that must form an integral part of the Union's policies. A premise that underpins this book is that, although the EU offers an admirable value system and has made a major contribution to the well-being of the peoples of Europe, it has not achieved its full potential owing to the lack of commitment by the Member States. The contributions address value creation in the EU by challenging what the authors perceive to be an eschewed conception of value creation and proposing its readjustment in the interests of social fairness and sustainability. The discussion unfolds against the backdrop of confluent crises that have bedevilled, and continue to challenge, the European integration model. Emerging from the shadow of the Eurozone crisis, whose ripple effects are still felt strongly in many European economies, the EU has to face Brexit, a migration crisis, regressive populism, an unprecedented pandemic and a sustainability deficit that poses an existentialist threat but has at last made it to the top of the political agenda. Each of these crises poses its own distinct challenges but they all strain the idea of EU solidarity and bring to the fore some fundamental questions regarding the future direction of the Union.

In the sixty or so years since its creation, the European integration project has proved resilient, going forward and mutating to meet emerging challenges. Although Brexit shattered the irreversibility outlook of the 'ever closer union' paradigm, wider centrifugal forces are currently contained. But huge challenges remain. Those posed by climate change are unprecedented. As the editors point out, economic development and social welfare are directly dependent on the stability of our ecosystem. How well placed is the EU to deal with such problems? Does it have the political will to meet them? Does it have a clear vision of what to do? Does it possess the requisite institutional arrangements and legal instruments?

The discussion is wide ranging and organised in four parts, exploring respectively the objectives of the EU's social market economy, the unsustainability of the EU's economic system, ways forward in the promotion of value creation, and a concluding set of reflections. The chapters offer, among others, an analysis of the EU's COVID-19 response, an appraisal of the EU's austerity model, a discussion of the role of the corporation in advancing social good and reflections on women's empowerment and their potential to enhance their contribution to the economy. The contributions examine the EU's prevailing value creation paradigm by reference, especially, to two areas: the EU's response to the Eurozone crisis; and the shareholder primacy model that underpins the harmonisation programme on corporate law. The link between economic sustainability and social, environmental and cultural sustainability is an underlying consideration present in many of the contributions.

A major theme of the book is the EU's response to the Eurozone crisis. The contributions are critical of the conditionality imposed on Greece, stressing the social consequences of budgetary discipline and its attenuating effect on inequalities. They elucidate the causes of the Greek sovereign crisis, assess the success of the Greek economic adjustment programme and debate the EU's fiscal austerity paradigm. Another major theme is the role of corporations on value creation. The shareholder primacy principle is placed under scrutiny with a more societally oriented corporate model being proposed as a better way of achieving long-term, sustainable business.

The book comes at a particularly opportune moment as the European project is under threat from convergent challenges. It calls for a departure from existing models of governance, which are debited with generating inequality, unbalanced growth and lack of wider stakeholder input, and it attempts to provide an alternative economic blueprint.

As the memory of the world wars fades, the EU can no longer rely on the catharsis model of European integration. Solidarity is in need of a forward-looking narrative. This book brings to the fore some important themes, critiques and prevailing policy models, and proposes solutions. The analysis is rigorous, relevant and original. It thus makes a very valuable contribution to the narrative debate and the conceptualisation of the integration model.

Takis Tridimas

Preface

As editors, our vision of a sustainable future for humankind has inspired our work with this volume on sustainable value creation in the European Union (EU). Our concern with the EU is not informed by a belief that a sustainable future contained within the EU is possible. This is obvious both because of the global nature of the sustainability challenges the world faces and because of the globalised business and finance that are themes in much of this volume. We see great potential in the EU's role in Europe and globally. Accordingly, the book centres upon the variables that have enabled the EU's rise, as well as those that appear to be leading to its gradual decline. A central aspect is the EU's social market economy value system as envisaged in theory and as it has evolved in practice. The inspiration for this volume originated with events that shook Greece and the rest of the EU during 2015. Following the Global Recession – the financial and economic crisis that occurred during the late 2000s, bringing with it a threat to the EU's common currency – Greece began to face a significant debt crisis. Capital controls were imposed on Greece and a referendum was conducted, in order for the public to decide whether Greece should accept the bailout conditions imposed by the European Commission, the International Monetary Fund and the European Central Bank that were intended to enable the country to resolve its government-debt crisis. The Greek prime minister at the time, Alexis Tsipras, reneged on a referendum he had initiated, in which a majority of over 61 per cent rejected the bailout, and he went ahead and applied for a third loan which he then signed off on alongside a raft of austerity measures that the country would have to endure.

In response to the crisis in Greece, which we saw as a symptom of broader European and global problems (rather than as a Greek problem), we organised a conference together with Professor Lina Papadopoulou, Jean Monnet Chair for European Constitutional Law and Culture at the Aristotle University of Thessaloniki. Our interdisciplinary conference, entitled 'Stimulating Business in an EU in Crisis: Evolving Trends and the Case of Greece', was held in Thessaloniki, Greece, at the Chamber of Commerce and Industry in June 2015. The conference brought together leading thinkers from different academic disciplines, established as well as early career researchers, all wishing to contribute to the discussions on the topic relating to the questions of how the European project was failing and what could be done further to support the private and public sector in the rapidly changing environment in Europe.

The Greek debt crisis presented a dramatic challenge to the integrity and solidarity of the EU, which began as a political project of solidarity after the Second World War. This solidarity came under further strain when Member States questioned their shared responsibility and demonstrated different national responses in the face of massive levels of global refugee migration. The Brexit vote of 2016, leading to the departure of the UK from the EU from 2021, has also shown up differences between Member States and between the central and periphery regions who see their experiences differently under the European project. The COVID-19 pandemic has also given rise to tensions as it has required regional and institutional co-operation to cope with the crisis as well as bringing out nationalistic and protectionist responses as European Member States have had to close their borders and have hoarded medical supplies. This EU backdrop exists alongside growing global climate change threats that have seen parts of the world ablaze with wildfires, dried out soils and ever more dramatic extreme weather events, and the horrific human suffering exacerbated by these and other environmental and social unsustainabilities. How are such challenges to be faced throughout the rest of this twenty-first century?

This book explores one major line of response through its focus upon sustainable value creation through corporate business and entrepreneurial activities as well as through the financing of business and, more broadly, monetary policies. The book observes that debates on *value creation* have turned towards demanding more sustainable business actions, looking for companies to create value not just through profit for themselves but for the benefit of society. As we recognise the urgent need to transition towards a sustainable future, *sustainable value creation* has become an increasingly referenced concept. However, despite repeated references to value creation, whether on its own or in respect of the creation of sustainable value, the term remains a contested concept and many companies adopt a narrow view of value creation, seeing it as a short-term goal to make profit that benefits only the company's shareholders and perhaps their boardroom actors. This book interrogates the concept more fully and then explores it as a central part of the EU's commitment to and efforts to ensure sustainable value creation and a sustainable future anchored in the EU Treaties. Indeed, sustainability is an overarching objective of the EU and is meant to be the guiding principle for the EU's policies and activities within Europe and in its relations with the rest of the world, to promote 'peace, its values and the well-being of its peoples' (Article 3(1) of the Treaty on European Union).

All books require the support and assistance of a great many people if they are going to be completed. In an edited collection such as this, the chapter authors deserve huge thanks for their expertise and efforts that have led to a set of chapters that contribute so coherently to the overall argument. This has been a long project and the authors have been patient and willing to work collectively to enable us to produce this set of chapters in a clear and structured examination of the overall topic and its related themes. Of course, the book would not have come to fruition at all without the conference for which we owe an enormous debt to Professor Lina Papadopoulou. We would also wish to thank the Thessaloniki Chamber of Commerce and Industry and specifically the President, Mr Dimitris Bakatselos, for hosting us and our conference in 2015 and generously supporting our event. We would like to pay special thanks to Bristol University Law School for the generous research funds provided that helped support, organise and promote the event. Georgina Tsagas would personally like to thank Focus Radio Station Thessaloniki, 103.6 FM Radio for interviewing her about the event and conference, notably radio spokespeople for the station, Evangelos Stefanis and Stefanie Efstathiou. We would also like to thank the Law School of the Aristotle University of Thessaloniki and especially Professor George Dellios, the appointed dean in 2015, who opened the conference with his introductory speech. We are enormously grateful to Professor Takis Tridimas for being so generous in providing his introductory speech to our conference held in 2015, and his positive and warm Foreword to this collection.

In 2015, we also received the good news that the proposal for EU funding for the interdisciplinary research project Sustainable Market Actors for Responsible Trade (SMART) was approved. Our work in the SMART project, of which all editors and several of the authors were members, has greatly contributed to developing our understanding of the multi-layered regulatory framework that aims to contribute to sustainable business and finance, and the research-based concept of sustainability within which the analysis of laws and policies should be positioned.

It was also in 2015 that, directly following the conference in Thessaloniki, we headed out to Vourvourou in Halkidiki for the very first workshop of Daughters of Themis: International Network of Female Business Scholars. Since 2016 these workshops have been held on the island of Kea in Greece (with a brief turn to digital workshops during the pandemic). Through the annual workshops and other events in this interdisciplinary and international network, of which the editors and several of the authors are members, we learnt much from each other and together about pathways towards sustainable business.

We gratefully acknowledge the contributions of the SMART team and of Daughters of Themis.

We have benefited from the invaluable assistance of our dedicated student research assistants, Pernille Bergan Yang and Madeleine Østenstad, who did a marvellous job in checking the references, proofreading manuscript drafts and in myriad other ways helping us bring the book to its final state. At Cambridge University Press, we have been supported immeasurably by Tom Randall, and his patience and faith in this project have been very inspiring.

Finally, this book goes to press at a critical time, following the United Nations Climate Change Conference in Glasgow (COP26) and as the COVID-19 pandemic has taken a new turn with the identification of a new variant, making the Greek alphabet famous all over again. These events alone highlight some of the major problems we face within the EU and globally. We hope that our book contributes to identifying some of the solutions necessary to respond to these and further challenges we will meet in the future.

PART I

THE OBJECTIVES OF THE EU'S SOCIAL MARKET ECONOMY REVISITED

1

Stimulating Value Creation in a Europe in Crisis

Charlotte Villiers, Beate Sjåfjell and Georgina Tsagas

1.1 SUPPORTING SUSTAINABLE DEVELOPMENT THROUGH THE LISBON TREATY

The Consolidated Treaty on European Union after Lisbon emphasises the overarching objectives of sustainable development and a highly competitive social market economy, aiming at full employment and social progress. In 2021, it is plain to see that these ambitions have not been fully achieved. Some writers have suggested that the European Union (EU) is currently facing its most significant existential crisis since it came into being after the Second World War.[1] The developments that have led to this crisis include the Global Recession, the financial and economic crisis that occurred during the late 2000s, bringing with it a threat to the EU's common currency. This instigated a punishing austerity programme that has brought about a deep income divide across Europe and with that a challenge to the solidarity of the European project of integration and union.

This solidarity came under further strain in the face of a global refugee crisis, with Member States questioning shared responsibility and demonstrating different national responses. The Brexit vote of 2016, leading to the departure of the UK from the EU in 2021, has also brought out several variations between Member States and between the central and periphery regions which see their experiences differently under the European project.[2] Further tensions have arisen from the COVID-19 pandemic, which has required regional and

---

[1] U. Bernitz, M. Mårtensson, L. Oxelheim and T. Persson, 'Analysing the Prosperity Gap: the Economic, Legal and Political Challenges Facing the EU', in U. Bernitz, M. Mårtensson, T. Persson and L. Oxelheim (eds.), *Bridging the Prosperity Gap in the EU: the Social Challenge Ahead* (Cheltenham: Edward Elgar, 2018), 1–21, p. 1. See also M. Riddervold, J. Trondal and A. Newsome (eds.), *The Palgrave Handbook of EU Crises* (Cham: Palgrave Macmillan, 2021).
[2] Bernitz et al., 'Analysing the Prosperity Gap'.

institutional co-operation to cope with the crisis but has also brought out nationalistic and protectionist responses as European Member States have had to close their borders and have hoarded medical supplies.[3]

The pandemic (ongoing at the time of writing), the continuing fall-out from Brexit and the resulting economic damage, a Grexit avoided and potential other exits – all of these may undermine the political consensus of the idea of a European Union.[4] The list of other challenges facing the EU is daunting: alongside rising Euroscepticism and populism, the EU has witnessed unemployment, especially amongst young people (in the Southern European countries beyond 50 per cent), fuelling social unrest and political instability; businesses closing down or moving overseas; xenophobia and the EU's inability to handle increased immigration; weak protection of basic human rights violations; and continued pressure on planetary boundaries. Whilst, following the exhausting and damaging Brexit, there now appears to be less enthusiasm for more breakaway moves, some Member States have sought to challenge the rule of law within the EU, and a rightwards political shift has been gaining strength.[5] At the same time, the EU faces challenges on the international stage as it seeks to protect its trade links and simultaneously strengthen its security and defence policies.[6] It therefore should not be considered an overstatement to suggest that the Treaty's goals are highly unlikely to be achieved in the foreseeable future.

Amidst these challenges to the EU, the debates on *value creation* have turned towards demanding more sustainable business actions, looking for corporations to create value not just through profit for themselves but for the benefit of society.[7] In acknowledgement of the urgency of transitioning towards a sustainable future, *sustainable value creation* has become an increasingly referenced concept. However, despite the repeated references to value creation, whether on its own or referring to the creation of sustainable value, the term remains a contested concept. The controversy arises because many companies

---

3 Z. Wang, 'From Crisis to Nationalism? The Conditioned Effects of the COVID-19 Crisis on Neo-Nationalism in Europe' (2021) 6 (1) *Chinese Political Science Review* 20–39.

4 A. Etiubon and J. Ibietan, 'European Union and Brexit Nationalism: A Historical' (2018) 6 (2) *International Journal of Innovative Social Sciences & Humanities Research* 26–39.

5 See e.g. D. Albertazzi and S. Van Kessel, 'Right-Wing Populist Party Organisation Across Europe: The Survival of the Mass-Party? Introduction to the Thematic Issue' (2021) 9 (4) *Politics and Governance* 224–227.

6 L. McGee, '2020 was a terrible year for Europe. 2021 is unlikely to be much better' (1 January 2021) *CNN*, available at: www.edition.cnn.com/2020/12/31/europe/eu-bad-2020-2021-analysis-intl/index.html.

7 M. E. Porter and M. R. Kramer. 'Creating Shared Value', in G. G. Lenssen and N. C. Smith, *Managing Sustainable Business* (Dordrecht: Springer, 2019), pp. 327–350.

adopt a narrow view of value creation, seeing it as a short-term goal of making profit that benefits only the company's shareholders and perhaps their boardroom actors.[8] This approach has had significant detrimental impact,[9] not least because it has involved negative externalities such as environmental degradation,[10] labour exploitation[11] and deepened wealth and income inequalities to excessive levels.[12] As the global economy faces many challenges, this approach to value creation has come under question. These global economic challenges put a further strain on the EU.

This volume is a response to the clear indications that the Lisbon Treaty goal of a social market economy has failed on many levels. It provides the space for in-depth discussion of the concept of *value creation* through the prism of sustainability, with particular focus on corporate law and governance and the financial markets and monetary policies in the context of the value system of the EU's social market economy. The inspiration for this book came from the interdisciplinary conference 'Stimulating Business in an EU in Crisis: Evolving Trends and the Case of Greece' that we organised in Thessaloniki, Greece, at the Chamber of Commerce and Industry in June 2015. The conference brought together leading thinkers from different academic disciplines, established, as well as early career researchers, all wishing to contribute to the discussions on the topic relating to the questions of how the European project was failing and what could be done further to support the private and public sector in the rapidly changing environment in Europe.

The conference took place during the summer of 2015, when capital controls had been imposed on Greece and a referendum was being implemented in order for the public to decide whether Greece should accept the bailout conditions in the country's government debt crisis. These conditions were proposed jointly by the European Commission (EC), the International Monetary Fund (IMF) and the European Central Bank (ECB) on 25 June 2015. Despite the bailout conditions having been rejected by a majority of

---

[8] Ibid.

[9] See F. H. Alexander, 'Saving Investors from Themselves: How Stockholder Primacy Harms Everyone' (2017) 40 (2) *Seattle University Law Review* 303.

[10] B. J. Richardson and B. Sjåfjell, 'Capitalism, the Sustainability Crisis, and the Limitations of Current Business Governance', in B. Sjåfjell and B. J. Richardson (eds.), *Company Law and Sustainability: Legal Barriers and Opportunity* (Cambridge: Cambridge University Press, 2015), 1–34.

[11] M. Alzola, 'Decent Work: The Moral Status of Labor in Human Resource Management' (2018) 147 (4) *Journal of Business Ethics* 835–853.

[12] See e.g. T. Piketty, *Capital in the 21st Century* (Cambridge, **MA**: Harvard University Press, 2014) and J. Hickel, *The Divide: A Brief Guide to Global Inequality and Its Solutions* (London: William Heinemann, 2017).

over 61 per cent to 39 per cent approving, Alexis Tsipras – who had initiated the referendum, urging Greeks to vote against the conditions – reneged on the referendum result and applied for a third loan. He signed off that loan on some of the most austere measures to that date, leaving political scientists dismayed at the turnaround.[13] The case of the Greek referendum was a precursor of what was yet to come in the UK. The non-binding referendum held in June 2016 on whether the UK should either remain a member of, or leave, the EU, contrary to opinion polls that had indicated otherwise, led to a referendum result of 51.9 per cent of voters voting in favour of leaving the Union, on a national turnout of 72 per cent. The referendum result was followed immediately by the resignation of the then Prime Minister, David Cameron, and led to the political demise of his successor, Theresa May, who failed to achieve an agreement on the terms of the UK's withdrawal from the EU. Britain's Parliament was paralysed by a lack of consensus on the terms of Britain's 'divorce' settlement and European politicians faced a threat of fall-out from a no-deal departure by the UK. The 27 Member States of the EU managed to show unity throughout the negotiations, and finally, Prime Minister Boris Johnson led the UK towards a very 'thin' deal in the Trade and Cooperation Agreement that took effect from 1 January 2021.[14]

As we complete this edited collection, Britain's economy is suffering from the strain of its Brexit terms, the Northern Ireland peace treaty of 1998 is under threat, the political union of the UK faces potential challenges from a Scottish independence movement and the Westminster government is plagued by accusations of corruption. The UK and Greek referenda concerned a vote on EU membership and on bailout conditions and the Eurozone respectively. Both showcase something important in relation to referenda on the EU and the inconsistent views and perceptions of the population with regard to the values and benefits encapsulated in the Eurozone and EU membership.[15]

---

[13] See H. Stewart, 'Memorandum of understanding: what exactly has Greece signed up for?' (12 August 2015) *The Guardian*, available at: www.theguardian.com/world/2015/aug/12/memorandum-understanding-what-exactly-has-greece-signed-up-for and N. Kiapidou, 'Greek elections: how Syriza managed to sign a bailout agreement yet retain its support base' (24 September 2015) *LSE Blogs*, available at: https://blogs.lse.ac.uk/europppblog/2015/09/24/greek-elections-how-syriza-managed-to-sign-a-bailout-agreement-yet-retain-its-support-base/.

[14] For an account of the Brexit developments, see C. Grey, *Brexit Unfolded: How No One Got What They Wanted (and Why They Were Never Going To)* (London: Biteback Publishing, 2021).

[15] Note that EU Membership and Eurozone Membership are different: being a member of the EU (currently twenty-seven member states) does not necessarily entail being a part of the Eurozone in which those countries included have adopted the euro as their currency (currently nineteen member states): for further details see European Commission, 'What

The referenda results may well indicate that the collective aim of value creation through EU objectives has been undermined by nationalism and protectionism. This perhaps indicates also that there is a need to reconsider and revise the meaning of value creation, its inherent value for the purposes of furthering sustainability in the EU and to consider in what respects the EU project has progressed and failed within this context.

This introductory chapter sets out the parameters of this book, which brings together contributions from experts from a range of academic disciplines, with legal scholarship at the core of the volume. Section 1.2 presents the context for our focus upon sustainable value creation and explores how this might be developed inside the EU and through the EU's institutions. Section 1.3 identifies a number of mileposts that have shaped the progress of the EU and its relevance for value creation, including the EU's ambitions, the financial and debt crises, Brexit and the urgent challenges presented by the COVID-19 pandemic and the broader environmental, social and economic aspects of sustainability. Section 1.4 gives a descriptive overview of the chapters that are presented in the book, and a short conclusion follows in Section 1.5.

1.2 THE VALUE OF SUSTAINABLE VALUE CREATION

The editors of this book share a joint academic interest, as well as life outlook, on the importance of building a sustainable future for humankind, which has led us to instigate this volume and to revisit a classic topic relating to the EU agenda, with a focus on sustainable value creation in the private and public sectors. The book focusses specifically on the variables that have enabled the EU's growth, as well as those that appear to be leading to its gradual decline. Emphasis is placed on the EU's social market economy value system as envisaged in theory and as it has evolved in practice.

Any discussion of sustainable value creation should start out with defining the concept of sustainable development – or sustainability, as it is often referred to today. Drawing on sustainability science, we see the recognition of planetary boundaries as crucial to an evidence-based understanding of sustainability. Planetary boundaries, as a term used for the limits of our planet, is the result of the work instigated by an international multidisciplinary group of environmental scientists, who, in 2009, pooled their knowledge of different Earth system processes to inform the world about the space for sustainable

is the euro area?', available at: https://ec.europa.eu/info/business-economy-euro/euro-area/
what-euro-area_en.

action within planetary boundaries.[16] Their work reflects the growing scientific understanding that life and its physical environment co-evolve. This pioneering effort brought together evidence of rising and interconnected global risks in several different contexts where environmental processes are being changed by human activities. The planetary boundaries framework flags a set of sustainability-critical issues. It presents policy makers with a dashboard of issues which arise from the collective impacts of humanity, impacts that are changing the fundamental dynamics of the Earth system upon which humans rely for their lives and livelihoods (Figure 1.1).[17]

Through the planetary boundaries work it is estimated that humanity has already transgressed at least five of the nine planetary boundaries currently identified, including climate change, biosphere integrity (biodiversity), biogeochemical flows, land system integrity and 'novel entities' (micro plastics, nano materials and various forms of chemical pollution).[18] At least two of these planetary boundaries, climate change and biodiversity, are what may be denoted *core boundaries*, where transgression of either of them may in itself

---

[16]   J. Rockström, W. Steffen, K. Noone, Å. Persson, F. S. I. Chapin, E. Lambin, T. Lenton, M. Scheffer, C. Folke, H. J. Schellnhuber, B. Nykvist, C. de Wit, T. Hughes, S. van der Leeuw, H. Rodhe, S. Sörlin, P. Snyder, R. Costanza, U. Svedin, M. Falkenmark, L. Karlberg, R. Corell, V. Fabry, J. Hansen, B. Walker, D. Liverman, K. Richardson, P. Crutzen and J. Foley, 'Planetary Boundaries: Exploring the Safe Operating Space for Humanity' (2009) 14 (2) *Ecology and Society* 32–64; W. Steffen, K. Richardson, J. Rockström, S. E. Cornell, I. Fetzer, E. M. Bennett, R. Biggs, S. R. Carpenter, W. de Vries, C. A. de Wit, C. Folke, D. Gerten, J. Heinke, G. M. Mace, L. M. Persson, V. Ramanathan, B. Reyers and S. Sörlin, 'Planetary Boundaries: Guiding Human Development on a Changing Planet' (2015) 347 *Science* 736–746; L. Persson, B. M. Carney Almroth, C. D. Collins, S. Cornell, C. A. de Wit, M. L. Diamond, P. Fantke, M. Hassellöv, M. MacLeod, M. W. Ryberg, P. S. Jørgensen, P. Villarrubia-Gómez, Z. Wang and M. Z. Hauschild, 'Outside the Safe Operating Space of the Planetary Boundary for Novel Entities' (2022) 56 (3) *Environmental Science & Technology* 1510–1521, https://doi.org/10.1021/acs.est.1c04158.

[17]   S. Cornell, 'Planetary Boundaries and Business: Putting the Operating into the Safe Operating Space for Humanity', Draft paper on file with current authors, University of Oslo (2016).

[18]   The other four being global freshwater use, ocean acidification, atmospheric aerosol loading and stratospheric ozone depletion: Steffen et al., 'Planetary Boundaries: Guiding Human Development on a Changing Planet'; Persson et al., 'Outside the Safe Operating Space of the Planetary Boundary for Novel Entities'. As more expert communities worldwide engage with putting the concept into practice, discussions continue (and become scientifically better evidenced) about the best control variables and the best placing of a truly precautionary boundary, as we see in this report, which indicates that the freshwater boundary is also transgressed: B. Campbell, D. Beare, E. Bennett, J. Hall-Spencer, J. Ingram, F. Jaramillo, R. Ortiz, N. Ramankutty, J. Sayer and D. Shindell, 'Agriculture Production as a Major Driver of the Earth System Exceeding Planetary Boundaries' (2017) 22 *Ecology and Society* 8–18.

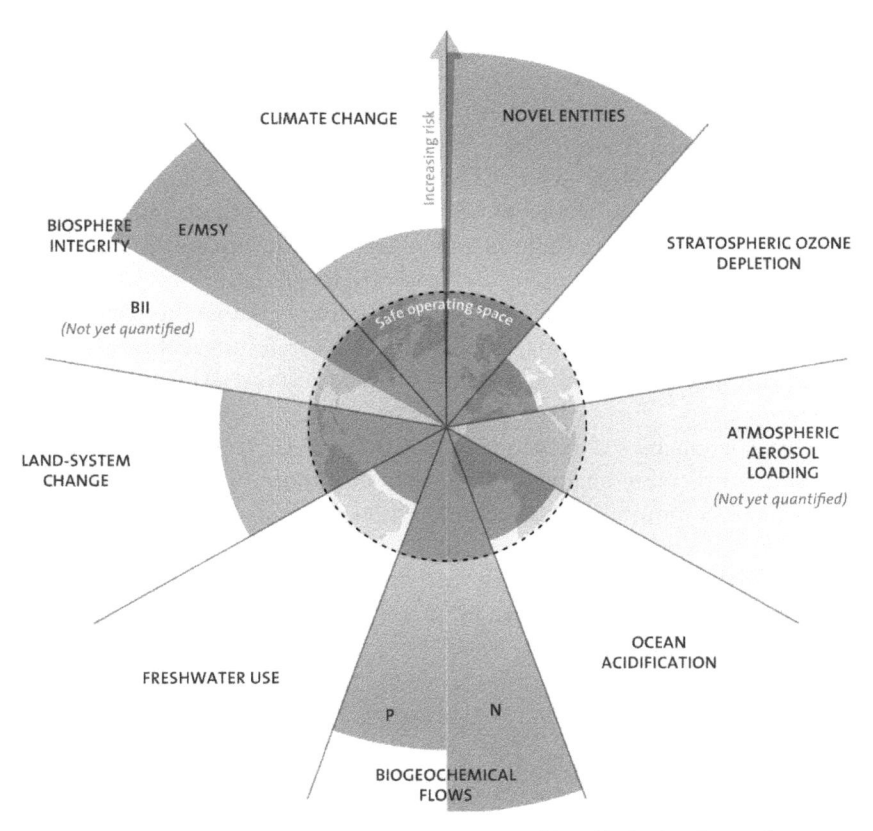

FIGURE 1.1 *Planetary boundaries. Source: Azote and Stockholm Resilience Centre, based on analysis in Persson et al., 'Outside the Safe Operating Space' and Steffen et al., 'Planetary Boundaries'.*

be sufficient to bring the Earth system out of the relatively stable state of the past few millennia, which the planetary boundaries scientists refer to as a 'safe operating space for humanity'.[19]

These environmental issues pose severe challenges for governance globally due to the inherent uncertainties and complex multi-level dynamics. Responding to these challenges entails contributing to preserving, protecting and regenerating natural resources and global geophysical processes at global,

---

[19] Rockström et al., 'Planetary Boundaries: Exploring the Safe Operating Space for Humanity'.

regional and local levels of society, and across public, private and hybrid institutions and organisations.

A research-based concept of sustainability naturally includes social issues too.[20] A broad approach to the social aspects of sustainability is crucial in an analysis of solidarity in the EU's social market and in consideration of the how global value chains of EU business and finance connect it with other parts of the world, including low-income countries falling within the EU's definition of 'developing' or 'least-developed' countries.[21] We therefore employ the broadly recognised definition of sustainability as securing social foundations for humanity now and for the future within planetary boundaries – encapsulated in the goal of a safe and just space for humanity (Figure 1.2).[22]

This encompasses a recognition that those most vulnerable, including workers across value chains in slavery-like conditions,[23] and traditional and indigenous communities whose land and other resources are exploited, are not always encompassed in sustainability initiatives.[24] To change this, it is not sufficient for experts to merely assess what is good for vulnerable people. Instead, inclusive and participatory processes are needed (as envisaged by

---

[20] B. Sjåfjell, 'How Company Law Has Failed Human Rights – and What to Do About It' (2020) 5 (2) *Business and Human Rights Journal* 179–199, available at SSRN: https://ssrn.com/abstract=3530956 and B. Sjåfjell, T. Häyhä and S. Cornell, 'A Research-Based Approach to the UN Sustainable Development Goals. A Prerequisite to Sustainable Business and Finance' (2020) 2020–02 *University of Oslo Faculty of Law Research Paper*, available at SSRN: https://ssrn.com/abstract=3526744.

[21] See e.g. The European Commission, www.ec.europa.eu/trade/policy/countries-and-regions/development/.

[22] M. Leach, K. Raworth and J. Rockström, 'Between Social and Planetary Boundaries: Navigating Pathways in the Safe and Just Space for Humanity', in ISCC and UNESCO, *World Social Science Report 2013* (Paris: OECD Publishing, 2013), pp. 84–90. See also the European Commission, 'General Union Environment Action Programme to 2020: living well, within the limits of our planet' (31 March 2014): https://ec.europa.eu/environment/pubs/pdf/factsheets/7eap/en.pdf.

[23] International Trade Union Confederation, 'New ITUC report exposes hidden workforce of 116 million in global supply chains of fifty companies' (18 January 2016), available at: www.ituc-csi.org/new-ituc-report-exposes-hidden.

[24] T. Novitz, 'Supply Chains and Temporary Migrant Labour: the Relevance of Trade and Sustainability Frameworks', in D. Ashiagbor (ed.), *Re-Imagining Labour Law for Development: Informal Work in the Global North and South* (Oxford: Hart Publishing, 2019), pp. 191–211; G. Christensen, 'What Does It Mean to Be Sustainable? Regulating the Relationship between Corporations and Indigenous People', in B. Sjåfjell and C. M. Bruner (eds.), *The Cambridge Handbook of Corporate Law, Corporate Governance and Sustainability* (Cambridge: Cambridge University Press, 2019), pp. 416–430; C. Y. Yu, 'An Application of Sustainable Development in Indigenous People's Revival: the History of an Indigenous Tribe's Struggle in Taiwan' (2018) 10 *Sustainability* 3259–3278.

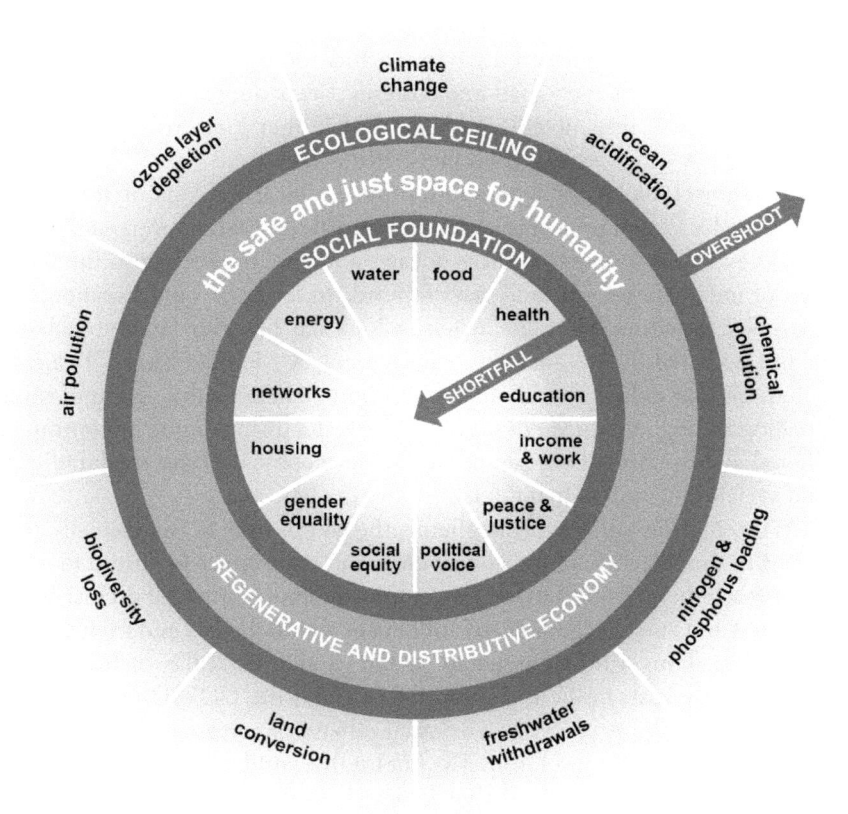

FIGURE 1.2 *The safe and just space for humanity. Source: Raworth,* Doughnut Economics.[25]

Goal 16 of the UN Sustainable Development Goals [SDGs]),[26] enabling vulnerable people to have access to justice and representative participation in the crafting of measures that affect their well-being.[27]

With this backdrop, reflecting on key milestones in the EU's historical evolution to date will make evident that the future of the EU is very uncertain

[25] K. Raworth, *Doughnut Economics: Seven Ways to Think Like a 21st-Century Economist* (New York: Random House, 2017).

[26] United Nations, *Transforming Our World: The 2030 Agenda for Sustainable Development*, General Assembly resolution A/RES/70/1 (25 September 2015), available at: www.un.org/en/development/desa/population/migration/generalassembly/docs/globalcompact/A_RES_70_1_E.pdf.

[27] For discussion, see T. Novitz, 'Engagement with Sustainability at the International Labour Organization and Wider Implications for Worker Voice' (2020) 159 (4) *International Labour Review* 463–482.

and will depend not only on the efforts of politicians but also on the actions of business leaders. If the various market actors continue to drive forward with short-term profit-oriented goals and austerity, deepening existing inequalities further, this will undoubtedly push the EU further into crisis and without providing any way of escape from that crisis.

The subject matter of the present volume is topical and important at a time when the European project is under such threat from this convergence of crises. The book contributes to these debates and tentatively suggests the direction of necessary reforms and ways forward. In terms of value creation, the EU offers an admirable value system, which has however failed to achieve its full potential due to a lack of commitment by Member States. The contributions that follow in this edited collection all address the notion of value creation through the prism of sustainability by focussing on the opportunities offered and the limitations present to the development of the legal, political and social value system that the EU aspires to offer.

As this is a constantly evolving theme, the editors have been especially conscious in the selection of the contributors and their topics to ensure that the volume will be of interest in the longer term and not connected exclusively to the latest and current changes and influences within the EU and from outside the region. Thus, whilst the spectre of Grexit and the reality of Brexit have been major threats to the EU project, so too has the COVID-19 pandemic. The unsustainability of business as usual remains a pervasive challenge with growing urgency, not just for the EU but for the world.

Marking the beginning of what is now known as the European Union, Robert Schuman, one of the founding fathers of the European Communities, made a Declaration on 9 May 1950 as Foreign Minister launching the 'Schuman Plan', proposing a supranational Community for coal and steel. In 2012 the EU was awarded the Nobel Peace Prize and was applauded for its contribution over six decades to 'the advancement of peace and reconciliation, democracy and human rights in Europe' and being instrumental in 'transforming most of Europe from a continent of war to a continent of peace'.[28] In its conception and development, the EU has undoubtedly offered an admirable set of values and standards to its citizens and at instances has been praised to be an admirable project which has helped transform living standards of Europe's people.[29]

[28] R. Belloni, 'Peace in Europe', in O. P. Richmond, S. Pogodda and J. Ramović, *The Palgrave Handbook of Disciplinary and Regional Approaches to Peace* (London: Palgrave Macmillan, 2016), pp. 411–423.

[29] J. FitzGerald, 'EU has helped transform living standards of Europe's people' (26 January 2018) *The Irish Times*, available at: www.irishtimes.com/business/economy/eu-has-helped-transform-living-standards-of-europe-s-people-1.3368611.

The EU's commitment to creating sustainable value and ensuring a sustainable future is anchored in the EU Treaties. Sustainability is an overarching objective of the European Union and meant to be the guiding principle for the EU's policies and activities within Europe and in its relations with the rest of the world, to promote 'peace, its values and the wellbeing of its peoples'.[30] The EU's treaty-based values and objectives further include respect for human dignity and human rights, social policy, minority peoples and rights of the child.[31] Together with the legal requirement for policy coherence for development (PCD), requiring that any area of EU law and policy must not work against developmental policies, this reinforces the sustainability aim of 'leaving no-one behind'.[32]

Any area of EU law and policy is as a matter of EU law meant to contribute to the overarching objectives of the EU as set out in the EU Treaties.[33] To reinforce this, the EU Treaties contain cross-cutting rules such as the environmental integration duty in Article 11 TFEU:[34]

> Environmental protection requirements *must* be integrated into the definition and implementation of the Union policies and activities, in particular with a view to promoting sustainable development.[35]

---

[30] Treaty on the European Union (TEU), signed at Maastricht, 7 February 1992, Article 3(1), with the values set out in Article 2: 'respect for human dignity, freedom, democracy, equality, the rule of law and respect for human rights, including the rights of persons belonging to minorities'. See further Article 3(3) and 3(5) TEU and Article 21 TEU.

[31] Article 2 TEU. See also the Preamble of the Treaty, where the Member States confirm their 'attachment to fundamental social rights as defined in the European Social Charter signed at Turin on 18 October 1961 and in the 1989 Community Charter of the Fundamental Social Rights of Workers'.

[32] Article 208 in the Treaty on the Functioning of the European Union (TFEU), signed at Rome, 25 March 1957. See C. Gammage, 'The EU's Evolving Commitment to Promoting Sustainability in its External Actions: Policy (In)Coherence for Development?' (2020) SMART working paper on file with this book's editors, University of Oslo. See also United Nations, *The 2030 Agenda for Sustainable Development*.

[33] The system of the Treaties as well as the case law of the Court of Justice shows that the general objectives function as a framework for EU law and thereby for the institutions of the EU, see B. Sjåfjell, 'The Legal Significance of Article 11 TFEU for EU Institutions and Member States', in B. Sjåfjell and A. Wiesbrock (eds.), *The Greening of European Business under EU Law: Taking Article 11 TFEU Seriously* (Abingdon: Routledge, 2017), pp. 51–72.

[34] Ibid. See also D. Grimeaud, 'The Integration of Environmental Concerns into EC Policies: A Genuine Policy Development?' (2000) 9 (7) *European Energy and Environmental Law Review* 207–218; G. M. Durán and E. Morgera, *Environmental Integration in the EU's External Relations: Beyond Multilateral Dimensions* (Oxford and Portland: Hart Publishing, 2012); J. Solana, 'The Power of the Eurosystem to Promote Environmental Protection' (2019) 30 (4) *European Business Law Review* 547–575.

[35] Emphasis added. B. Sjåfjell, *Towards a Sustainable European Company Law: A Normative Analysis of the Objectives of EU Law, with the Takeover Directive as a test case* (Alphen aan den Rijn: Kluwer Law International, 2009), pp. 204–214 and 217–228; inter alia Ludwig Krämer,

This rule encapsulates a legal principle that constitutes one of the most important elements of EU environmental law.[36] Article 11 TFEU entails that any legal basis in the Treaties is also a basis for environmental protection requirements, with its aim of contributing to sustainability. It constitutes a core tool to implement the concept of sustainability in EU policies and to facilitate the transition towards sustainability. With its explicit aim of 'sustainable development', complying with the duty contained in Article 11 TFEU entails integrating environmental protection requirements in such a way as to achieve sustainable development.[37]

In addition to the environmental integration principle in Article 11 TFEU and the principle of social policy integration in Article 9 TFEU,[38] we have a general principle of integration of policy objectives contained in Article 7 TFEU requiring that the EU must ensure consistency between its policies and activities.[39]

Economic development and social welfare, or as formulated as an objective of EU law: achieving 'a highly competitive social market economy, aiming at full employment and social progress',[40] is in the long run fully dependent on the stability of our ecosystems. Likewise, societal stability is dependent on ensuring fundamental social rights. Thereby the social dimension is also included in the aim of a sustainable development, while a number of other EU sources, including the values and aims expressed in Articles 2 and 3(5) TEU, the Charter of Fundamental Rights and the EU's own case law, provide further bases for the inclusion and promotion of fundamental human and social rights.[41]

'The Genesis of EC Environmental Principles', in R. Macrory, I. Havercroft and R. Purdy (eds.), *Principles of European Environmental Law* (Groningen: Europa Law Publishing, 2004), pp. 29–47.

[36] See C. Voigt, 'Article 11 TFEU in the Light of the Principle of Sustainable Development in International Law', in Sjåfjell and Wiesbrock (eds.), *The Greening of European Business under EU Law*, pp. 31–50.

[37] Arguably even more clearly expressed in the Charter of Fundamental Rights of the European Union, OJ 2000 C-364/1 Article 37: 'A high level of environmental protection and the improvement of the quality of the environment must be integrated into the policies of the Union and ensured in accordance with the principle of sustainable development'.

[38] Article 9 TFEU: 'In defining and implementing its policies and activities, the Union shall take into account requirements linked to the promotion of a high level of employment, the guarantee of adequate social protection, the fight against social exclusion, and a high level of education, training and protection of human health'.

[39] Article 7 TFEU: 'The Union shall ensure consistency between its policies and activities, taking all of its objectives into account'.

[40] Article 3(3) TEU.

[41] For a discussion of the legal status of human rights protection after the Lisbon Treaty, which, inter alia, gives binding, primary law status to the Charter of Fundamental Rights, see

Through a milepost analysis of successes and crises facing the EU provided for in the following section, the value creation offered by the EU and the drawbacks will be made evident and will help showcase the narrative on sustainable value creation that the chapters of this edited collection seek to address.

1.3 MILEPOSTS: SUCCESSES AND CRISES IN THE EU'S HISTORICAL EVOLUTION

1.3.1 *The EU as a Foundation for Peace, Economic Success – and Decline*

The EU, as it is known today, was from the start not only aiming at the economic unity of neighbouring Member States but also ultimately helped end the frequent and destructive wars between neighbours, which culminated in the Second World War. After communism collapsed across Central and Eastern Europe, Europeans became closer neighbours.[42] In 1993, the Single Market was completed with the 'four freedoms' of: movement of goods, services, people and money. The 'Schengen' agreement allowed people to travel without having their passports checked at the borders.[43]

It is safe to say that the EU has brought with it many benefits to European citizens ranging from freedom of movement to work and study in Europe to indirect benefits from structural and cohesion funds enabling development of transport and environment and energy development.[44] Workers across Europe have seen their working conditions improve as a result of Europe-wide labour protections such as those found in the Working Time Directive[45] or in European health and safety requirements.[46]

S. Douglas-Scott, 'The Court of Justice of the European Union and the European Court of Human Rights after the Treaty of Lisbon', in S. Weatherill, S. de Vries and U. Bernitz (eds.), *The Protection of Fundamental Rights in the EU After Lisbon* (London: Bloomsbury Publishing, 2013), pp. 153–180.

[42] See European Union Website, 'The History of the European Union', available at: www.europa.eu/european-union/about-eu/history_en.

[43] Originally signed in 1985, supplemented with Schengen Convention in 1990 and incorporated into EU law in 1999 with the Treaty of Amsterdam.

[44] See e.g. European Commission, 'European Structural and Investment Funds', available at: www.ec.europa.eu/regional_policy/en/funding/.

[45] Directive 2003/88/EC of the European Parliament and of the Council of 4 November 2003 concerning certain aspects of the organisation of working time, OJ L 299, 18.11.2003, pp. 9–19.

[46] See e.g. Trade Union Congress (TUC), 'EU Membership and Health and Safety: The Benefits for UK Workers – A TUC Report' (2016) available at: www.tuc.org.uk/sites/default/files/EU_Health_Safety_Report_0.pdf.

The single currency was a major, ambitious EU project that had been conceived with the passing of the Treaty of Maastricht in 1993 and which came to fruition in 2002, with the introduction of the Euro, which replaced 12 of 15 national currencies in the EU, who became members of the European Monetary Union. During the 2000s the EU saw two further expansions ending with 27 members in 2007 after Bulgaria and Romania joined. In 2008 the euro's value had reached more than 1.5 to the dollar but in that year a worldwide recession took hold and caused damage to the euro's value. The Treaty of Lisbon was ratified by all EU countries before entering into force in 2009. It provides the EU with modern institutions and more efficient working methods.[47]

In 2009 Greece's level of debt led to a credit downgrade by three credit ratings agencies and to major falls in the financial markets with further problems arising for other European economies including Spain, Italy, Portugal and Ireland. By 2010 Greece's debt had been downgraded to junk status by Standard and Poor, and Spain and Portugal also saw their credit ratings cut. A 110 billion euro loan was granted to Greece but the euro value fell to a four-year low. The EU established the Banking Union to ensure safer and more reliable banks. Croatia became the 28th member of the EU in 2013.

In the 2014 European elections, more Eurosceptics were elected into the European Parliament. In the 2019 elections, the picture was rather more complicated, with soft Eurosceptic numbers decreased, but harder Eurosceptic representation increased.[48] A migration crisis in which millions of people have fled their homes and sought refuge in Europe has placed pressure on the EU. In 2015 alone, 1.3 million came to the EU, Norway and Switzerland, half of them from Syria, Afghanistan and Iraq.[49] With the reasons for flight unresolved, refugees have continued to try to access Europe. The EU was faced with the dilemma of how to take care of the refugees, who headed towards some EU countries such as Germany and Greece in much greater numbers than other countries saw, leading to divisions among the member states over refugee quotas and responsibilities.[50] The islands of the coastal state of Greece,

---

[47] Treaty of Lisbon amending the Treaty on European Union and the Treaty establishing the European Community, signed at Lisbon, 13 December 2007, OJ C 306, 17.12.2007, pp. 1–271.

[48] See for an account: A. Ripoll, 'The New European Parliament: more Eurosceptic?', *UK in a Changing Europe* (16 September 2019), available at www.ukandeu.ac.uk/the-new-european-parliament-more-eurosceptic/.

[49] Pew Research Center, 'Number of Refugees to Europe Surges to Record 1.3 Million in 2015' (2 August 2016), available at: www.pewglobal.org/2016/08/02/number-of-refugees-to-europe-surges-to-record-1-3-million-in-2015/.

[50] B. Riegert, 'Opinion: The EU is Divided by Refugee Policy', *DW* (15 December 2017), available at: www.dw.com/en/opinion-the-eu-is-divided-by-refugee-policy/a-41816730.

and the Italian island of Lampedusa, have been left with a disproportionate responsibility in practice for the refugees. In the second quarter of 2021, a more than 35,000 migrants and refugees into Europe were registered – more than 3 times higher than the 10,334 arrivals registered in the same period in 2020, and 56 per cent more than the 22,626 registered in that period in 2019. Forty-five per cent of those entering Europe came via the Western Mediterranean and Western African Atlantic routes (15,948) to Spain, whilst 38 per cent arrived in Italy and Malta and the remainder 17 per cent travelled to Greece, Cyprus and Bulgaria.[51]

And the extreme plight of the refugees on their way to Europe and in Europe for those who survive the journey, as well as the often horrific conditions that make highly unsafe journeys to Europe with uncertain outcomes a better choice, remains an unsolved issue for the EU, wishing to pride itself on solidarity.[52] The EU also finds itself the target of several terrorist attacks,[53] which may also have exacerbated xenophobia.[54]

All these stages of the EU's development are testament both to its strengths as a project but also to its weaknesses. Major growth of the membership has benefited huge numbers of citizens but the political impact of that growth has brought with it also a growth in Euroscepticism, fuelled in part by the debt crisis within the Eurozone.

1.3.2 *Account of the Euro Debt Crisis*

The global financial crisis that emerged in 2008 following the collapse of Lehman Brothers evolved into a sovereign debt crisis for certain European Member States, and subsequently the EU as a whole, leading to high unemployment rates, especially in the Southern European countries and to businesses closing down or moving overseas, and to xenophobia, social unrest and human rights violations.[55]

---

51 DTM, 'Europe – Mixed Migration Flows to Europe, Quarterly Overview (April–June 2021)' (27 August 2021), available at: https://dtm.iom.int/reports/europe-%E2%80%94-mixed-migration-flows-europe-quarterly-overview-april-june-2021.

52 See further: International Rescue Committee, 'Refugees in limbo – Greece', available at: www.rescue-uk.org/country/greece and see also M. Lowen, 'Lampedusa: Italy's gateway to Europe struggles with migrant influx', *BBC News* (13 May 2021), available at: www.bbc.co.uk/news/world-europe-57087818.

53 European Union Website, 'The History of the European Union'.

54 Open Society Foundations, 'Islamophobia in Europe' (May 2019), available at: www.opensocietyfoundations.org/explainers/islamophobia-europe.

55 See e.g. G. Friedman, 'Europe, Unemployment and Instability' (5 March 2014) *Stratfor Global Intelligence*, available at: www.businessforum.com/STRATFOR_Europe-Unemployment-Instability.pdf.

It is not easy to state conclusively what brought about the euro debt crisis. There are competing explanations, including: excessive public debt, diverging competitiveness and weak regulation of the financial sector.[56] Excessive public debt arose because many member states of the European Monetary Union failed to conduct sound fiscal policies and did not follow the Stability and Growth Pact. Consequently, when the economy slowed down they found themselves pushed out of the market as they were burdened by an unsustainable sovereign debt position.[57] There were different levels of competitiveness among the member states with the result that labour costs could not be met in some whilst others retained cost stability. The result was current account imbalances and external financing came to an end.[58] The financial sector had not been regulated adequately and loans were being granted without proper precautions. Banks then required to be bailed out by their governments, leading to them being burdened with debt.[59] In summary, the Eurozone was characterised by debt imbalances that led to financial instability.[60] There were asset bubbles caused by a flow of capital stimulated by cheap credit. As imbalances emerged the Eurozone had no real means of adjustment that single countries might otherwise have such as currency devaluation.[61] The European-level monetary policy of one interest rate served to increase the imbalances across the Eurozone so that for high-growth, high-inflation countries such as Spain and Ireland, the real interest rate was too low, causing the economy to overheat whereas for low-growth, low-inflation countries such as Germany, the real interest rate was too high, leading to depressed levels of growth and investment.[62]

Alongside this financial instability and growing distrust in the monetary policy there were louder complaints about the lack of trust in the political framework, with criticisms, not just from Eurosceptics, of the EU's democratic deficit, lack of transparency and too much intrusion upon member states' sovereignty.

The Greek financial crisis had two key causal factors. First, there was internal economic mismanagement within Greece including a lack of public accountability and fraud on a large scale. These resulted in unsustainable

---

[56] J. Haas and K. Gnath, 'The Euro Area Crisis: A Short History' (15 September 2016) 172 *Policy Paper Jaques Delors Institut*, at 3.
[57] Ibid.
[58] Ibid.
[59] Ibid.
[60] Ibid.
[61] Haas and Gnath, 'The Euro Area Crisis: A Short History'.
[62] Ibid.

debt levels, excessive public spending, high wage growth not supported by productivity growth, which led to a decline in Greece's competitiveness, a surge in credit growth, and massive tax evasion. Second, Greek membership in the Eurozone meant that Greece was subject to requirements that were not compatible with its own political and financial aspirations. As Greece's fiscal deficits rose in 2008–2010, interest rates on government and private debt in Greece increased rapidly. Handcuffed by the ECB, however, Greece was held captive and therefore could not reduce interest rates or devalue its currency to encourage economic growth and thereby protect is economic needs.[63] The numerous bailouts granted to Greece by the 'Troika' from 2010 were accompanied by demands for 'haircuts' and austerity. Despite the Greek people voting against the third bailout's terms in 2015, the government went ahead and pushed it through with the required austerity measures.[64] Today, Greece still struggles at the edge of recovery, showing that the technical measures and austerity measures ultimately did little to stimulate economic well-being, prosperity or sustainability.[65]

1.3.3 *Brexit, the Close Call of the Non-Grexit – and the Future of the EU*

Britain had been a member of the EU (and its predecessor European Economic Communities) since 1973, although it has often been described as an awkward partner, a reluctant member on many fronts.[66] The voice of the Eurosceptics in the UK grew louder over many years but the financial recession became a reason for challenging the country's continued presence in the Union. The ECB's response to the financial crisis resulted in mass unemployment in Greece and Spain and the refugee crisis presented a major challenge to Europe's open-borders policy and caused fears of an influx of migrants into Britain.

The UK's Brexit vote in June 2016 signified a further blow to the EU, and the vote to leave arguably shocked many in the UK as much as it shocked the EU. Then Prime Minister David Cameron called the Referendum in 2014 even though he personally believed that it would be a mistake for Britain to leave the EU. He was worried about gains by the far-right United Kingdom

[63] A. Kindrich, 'The Greek Financial Crisis (2009–2016)', *CFA Institute* (20 July 2017), available at: www.econcrises.org/2017/07/20/the-greek-financial-crisis-2009-2016/.

[64] Ibid.

[65] See OECD, 'Economic Policy Reforms 2021: Going for Growth – Greece', available at: www.oecd.org/economy/growth/Greece-country-note-going-for-growth-2021.pdf.

[66] S. George, *An Awkward Partner: Britain in the European Community* (New York: Oxford University Press, 1990).

Independence Party and so sought to appease anti-immigration voters in his party by promising the referendum on British exit from the EU if he won the 2015 election. His gamble back-fired and the British public voted by a small majority of 52 per cent in favour leaving.[67]

It may be said that the United Kingdom was never really invested in the EU to begin with. Whilst the Brexit votes were only *marginally* in favour of leaving, the referendum result in fact triggered a strong response that the outcome vote definitely needed to be respected. The experience was somewhat different in Greece where, despite citizens voting against the suggested measures, the government did not feel that the public vote was a binding vote and proceeded to sign up to the new measures proposed anyway.[68]

The complex Brexit negotiations were a source of tension, with no clear settlement in sight even after the formal exit date of 29 March 2019. Ultimately, an unsatisfactory deal was settled which barely went beyond an earlier feared no-deal and since the end of the transition period there has been much disquiet about the economic reality of the deal for people in the UK.[69]

In light of Brexit, terrorist threats, climate change and other environmental and social sustainability challenges, we need, more than ever, economic stimulus that is sustainable and that will nurture social well-being of all and reduce inequality. The EU has offered and offers an admirable value system. Yet, it has failed to achieve its full potential due to a lack of commitment on Member States' part.

These crises and current threats highlight to us the continued relevance of the EU. It may be too easy to lose sight of the EU's strengths and successes. Integration and close co-operation have helped to create wealth, higher social standards and increased opportunities for its citizens.[70] We should value the endeavours to create common principles and values of democracy, to protect human rights, and to support the rule of law in a social, economic and political EU. Now, in the face of these threats, it is our opinion that the EU should not retreat, but move forward and lead the way for the rest of the world in pursuit of sustainability – of securing social foundations for humanity within planetary boundaries.

---

[67] C. Oliver, *Unleashing Demons: The Inspiration Behind Channel 4 Drama Brexit: The Uncivil War* (London: Hodder & Stoughton, 2016).

[68] See e.g. I. Terzi, 'Grexit and Brexit: Lessons for the European Union', *E-International Relations* (May 2020), available at: www.e-ir.info/2020/05/04/grexit-and-brexit-lessons-for-the-eu/.

[69] J. Smith, 'Brexit: Five Charts Show the Impact on the UK Economy This Year', *ING* (8 March 2021), available at: https://think.ing.com/articles/measuring-the-brexit-effect-its-complicated.

[70] European Commission, Reflection Paper: Towards a Sustainable Europe by 2030, 30.01.2019, COM(2019)22 final.

1.4 ROADMAP OF THE BOOK

Through four Parts, the chapters in this book analyse why the EU is struggling, the challenges it faces in achieving sustainable value creation and suggestions as to what the EU – and all of us together – ought to do now. Starting in Part I, following this introductory chapter, Zetzche and Consiglio undertake a highly topical analysis of the EU's COVID-19 response, reflecting not only on the tragic consequences of the pandemic across the world but also putting forward proposals to mitigate the impact of the pandemic not only for the EU, but also for the developed and developing countries (see Chapter 2). Their suggestions are necessary ones for making the sustainability agenda possible. Lynch Fannon and Boland go the heart of the unsustainability of the corporation in their chapter, and they suggest how a more value-focused approach may provide a basis for change.

In Part II, the authors discuss the unsustainability of the European economic system. Johnston and Pugh's analysis proves particularly insightful for the purposes of our discussion on value creation, as it demonstrates that although quantitative easing policies boosted asset prices and made the wealthy even wealthier by lowering borrowing costs for governments and large companies, it did not necessarily stimulate economic activity. This failure resulted because, whilst Member States made adjustments to stimulate innovation and competitiveness, there were also public spending cuts, more flexible labour markets and commitment to shareholder primacy, all of which created barriers to economic recovery. As Johnston and Pugh make clear in their chapter, too much reliance on monetary policy to stimulate the economy leads to more private debt and more wealth inequality.

Kyriakides explores sustainability and what is denoted as 'Eurozone 2' and he suggests that this is a significantly modified version of the Eurozone following the financial crisis. He investigates whether or not we have a more sustainable Eurozone. He pinpoints existing imbalances and queries the extent to which the changes have had a beneficial effect. In his discussion, he draws links between economic sustainability and socio-environmental-cultural sustainability. For Kyriakides, sustainability encompasses future (preservation) and present (equitable/efficient resource allocation) generations, and economic, social, ecological dimensions that allow it to withstand external shocks. Kyriakides argues that the Eurozone measures are one-dimensional and thus limited because they focus only on the economic dimension; that they are geared towards austerity; that budgetary discipline increases inequality; and that there have been unbalanced fortifications against shocks and lack of a wider stakeholder input.

Liarvogas and Kratimenou tell us that the measures to restore Greece failed because they relied on extreme austerity with the effect of decelerating economic growth and increasing the ratio of debt to gross domestic product (GDP). Liarvogas and Kratimenou also note that severe austerity was not socially accepted, it provoked a rise of nationalism that continues to threaten European integration. They argue that austerity was a trap that led to worse economic outcomes and few sustainability gains. In their view, sustainable growth would have been a better alternative, as that depends on relief of public debt, quality of the outstanding structural reforms, political stability, and ability to cope with sudden external shocks. The answer for these authors is less austerity, more and deeper structural reforms, and European solidarity regarding growth and employment.

Mahönen focusses on the role of shareholders and the barriers and the opportunities for shareholders to support a sustainable economy. Mahönen challenges the EU's favoured approach in stimulating more long-term and sustainable business: nudging shareholders to be more active, through his analysis of the threats and possibilities in shareholder participation.

All these chapters point to what went wrong, suggesting primarily that qualitative easing and austerity worsened the situation by creating greater levels of inequality and doing nothing to reduce the debt burden, and highlighting the limitations of shareholder activism as the way to promote sustainable value creation.

In light of Greece's experience and what has happened across Europe we need more creative and socially beneficial responses than those we have witnessed so far. In Part III, the chapters put forward some suggestions that may contribute towards stronger and more lasting solutions. In their chapter, Cullen, Mahönen and Rapp Nilsen analyse the EU's sustainable finance initiative, which the EU launched with its action plan in 2018 and followed up quickly with legislative measures in 2019, 2020 and 2021, identifying the potential it provides for financing sustainable value creation as well as its weaknesses and possibilities for reform.

Sjåfjell and Tsagas discuss different ways of integrating sustainable value creation into the governance of European business. With the starting point that sustainable value creation is an emerging concept in corporate law and corporate governance, they discuss the potential of securing sustainable value creation in Europe through a company law reform, and through reform of corporate governance codes. While corporate governance codes have been proponents of shareholder primacy, codes are also where we find the most examples in Europe of the emergence of the concept of sustainable value creation. Integrating this more fully into corporate governance codes could be envisaged as a support for a law reform or as an alternative way to promote sustainable business while waiting for legislative reform. Recognising that the individual company ultimately will need to integrate sustainability into its governance, whether that is a result of effective legislative reform in Europe, or of corporate governance codes that are revised to promote sustainability, or in the absence of either, the authors also discuss the potential of integrating sustainable value creation in company constitutions as a way to realise the shift of business towards sustainability.

Corporate creativity is essential for achieving sustainable value creation and in Chapter 10 Lambooy and colleagues explore the creativity that is possible through social enterprise. They note the potential ability of social enterprises to contribute to economic development and to offer efficient solutions to socio-economic problems. They note also the desirability of providing an enabling and favourable legal environment that would recognise and support social enterprises. The positive contribution that social enterprises might make is through their ability to be inclusive and to offer participatory governance models, with input from stakeholders and society. Lambooy et al. showcase the innovative use of the corporate form in the creation of the social enterprise, Dopper. In the Netherlands, there are no specific laws or structures for social enterprises, yet Dopper is one of a growing number of social enterprises in the Netherlands. A noteworthy feature of Dopper is its highly participatory structure as well as its contribution towards a solution for stimulation and sustainability.

Villiers and Russell discuss women's empowerment and the potential for women to contribute to the economy and to benefit from it more meaningfully. Their starting point is that women have been more negatively affected by the financial crisis and by subsequent austerity measures and the COVID-19 pandemic. They consider women's experience of the Greek debt crisis and note that how women fared in Greece could be seen also in other contexts as regards women's experience of disadvantage. Villiers and Russell argue that efforts to encourage and assist women's participation in the labour market and the economy are positive steps, but such efforts remain limited. They argue that it is important to avoid instrumentalising women's roles and instead to think about their human rights and the need to empower them. That would be a more sustainable approach.

Finally, as editors of this book, we conclude in Chapter 12 with some suggestions for the future.

1.5 CONCLUSION

There is inherent value in the EU, which is made most evident if recourse is made to the freedoms and standards it has exported to its citizens and globally, and to the respect it provides to the rule of law. Sandy Tsagas, in a celebration of Europe Day on 9 May 2012, eloquently outlines the following:

> A union by far complete, yet characterised by truly outstanding and admirable founding principles. A union comprised of equal yet diverse European member states and a supranational authority actively created in accord by its very member states. A union that holds as equals all of its member states while at the same time respects each one's individual diversities. A union that created an internal single market for its members based on four fundamental freedoms: of goods, of persons, of capital, of services. A union that supports research, growth and development. A union that, despite all odds, created and sustained, thus far, a single currency. A union that respects the rule of law and possesses for this purpose appropriate legal mechanisms to uphold it. A union that actively respects democracy and human rights. A union that has come to play a very important role, political and financial, in the international community. What other union do you know of that can boast all of these attributes put together? Few, in their right mind, if given the opportunity, would not want to be part of this union.[71]

The EU offers an admirable value system comprising overarching goals of sustainability, including environmental protection, the achievement of peace and the promotion of human rights and welfare, combining this with instrumental goals of free movement of people, goods, services, capital, the free establishment and cross-border activity of business and fair competition amongst market actors. Yet this has failed to achieve its full potential due to a lack of commitment on Member States' part. The contributions in this edited collection all address the notion of value creation in the EU by focussing on some of the opportunities and the limitations present to the development of the legal, political and social value system that the EU aspires to offer.

It is clear that the Eurozone crisis was tied up with faulty governance and economics and there is a need for new economic and political approaches. The traditional capitalism model and the corporate law models of shareholder primacy and the growing influence of financialisation have proven to be problematic for all and disastrous for some countries and citizens. Inequality, poor governance, and strict austerity measures are challenges that need to be dealt

---

[71] S. Tsagas 'A Day for Europe – there is still hope', published in *EurActive* (9 May 2012) [no longer available online].

with, not ways to solve the problems of the region. To achieve a sustainable future, new, sustainable ways of acting in the economic arena must be found. The corporation has long been regarded as an innovative invention but it has not always led to sustainable or good social or economic outcomes for everyone. Through neo-liberal policies and an emphasis on shareholder primacy, the corporation has instead often been a vehicle which has been used for business activities that have resulted in greater inequality, human exploitation and environmental harm. It is time to reinvigorate the corporation's potential for positive innovation and financial support. This requires us to reframe our corporate laws and to find ways of supporting sustainable and social entrepreneurial activities. We must also be more inclusive, especially to involve women generally as well as vulnerable groups across global value chains in more empowering, non-instrumental ways. The chapters in this book have shown that there are examples of good practice that could be transformative and we need to build on these.

Ten Million or One Hundred Million Casualties? COVID-19 and Europe's Sustainability Agenda

Dirk Andreas Zetzsche and Roberta Consiglio

2.1 INTRODUCTION

The COVID-19 crisis has had a profound impact on human life in the Global North, which has been burdened by hundreds of thousands of deaths, social distancing, the shutting down of whole industries and an immediate economic decline. Strict measures were put in place as the number of casualties soared worldwide in an attempt to limit the spiralling human cost. As of 31 December 2020, the number of COVID-19 casualties has approached 2 million; the death toll keeps rising. In the end, the overall number of direct casualties of the crisis may be anything up to 10 million in total.

Such a heavy loss of human life is clearly a reason for mourning. However, we make the argument that for developing countries (for which we use herein, synonymously, the term Low- and Middle-Income Countries – LMICs)[1] the impact of the crisis is potentially far greater. Yet owing to the age structure in developing countries the impact there is less about direct casualties, and far more about the social and economic tragedies caused indirectly by the epidemic such as hunger and famine. To put the potential scale of the devastation into perspective, we present an estimate that, if poorly managed, the COVID-19 crisis could take 100 million or more lives in developing countries. In order to reach this number, we have considered and collected the different ways in which COVID-19 may hit these countries by engaging in a literature and policy review. We show that, if poorly managed, the crisis may reverse the positive development trend of the last twenty years, by providing an overview on how COVID-19 is hindering the progress on the United Nations (UN) Sustainable Developments Goals (SDGs), and submit that it may even put the realisation of the SDGs at risk. We further show that the

---

[1] LMICs include all Least Developed Countries (LDCs) according to UN classification.

measures taken by European countries and the European Union (EU) so far are insufficient to mitigate the economic and social impact of the crisis. To address the threat of an enormous number of *indirect* casualties (on top of direct casualties) and the potential departure from, or delay of implementation of, sustainability commitments worldwide (and in Europe in particular), we propose policy measures to mitigate the most severe impacts of the crisis on developing countries.

This chapter is structured as follows: Section 2.2 argues that whatever the direct impact may be according to various statistics, the number of casualties in developing countries is potentially underestimated. In Section 2.3 we present the first and most severe indirect impact of the crisis, namely the return of hunger and famine. In Section 2.4 we go on to present a second possible result of the crisis, specifically a departure from the SDGs. In Section 2.5 we show that the global support is inadequate to reverse the trend. We also take a closer look at the European countries and their policy responses. This closer look confirms the view that publicly announced policy actions so far are most likely inadequate, with potentially severe consequences for the European sustainability agenda. In Section 2.6 some policy considerations to reduce the impact of COVID-19 on developing countries are outlined, in an effort to awaken decision-makers and prevent the aforementioned 100 million casualties prediction from becoming a horrifying reality. Section 2.7 concludes.

2.2 UNDERESTIMATED NUMBERS?

The Johns Hopkins Institute reports, per 31 December 2020, more than 83 million reported COVID-19 and/or SARS-Cov-2 cases worldwide, with more than 1.8 million casualties. For all LMICs combined, as defined by the World Bank,[2] the Institute reports about 42 million cases and 988,000 casualties[3]. Even though high in absolute terms, given that 80 per cent of the world's population resides in the developing countries, the figures for this part of the world are lower than expected. The relative distribution of COVID-19 casualties reported in LMICs and developed countries is not matching the relative distribution of the world population in the two areas, given that 80 per cent of the world's population live in LMICs; while the relative percentage

---

[2] World Bank, 'Low & middle income [dataset]' (2020), available at: data.worldbank.org/income-level/low-and-middle-income.
[3] Rounded numbers based on own calculation of HDX data of low- and middle-income countries. Humanitarian Data Exchange (HDX), 'Novel Coronavirus (COVID-19) cases data [dataset]' (2020), available at: data.humdata.org/dataset/novel-coronavirus-2019-ncov-cases.

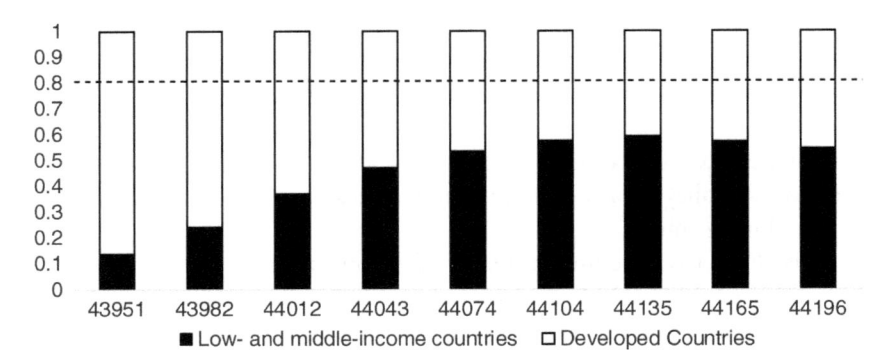

FIGURE 2.1 *Number of COVID-19 deaths reported (in per cent) in LMICs and developed countries (data as of 31 December 2020). Authors' creation based on Johns Hopkins Institute data (Humanitarian Data Exchange (HDX), 2020).*

of COVID-19 casualties have risen throughout 2020, they are yet lower than expected (see Figure 2.1).

Apparently, the COVID-19 virus started spreading later in most of the LMICs; indicating they could eventually reach levels of contagion similar to (or even higher) than those reported in developed countries at a later stage[4]. Regardless of the former, the direct impact of the COVID-19 crisis was for long most likely underestimated in the official statistics.[5] For instance, official data did not take into account people who did not die in hospital or people who did not test positive for the virus.[6]

In developing countries, the hospitalisation and testing rates are relatively low and thus so too are the COVID-19 numbers. For instance, in Luxembourg – a tiny country with a very well-developed healthcare system and a testing strategy targeting the whole population – there have been a high number of COVID-19 cases but a relatively low number of casualties. If the rate of infection in Luxembourg was to be replicated in developing countries, the number

---

[4] B. Choon-Looi., C. Brasher, E. Chikumba, R. McDougall, J. Mellin-Olsen and A. Enright, 'The COVID-19 Pandemic: Effects on Low- and Middle-Income Countries' (2020) 131 *Anesthesia & Analgesia*, 86–92, available at: https://doi.org/10.1213/ANE.0000000000004846.

[5] P. Schellekens and D. Sourrouille, 'COVID-19 Mortality in Rich and Poor Countries: A Tale of Two Pandemics?' (2020) 9260 *Policy Research Working Paper*, available at: https://openknowledge.worldbank.org/handle/10986/33844. See also BBC, 'Coronavirus: Health chief hails Africa's fight against Covid-19', *BBC*, 23 September 2020, available at: www.bbc.com/news/world-africa-54248507.

[6] The Economist, 'Tracking Covid-19 excess deaths across countries', *The Economist*, 16 April 2021, available at: www.economist.com/graphic-detail/2020/07/15/tracking-covid-19-excess-deaths-across-countries.

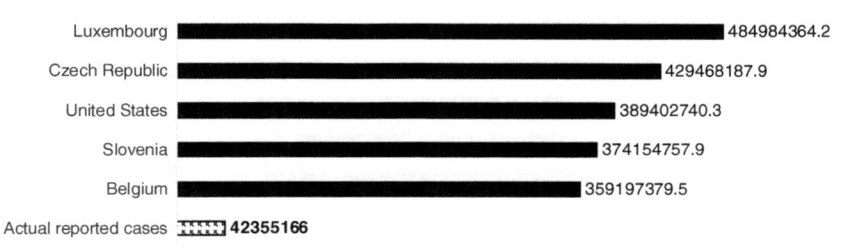

Luxembourg ████████████████████████████ 484984364.2
Czech Republic ████████████████████████ 429468187.9
United States ██████████████████████ 389402740.3
Slovenia █████████████████████ 374154757.9
Belgium ████████████████████ 359197379.5

Actual reported cases ▨ **42355166**

FIGURE 2.2 *Estimated number of total COVID-19 cases in all LMICs combined, extrapolated from the highest five COVID-19 cases country ratios of OECD (high-income) countries versus actual reported cases in all LMICs combined. COVID-19 cases country ratios = total number of confirmed COVID-19 cases per total population (data as of 31 December 2020). Authors' creation based on Johns Hopkins Institute data (Humanitarian Data Exchange (HDX), 2020).*
Note: COVID-19 cases country ratios = total number of confirmed COVID-19 cases per total population (data as of 31 December 2020).

of COVID-19 cases would be around 485 million – ten times the number reported so far (Figure 2.2).

We thus have reason to believe that the true numbers in LMICs are also higher, or at least will be in the near future. This is because, in principle and with some exceptions (Hong Kong and Singapore among them), dense living makes transmission of the disease much more likely: the closer people live the higher the transmission rates. This doesn't bode well at all for super-cities in poorer countries, with Delhi, Jakarta, Karachi, Lagos, Manila, Mexico City, Mumbai and São Paulo all in the more than-20 million inhabitants range. This may explain why for Mexico City alone some studies report an excess mortality of 122,765 casualties until early September 2020.[7]

At the same time, a lockdown is very difficult to manage in countries where people have to work to eat. How does one stop people leaving their homes when a week at home equals starvation?

Figure 2.3 estimates the *number of casualties* for developing countries based on the numbers we currently have from developed Organisation for Economic Co-operation and Development (OECD) countries. Applying the ratios for the USA and the UK – developed economies with vast resources compared with developing countries – to the approximate 6.4 billion people[8] residing in developing countries would lead to 6,725,314 casualties (US ratio)

---

[7] D. Jorgic, 'Mexico says 122,765 extra people died during pandemic in "excess deaths" study', *Reuters*, 6 September 2020, available at: www.reuters.com/article/us-health-coronavirus-mexico-excessdeath-idUSKBN25X00K.

[8] World Bank, 'Low & middle income [dataset]'.

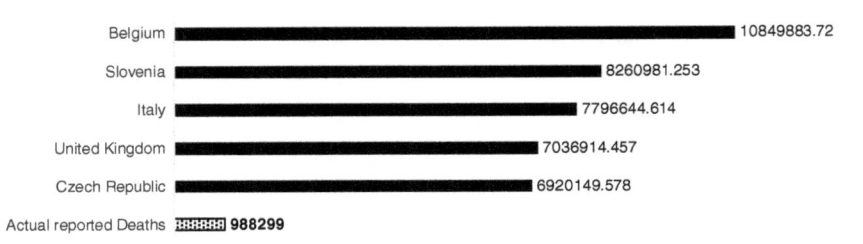

FIGURE 2.3 *Estimated number of total COVID-19 casualties in all LMICs combined, extrapolated from the highest five COVID-19 deaths country ratios of OECD (high-income) countries versus actual reported casualties in all LMICs combined. COVID-19 deaths country ratios = total number of confirmed COVID-19 deaths per total population (data as of 31 December 2020). Authors' creation based on Johns Hopkins Institute data (Humanitarian Data Exchange (HDX), 2020).*
Note: COVID-19 deaths country ratios = total number of confirmed COVID-19 deaths per total population (data as of 31 December 2020).

and 7,036,914 casualties (UK ratio), respectively. If we applied the scenarios from Luxembourg and Germany – two countries at the heart of Europe with well-developed public social and medical systems – the number of COVID-19 casualties would still amount to 5,172,191 (Luxembourg ratio), and 2,589,128 (Germany ratio), respectively.

However, according to some studies, demography and age structure in a population 'may help explain differences in fatality rates across countries'.[9] The virus could have a lower impact on casualties in LMICs as the population in this region is younger than in developed countries, and it is primarily elderly people who are most vulnerable to the virus.

Estimating COVID 19 casualties is not an exact science, for sure. Given that the epidemic's direct impact depends on a combination of multiple factors,[10] and experiences with COVID-19 in wealthy countries may not be easily transferred to developing countries,[11] a precise figure is beyond reach. But our

[9] J. B. Dowd. L. Andriano, D. M. Brazel, V. Rotondi, X. Ding, Y. Liu and M. C. Mills, 'Demographic Science Aids in Understanding the Spread and Fatality Rates of COVID-19' (2020), 117 *PNAS*, 9696–9698, available at: https://doi.org/10.1073/pnas.2004911117.

[10] M. R. Nepomuceno, E. Acosta, D. Alburez-Gutierrez, J. M. Aburto, A. Gagnon and C. M. Turra, 'Besides Population Age Structure, Health and other Demographic Factors Can Contribute to Understanding the COVID-19 Burden' (2020), 117 *PNAS*, 13881–13883, available at: https://doi.org/10.1073/pnas.2008760117; F. Natale, D. Ghio, D. Tarchi, A. Goujon and A. Conte, 'COVID-19 cases and case fatality rate by age' (2020) *European Commission*, available at: https://knowledge4policy.ec.europa.eu/publication/covid-19-cases-case-fatality-rate-age_en.

[11] G. Demombynes, 'COVID-19 Age-Mortality Curves Are Flatter in Developing Countries' (2020) 9313 *Policy Research Working Paper*, available at: https://openknowledge.worldbank.org/handle/10986/34028.

rough estimate supports the intermediate result that numbers of COVID-19 cases in LMICs are likely misrepresented on the lower end – a factor that we need to take into account for all crisis-related policy steps.[12]

2.3 RETURN OF HUNGER AND FAMINE

While these 10 million casualties would already amount to a nightmare scenario, the true horror only materialises once we take the indirect impacts of the crisis into account. The UN's World Food Programme expects the number of undernourished people in 2020 to be up to 19 per cent higher than the baseline scenario; this translates into 132 million additional undernourished people, attributable to the COVID-19 crisis.[13]

To provide some background, in the last fifty years, mankind had won its age-old battle against hunger. While famines in the 1960s killed more than 50 million people, hunger was relatively non-existent in the 2010s, with fewer than 500,000 people dying of starvation during the decade.[14] This prompted policy bodies around the world to announce that the world would be close to realising SDG No. 2 (zero hunger), which foresees the eradication of hunger and under-nutrition by 2030.[15]

We argue in this section that the COVID-19 crisis will bring hunger and starvation back on to the regulatory agenda. One major contributing factor on which we focus in this chapter is that the hard currency that has allowed developing countries to feed its populations will cease to flow in from developed countries.

We formulate this argument in three steps. First, we argue that hard currency is a necessity for large-scale economic well-being. Second, we argue

---

[12] According to data at 31 December 2020.

[13] FAO, IFAD, UNICEF, WFP and WHO, 'The state of food security and nutrition in the world 2020: transforming food systems for affordable healthy diets' (2020) *FAO*, available at: https://doi.org/10.4060/ca9692en. World Bank, 'For Sub-Saharan Africa, Coronavirus Crisis Calls for Policies for Greater Resilience', *World Bank*, 9 April 2020; World Bank, 'COVID-19 (Coronavirus) Drives Sub-Saharan Africa Toward First Recession in 25 Years', 9 April 2020, available at: www.worldbank.org/en/region/afr/publication/for-sub-saharan-africa-coronavirus-crisis-calls-for-policies-for-greater-resilience; The Economist, 'The race to feed Africa during a pandemic', *The Economist*, 23 April 2020, available at: www.economist.com/middle-east-and-africa/2020/04/23/the-race-to-feed-africa-during-a-pandemic; Food Security Information Network (FSIN), '2020 Global Report on Food Crises' (2020), available at: www.fsinplatform.org/global-report-food-crises-2020.

[14] J. Hasell and M. Roser, 'Famines' (2017), Our World in Data, available at: ourworldindata.org/famines.

[15] United Nations, 'Sustainable Development Goals. Goal 2: Zero Hunger' (2020), *United Nations*, available at: www.un.org/sustainabledevelopment/hunger/.

that the main wells of hard currency have dried up owing to the crisis. Third, we argue that there are no substitutes for the availability of hard currency as rising populations are dependent on a *developing*, rather than stagnant, economy.

2.3.1 *Dependency on Hard Currency to Prevent Hunger and Famine*

The economies of developing countries, and the long-term prevention of hunger and famine, depend on the influx of hard currencies.[16]

This is because some of the developing countries never had any, or have long neglected, their agriculture, production and manufacturing sectors, owing to the availability of inexpensive alternatives facilitated through a hitherto uninterrupted global supply chain. In turn, these countries need to buy food, or at least engineering products, information and communications technology goods, advanced agricultural goods (e.g. modified seeds) and other technical goods, as well as seeds (necessary for industrial agricultural production) and crucial commodities (e.g. oil and gas), all of which are produced by more developed countries and are traded on a global level in hard currencies.

If developing countries lack hard currency, they can neither buy food nor the goods necessary to produce it. This will lead to their own economic downturn, with their currency value tanking against hard currencies. In turn, farmers in these countries will lack sufficient funds to buy seeds *and* oil and gas, hence their productivity will suffer, resulting in insufficient domestic food production. The situation is particularly dire if we assume that food production has already suffered from social distancing measures, which have prevented migrant workers from travelling to their work places and assisting in agricultural work. Accordingly, the lack of hard currency will hit developing countries at a time when local supply is already weak and many farmers' resources are depleted.

In developing countries, populations grow at a rate that exceeds their capacity to produce food.[17] In turn, these countries need to import food at an increasing rate. This makes net-food-importing countries particularly

---

[16] FAO, IFAD, UNICEF, WFP and WHO, 'The state of food security and nutrition in the world 2017 – building resilience for peace and food security' (2017), available at: www.fao.org/3/a-i7695e.pdf; FAO, 'Financing normal levels of commercial imports of basic foodstuffs in the context of the Marrakesh decision on the least-developed and net food-importing developing countries' (2003), available at: www.fao.org/3/y5109e/y5109e00.htm.

[17] FAO, 'The future of food and agriculture – trends and challenges' (2017), available at: www.fao.org/3/a-i6583e.pdf.

vulnerable to economic shocks and currency depreciations. Indeed, the Food and Agriculture Organization of the United Nations (FAO) outlined that: 'Seventy-five percent of the countries with food crises that also suffered from economic shocks are net food importers'.[18]

2.3.2 *Main Wells of Hard Currency Dried Out*

At the same time, developing countries cannot purchase food on world markets where hard currency is expected in return (i.e. where the buyer has to effectively pay more due to using their own local (non-hard) currency). This section argues that the main sources of hard currency are about to dry out owing to the crisis. These sources are the global supply chain (GSC), tourism, commodities, remittances and foreign investments.

2.3.2.1 Disruption of Global Supply Chain

The GSC relies on developing countries as part of the global workbench. In recent years, participation in the GSC has become very important for many, in particular developing countries.

Some insights into the contribution of the GSC to the gross domestic product (GDP) of developing economies can be inferred by looking into trade data.[19] In the last three years, trade boosted the GDP of LMICs by an average of 50 per cent; in some countries, this figure reached 120 per cent (e.g. Liberia, Cambodia and Malaysia), while for others it was more modest, at around 30 per cent (e.g. Sudan, Turkmenistan and Kenya).[20]

According to the OECD's Trade in Value Added (TiVA) database, presenting data up to 2015, developed economies and developing economies show the same rate of participation in Global Value Chains (GVCs), which is estimated to contribute to 41.4 per cent of their total exports (Figure 2.4).[21]

---

[18] FAO, IFAD, UNICEF, WFP and WHO, 'The State of Food Security and Nutrition in the World 2019 – Safeguarding against Economic Slowdowns and Downturns', Rome, FAO (2019), p. 61, available at: www.wfp.org/publications/2019-state-food-security-and-nutrition-world-sofi-safeguarding-against-economic-.

[19] A. Nicita, V. Ognivtsev and M. Shirotori, 'Global Supply Chains: Trade and Economic Policies for Developing Countries' (2013) 55 *Policy Issues in International Trade and Commodities Study Series*, available at: unctad.org/en/PublicationsLibrary/itcdtab56_en.pdf.

[20] World Bank, 'Trade (per cent of GDP) [dataset]' (2020), World Bank, Washington, DC. © World Bank, License: CC BY-4.0, available at: data.worldbank.org/indicator/NE.TRD.GNFS.ZS.

[21] World Trade Organization, 'Trade in value-added and global value chains: statistical profiles' (2020) Geneva: © 2020, World Trade Organization, underlying data from OECD, TiVA Database.

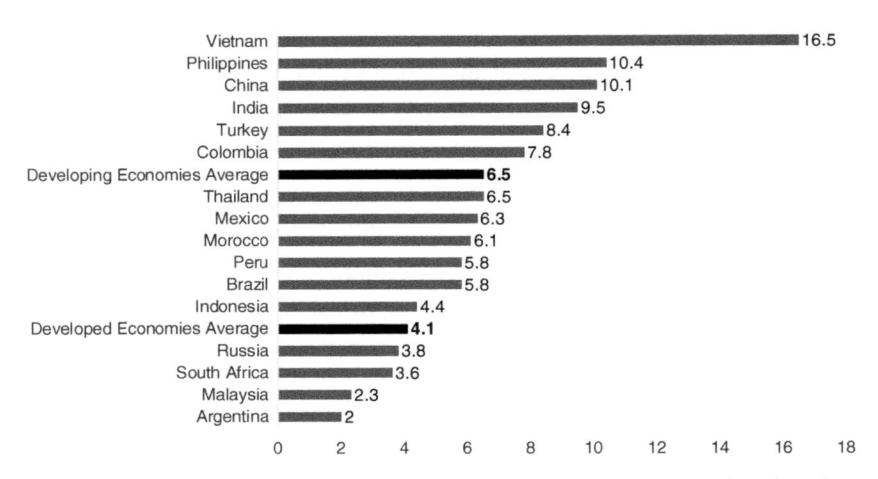

FIGURE 2.4 *Annual percentage growth-rate of participation in GVCs for selected developing countries, 2005–2015. Source: World Trade Organization based on TiVA Database*[22]

The numbers given here make it abundantly clear how the disruption of the GSC will both impact developed and developing countries, mutually connected through global tangled trade networks.

Even though the industry most impacted by COVID-19 is the services industry, merchandise trade was also highly affected by the crisis (Figure 2.5).[23]

Overall, according to the World Bank, global trade is expected to decline about 13.4 per cent in 2020, a much more severe contraction than during the global financial crisis.[24] Such a fall is exacerbated by the negative impacts of the crisis on trade in services (e.g. tourism, see Section 2.3.2.2) and by delays in shipments.[25]

[22] © World Trade Organization, 'Trade in value-added and global value chains: statistical profiles' and underlying data from © Organisation for Economic Co-operation and Development (OECD), TiVA Database, available at: www.wto.org/english/res_e/statis_e/miwi_e/all_Profiles_e.pdf.

[23] World Trade Organization, 'Trade falls steeply in first half of 2020', World Trade Organization, 22 June 2020, available at: www.wto.org/english/news_e/pres20_e/pr858_e.htm; S. Miroudot, 'Reshaping the policy debate on the implications of COVID-19 for global supply chains' (2020) *Journal of International Business Policy*, available at: https://doi.org/10.1057/s42214-020-00074-6.

[24] World Bank, *Global Economic Prospects, June 2020*, Washington, DC: World Bank © World Bank, Licence: CC BY 3.0 IGO, available at: openknowledge.worldbank.org/handle/10986/33748.

[25] Ibid.

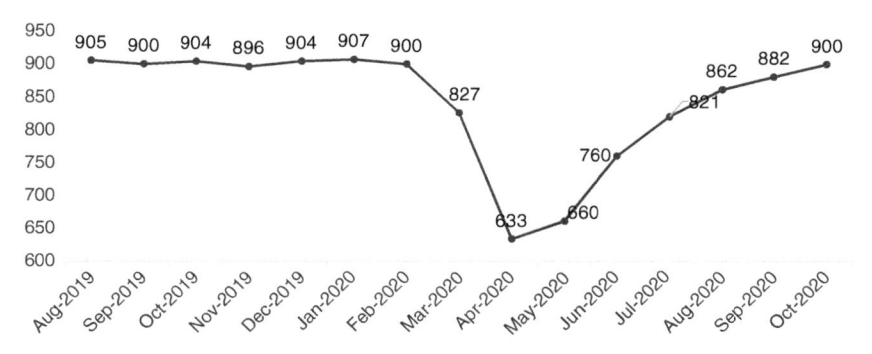

FIGURE 2.5 *Monthly international merchandise trade volume (OECD countries), exports in goods (value). Authors' creation based on OECD, 'Monthly International Merchandise Trade (IMTS) – Headline Series [dataset]'*[26]

2.3.2.2 Halt of Global Tourism

Another main source of hard currency is tourism. In order to measure the impact of tourism on GDP, we have used as an indicator international tourism receipts as a percentage of exports.[27]

In recent years, international tourism receipts have contributed on average to 6 per cent of exports in LMICs:[28] in some countries the contribution has been closer to 80 per cent (e.g. Maldives), while in other countries it has been negligible (e.g. Guinea, Mauritania and South Sudan).

Global tourism has essentially stopped in the wake of the COVID-19 crisis and the UN World Tourism Organization (UNWTO) estimates a drop in export revenues from international tourism of US$935 billion and a 72 per cent decline in international arrivals in the first ten months of 2020.[29] This disruption to the tourism industry will lead, in some LDCs and developing countries to significantly less hard currency being available.

2.3.2.3 Commodities Market Downturn

In recent years, total natural resources rents have contributed 3.75 per cent to the GDP of LMICs.[30] Again, the numbers vary notably, though. In some

[26] OECD statistics, available at: stats.oecd.org/Index.aspx?DataSetCode=MEI_TRD.

[27] World Bank, 'International tourism, receipts (current US$) [dataset]' (2020), World Bank, Washington, DC. © World, Bank, Licence: CC BY-4.0, available at: data.worldbank.org/indicator/ST.INT.RCPT.CD.

[28] Ibid.

[29] UNWTO, 'Latest tourism data' (2021), www.unwto.org/unwto-world-tourism-barometer-data.

[30] World Bank, 'Total natural resources rents (per cent of GDP) [dataset]' (2020), World Bank, Washington, DC. © World Bank, Licence: CC BY-4.0, available at: data.worldbank.org/indicator/NY.GDP.TOTL.RT.ZS.

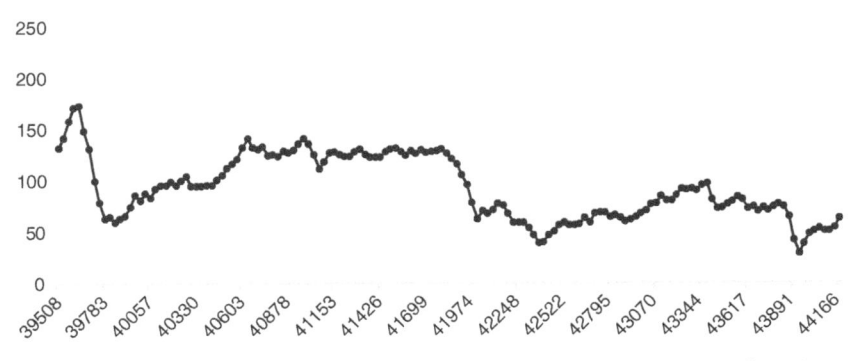

FIGURE 2.6 *Monthly indices based on nominal US dollars, 2010=100, March 2008 to December 2020. Authors' creation based on World Bank data.*[31]

countries the contribution has been closer to 40 per cent (e.g. Iraq, Libya and Republic of Congo), while in other countries it has been minimal (e.g. Bangladesh, Cuba and Namibia).

Less industrial production in developed countries leads to less demand for commodities.[32] Less demand has led to lower prices,[33] and in turn less income from commodities sales in *some* developing countries (while developing countries that have hard currency could in fact have mitigated the effect of this decline). South Sudan, for example, relies heavily on oil exports, which account for 97 per cent of national exports and 88 per cent of government revenues.[34] The drop in oil price has caused a massive decline in national revenues.[35]

Figure 2.6 and Figure 2.7 show the drop in energy commodities prices.

The decline of the commodities market will lead to less hard currency being available in some developing countries, with those countries heavily dependent on commodity-based income suffering the most.

2.3.2.4 Significant Reduction in Remittances

Another of the main sources of hard currency is remittances. In 2019, about US$548 billion flew into LMICs through funds wired by relatives (equivalent

---

[31] World Bank, 'Commodity price data (the pink sheet) [dataset]', available at: www.worldbank.org/en/research/commodity-markets.

[32] World Bank Group, 'Commodity Markets Outlook' (2020), World Bank, Washington, DC. © World Bank, Licence: CC BY 3.0 IGO, available at: https://openknowledge.worldbank.org/handle/10986/33624; World Bank, 'A Shock Like No Other: Coronavirus Rattles Commodity Markets' (2020).

[33] World Bank, *Global Economic Prospects, June 2020*.

[34] A. Lahreche and N. A. Hobdari, 'Four Things to Know about how Fragile States like South Sudan Are Coping with COVID-19', *IMF News*, 20 November 2020.

[35] Lahreche and Hobdari, 'Four Things to Know'.

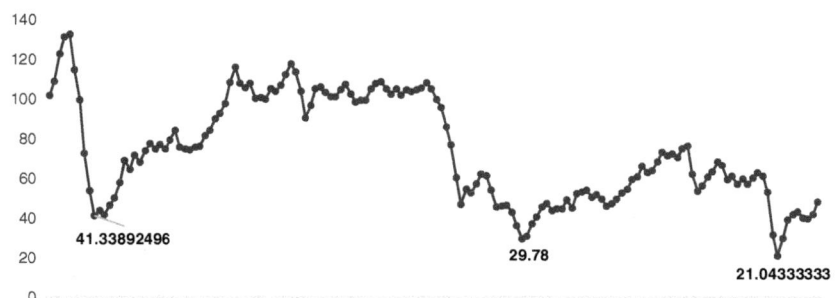

FIGURE 2.7 *Monthly prices in nominal US dollars of crude oil, average (in $/bbl.), March 2008 to December 2020. Authors' creation based on World Bank data.*[36]

on average to about 2 per cent of their GDP; the share of remittances on GDP reaches 9.2 per cent in countries in fragile and conflict-affected situations).[37] However, such remittances are reliant on migrant workers being able to earn money. With developed countries in crisis mode and restrictions affecting access to workplaces, the capacity of migrant workers to travel to their workplace and in turn send money home is significantly diminished.

By some estimates, remittances to LMICs are expected to decline by about 7 per cent in 2020 and by a further 7.5 per cent in 2021; this equates to a substantial total drop of around US$78 billion.[38] Yet others predict a speedy recovery of remittances in certain regions, in particular Latin-America.[39] For the remainder of this chapter we will rely on the negative scenario – while hoping for a better state.

2.3.2.5 Decline of Foreign Investments

The final main source of hard currency is foreign investments. Foreign Direct Investment (FDI) in developing economies amounted to US$685 billion in 2019 (equivalent to about 2 per cent of their GDP).[40]

---

[36] Ibid.

[37] World Bank, 'GDP (current US$) [dataset]' (2020), World Bank, Washington, DC. © World Bank, Licence: CC BY-4.0, available at: data.worldbank.org/indicator/NY.GDP.MKTP .CD; World Bank, 'COVID-19: remittance flows to shrink 14 per cent by 2021' (2020), available at: www.worldbank.org/en/news/press-release/2020/10/29/covid-19-remittance-flows-to-shrink-14-by-2021.

[38] World Bank, 'COVID-19: remittance flows to shrink 14 per cent'.

[39] UNDP, 'Stand by me: COVID-19 and the resilience of remittance flows to LAC' (2020), available at: www.latinamerica.undp.org/content/rblac/en/home/presscenter/director-s-graph-for-thought/stand-by-me--covid-19-and-the-resilience-of-remittance-flows-to-.html.

[40] UNCTAD, 'World Investment Report 2020 International Production Beyond the Pandemic' (2020), New York: © 2020, United Nations, available at: unctad.org/en/PublicationsLibrary/wir2020_en.pdf.

A decline in global FDI of about 40 per cent is projected for 2020, resulting in a dramatic fall of FDI in the range of US\$205–305 billion in developing countries.[41] Plummeting foreign investments will constrain private sector development and employment in these countries.

2.3.3 *No Substitutes Available*

Worryingly, there are no immediately apparent substitutes for the inflow of hard currencies into developing countries that could counter or at least dilute the substantial negative effects of the crisis on the economies, and in particular the food production, of developing countries.

2.3.3.1 Hard Currency to Remain Hard

The prospect of the crisis softening hard currencies shows no sign of materialising, as we see no evidence of the US dollar, euro, Swiss franc and Japanese yen weakening against the currencies of developing countries. Indeed, as Figure 2.8 shows, many emerging and developing countries' currencies have actually lost value in the wake of the crisis.[42]

2.3.3.2 No Fast Recovery

The broad consensus is that the crisis impaired the entire year 2020.[43] The International Monetary Fund (IMF) has estimated – so far – a contraction in the global economy of 4.4 per cent in 2020, after revising its first projections.[44] In December 2020 the OECD has forecasted a decline of 4.2 per cent in global GDP,[45] adjusting its more negative predictions from June and September 2020.[46] The OECD highlights a less strong decline in global output and at

---

[41]　Ibid.

[42]　IMF, 'A crisis like no other, an uncertain recovery. World economic outlook update' (2020), available at: www.imf.org/en/Publications/WEO/Issues/2020/06/24/WEOUpdateJune2020.

[43]　IMF, 'G-20 surveillance note. COVID-19 – impact and policy considerations' (2020), available at: www.imf.org/external/np/g20/pdf/2020/041520.pdf; IMF, 'World economic outlook: a long and difficult ascent' (2020), available at: www.imf.org/en/Publications/WEO/Issues/2020/09/30/world-economic-outlook-october-2020.

[44]　IMF, 'G-20 surveillance note. COVID-19'; IMF, 'World economic outlook: a long and difficult ascent'; IMF, 'A crisis like no other'.

[45]　OECD, 'OECD interim economic assessment. Coronavirus: living with uncertainty' (2020), available at: www.oecd-ilibrary.org/docserver/34ffc900-en.pdf?expires=1600683032&id=id&accname=guest&checksum=2E65716A8A29CA72CBF8565FA1BD645A.

[46]　OECD, 'OECD economic outlook volume 2020 Issue 1' (2020), available at: www.oecd-ilibrary.org/economics/oecd-economic-outlook_16097408; OECD, 'OECD interim economic assessment'.

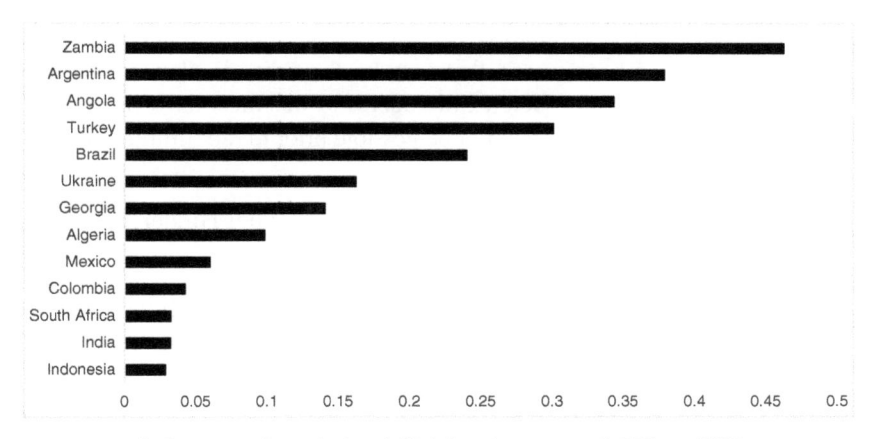

FIGURE 2.8 *Currency depreciation (official exchange rate, LCU per USD, per cent change between January 2020 and December 2020). Authors' creation based on data from the World Bank.*[47]

the same time higher discrepancies in the COVID-19 pandemic effects on output, with some LMICs (e.g. India, Mexico and South Africa) hit harder than expected.[48] The World Bank in January 2021 predicts a decline of world GDP of 4.3 per cent in 2020.[49] While varying in detail, all forecasts present a more significant decline than that caused by the 2008–2009 financial crisis.[50] The impact of COVID is expected to have even more severe consequences in countries in fragile and conflict situations, where in the baseline scenario GDP is expected to shrink by 7 per cent in 2020.[51]

At the same time, projected growth for 2021 is estimated at about 4 per cent according to the World Bank January 2021 economic prospects, *if certain conditions are in place* (e.g. strong policy support).[52] We will see whether the assumption of a fast recovery holds true – from the current perspective this looks wildly

[47] World Bank, 'Global economic monitor [dataset]'. Available at: https://datacatalog.worldbank.org/dataset/global-economic-monitor.

[48] Ibid.

[49] World Bank, *Global Economic Prospects, June 2020*; World Bank, *Global Economic Prospects, January 2021*, Washington, DC: World Bank. © World Bank, CC BY 3.0 IGO, 10.1596/978-1-4648-1612-3.

[50] IMF, 'G-20 surveillance note. COVID-19'; IMF, 'A crisis like no other'; United Nations, 'World economic situation and Prospects as of mid-2020' (2020); A. Shalal and D. Lawder, 'IMF chief says growth forecast cuts "very likely" as coronavirus hits economies hard', *Reuters*, 12 May 2020, available at: www.reuters.com/article/us-health-coronavirus-imf-georgieva-idUSKBN22O254.

[51] IMF, 'COVID-19 Poses Formidable Threat for Fragile States in the Middle East and North Africa', *IMF News*, 13 May 2020.

[52] World Bank, *Global Economic Prospects, January 2021*.

optimistic, given that new variants of the virus seem to spread much faster than the version original known, and that even in the most developed countries (where vulnerable parts of society have access to vaccines) mass vaccination of *all* parts of the population will not be possible prior to the summer of 2021.

2.3.3.3 Publicly Sponsored Nutrition of the Poor Hindered by COVID-19 Measures

Another factor increasing the vulnerability of those in developing countries exposed is the fact that many such countries have countered famine through public food programmes, particularly for children in schools and kindergartens.[53] In many cases, when schools and kindergartens are closed, children cannot access the public support they usually receive, and hence lack nutrition. This stretches the already-scarce resources of these children's households even further, resulting in otherwise preventable casualties especially among the very young and elderly. The income uncertainty caused by lockdowns will probably exacerbate such grave problems. Hence, labour-market policy interventions must be carefully administered using a coordinated approach among different regulators, taking into account the various phases of the pandemic.[54]

2.3.4 *Impact*

To substantiate the dimension of up to 100 million casualties, we put two factors together. On the one hand, the World Bank estimated for 2017 that 689 million people were living in extreme poverty.[55] Extreme poverty is defined as the minimum amount below which a 'person's minimum nutritional,

---

[53] World Food Programme, 'World Food Programme gears up to support children left without meals due to COVID-19 school closures', *World Food Programme News releases*, 20 March 2020, available at: www.wfp.org/news/world-food-programme-gears-support-children-left-without-meals-due-covid-19-school-closures.

[54] GIZ, 4B10: Unit for Education, VET and Labour Markets, 'Labour market policy in times of the COVID-19 pandemic' (2020), available at: sea-vet.net/images/seb/e-library/doc_file/721/working-paper-labour-market-policy-in-times-of-the-covid-19-pandemic-and-during-its-aftermath.pdf.

[55] World Bank, 'Poverty and shared prosperity 2018: piecing together the poverty puzzle (2018), World Bank, Washington, DC. © World Bank, Licence: Creative Commons Attribution CC BY 3.0 IGO, available at: openknowledge.worldbank.org/bitstream/handle/10986/30418/9781464813306.pdf; World Bank, 'Foreword – poverty and shared prosperity 2020' (2020), available at: blogs.worldbank.org/voices/october-7-2020-foreword-poverty-and-shared-prosperity-2020.

clothing, and shelter needs cannot be met'.[56] For any one percentage point slow-down of the global economy, the number of people in extreme poverty (with purchase power parity of US$1.90 per day) would increase by about 2 per cent (14 million people) and by about 3 per cent (21 million people) if trade channels were interrupted.[57] According to the Vos, Martin and Laborde model and June projections for 2020 of minus 4.4 per cent in GDP,[58] we would expect an additional 61 million people living in extreme poverty in the 'best' scenario (increase by 2 per cent), and about 91 million in the worst (increase by 3 per cent). While the World Bank estimates for 2020 an increase of 88–115 million people living in extreme poverty,[59] another study from UNU-Wider, in the scenario of a 5 per cent contraction in per capita incomes, envisages 80 million more people.[60] All in all, the UN estimates an increase up to 160 million people living in extreme poverty by 2030.[61] Although these estimates might appear volatile, conflicting and highly dependent on many still uncertain variables, they all present the same trend: a substantial increase in people living in poverty in the near future. At the same time, those already in extreme poverty will suffer additional setbacks in their daily struggle for food. In plain words: they will starve, and where people starve without help, some of them die.

On the other hand, almost 400 million people live in ultra-poverty;[62] they are people living in 'extremely poor' (as just defined) communities facing *additional* challenges, preventing them from benefiting from any government-led social protection programs or market-led initiatives, such as microfinance. Bringing digital development aid and government support to these ultra-poor is virtually impossible since these people do not exist in any ledger at all; where on the ground assistance is inhibited owing to the crisis, these people are very likely to be completely sidelined.

The important point here is the insight that if developed countries focus on themselves and global trade connections are interrupted, developing

[56] World Bank, 'Poverty and shared prosperity 2018'.

[57] R. Vos, W. Martin and D. Laborde, 'How much will global poverty increase because of COVID-19?' (2020), available at: www.ifpri.org/blog/how-much-will-global-poverty-increase-because-covid-19.

[58] IMF, 'World economic outlook: a long and difficult ascent'.

[59] World Bank, 'Foreword – poverty and shared prosperity 2020'.

[60] A. Sumner, C. Hoy and E. Ortiz-Juarez, 'Estimates of the Impact of COVID-19 on Global' (2020), *United Nations University*, Working Paper 43/2020, available at: www.wider.unu.edu/publication/estimates-impact-covid-19-global-poverty.

[61] UN, 'World economic situation and prospects as of mid-2020'.

[62] Uplift and The RESULTS Educational Fund, 'The global state of ultra-poverty 2017' (2017), available at: www.ultra-poverty.org/assets/downloads/gsup-2017-report.pdf.

countries suffer, with the number of casualties being potentially astronomi-
cal. At the same time, we cannot claim precision with regard to the prediction
of 100 million casualties – and the authors of this chapter would be more than
happy to be proved wrong. To clarify, we use this figure as a rough but drastic
forecast to convey the message that the crisis *will* have a very severe impact on
developing countries, much more severe than has yet been realised owing to
the circumstances on the ground and the slow-down of economic interactions
between developed countries and developing countries.

Our key message is to warn politicians and regulators to see the wider global
picture and undertake steps to avoid a looming human catastrophe, not only
in the interest of the poor, but also the rich countries: a number of casualties
close to 100 million will threaten the moral right of rich country citizens to
live on this planet.

2.4 DEPARTURE FROM THE SUSTAINABLE DEVELOPMENT GOALS

The second indirect impact of the crisis is even harder to prove than the first.
But as our aim here is to alert relevant actors to the less-obvious crisis consequences for developing countries, it is legitimate to raise our concern that the
crisis will mark a departure from, or at least a significant slow-down in, the
realisation of the SDGs. Drawing on the previous sections, this seems obvious
for SDGs 1 (no poverty), 2 (zero hunger), 3 (good health and well-being) and
8 (decent work and economic growth), but most of the other SDGs are also
at risk.

2.4.1 *Inequality Reduction Thwarted by Crisis*

The crisis will have a direct impact on the realisation of SDG 10,[63] which is
aimed at reducing inequality: the crisis and related lockdowns have instead
reinforced inequalities at all levels.

The socio-economic impacts of crisis-related restrictions to labour and
schooling generally vary according to income level: high-income earners can
usually buffer the crisis impact the best, while low-income earners struggle
more as they lack both the skills and resources to buffer.[64]

---

[63] United Nations, 'Special edition: progress towards the Sustainable Development Goals'
(2019), available at: undocs.org/E/2019/68.
[64] Vos et al., 'How much will global poverty increase because of COVID-19?'.

For instance, the quality of home-schooling is strongly correlated with the background, income and education level of the parents.[65] This leads to a disproportionately negative effect on the education of children from low-income and poor families, which have less access to the internet and other educational resources.[66] In relation to inequalities between developed and developing countries, 86 per cent of children in primary education were out of school in low-development countries, in contrast to 20 per cent in more advanced economies.[67]

In a similar vein, small firms register significantly higher cash flows-to-asset ratios than big enterprises and mainly rely on cash sales rather than assets-to-pledge to access credit. Accordingly, it is small firms that are suffering the most from the slow-down in consumption.[68] Meanwhile, high-income earners are at more of an advantage compared with low-income earners because they are more likely to be able to work from home.[69]

2.4.2 *Unemployment, 'Uneducating', 'Ungendering' and 'Ungreening'*

The ongoing crisis represents a litmus test for several SDGs at once. Rising unemployment will be an immediate result of the crisis, which will in turn widen inequality at all levels and potentially harm the prospects of future generations, owing to a lack of resources to fund their education. This would threaten SDG No. 4 (quality education). Children who have to be schooled at home rather than in school are generally being taught by women in developing countries. Accordingly, we would expect this to hinder the achievement of SDG No. 5 (gender equality). And where there is an urgent short-term need, we would expect fewer long-term perspectives to be taken into account, resulting in less attention being paid to environmental concerns and sustainable handling of resources (SDGs 11–15).

Simple examples reported in the press in one way or another support our thesis about the forced departure from SDGs. Where people cannot generate

---

[65] J. J. Heckman, 'Skill Formation and the Economics of Investing in Disadvantaged Children' (2006) 312 *Science* 1900–1902.

[66] P. Surico and A. Galeotti, 'The economics of pandemics: the case of Covid-19', 27 April 2020, available at: www.youtube.com/watch?v=FHDmyiWpldY&feature=youtu.be.

[67] M. Rowling, 'Pandemic may reverse human development for first time in 30 years, UN says', *Reuters*, 20 May 2020, available at: www.reuters.com/article/healthcoronavirus-global-development/pandemic-may-reverse-human-development-for-first-time-in-30-years-un-says-idUSL8N2D251B.

[68] Ibid.

[69] Surico and Galeotti, 'The economics of pandemics'.

income through services (such as tourism), they will turn to natural resources that no one defends. For instance, a Mexican owner of horses who has previously rented them out to tourists to make a living may turn into a predator of marine resources by hunting for fish and oysters; the unpaid guide of a natural park in Africa may be forced to hunt the very animals s/he is supposed to protect to survive; where petrol, gas and coal become unaffordable owing to a decline in local currencies people turn to cutting down trees and burning the timber of rain forests; where renewable energy requires expensive spare parts to be paid in hard currencies, the production facilities will be sold, to be replaced by local forms of energy production (burning wood); and so on. Years of progress to substitute use of natural resources with service-oriented wealth generation are about to be lost.

The current crisis also threatens traditional financial inclusion, which is an enabler of at least eight (if not all) of the seventeen SDGs.[70] In particular, microfinance is often the tool of choice for people with low technical and financial sophistication as well as micro, small and medium enterprises (MSMEs), representing about 90 per cent of businesses and more than 50 per cent of employment worldwide.[71] Many of these businesses are excluded from the traditional banking sector and are served by microfinance institutions (MFIs) and other non-bank financial companies.[72] Since traditional microfinance relies on personal contact, the current crisis is putting the microfinance sector at risk, with repayment rates consistently falling.[73] Efforts to improve under challenging conditions have been undertaken,[74] but it is difficult to

---

[70] D. W. Arner, R. P. Buckley, D. A. Zetzsche and R. Veidt, 'Sustainability, FinTech and Financial Inclusion' (2020) 21 *European Business Organization Law Review*, 7–35, available at: https://link.springer.com/article/10.1007%2Fs40804-020-00183-y; UNCDF, 'Financial Inclusion and the SDGs' (2020), © UNCDF, available at: www.uncdf.org/financial-inclusion-and-the-sdgs.

[71] United Nations, 'Supporting small businesses through the COVID-19 crisis' (2020), available at: www.un.org/en/observances/micro-small-medium-businesses-day; M. Schlein, 'The financial engine for half the world's jobs is about to seize up' (2020) *Accion*, available at: www.accion.org/the-financial-engine-for-half-the-worlds-jobs-is-about-to-seize-up.

[72] M. G. Moritán, 'Financial Inclusion for MSMEs and Women's Economic Empowerment' (2020) 1 (1) *Journal of the International Council for Small Business* 7–9, available at: https://doi.org/10.1080/26437015.2020.1714348.

[73] G. Bull and T. Ogden, 'COVID-19: How does microfinance weather the coming storm?', *CGAP*, 25 March 2020, available at: www.cgap.org/blog/covid-19-how-does-microfinance-weather-coming-storm; The Economist, 'For microfinance lenders, Covid-19 is an existential threat', *The Economist*, 5 May 2020, available at: www.economist.com/finance-and-economics/2020/05/05/for-microfinance-lenders-covid-19-is-an-existential-threat.

[74] H. Hekkenberg and W. Medrano-Lazo, 'Attention Points Business Continuity for MFIs in View of the COVID-19 Outbreak', *Luxembourg: ADA-Microfinance*, 16 April 2020; D. W. Arner, J. N. Barberis, J. Walker, R. P. Buckley, A. M. Dahdal and D. A. Zetzsche, 'Digital Finance & The COVID-19 Crisis' (2020) 2020/017 *University of Hong Kong Faculty of Law Research Paper*, available at: papers.ssrn.com/sol3/papers.cfm?abstract_id=3558889.

achieve good results in the absence of technological infrastructure and technical expertise on the side of both MFIs and their clients – as hard currency is required to pay for it.

2.4.3 *Brain Drain and Mass Migration*

The estimated impact of a departure from the SDGs is less certain in terms of actual casualties. Yet such a departure will lead to political instability resulting in civil disobedience and unrest, thereby prompting further self-preserving reactions from those yielding political power and undermining civil institutions (at odds with SDG No. 16).

Meanwhile, developed countries will feel an impact in terms of increasing migration. Where economic need and political angst coincide, people who can afford to do so will emigrate. This could create new waves of mass migration similar to those regularly seen at the Mexican–American border or on the shores of the Mediterranean Sea.

Many of the most likely migrants are from countries that have made significant progress in the last decade, including India and Vietnam in Asia and Kenya and Rwanda in Africa. These countries have built up human resources to maintain and grow their economies but are now at great risk of losing these resources in a seemingly inevitable brain drain prompted by economic decline and lack of opportunities.

2.4.4 *Fintech as a Countermeasure?*

One counter-argument to the departure thesis is that financial technology (fintech) has never been better. Indeed, fintech may be a significant driver in reaching the SDGs,[75] and the need for digital finance in the COVID-19 crisis is obviously massive.[76] Yet fintech is a mere facilitator in pursuing the SDGs. It cannot work alone in the absence of a comprehensive strategy pursuant to the realisation of the SDGs.[77]

---

[75] D. A. Zetzsche, R. P. Buckley and D. W. Arner, 'FinTech for Financial Inclusion: Driving Sustainable Growth', in J. Walker et al. (eds.), *Sustainable Development Goals: Harnessing Business to Achieve the SDGs through Finance, Technology and Law Reform* (Chichester: Wiley, 2019), pp. 179–204.

[76] Arner et al. 'Digital Finance & The COVID-19 Crisis'.

[77] E. Solberg and N. Addo Dankwa Akufo-Addo, 'Why we cannot lose sight of the Sustainable Development Goals during coronavirus', 23 April 2020, available at: www.weforum.org/agenda/2020/04/coronavirus-pandemic-effect-sdg-un-progress; D. W. Arner, R. P. Buckley and D. W. Arner, 'Fintech for Financial Inclusion: A Framework for Digital Financial Transformation' (2018), 18–87, UNSW *Law Research Paper*, available at: https://ssrn.com/abstract=3245287 or http://dx.doi.org/10.2139/ssrn.3245287.

Indeed, in the absence of such a comprehensive strategy, fintech could be applied negatively to control people, suppress females and minority groups, violate data privacy rights and erode trust in the emerging financial systems of developing countries.

2.5 INSUFFICIENT POLICY RESPONSE
TO REVERSE THE TREND

Global support could reverse the trend toward a return of hunger and famine and the departure from the SDGs. While many initiatives have been taken, indeed, whether these have the volume and impact to reverse the trend is in doubt.

2.5.1 *Shortage of Global Support*

Development aid could be a viable short-term substitute for the lack of hard currencies. The IMF and the World Bank have organised unprecedented liquidity inflows to developing countries and developing countries. Yet while the liquidity support may help countries to stay afloat in the short run, the amount is not enough in the mid- and long term.

While the relatively well-off Western and Asian economies are currently undertaking huge efforts to support themselves, few efforts are being made to support developing economies. Indeed, some developed economies have even reduced their development assistance to developing countries,[78] compared with the US$ 152.8 billion committed as official development assistance from members of the OECD's Development Assistance Committee (DAC) in 2019.[79] To counter the crisis, the UN has called for a US$2.5 trillion package to be provided for developing countries. The proposed package would comprise the following:

---

[78] J. Mason, 'Exclusive: Trump proposes 21 per cent cut in U.S. foreign aid in budget proposal – officials', *Reuters*, 9 February 2020, available at: www.reuters.com/article/us-usa-trump-budget-foreign-exclusive/exclusive-trump-proposes-21-cut-in-u-s-foreign-aid-in-budget-proposal-officials-idUSKBN2030Q5; R. Gramer and C. Lynch, 'Trump's plan to slash foreign aid puts humanitarian programs in jeopardy', *Foreign Policy*, 16. August 2019, available at: foreignpolicy.com/2019/08/16/donald-trump-plan-to-slash-foreign-aid-puts-humanitarian-programs-in-jeopardy/.

[79] OECD, 'OECD and donor countries working to focus development efforts on Covid-19 crisis, building on a rise in official aid in 2019' (2020), available at: www.oecd.org/development/oecd-and-donor-countries-working-to-focus-development-efforts-on-covid-19-crisis-building-on-a-rise-in-official-aid-in-2019.htm.

- US$1 trillion made available through the use of special drawing rights;
- US$1 trillion of debts owed by those countries to be cancelled; and
- US$500 billion to fund a Marshall Plan for health recovery to be dispersed as grants.[80]

These amounts look large in absolute terms, and especially so when compared with the DAC's assistance of previous years.

Yet they are *not* large[81] if one considers that these funds would potentially help 80 per cent of the world's population to effectively and sustainably contain the pandemic by achieving economic recovery, improving healthcare systems and financing and organising vaccinations. To put the US$2.5 trillion package into perspective,[82] the EU and EU Member States together are investing about US$4.5 trillion to battle the crisis (29 per cent of 2019 GDP);[83] and the US has promised to invest a total of about US$3 trillion into its economy and healthcare system, equivalent to 14 per cent of its 2019 GDP;[84] on top comes the US$1.9 trillion COVID 19 Relief Package announced in 2021 by the Biden administration, bringing support beyond 23 per cent GDP. Assuming the world's GDP to be around US$88 trillion, with some US$55 trillion attributable to high-income countries,[85] if the world was to support LMICs to the equivalent level of the US and the EU in terms of percentage of GDP, this would equate to assistance ranging from US$7.6 trillion (US level) to US$9.6 trillion (EU level). What has been done so far is significantly less ambitious.

First, the G20 countries agreed to freeze the repayment of the debt of the world's seventy-six poorest countries plus Angola until the end of the year 2020 through the Debt Service Suspension Initiative (DSSI).[86] In October

---

[80] See UNCTAD, 'UN calls for $2.5 trillion coronavirus crisis package for developing countries' (2020), available at: unctad.org/en/pages/newsdetails.aspx?OriginalVersionID=2315.

[81] Shalal and Lawder, 'IMF chief says growth forecast cuts "very likely"'.

[82] J. Anderson, E. Bergamini, S. Brekelmans, A. Cameron, Z. Darvas, M. Domínguez Jíménez, K. Lenaerts and C. Midões, 'The fiscal response to the economic fallout from the coronavirus', *Bruegel*, 5 August 2020, available at: www.bruegel.org/publications/datasets/covid-national-dataset#usa.

[83] L. Hurst, 'EU agrees massive aid package of immediate support for member states', *Euronews*, 24 April 2020, available at: www.euronews.com/2020/04/23/eu-agrees-massive-aid-package-of-immediate-support-for-member-states; Anderson et al., 'The fiscal response to the economic fallout from the coronavirus'.

[84] Anderson et al., 'The fiscal response to the economic fallout from the coronavirus'.

[85] World Bank, 'GDP (current US$) [dataset]' (2020).

[86] A. England, J. Wheatley and J. Politi, 'G20 nations close in on debt deal for poor countries', *Financial Times*, 12 April 2020, available at: www.ft.com/content/30321fc4-e77c-4688-8d87-ef344108ed6b; J. Wheatley, M. Stott and D. Pilling, 'Emerging economies call for more financial help after G20 deal', *Financial Times*, 17 April 2020, available at: www.ft.com/content/203ed8f5-6bb2-4016-80a9-dd99269bfa26.

2020 the DSSI was extended until mid-2021. The Council of Europe endorsed this initiative and recognised the necessity for potential debt restructuring for the most vulnerable countries, agreeing on a 'Common Framework for Debt Treatments beyond the DSSI'.[87] The G20 agreement of April 2020 to freeze principal repayments and interest payments is expected to equate to around only 0.8 per cent[88] of the US$2.5 trillion package for developing countries called for by the UN. This measure should be extended to other LMICs facing considerable economic tensions and involve private creditors as well, whose participation to debt relief cannot just be 'voluntary'.[89] Following the G20 initiative, China announced the provision of US$2 billion over two years 'to help other countries respond to the impact of the COVID-19 pandemic',[90] and the EU increased the allocation for 'external action' in the proposals of the EU budget 2021–2027 to €10.5 billion as part of the measures aimed to 'fight the negative consequences of COVID-19'.[91]

Second, the World Bank Group announced in 2020 that it expects to grant developing countries up to US$160 billion over the next fifteen months.[92]

Third, the IMF has initiated a $100 billion emergency financing programme (overall $250 billion has been made available to its members). The emergency financing programme includes Rapid Credit Facilities – US$4.4 billion approved so far to LDCs – and Rapid Financing Instruments – US$1.3

[87] Council of the European Union, 'Debt relief efforts for African countries: Council approves conclusions' (2020), available at: www.consilium.europa.eu/en/press/press-releases/2020/11/30/debt-relief-efforts-for-african-countries-council-approves-conclusions.

[88] D. Barbuscia, M. Rashad and A. Shalal, 'G20 countries agree debt freeze for world's poorest countries', *Reuters*, 15 April 2020, available at: www.reuters.com/article/us-health-coronavirus-g20-statement/g20-countries-agree-debt-freeze-for-worlds-poorest-countries-idUSKCN21X29A.

[89] P. Bolton, L. Buchheit, P.-O. Gourinchas, M. Gulati, C.-T. Hsieh, U. Panizza and B. Weder di Mauro, 'Born Out of Necessity: A Debt Standstill for COVID-19' (2020) 103 *CEPR Policy Insight*, available at: https://cepr.org/sites/default/files/policy_insights/PolicyInsight103.pdf; Institute of International Finance, 'IIF letter to IMF, World Bank, OECD and Paris Club on Debt of LICs', 9 April 2020, available at: www.iif.com/Publications/ID/3849/IIF-letter-to-IMF-World-Bank-OECD-and-Paris-Club-on-Debt-of-LICs; World Bank, 'World Bank Group President David Malpass: remarks for G20 finance ministers and Central Bank governors meeting' (2020), available at: www.worldbank.org/en/news/statement/2020/07/18/world-bank-group-president-david-malpass-remarks-at-the-g20-finance-ministers-and-central-bank-governors-meeting.

[90] I. Luan, 'China suspends debt repayments for 77 developing countries battling Covid-19', *Caixin*, 8 June 2020, available at: www.caixinglobal.com/2020-06-08/china-suspends-debt-repayments-for-77-developing-countries-battling-covid-19-101564592.html.

[91] European Commission, 'Questions and answers: the EU budget for external action in the next Multiannual Financial Framework', European Commission, 2 June 2020, available at: https://ec.europa.eu/commission/presscorner/detail/es/qanda_20_988.

[92] World Bank, 'World Bank COVID-19 Response, 14 Oct. 2020' (2020), available at: www.worldbank.org/en/news/factsheet/2020/10/14/world-bank-covid-19-response.

billion approved until end of 2020 to LDCs.[93] On top of the emergency financing programme the IMF approved some grant-based debt relief, amounting to US$1.4 billion for its twenty-five poorest member countries for six months in the form of a Catastrophe Containment and Relief Trust – US$ 471 million approved until end of 2020 to LDCs.[94] The IMF is also 'augmenting existing lending programs' – Extended Credit Facilities and Extended Fund Facilities, with approved funds to LDCs amounting in 2022 to US$1.8 billion.[95]

Fourth, regional development banks started to provide support facilities, such as the European Bank for Reconstruction and Development and the Asian Infrastructure Investment Bank with €21 billion and €10 billion respectively.

These measures together result in some $300 to $350 billion for developing countries (data as of 1 December 2020). Even if we suppose some bilateral assistance we will find ourselves clearly below the UN's target – not even speaking of US or EU support levels.

On top of this comes the introduction of a new IMF tool, the Short-Term Liquidity Line,[96] and the potential issuance of new special drawing rights.[97]

Overall, financial assistance and lending programmes launched so far have been largely criticised, as the amounts are considered inadequate given the dimension of the crisis.[98] The intermediate results confirm that much less global support has been announced than necessary, and even less announced than achieved as of 2020.

---

[93] IMF amounts reported in this sub paragraph are based on data relative to LDCs at 1 December 2020, IMF, 'The IMF's response to COVID-19' (2020), available at: www.imf.org/en/About/FAQ/imf-response-to-covid-19; IMF, 'COVID-19 financial assistance and debt service relief' (2020), available at: www.imf.org/en/Topics/imf-and-covid19/COVID-Lending-Tracker.

[94] IMF, 'The IMF's response to COVID-19'; IMF, 'COVID-19 financial assistance and debt service relief'; IMF, 'IMF Executive Board approves immediate debt relief for 25 countries' (2020), available at: www.imf.org/en/News/Articles/2020/04/16/pr20165-board-approves-immediate-debt-service-relief-for-25-eligible-low-income-countries.

[95] IMF, 'The IMF's response to COVID-19'; IMF, 'COVID-19 financial assistance and debt service relief'.

[96] G. Okamoto, 'The short-term liquidity line: a new IMF tool to help in the crisis', *IMFBlog*, 22 April 2020, available at: blogs.imf.org/2020/04/22/the-short-term-liquidity-line-a-new-imf-tool-to-help-in-the-crisis/.

[97] M. Jones, 'Explainer: which countries will benefit most from an IMF SDR increase', *Reuters*, 7 April 2021, available at: www.reuters.com/article/us-imf-sdr-idUSKBN2BU1BQ.

[98] UNCTAD, 'The Covid-19 shock to developing countries: towards a "whatever it takes" programme for the two-thirds of the world's population being left behind' (2020), *Trade and Development Report Update*, available at: unctad.org/en/PublicationsLibrary/gds_tdr2019_covid2_en.pdf; A. Kentikelenis, D. Gabor, I. Ortiz, T. Stubbs, M. McKee and D. Stuckler, 'Softening the blow of the pandemic: will the International' (2020) 8 (6) *The Lancet*, available at: https://doi.org/10.1016/S2214-109X(20)30135-2.

2.5.2 *EU Support Falling Short of Expectations*

European institutions have supported developing economies through a number of initiatives, ranging from budget support and financing to guarantees and technical assistance.

First, in November 2020 the Council of Europe endorsed the DSSI, leading to delayed debt services. While a potential debt restructuring for the most vulnerable countries was deemed necessary (see Section 2.5.1), it did not come to that; we note some progress, though, on a 'Common Framework for Debt Treatments beyond the DSSI'.[99]

Second, the European bilateral development finance institutions and the European Investment Bank announced to initiate €280 million financing to support small and medium enterprises in developing countries to reduce the economic impact of COVID-19.

Third, in December 2020 the European Council endorsed a provisional agreement to set-up a unique instrument named Neighbourhood, Development and International Cooperation Instrument 'aiming at streamlining and simplifying the EU's external action financing instruments for international and development cooperation, crisis response or peace-building actions in partner countries'.[100] Such an instrument will have a financial capacity of about €80 billion for the period 2021–2027. Out of the total amount, only €29 billion will go to Sub-Saharan Africa and a total of €3 billion will be dedicated to 'quick response capacity for crisis management'.[101]

Fourth, some pre-existing facilities, such as the European Fund for Sustainable Development (EFSD), have been partially re-adapted to support countries (including developing countries, in particular EU neighbourhood countries and Africa) facing the negative economic impact of the COVID-19 crisis. An example is the EFSD Guarantee that was re-focused to address the COVID-19 pandemic through a number of guarantee agreements, such as: Agricultural and Rural Finance Guarantee Programme (AgreenFi), European Health Platform, European Guarantee for Renewable Energy (non-sovereign), EU Market Creation Facility, EU Municipal, Infrastructure and Industrial Resilience Programme, Financial Inclusion Programme

---

[99] Council of the European Union, 'Debt relief efforts for African countries'.
[100] Council of the European Union, 'Neighbourhood, Development and International Cooperation Instrument: Coreper endorses provisional agreement with the European Parliament' (2020), available at: www.consilium.europa.eu/en/press/press-releases/2020/12/18/neighbourhood-development-and-international-cooperation-instrument-coreper-endorses-provisional-agreement-with-the-european-parliament.
[101] Ibid.

(InclusiFi), Renewable Energy Support Programme for mainly rural areas in Sub-Saharan Africa, Small Loan Guarantee Programme.[102]

Fifth, Team Europe approved the provision of up to €38.5 billion,[103] to partner countries to recover from the COVID-19 pandemic.[104] Among Team Europe's initiatives, the EU partnered with Germany to contribute over €200 million in assistance for Senegal.[105] Team Europe also contributed €500 million to the COVAX initiative to provide a billion COVID-19 vaccine doses for LMICs.[106]

Sixth, other support measures to developing economies/LDCs include country-based measures of European Economic Area countries and Switzerland. For instance, Switzerland committed about €464 million in total to respond to COVID-19 pandemic 'particularly in developing countries',[107] while Norway approved an additional €4 million to the 'record-high' humanitarian budget for 2020, equal to about €535 million.[108]

Although the EU has 'committed in leading … towards a truly global recovery, notably though joint coordination with the United Nations, the G20 and G7, the International Monetary Fund, the World Bank or the International Labour Organisation',[109] we miss a long-term vision of how the recovery in the most vulnerable countries may be supported. Moreover, guarantees

---

[102] European Commission, 'EU external investment plan' (2021), available at: ec.europa.eu/eu-external-investment-plan/about-plan/progress_en.

[103] Team Europe is an initiative aimed to 'combine resources from the EU, its Member States, and financial institutions, in particular the European Investment Bank and the European Bank for Reconstruction and Development', EEAS.

[104] European Commission, 'Team Europe steps up delivery to its COVID-19 recovery package up to €38.5 billion for partner countries' (2020), available at: ec.europa.eu/commission/presscorner/detail/en/ip_20_2195.

[105] Federal Ministry for Economic Cooperation and Development, 'European Union and Germany provide over 200 million euros in assistance for Senegal' (2020), available at: www.bmz.de.

[106] European Investment Bank, 'Team Europe contributes €500 million to COVAX initiative to provide one billion COVID-19 vaccine doses for low and middle income countries' (2020), available at: www.eib.org/en/press/all/2020-366-team-europe-contributes-eur500-million-to-covax-initiative-to-provide-one-billion-covid-19-vaccine-doses-for-low-and-middle-income-countries.

[107] Federal Department of Foreign Affairs FDFA, 'COVID-19: Switzerland strengthens international cooperation' (2020), available at: www.eda.admin.ch/eda/en/fdfa/fdfa/aktuell/newsuebersicht/2020/04/corona-internationale-zusammenarbeit.html.

[108] Norwegian Government Security and Service Organisation (GSSO), 'Norway allocates a further NOK 38.2 million to humanitarian efforts' (2020), available at: www.regjeringen.no/en/aktuelt/rnb_hum/id2701821/.

[109] European Commission, 'Europe's moment: repair and prepare for the next generation' (2020), available at: ec.europa.eu/commission/presscorner/detail/en/ip_20_940.

and suspension of interests do not help sustain increasing liquidity needs or long-term growth, nor do they represent a solution for the government over-indebtedness of most of the LMICs.

All in all, the overall amount committed by the EU is below the need that has been identified here, and also below the (low) target set by international institutions. If the EU, representing 16 per cent of the world's GDP, contributes in all only €120 billion to the recovery of LMICs, how can we expect other major economies to commit higher amounts?

2.5.3 *Impact on Europe's Sustainability Agenda*

The observation of (too) low EU support for LMICs is particularly striking in light of the EU's exposure to the social and economic consequences of the COVID 19 crisis. If the gloomy scenario we have sketched comes true, the impact on Europe will be profound. We expect a direct impact on Europe's sustainability agenda.

As an obvious consequence, we expect the return of mass migration, with all the individual harm that this brings about, and also unwanted consequences for social infrastructure and the political establishment in Europe. Political dependency on 'barrier countries' (such as Turkey, Libya and others) with doubtful approaches to human rights and sustainability will undermine Europe's political commitment to human rights and the rule of law.

In addition, we see three direct consequences for the EU's Green Deal, adopted in December 2019. First, fewer investments with links to LMICs will meet the sustainability definition as defined within the Sustainable Finance Taxonomy, either since more production and services do 'significant harm to one of the environmental objectives' (cf. Articles 9, 17 Taxonomy Regulation (EU) 2020/852,[110] hereafter Taxonomy Regulation), or for violation against the social standards laid out in Article 18 Taxonomy Regulation; under that provision a conduct must not be called sustainable if it violates the OECD Guidelines for Multinational Enterprises (addressing for instance, supply chain issues),[111] the UN Principles for Business and Human Rights,[112] and the Declaration of the International Labour Organisation on Fundamental

---

[110] Regulation (EU) 2020/852 of the European Parliament and of the Council of 18 June 2020 on the establishment of a framework to facilitate sustainable investment, and amending Regulation (EU) 2019/2088, OJ L 198, 22 June 2020, p. 13–43.

[111] OECD guidelines for multinational enterprises, available at: www.oecd.org/corporate/mne/.

[112] UN Human Rights, 'Guiding principles on business and human rights, available at: www .ohchr.org/documents/publications/guidingprinciplesbusinesshr_en.pdf .

Principles and Rights at Work and the International Bill of Human Rights providing minimum standards for labour, work safety and social insurance.[113]

Given that global enterprises aggregate the country-specific sustainability impact based on capital expenditure and operational expenses, if a part, or several parts, of a global conglomerate's investment does not qualify as sustainable, the overall share of sustainability of that conglomerate will also be impaired.

Second, political stability and the influence of human rights and the rule of law lost during the COVID 19 crisis will not be reinstalled once the virus is under control. A discussion about whether the Western libertarian model is fit to combat the crisis is already under way. Countries with a pro-Western approach could be destabilised through the social and economic impact of the COVID 19 crisis for lack of economic support from the US and the EU, while autocrats, less concerned about the individuals within their domain, may come out strengthened by crisis support from less human rights-oriented economic superpowers.

Third, while the COVID 19 crisis had reduced carbon emissions owing to reduced business and leisure traffic, its impact on the SDGs could potentially delay the long-term sustainable transformation of the EU's, and the world's, economy, with carbon reductions and the effectiveness of combatting global warming through natural resources under threat: as an example, the circular economy depends on glass and paper collection, a labour-intensive service; accelerated by low oil prices during the crisis, the European Environmental Protection Agency (EEA) reported a higher share of single use items.[114] The long-term impact, however, is more profound, and negative: COVID 19, being a 'zoonic' disease that spreads from animals to humans and vice versa, threatens biodiversity. In a similar way, trees cut for heating and cooking during the COVID 19 crisis do not grow again overnight (even if immediately planted), as fish and oysters killed to feed people will take time to recover; while infrastructure relying on electricity and renewable power generation may be lost owing to a lack of maintenance and spare parts, as a result of a shortage of hard currency. For all we know, we lack insights into the long-term environmental impact of the COVID 19 crisis; yet history tells us that the immediate need of many people comes at the cost of long-termism, while Europe's sustainability agenda is all about making long-termism the new mainstream.

---

[113] ILO Declaration on Fundamental Principles and Rights at Work, available at: www.ilo.org/declaration/lang–en/index.htm.

[114] EEA, 'COVID-19 and Europe's environment: impacts of a global pandemic' (2020), available at: www.eea.europa.eu/post-corona-planet/covid-19-and-europes-environment.

As such, the social and economic impact of COVID 19 goes far beyond a regional and human disaster. Regulators worldwide, including in Europe, are well advised to deal with it, to ensure that the sustainability agenda can be implemented as hoped for – for the good of the future of our planet.

2.6 POLICY CONSIDERATIONS

We have drawn a gloomy picture of some 100 million people passing away owing to the direct and – to a much greater extent – the indirect impacts of the crisis, with many developing countries being diverted off the successful paths they have been taking towards the realisation of the SDGs to overcome hunger,[115] and to make excellent advances in education, literacy, gender equality, and infrastructure.[116]

What could be done to avoid the catastrophic scenario foreseen? What started as a health crisis in some regions is going to be a *global* health, economic and financial crisis, hence there is a dire need for well-coordinated efforts with a global perspective. We see five elements of the coordinated efforts as crucial.

First, financial support must consider developing countries' needs. In particular, if developed countries support firms, support should not be conditional on spending support or retaining labour within the confined economic region of the supporting body (i.e. Europe for the EU). Rather, support should be aimed at restarting global rather than domestic economic activity. This support must, particularly but not only, include food supply over 2022 and 2023. International coordination is necessary to limit negative economic spillover effects across countries; inadequate policies in some countries can have direct or indirect adverse effects on partner economies, making unilateral macroeconomic policies ineffective from the global perspective.[117] Appropriate coordination could take the form of a global crisis recovery system, steering, among others, coordinated and global investments into healthcare systems, funded by a global crisis recovery fund.[118] Recovery packages should be designed

---

[115] United Nations, 'The Sustainable Development Goals report 2019' (2020), available at: unstats .un.org/sdgs/report/2019/The-Sustainable-Development-Goals-Report-2019.pdf.

[116] United Nations, 'The Sustainable Development Goals Report 2019'.

[117] E. Kohlscheen, B. Mojon and D. Rees, 'The macroeconomic spillover effects of the pandemic on the global economy' (2020) 4 *BIS Bulletin*, available at: www.bis.org/publ/bisbullo4.pdf.

[118] R. Ayadi, 'Time for a decisive coordinated response to a costly global COVID-19 systemic crisis. Towards a resilient global system' (2020), *Euro-Mediterranean Economists Association*, available at: euromed-economists.org/download/time-for-a-decisive-coordinated-response-to-a-costly-global-covid-19-systemic-crisis-towards-a-global-resilient-system/?wpdmdl=3222&refresh=5f325-60d55be81597134349.

promptly and with particular attention to productive investment and sustainable development, as if they are based only on consumption 'they could exacerbate intergenerational inequities'.[119] At the same time, new forms of collaboration at local and regional levels, although globally connected, coordinated and (potentially) financed, could focus on enhancing local investments and outputs (i.e. local agricultural development and local value chains).

In addition, financial support should be combined with an extended and well-coordinated debt standstill in order to avoid that these new financial resources will be spent to service outstanding debt obligations and to effectively orient capital flows towards productive investments.[120] Financial assistance and policy response should also specifically target the poorest segments of society, especially in areas where informal work and self-employment are prevalent components of the economic system, in order to control increasing inequality.[121] Global human development is expected to decline during the pandemic for the first time since 1990.[122]

Second, global economic, travel and digital connections must be reinstalled as quickly as possible to maintain existing economic ties. This does not have to coincide with the bearing of additional risk for developed economies: travel could be conditional on up-to-date or on-the-spot COVID-19 tests, short quarantine periods and eventually vaccination. The revival of air services and supply chains is crucial if we are to avoid a scenario in which developed countries pursue highly-automated industrial production at the national level to replace goods usually imported from developing countries, thereby leaving those countries in even greater economic peril.

Third, it is imperative that medical resources like vaccines and pharmaceutical products be shared with developing countries, not only to avoid the human tragedy predicted herein as a direct and indirect impact of the crisis, but also to rebuild as soon as possible an integrated world economy.[123] A sustainable approach here requires that developed countries share resources with

---

[119] C. Hepburn, B. O'Callaghan, N. Stern, J. Stiglitz and D. Zenghelis, 'Will COVID-19 fiscal recovery packages accelerate or retard progress on climate change?' (2020) 36 *Oxford Review of Economic Policy*, 359–381, available at: https://doi.org/10.1093/oxrep/graa015.

[120] Bolton et al., 'Born Out of Necessity'.

[121] D. Furceri, 'How pandemics leave the poor even farther behind', *IMF Blog*, 11 May 2020, available at: blogs.imf.org/2020/05/11/how-pandemics-leave-the-poor-even-farther-behind/.

[122] United Nations Development Programme, 'COVID-19 and human development: assessing the crisis, envisioning the recovery', available at: https://hdr.undp.org/content/covid-19-and-human-development-assessing-crisis-envisioning-recovery; for examples of policy response see Furceri, 'How pandemics leave the poor even farther behind'.

[123] T. Murithi, 'COVID-19 reminds us that we are one global society', *Accord*, 10 May 2020, available at: www.accord.org.za/analysis/covid-19-reminds-us-that-we-are-one-global-society/.

those in greater need, even though there will be a clamour at national level to look after their own citizens first.

Fourth, all public and private resource-rich bodies should focus on how to make use of innovation (in technology, relationships, human well-being services, etc.) to devise new solutions to fight hunger *and* to keep on course towards the realisation of the SDGs in developing countries. For instance, developing countries continuing to pursue fulfilment of the SDGs should benefit first from digital screening for their people and digital farming for their farmers, by applying new technologies, the provision of which would act as an implicit subsidy for SDG compliance.

Innovation includes *financial* innovation. Private and public actors around the world must look for financial innovation that mitigates the impact of developing countries' currency decline, for instance through barter deals or the use of price indices that result in a mix of hard and soft currency.

This leads to the fifth principle: most of the tools mentioned here work best when the recipient country has some purchasing power to ensure that local investment, output and innovation can take place. Therefore, it is crucial to think about financial products that bridge the hard currency gap. Currency transactions in the scarcely-traded currencies of developing countries come with severe transaction costs and fees up to a two-digit percentage. Assistance for developing countries could focus on temporary measures that limit the negative impact of currency devaluation on domestic production and infra-structure investments. We could envisage the establishment of a currency mechanism that buffers the crisis-related currency devaluation of develop-ing countries. For instance, this could offer to smoothen some of the crisis-incurred losses by participating in currency trade as counterparty for certain transactions for certain countries and market participants when crucial for daily life. For example, one Guatemalan quetzal was equal to US$0.13048 on 1 February 2020, before the crisis. The currency mechanism could swap quetzal (within a limited monthly budget) at that same rate, with the monthly budget set in correlation with the uptake of local production. This means that in the beginning the budget is bigger, while in correlation with economic recovery the monthly budget will be reduced. Through such a currency mechanism, certain locally traded goods could effectively be priced at pre-crisis levels in external trade relations, so that developing countries would maintain some of their purchasing power on the world markets, resulting in faster recovery for both developing and LDCs'/developed countries' economies. The envis-aged currency mechanism would partially set aside pricing effects at currency exchanges around the world. We are aware that such a proposal attracts criti-cism for a plethora of reasons, yet it could be a faster way of achieving global recovery than directly channelling funds to many countries around the globe that come with other unwanted effects, from curtailing local production to enhanced corruption. Naturally, this currency mechanism would require significant resources in an amount only available at the largest central banks of developed countries.

All of the five alternatives are difficult to sell politically at a time when national rather than global matters are treated as the priority by most governments. Yet the cost of failing to adopt a global approach to counter the crisis is a decade with declining world trade and a lost decade for humanity. Any responsible and humane decision-maker will understand that foregoing all of the five choices sketched out here will tip the tide towards the ghastly realisation of our prediction of 100 million casualties.

2.7 CONCLUSION

We have argued in this chapter that, while the crisis has taken many lives in many *developed* countries, the impact of the crisis on *developing* countries is potentially far greater than the numbers so far reveal (or have for long revealed). In addition to the direct impact, we expect the social and economic tragedies caused indirectly by the epidemic such as hunger and famine, inequality, unemployment and other departures from the SDGs to affect 80 per cent of the world's population, since the crisis and crisis response measures in developed countries have all but erased the basis for economic and financial stability in LMICs. Further, we have shown that the social and economic consequences of COVID 19 may have severe effects on the efforts directed at achieving the SDGs, and Europe's sustainability agenda in particular.

We have proposed five policy measures to mitigate the most severe impacts of the crisis on developing countries: (1) financial support provided by developing countries to their economies must consider developing countries' needs; (2) global economic, travel and digital connections must be reinstalled as soon as possible; (3) medical achievements must be shared with developing countries; (4) use must be made of innovation (in technology, relationships, human well-being services, etc.) to devise new solutions to fight hunger *and* to keep on course the realisation of the SDGs in developing countries; and (5) developed countries (or their central banks) should work on a temporary currency mechanism that functions as a buffer against the crisis-related currency devaluation of developing countries to allow for the purchase of crucial goods for local food supply and economic recovery.

Despite difficulties in selling these costly measures to their people, policy makers in *developed* countries must decide whether they want to undermine the global sustainability agenda, as well with which number the COVID-19 epidemic will be listed in the annals of mankind: 100 million casualties?

3

The Corporation and the EU Social Market Economy

A Renewed Commitment

Irene Lynch Fannon and Michael James Boland

3.1 INTRODUCTION

3.1.1 *The Corporation and Value Capitalism*

A thematic aim of this collection is to critically examine the 'values of the EU social market system'. The introductory chapter describes how in terms of wealth creation 'the EU has offered a strong value system, yet one that has failed to achieve its full potential'.[1] We provide a different perspective from which we build a different hypothesis. We begin with a focus on the corporation as an engine of capitalism and wealth creation, and we end this chapter with our hypothesis about how corporations in Europe may renew their commitment to European values. External regulation of the corporation, aimed at giving expression to the European project, has travelled quite a distance in terms of the creation of a society where the corporation is viewed as having a central role along with other social actors in shaping European society, which is underpinned by a principle of equitable distribution of the wealth it generates. In comparing different regulatory responses we reiterate our view that different political contexts yield different answers regarding corporate function and present the reader with a vision of a European future.[2]

---

[1] C. Villiers, B. Sjåfjell and G. Tsagas, 'Stimulating Value Creation in a Europe in Crisis', Chapter 1 in this volume.

[2] A recent iteration of the regulatory approach of the EU is exemplified by the Sustainable Corporate Governance initiative, which 'aims to improve the EU regulatory framework on company law and corporate governance', which would 'enable companies to focus on long-term sustainable value creation rather than short-term benefits'. The proposed directive is currently in a consultation phase. See further https://ec.europa.eu/info/law/better-regulation/have-your-say/initiatives/12548-Sustainable-corporate-governance. This is discussed in B. Sjåfjell and G. Tsagas, 'Integrating Sustainable Value Creation: Company Law, Corporate Governance Codes and the Constitution of the Company', Chapter 9 in this volume.

The corporation as a social actor reflecting European values is considered in Section 2. Moving on from regulation we continue our analysis of corporate action with a focus on non-regulatory movements, the Corporate Social Responsibility (CSR) movement in particular, which is popular in many developed economies, ranging from the European social market economy to the neo-liberal market economy, often exemplified by the US in academic literature. In the European Union (EU), the CSR movement has been given the additional imprimatur of official policy reflected in policy documents issued on this matter over many years.[3] We consider the importance of the CSR movement in Section 3. We ask questions as to the nature of CSR as it influences corporate action. Is CSR properly viewed as a type of quasi-regulatory movement, acting externally to influence corporate action, with an emphasis on voluntarism rather than mandated regulation? In this sense is CSR a vehicle, used by some of its proponents at least, as a way of resisting regulation? Alternatively, is CSR in fact a more authentic voluntary movement coming from within the corporation demanding the corporation acts in certain ways? Or can it be, and is it in fact, a combination of both types of influences?

Even though the EU has espoused a comparatively more assertive approach towards the corporation in regulating certain types of activities and even though support has simultaneously been given to CSR by the EU at institutional level, we seem to have again reached an impasse, a point of failure and disappointment that broadly speaking is the subject matter of this collection.

Our hypothesis is presented in Section 4. Rather than adhere to attractively neat divisions between social market economies on the one hand, and neo-liberal economies on the other, reflected in a binary presentation of contractarianism versus communitarianism; and rather than positing regulatory models as being in conflict with voluntarist models such as the CSR model, we argue that the true resolution of our difficulties with capitalism lies in the development of a new theoretical framework driven by an ethical challenge

---

[3] Section 3 describes these in detail. On 20 March 2019 the EU described its CSR programme as follows: 'In 2011, the Commission adopted its renewed strategy for CSR, which combines horizontal approaches to promote CSR/RBC with more specific approaches for individual sectors and policy areas. Following up on its strategy, the Commission published a staff working document (SWD (2019) 143) in March 2019. It gives an overview of the Commission's and the European External Action Service's (EEAS) progress implementing CSR/RBC and business and human rights'; see European Commission, 'Corporate Social Responsibility, Responsible Business Conduct, and Business & Human Rights: Overview of Progress', SWD (2019) 143 final, available at: https://ec.europa.eu/growth/industry/corporate-social-responsibility_en.

to those acting behind the corporate veil or under its shadow. We cannot really effect the changes we would like unless we present an ethical challenge to those who are actors within the corporate myth,[4] whether they are directors, shareholders, consumers or other stakeholders such as lenders. Our argument is that the corporation is so simple a construct that in itself it makes very few value laden claims. Corporate actors such as directors, shareholders and others have in the past hidden behind theoretical myths. Examples include ideas such as shareholder wealth maximisation,[5] and the insistence in most jurisdictions on a strict lack of relationship between a parent and its subsidiaries.[6] Our hypothesis is that if we move on from present arguments and present a meaningful ethical challenge to corporate actors, we can ensure better outcomes. The conclusion in Section 5 will strike an optimistic note in this regard.

In the rest of this introduction, we begin by considering the simplicity of the limited liability corporation as a business vehicle.

---

[4]   In his book *Sapiens* the author Yuval Noah Harari speaks of the human capacity to invent myths such as the state, God and corporations. Taking the French company Peugeot as an example, he says: 'Ever since the Cognitive Revolution, Sapiens have thus been living in a dual reality. On the one hand, the objective reality of rivers, trees and lions; and on the other hand, the imagined reality of gods, nations and corporations. As time went by, the imagined reality became ever more powerful, so that today the very survival of rivers, trees and lions depends on the grace of imagined entities such as the United States and Google.' Y. Harari, *Sapiens: A Brief History of Humankind* (New York: HarperCollins, 2015), 21.

[5]   J. F. Sneirson, 'The History of Shareholder Primacy, from Adam Smith through the Rise of Financialism' in B. Sjåfjell and C. Bruner (eds.), *Cambridge Handbook of Corporate Law, Corporate Governance and Sustainability* (Cambridge: Cambridge University Press, 2020) 73–85; D. Katelouzou, 'Shareholder Stewardship: A Case of (Re) Embedding Institutional Investors and the Corporation', in B. Sjåfjell and C. Bruner (eds.), *Cambridge Handbook of Corporate Law, Corporate Governance and Sustainability* (Cambridge: Cambridge University Press, 2020) 581–595. See L. A. Stout, *The Shareholder Value Myth: How Putting Shareholders First Harms Investors, Corporations, and the Public* (California: Berrett- Koehler Publishers, 2012), 1–24; see also D. Millon, 'Shareholder Primacy in the Classroom after the Financial Crisis' (2013) 8(1) *Journal of Business and Technology Law*, 191–195. See generally C. Myers, *Firm Commitment-Why the Corporation is Failing Us and How to Restore Trust in It* (Oxford: Oxford University Press, 2013); S. Mansell, 'Shareholder Theory and Kant's 'Duty of Beneficence' (2013) 117(3) *Journal of Business Ethics*, 583–599.

[6]   See, generally, Y. S. Ang, 'Exploring Spatial Justice and the Ethic of Care in Corporations and Group Governance', in B. Sjåfjell and I. Lynch Fannon (eds.), *Creating Corporate Sustainability: Gender as an Agent for Change* (Cambridge: Cambridge University Press, 2018). This chapter discusses the significant decision of the Court of Appeal of England and Wales in *Chandler v. Cape Industries Plc*, [2012] EWCA Civ 525 where Arden LJ (as she was) held that the parent company owed a duty of care to the employees of its subsidiary. For discussion of the concept of separate legal personality in an Irish context see Company Law Review Group, *Report on the Protection of Employees and Unsecured Creditors* (Dublin: Company Law Review Group, 2017), at pp. 43–56 and pp. 106–124.

3.1.2 *The 'Genius' of the Corporation*[7]

In legal systems generally, the limited liability corporation possesses some core characteristics that are commonly accepted. In successive editions of their seminal work, *The Anatomy of Corporate Law*, the authors summarise these fundamental characteristics of the corporation as (1) legal personality, (2) limited liability, (3) transferable shares, (4) centralised management under a board structure and (5) shared ownership by contributors of equity capital.[8] With this as a starting point, we add some additional commentary relevant to our argument.

Limited Liability for Those Investing in the Company: Shareholders
Limited liability means that even where the shareholders buy sufficient shares to control the corporation similar to that of an owner, their liability for any of the downsides of the risks of the business is strictly limited to the value of their initial investment. Although now well established, the significance of the legal invention that is limited liability calls for reflection. The limitation of the liability of the shareholders to the value of the initial price of the share allows business owners (shareholders) to constrain the nature of their investment in the downside of the business risk. If the shareholder buys 100 €1 shares, he or she knows that normally even in the worst case scenario, €100 is the value of their loss, whereas the potential for the upside of the risk is limitless. This simple fact has added resonance in jurisdictions, which are numerous,[9] where there is no requirement that the initial value of a share in a corporation should have any significant minimal value, regardless of the value of assets held by the corporation itself.[10] Moreover, once the share's nominal value is paid up

---

7 This is an adaptation of Roberta Romano's famous claim for the 'Genius of Corporate Law', discussed later. See, R. Romano, *The Genius of American Corporate Law* (Washington DC: AEI Press, 1993).

8 J. Armour, H. Hansmann, R. Kraakman and M. Pargendler, 'What is Corporate Law?' in R. Kraakman, J. Armour, P. Davies, L. Enriques, H. Hansmann, G. Hertig, K. Hopt, H. Kanda, M. Pargendler, W. G. Ringe and E. Rock (eds.), *The Anatomy of Corporate Law: A Comparative and Functional Approach*, 3rd edition (Oxford: Oxford University Press, 2017).

9 In this context a distinction must be made between requirements that the nominal value of a share must be at a minimum, whether this is a share in a private or public company, and requirements regarding minimum capitalisation of a company overall. The United Kingdom, Ireland, Delaware, New York and California are all examples of jurisdictions with which the authors are familiar where there is no requirement that a share, whether in a private or public company, has a particular minimum value.

10 It is the case that even in relation to public quoted companies that will have a minimum overall capital requirement (mandated by European Directives within the EU plus the European Free Trade Association states of the European Economic Area), the nominal value of a particular share can be very low, and thus the individual shareholders' liability to contribute is

in the first transfer or issue, the liability of subsequent owners of the share is normally non-existent.[11] For subsequent shareholders of the corporation, therefore, their risk relates to the market value of the share and the possibility of this value rising or falling.

Separate Legal Personality for the Company

The doctrine of corporate personality means that the assets of the firm are held by the corporate identity and these assets (in addition to liabilities) belong to the corporation. The main consequence of this doctrine is the negative assertion that the assets of all of the corporate actors, whether these are shareholders (theoretically considered as owners) or directors and senior management (the controllers) are not generally available to creditors or other stakeholders who bear the risk of corporate failure.[12] This simple proposition describes the original purpose of the doctrine of corporate personality combined with limited liability, namely to facilitate business risk. However, as corporations have become more powerful and more pervasive in our society, the additional point is that shareholders and directors are also insulated from accountability for all sorts of corporate actions, whether these are acts of damage to natural resources,[13] acts of ill treatment of workers,[14] or other

---

low. As regards privately held companies, interestingly, in many European jurisdictions there was historically a requirement that a shareholder would contribute a minimum capital investment for private companies. However, under the influence of Anglo-American corporate law, there has been a gradual erosion of this concept. See, generally, O. Kahn-Freund, 'Some Reflections on Company Law Reform' (1944) 7 *Modern Law Review*, 54, where the author proposes, inter alia, that companies have a minimum capital in advance of incorporation as a way of addressing the disadvantages to creditors posed by limited liability.

[11] For discussion on how limited liability promotes, inter alia, the free transferability of shares, see F. H. Easterbrook and D. R. Fischel, 'Limited Liability and the Corporation' (1985) 52 *University of Chicago Law Review*, 89, 93–101.

[12] In the English law context, which has influenced many common law countries of the former and current commonwealth, see R. Grantham and C. Rickett, 'The Bootmaker's Legacy to Company Law Doctrine', in R. Grantham and C. Rickett (eds.), *Corporate Personality in the 20th Century* (Oxford: Hart Publishing, 1998).

[13] See, generally, A. Okoye and E. Osuteye, 'Ascertaining Corporate Sustainability from 'Below': The Case of Ghanaian Rural Mining Communities', in Sjåfjell and Lynch Fannon (eds.), *Creating Corporate Sustainability*, p. 67.

[14] See, for example, L. Talbot, 'Reclaiming Value and Betterment for Bangladeshi Women Workers in Global Garment Chains' in Sjåfjell and Lynch Fannon, (eds.), *Creating Corporate Sustainability*, 17, 28, where the author describes the conditions for the largely female garment factory workers in Bangladesh. She refers to the pay disparity to illustrate the dominance of global retail brands such as H&M compared with workers in its supplier factories. Talbot explains how the Bangladeshi female factory worker earns €3 for a ten- to twelve-hour workday in which 250 T-shirts are produced an hour, while H&M earn €1,500 from the same workday; see T. Norfield, 'T-Shirt Economics: Labour in the Imperialist World Economy'

actions that in a number of cases can only be described as egregious acts of corporate greed.[15]

The Concept of the Corporate Share

As is generally acknowledged by corporate lawyers, the simple concept of the share facilitates investor ownership, easy transferability of what is normally considered to be the legal ownership of the business, and also allows for continuity of the company over generations and through change of individual ownership. As compared with the unwieldy piecemeal transfer of assets in other forms of business ownership, or the dissolution and reconstitution of partnerships, the share transfer allows for a simple transfer of ownership and for the creation of secondary markets in investment in corporate ownership.

Although some corporate law theorists entirely reject the proposition that shareholders are viewed as owners of the corporation, we believe the argument must be presented in a more nuanced fashion.[16] In practical terms there is an equation between the shareholder as owner in terms of company formation and growth, transfer of ownership of business and so on. However, there are two important theoretical arguments accompanying our nuanced view of the role of the shareholder. The first, an argument developed elsewhere by Lynch Fannon, is that 'ownership', shareholder primacy and shareholder wealth maximisation are all different propositions, which do not necessarily follow each other. Rejecting shareholder wealth maximisation does not necessarily imply we must reject the concept that the shareholder is the closest thing to legal owner of the company. This is important because the argument is that as owner of residual corporate wealth, shareholders should be more responsible, not less. In that context the second theoretical argument relies on the development of company law on the basis that the unusual type of

(August 2012) *Global Labour Column*, available at: http://column.global-labour-university .org/2012/08/t-shirt-economics-labour-in-imperialist.html. See also E. Prügl, 'Neoliberalising Feminism' (2015) 20(4) *New Political Economy*, 614, 621–624, where the author considers Unilever's Shakti Project. This involves Unilever in India providing training to rural women so that they can sell Unilever's products in small Indian villages. Prügl criticises the project on the basis that it puts women in the service of corporate interests and thus represents a disingenuous attempt by Unilever to improve the lives of women. For further discussion of some of these issues, see M. J. Boland, 'Using Gender to Reimagine Corporate Purpose', *Trinity College Law School Colloquium, Trinity College Dublin*, 9 February 2019. Notes with author.

[15] See, for example, discussion about the actions of Apple Inc. in relation to tax avoidance in I. Lynch Fannon, 'Apple Tax: The Core Issues', in C. Gammage and T. Novitz, (eds.), *Sustainable Trade, Investment and Finance: Toward Responsible and Coherent Regulatory Frameworks* (Cheltenham: Elgar Publishing, 2019), p. 331.

[16] See P. Ireland, 'Company Law and the Myth of Shareholder Ownership' (1999) 62 *Modern Law Review*, 32–57.

splintered ownership exercised by shareholders must be recognised before we can move forward:

> To talk of the shareholders as owners is not an accurate description of reality. If the use of the word 'owner' is intended to convey the notion of full owner-ship with which we are familiar when we consider ownership of other types of property, then in many cases shareholders are not owners in that sense …. we should confine that understanding of ownership … to shareholders of close corporations … descriptions of the shareholder as owner where the shareholding is diverse and publicly traded describes no *ab initio* entitlement to other incidents of ownership such as control or voice.[17]

The Division between Ownership (the Shareholders) and Control (the Management)

A further characteristic of the corporation is that the theory of ownership through the share allows for the delegation of control from the alleged or putative own-ers of the corporation to management. This characteristic has thus become an important feature of the corporation, leading to problems created by the ongo-ing accountability of the board to the owner. These are generally described as agency problems and have occupied the minds of many corporate lawyers.[18]

From these simple conceptual ideas, the limited liability corporation has been described as 'the greatest invention since the wheel'.[19] Roberta Romano has considered 'the genius of corporate law' as a real conceptual and legal achieve-ment.[20] The present authors would not consider either of these descriptions to

---

[17] I. Lynch Fannon, *Working Within Two Kinds of Capitalism: Corporate Governance and Employee Stakeholding – US and EC Perspectives* (Oxford: Hart Publishing, 2003), pp. 80–83. See also J. W. Singer, 'The Reliance Interest in Property' (1987–1988) 40 *Stanford Law Review*, 713. M. Blair, *Ownership and Control: Rethinking Corporate Governance for the Twenty-First Century* (Washington DC: Brookings Institute Press, 1995), pp. 224–225.

[18] For an excellent discussion of externalities associated with the fundamental characteristics of the corporation, specifically limited liability, corporate personality, agency, and the easy transferability of the share, see F. H. Easterbrook and D. R. Fischel, 'Limited Liability and the Corporation' (1985) 52 *University of Chicago Law Review*, 89; See also S. M. Bainbridge, 'In Defence of the Shareholder Wealth Maximisation Norm: A Reply to Professor Green' (1993) 50(4) *Washington and Lee Law Review*, 1423; see C. Mayer, *Firm Commitment: Why the Corporation is Failing Us and How to Fix it* (Oxford: Oxford University Press, 2013); see W. H. Clark and D. A. Hickok, 'Repricing Limited Liability and Separate Entity Status' (2017) 40 *Seattle University Law Review*, 497.

[19] See N. M. Butler in W. Fletcher, *Cyclopedia of the Law of Corporations* (Chicago: Callaghan, 1917), p. 21.

[20] See R. Romano, *The Genius of American Corporate Law* (Washington DC: AEI Press, 1993). At its core this text addresses the continuing debate in the US regarding Federal versus State regulation; however, the text also describes the flexibility of the core concepts of corporate law. The importance of maintaining the quintessentially enabling and responsive characteristics of corporate law is an important assertion in Romano's work.

amount to hyperbole when one considers how the limited liability corporation has been an engine for economic growth in many capitalist societies. Indeed, anybody surveying the history of the corporation since its beginning cannot but deny the effectiveness of the limited liability corporation as a vehicle for business growth and also the usefulness of the concept of the share as part of the structure of the limited liability corporation for the transfer of business ownership over generations, and as a means of generating wealth through the extension of business ownership through investment. This has allowed for the generation of wealth, across social boundaries and across generations. But at the centre of this capitalist achievement is a myth the nature of which only the human mind is capable. In his book *Sapiens: A Brief History of Humankind*, Harari compares the limited liability corporation and the creation of its underlying concepts as having a similar place in human development as the concept of deity.[21] The importance of this insight in his argument is to identify the ability of humans to co-operate in the pursuit of a grander ideal. He observes that 'large numbers of strangers can cooperate successfully by believing in myths'. He makes exciting comparisons for the humble corporate lawyer:

> How exactly did Armand Peugeot, the man, create Peugeot, the company? In much the same way that priests and sorcerers have created gods and demons throughout history ... In the case of Peugeot SA, the crucial story was the French legal code, as written by the French parliament. According to French legislators, if a certified lawyer followed all the proper liturgy and rituals, wrote all the required spells and oaths on a wonderfully decorated piece of paper, and affixed his ornate signature to the bottom of the document, then hocus pocus- a new company was incorporated ... Once the lawyer had performed all the right rituals and pronounced all the necessary spells and oaths, millions of upright French citizens behaved as if the Peugeot company really existed.[22]

3.2 THE CORPORATION AND THE EUROPEAN PROJECT

3.2.1 *Contracts and Communities*

The contractarian versus the communitarian view of the corporation is often adopted as a theoretical model explaining the divergence of approach in relation to the regulation of the corporation.[23] The former is described as being

---

[21] Harari, *Sapiens*, Ch. 2, p. 26.
[22] Harari, *Sapiens*, Ch. 2, p. 20.
[23] For an example of communitarian writing, see Stout, *The Shareholder Value Myth*; see also L. E. Mitchell (ed.), *Progressive Corporate Law: New Perspectives on Law, Culture and Society* (Boulder, CO: Westview Press, 1995); see L. E. Mitchell, *Corporate Irresponsibility: America's Newest Export* (New Haven: Yale University Press, 2001).

'root[ed] in "realist" conceptions of the company as a body autonomous from the state',[24] and tends to regard maximisation of shareholder wealth as the sole function of the corporation.[25] In contrast to the *monist* perspective of contractarian writers, communitarian writers view the corporation in *pluralist* terms.[26] They have argued that the corporation should be viewed not just as a business enterprise but as a social organisation owing varying duties to all stakeholders and society at large.[27] Commentators have described how the contractarian view regards corporate law as being individualistic in inclination and 'enabling in character, not regulatory';[28] it treats the corporation as 'the market writ small',[29] and conceives of it as a purely causal nexus of *self-regarding individuals; an agglomeration of explicit and implicit contracts through which each stakeholder can establish their standing within the firm.[30]

In contrast, and as explained in the elegantly written article by William T. Allen published some years ago,[31] what is now described as the communitarian or progressive movement reflecting the values of the European social model is 'grounded in the dominant concepts of continental Europe',[32] and sees the corporation as a 'social partner' in the pursuit of broad-based social, employment and economic policies.[33] In contrast to the Anglo-American/contractarian school, the European/communitarian school more readily looks to legal rules to govern the corporation's internal and external relationships reasoning that *ex ante* legal ordering – favoured by contractarians – fails

---

[24] R. Parry, 'Directors' Duties within the United Kingdom', in S. Tully (ed.), *Research Handbook in Corporate Legal Responsibility* (Cheltenham: Edward Elgar Publishing, 2005), p. 74.

[25] Lynch Fannon, *Working Within Two Kinds of Capitalism*, p. 77.

[26] B. Sjåfjell, A. Johnston, L. Anker-Sørensen and D. Millon, 'Shareholder Primacy: The Main Barrier to Sustainable Companies', in B. Sjåfjell and B. J. Richardson (eds.), *Company Law and Sustainability: Legal Barriers and Opportunities* (Cambridge: Cambridge University Press, 2015), pp. 79–147, 94.

[27] Lynch Fannon, *Working Within Two Kinds of Capitalism*, p. 78.

[28] Ibid.

[29] Ibid.

[30] A. A. Alchian and H. Demsetz, 'Production, Information Costs, and the Economic Organisation' (1972) 62 *The American Economic Review*, 777, who posited that the corporation is a team of inputs monitored by another contracting party, the shareholders; see M. C. Jensen and W. H. Meckling, 'The Theory of the Firm: Managerial Behaviour, Agency Costs, and Ownership Structure' (1976) 3 *Journal of Financial Economics*, 305 who coined the phrase 'nexus of contracts'; for a clear explanation of the nexus of contracts paradigm see W. T. Allen, 'Contracts and Communities in Corporation Law' (1993) 50(4) *Washington and Lee Law Review*, 1400.

[31] Allen, 'Contracts and Communities in Corporation Law', 1395.

[32] Ibid., 1397.

[33] I. Lynch Fannon, 'The European Social Model of Corporate Governance: Prospects for Success in an Enlarged Europe', in G. N. Gregoriou and P. U. Ali (eds.), *International Corporate Governance after Sarbanes-Oxley* (Hoboken, NJ: Wiley, 2006), chapter 20.

to foresee events that occur *ex post,* leaving certain non-shareholder groups unprotected.[34]

Recent examples of the type of regulation more closely associated with the European social model of regulation include compulsory employee or creditor representation on corporate boards;[35] the use of quotas to achieve gender diversity in the boardroom;[36] compulsory rules on the disclosure of gender, employee and environmental information, so-called triple bottom line reporting.[37] In contrast, in the contractarian model, exemplified in this theoretical construct by the US, regulation of the internal structures of boards to include employee, creditor or gender representation has appeared to be unthinkable.

3.2.2 *Regulating the Corporation: The Corporation and Employees as Stakeholders*

Developing these contrasting approaches, key differences between the EU value capitalism model[38] and that which pertains in the US seem to lie in the more assertive regulatory model adopted by the EU, where issues of distributive justice are at stake. In particular, a stark contrast can be made between the regulation of corporate action regarding stakeholders such as employees.[39] The EU has issued many Directives to its member states regarding not only equal pay and equal opportunities,[40] interestingly originally concerned mainly with gender equality, but also regarding a broader range of employment related issues, such as working time, shift work and holiday leave,[41] in addition to the pan-European regulation of minimum standards concerning family and

---

[34] D. Millon, 'New Directions in Corporate Law: Communitarians, Contractarians, and the Crisis in Corporate Law' (1993) 50(4) *Washington and Lee Law Review*, 1373, 1379.

[35] A mandatory two-tier board structure exists in seven EU member states, including Germany and Austria. The first tier consists of the executive and non-executive directors and the second tier sits employee and other stakeholder representatives. See B. Clarke, 'The Role of Board Directors in Promoting Environmental Sustainability' in Sjåfjell and Richardson (eds.), *Company Law and Sustainability*, p. 150.

[36] Ibid., p. 168; see I. Lynch Fannon, 'A Toad We Have to Swallow: Perceptions and Participation of Women in Business and the Implications for Sustainability', in Sjåfjell and Lynch Fannon (eds.), *Creating Corporate Sustainability*,) 114, pp. 133–134.

[37] Clarke, 'The Role of Board Directors in Promoting Environmental Sustainability', 158.

[38] For a consideration of these contrasting approaches, see generally Lynch Fannon, *Working Within Two Kinds of Capitalism.* See, in particular, Chs. 6, 7 and 8.

[39] Ibid., pp. 108–113.

[40] See original EU Treaty 1957. Issues concerning the gender pay gap are of continued concern to the EU, available at: https://ec.europa.eu/info/policies/justice-and-fundamental-rights/gender-equality/equal-pay_en.

[41] Directive 2003/88/EC of the European Parliament and of the Council of 4 November 2003 concerning certain aspects of the organisation of working time OJ L 299, 18.11.2003, pp. 9–19.

caring related leave.[42] Essentially, this model is based on an assumption that the state has legitimate authority to regulate the corporation to these ends and in addition has a legitimate interest in regarding corporations as organisations with a role in delivering a comprehensive European Social Policy.[43] In contrast, in the US, the regulation of corporate action in the sphere of equality derived from a different concern regarding racial inequality as distinct from gender equality;[44] and again, in contrast to the EU, there is no federal regulation of working time, vacation leave and very little regulation even regarding the availability of paid family leave.[45]

However, even though the contrast between the EU and the US in relation to the regulation of the employment issues is clear, the presentation of such a stark, theoretically based divergence is not convincing when the regulation of other issues such as corporate criminality, environmental degradation and corporate tax avoidance are added to the mix. Tax is chosen as a comparator in this piece, as with regulation aimed at achieving fair and equitable working conditions, which in turn impacts on both employment and quality of life issues, taxation is equally concerned with distributive justice, having the effect of ensuring that the wealth created by corporations is distributed in an equitable manner.[46]

3.2.3 *Regulating the Corporation: Tax and Multinationals*

Table 3.1, compiled by the authors based on a number of sources of information, including KPMG and the Organisation for Economic Co-operation and Development (OECD), US and Irish tax codes, provides corporate tax rates in the US and a handful of comparator European countries:

---

[42] Council Directive 92/85/EEC of 19 October 1992 on the introduction of measures to encourage improvements in the safety and health at work of pregnant workers, Official Journal L 348, 28/11/1992 P. 0001 – 0008; Council Directive 2010/18/EU of 8 March 2010 implementing the revised Framework Agreement on parental leave concluded by BUSINESSEUROPE, UEAPME, CEEP and ETUC and repealing Directive 96/34/EC (Text with European Economic Area relevance), OJ L 68, 18.3.2010, pp. 13–20.

[43] See Reflection Paper on the Social Dimension of Europe European Commission, COM(2017) 206 of 26 April 2017. In this somewhat alarming document questions are asked as to how Europe will proceed with its social policy. The corporation is again seen as a social actor. In addition three options are considered: reducing social protections across Europe; continuing with an ongoing agenda confined to countries of the Eurozone; or pursuing a pan-twenty-seven Member State approach.

[44] See the text of the 14th Amendment of US Constitution. Civil Rights Act 1964.

[45] Family and Medical Leave Act 1993.

[46] This has been recognised by international organisations. See, for example, OECD/G20, *Base Erosion and Profit-Shifting Project: Executive Summary* (OECD, 2015), available at: www .oecd.org/tax/beps-2015-final-reports.htm.

TABLE 3.1 *Comparative tax rates**

Country	Rate	Comment
United States	Federal tax rate is normally around 35%. Average corporate tax rate 27%	US Companies are also subject to State and local taxes[47]
France	33.%–25%[48]	Planned reduction to 25%
Germany	30%[49]	
Ireland	12.5%	If the OECD's global corporate tax deal discussed below comes into effect, Ireland will tax corporations with annual earnings of over €750 million at a rate of 15%. The existing rate of 12.5% will apply to every other company.
Netherlands	16%–25%[50]	Varied rates.
Norway	22%[51]	

* The table is compiled by the authors of this chapter.

From this we can see that the current US corporation tax rate is effectively 27 per cent, with some European countries having lower rates and increasingly moving towards lower rates since 2018 with the exception of Germany. Interestingly, in April 2017, the Trump administration promised to introduce an effective flat tax rate of 21 per cent at federal level and this was done under the Tax Cuts and Jobs Act 2017, which not only reduced the corporate tax rate but

47 KPMG Corporate Tax Rates Table for 2010–2020. Regarding the US, a corporation is liable to federal tax averaging 27 per cent, then state and possibly local taxes. 'A corporation may deduct its state and local income tax expense when computing its federal taxable income, generally resulting in a net effective rate of approximately 27 per cent. The effective rate may vary significantly depending on the locality in which a corporation conducts business.' Furthermore, other special rules may apply to a corporation, resulting in a greater or lesser federal taxable income. This tool does not take into account those other special rules.

48 Ibid. 'The French Finance Law for 2018 followed by the French Finance Law for 2019 decided a progressive reduction of the CIT rate from 33.1/3 per cent down to 25 per cent. However, increased budget spending forced the government and French lawmakers to slowdown the scheduled decrease of the CIT rate for large corporate taxpayers.'

49 Ibid.

50 Ibid. 'The corporate tax rate is 16.5 per cent on taxable profit up to EUR 200,000 and 25 per cent for taxable profits exceeding EUR 200,000.'

51 Ibid. 'Special rates apply for petroleum companies and in the power sector.'

also allowed for a once off tax amnesty at the rate of 15 per cent.[52] However, even within this legislation the tax rate will be restored to pre-2017 levels by 2025.

The Biden administration has pledged to increase the federal rate of corporation tax to 28 per cent,[53] and has also promised to tax the earnings of US multinationals abroad. Most recently, the Biden administration has signed the US up to the OECD's corporate tax reform deal, which would align taxing rights with markets where the economic activity that generated the profit took place and would introduce an effective global minimum corporate tax rate of 15 per cent. In total, 136 of 140 OECD members have now signed up to the deal.[54] G20 leaders also endorsed the deal at their Summit in Rome in October 2021.[55] At the time of writing, progress towards the implementation of the OECD deal is slow with some speculating that Pillar Two of the deal – the part relating to a global minimum rate of corporate tax – may not be given effect to until 2024.[56] The timeline for Pillar One of the deal relating to taxing rights is also uncertain. The delays are reportedly due to political opposition in the US and Hungary to aspects of the deal.[57]

A number of US multinational corporations came under scrutiny from tax authorities on both sides of the Atlantic regarding tax avoidance practices. Taking one of the most well-known companies, Apple Inc., as a point of discussion, in 2014 the European Commission began an investigation into the company and concluded that two specific tax rulings given to Apple by Ireland, a member state of the European Eurozone, 'substantially and artificially lowered the tax paid by Apple in Ireland … (and Europe) … since 1991'.[58]

The Commission asserted that these two rulings did not reflect the reality of Apple's trading operations. It found that:

---

[52] 115th Congress Public Law 115–97 'An Act To provide for reconciliation pursuant to titles II and V of the concurrent resolution on the budget for fiscal year 2018.' Dec. 22, 2017 131 Stat. 2054.

[53] T. Luhmy and K. Lobosco, 'Here's how Biden wants to raise taxes on the wealthy and corporations', *CNN* (23 April 2021), available at: https://edition.cnn.com/2021/03/18/politics/biden-tax-plan-explainer/index.html.

[54] OECD, 'International community strikes a ground-breaking tax deal for the digital age' (Paris: 2021), available at: www.oecd.org/tax/international-community-strikes-a-ground-breaking-tax-deal-for-the-digital-age.htm.

[55] G20, 'G20 Rome Leaders' Declaration' (Rome: G20 Leaders' Summit, 2021) at 9, available at: www.consilium.europa.eu/media/52732/final-final-g20-rome-declaration.pdf.

[56] M. McDougall, 'Joe Biden tax proposals fall short of OECD standards for minimum rate', *Financial Times* (9 August 2022), available at: www.ft.com/content/ffoc15b7-2e34-469f-8c5e-9168bbb30c51; see further S. Collins, 'US can't deliver tax deal Yellen convinced Donohoe to support', *Irish Independent* (20 July 2022), available at: www.independent.ie/business/world/us-cant-deliver-tax-deal-janet-yellen-convinced-paschal-donohoe-to-support-41853428.html.

[57] *Ibid.*

[58] European Commission, 'State aid: Ireland gave illegal tax benefits to Apple worth up to €13 billion' (Brussels: 2016), available at: https://ec.europa.eu/commission/presscorner/detail/en/IP_16_2923.

[A]lmost all sales profits recorded by the two companies were internally attributed to a 'head office'. The Commission's assessment showed that these 'head offices' existed only on paper and could not have generated such profits. These profits allocated to the 'head offices' were not subject to tax in any country under specific provisions of the Irish tax law, which are no longer in force. As a result of the allocation method endorsed in the tax rulings, Apple only paid an effective corporate tax rate that declined from 1 per cent in 2003 to 0.005 per cent in 2014 on the profits of Apple Sales International.[59]

Soon after the Commission's ruling in respect of Apple Inc.'s Irish operations, the Irish government and Apple Inc. as co-appellants announced their intention to appeal the Commission's ruling to the General Court of the European Union (GCEU). On 15 July 2020, the GCEU delivered its judgment in Ireland's appeal, finding that Ireland did not give illegal state aid to Apple in the form of undue tax benefits of up to €13 billion and that Apple's Irish subsidiaries had legitimately benefitted from an exemption in Ireland's tax code that, as the Commission acknowledged, is no longer in force. Most recently, on 25 September 2020, the Commission announced that it will appeal the General Court's decision to the Court of Justice of the European Union (CJEU), which is expected to be heard in two years' time.[60] The Commission's underlying position is that all companies must pay their 'fair share of tax',[61] that selective tax treatment of individual companies distorts competition and that tax avoidance practices hinders the ability of member states to invest in public services.[62] On 15 December 2020, the Irish government lodged its response to the Commission's appeal with the CJEU, although it did not set out the legal arguments made in its response to the Commission's appeal.[63]

---

[59] Ibid.

[60] European Commission, 'Statement by Executive Vice-President, Margrethe Vestager, on the Commission's decision to appeal the General Court's judgment on the Apple tax State aid case in Ireland' (Brussels, 25 September 2020), available at: https://ec.europa.eu/commission/press-corner/detail/en/statement_20_1746; see Department of Finance (Ireland), 'Minister Donohoe notes EU Commission's decision to appeal Apple State aid case to the Court of Justice of the EU' (25 September 2020), available at: www.gov.ie/en/press-release/77ec6-minister-donohoe-notes-eu-commissions-decision-to-appeal-apple-state-aid-case-to-the-court-of-justice-of-the-eu/.

[61] European Commission, 'Statement by Executive Vice-President, Margrethe Vestager, on the Commission's decision to appeal the General Court's judgment on the Apple tax state aid case in Ireland'.

[62] Ibid.

[63] The authors contacted the Irish Department of Finance in October 2020 and, more recently, in January 2021 seeking guidance as to when formal notice of appeal was expected and whether Ireland's legal arguments in respect of the Commission's appeal would be published. The authors received a response from the Department of Finance on 11 January 2021 confirming when the Irish government lodged its response with the CJEU but declining to comment further, citing possible prejudice to the forthcoming appeal.

Similarly, in August 2016, the US Department of Treasury issued a White Paper on 'The European Commission's Recent State Aid Investigations of Transfer Pricing Rulings'.[64] Part of the rationale behind this paper was to assert that the taxes were owed to the United States government and not the EU. The tax amounts totalled between €13 and €16 billion. The main thrust of the argument by the US Federal agency was that the international community had developed a set of standards including a reference to economic realities, regarding 'the allocation of corporate income among jurisdictions' in a group context, which included the use of an 'arm's length principle for transfer pricing and the development of a network of treaties to resolve disputes'. In addition, the OECD principles were invoked, particularly those relating to economic realities, noting that Ireland and the US, and other European states such as Luxembourg, Belgium and the Netherlands (all of which benefit from the location of US subsidiaries in their jurisdictions), have maintained a consensus regarding these matters.[65]

3.2.4 *Moving Away from a Binary Theoretical Construct to a Multifaceted Approach*

The key point we wish to make here is that whilst there may be particular sectoral areas such as the regulation of the corporation's relationship with employees as stakeholders where the differences in approach are significant, the similarities of approach to regulation of the corporation's actions in other sectoral areas such as tax are equally compelling. For this reason, we present a challenge to the binary understanding of contractarian and communitarian analysis of corporate regulation, and how this is translated into the identification of political and economic analysis of particular trading groups such as the EU and the US. In reality, the picture is more complex, and there is no really obvious dividing line between the contractarian and communitarian who both can easily accept that the corporation can be regulated to achieve an equitable tax yield. Perhaps this is one reason why what is usually termed 'progressive corporate law scholarship' has not yielded as many insights in different areas as we would have expected. As Liao observed:

> [T]here has been very little development of theory under the flag of 'progressive corporate law' for some time now. The inability to find common terminology and consensus created a significant stumbling block to internal organisation and cohesion. Other positions, such as more advanced versions of progressive

---

[64] US Department of the Treasury, 'The European Commission's Recent State Aid Investigations of Transfer Pricing Rulings' (2016) *US Department of the Treasury White Paper*, available at: www.treasury.gov/resource-center/tax-policy/treaties/Documents/White-Paper-State-Aid.pdf.
[65] Ibid., pp. 18–19.

corporate law theory emanating from a pragmatic European perspective on corporate function, or the fact that nations have adopted more stakeholder-based models of governance, have not been recognised sufficiently in academic scholarship and have struggled to gain traction in popular discourse.[66]

In concluding this section, we argue that the neat conceptual divide that we mentioned in the introductory part of this chapter and that will be considered further in Section 4, between social market economies and neo liberal economies and their distinct and contrasting approaches to the regulation of the corporation, is not as sustainable as many theorists assume. There are other political factors at play, presenting a much more nuanced approach.

3.3 CSR AND REGULATION

This section considers the effect of CSR movements on corporate action. As described in the introduction, there are many variants of CSR, but for our purposes there are two approaches, which are quite different. The first considers the encouragement of CSR as an alternative to regulation and, even more assertively, as a substitute to regulation.[67] Here, there is a binary presentation of deregulation rather than regulation and an adoption of a haphazard assortment of voluntary standards rather than universal minimum standards. In contrast, a second variant of CSR is to set out norms of behaviour, which can be pursued by corporations on a voluntary basis as a precursor to regulation or indeed as a compliment to regulation.[68] The approach of the EU to CSR is reflective of this variant of CSR.[69] However, as stated, the presentation and scholarly debate around CSR is sometimes reflected in a binary understanding of the corporation as being based in a contractarian or communitarian context. The following is an example of this presentation from Avi-Yonah:

> Fundamentally, therefore, the debate around CSR is linked to another widespread debate in corporate law: Whether corporate law is destined to 'converge' on the US model of publicly traded corporations with dispersed share

---

[66] C. Liao, 'Power and the Gender Imperative in Corporate Law', in Sjåfjell and Lynch Fannon (eds.), *Creating Corporate Sustainability*, pp. 296–297.

[67] The danger of regarding CSR in this way is discussed in I. Lynch Fannon, 'The Corporate Social Responsibility Movement and Law's Empire: Is there a Conflict?' (2007) 58 *Northern Ireland Legal Quarterly*, 1.

[68] A. Vives, 'Corporate Social Responsibility: The Role of Law and Markets and the Case of Developing Countries' (2008) 83(1) *Chicago-Kent Law Review*, 199.

[69] European Commission, *Corporate Social Responsibility: National Public Policies in the European Union (Compendium 2014)* (European Commission: Directorate-General for Employment, Social Affairs and Inclusion, 2014), available at: https://ec.europa.eu/digital-single-market/en/news/corporate-social-responsibility-national-public-policies-european-union-compendium-2014; see Section 3.3.2 for further references to EU CSR.

ownership, or whether other models (such as the German and Japanese models) are viable. The aggregate, nexus of contracts theory is closely linked to the US corporate governance model, while other models are much more open to CSR. Recent literature has given rise to doubts about the convergence hypothesis, but this debate will no doubt continue.[70]

Again, the binary approach between social market economies and outcomes, and neo-liberal economies and outcomes reflected in contractarian versus communitarian debates is also reflected in this presentation of CSR and in the arguments surrounding it.

3.3.1 *Similar Approaches to CSR in the EU and the US*

In contrast, we suggest that both the EU and the US share a similar approach to CSR. Specifically, it is suggested that the constituency approach to CSR is applied across the EU and the US. The constituency approach, which is arguably inspired by Dodd's seminal article in 1932,[71] attempts to balance all of the constituent interests affected by corporate activity. It recognises the competing interests of stakeholders and shareholders, and has regard for the broader social effects of the corporation on employees, their families and the local community.[72] Moreover, the constituency approach finds expression in the feminist

---

[70] R. S. Avi-Yonah, 'Corporate Social Responsibility and Strategic Tax Behaviour' (2006) 69 *University of Michigan Public Law Working Paper* and 06–008 *University of Michigan Law & Economics, Olin Working Paper*, available at: https://papers.ssrn.com/sol3/papers .cfm?abstract_id=944793.

[71] E. M. Dodd, 'For Whom Are Corporate Managers Trustees?' (1932) 45(7) *Harvard Law Review*, 1145. Professor Dodd was among the first who sought to sideline *exclusive* profit-making for social responsibility. A similar attempt had been made two years earlier by John Maynard Keynes in his paper 'Economic Possibilities for our Grandchildren' (1930), which predicted that by the year 2030 we would be working a fifteen-hour week as we would have realised by then the 'good life', that is, a life where humans' insatiable desires for growth and wealth would be quenched thus obviating the need to work long hours. For discussion about why Keynes's prediction has failed to materialise, see R. Skidelsky and E. Skidelsky, *How Much Is Enough? Money and the Good Life* (London: Penguin Books, 2013). It is noteworthy, however, that some organisations such as Microsoft are currently experimenting with a four-day working week. See B. Chappell, '4-Day Workweek Boosted Workers' Productivity By 40 per cent, Microsoft Japan Says' *NPR – All Things Considered*, 4 November 2019, available at: www.npr.org/2019/11/04/776163853/ microsoft-japan-says-4-day-workweek-boosted-workers-productivity-by-40.

[72] D. Millon, 'Two Models of Corporate Social Responsibility' (2011) 46 *Wake Forest Law Review*, 523, 525–526. Other models of CSR include the 'strategic' approach and the 'holistic' approach. Strategic CSR strives to create long-term benefits for the corporation and can thus be said to accommodate both shareholder and non-shareholder interests. Holistic CSR, on the other hand, is an idea from feminist legal theory. Ruth Pearson writes about it in the context of global supply chains and urges that CSR should take account of both the work-life and home-life of women working in export production. The reason for this is that business will

ethical theory called the 'ethics of care',[73] which can clarify what is meant by CSR in this context. This approach concerns relationships with 'concrete others' as opposed to 'generalised others'.[74] In the context of the corporation, viewed as a 'web of relationships',[75] this means that each individual within the organisation owes caring responsibilities to those they are closest to. The rationale for this is that effective caregiving requires that the caregiver be able to identify and empathise with the needs of others, which can only be achieved in close, proximate relationships.[76] Therefore, employees are in a caring relationship with other employees, the board of directors owe caring ethics to other members of the board and management have an obligation to care for the needs of shareholders.[77] The ethics of care thus avoids making trade-offs between diverse interests;[78] it achieves a reconciliation between shareholder and non-shareholder interests by placing every corporate constituent within the ambit of care.

3.3.2 CSR and the EU

There is evidence of the constituency approach across all of the European Commission's policy documents on CSR. The Commission's Green Paper on Promoting a European Framework for CSR looked to the CSR movement as an antidote to the perceived threats of globalisation,[79] in particular, the exploitation of workers and communities in developing countries where EU companies are established.[80] The importance of the global context is a constant across all EU policy documents relating to CSR; however, each is also incremental in the sense that every CSR-related proposal identifies new

   benefit from the 'reproductive' work of women in rearing and educating the future workforce and should, therefore, consider the *families* of its labour force as another subject of CSR concern. For discussion on the 'strategic' approach, see Millon, 'Two Models of Corporate Social Responsibility', 530–533; see R. Pearson, 'Beyond Women Workers: Gendering CSR' (2007) 28(4) *Third World Quarterly*, 731, 739–745 for discussion on the 'holistic' approach.

73 S. Machold, P. K. Ahmed and S. S. Farquhar, 'Corporate Governance and Ethics: A Feminist Perspective' (2008) 81 *Journal of Business Ethics*, 665.

74 Ibid., 670.

75 Ibid., 673.

76 Ibid., 671.

77 Ibid., 673–674.

78 The constituency approach can be criticised on the basis that it often involves making trade-offs between shareholder and non-shareholder interests: what is advantageous to shareholders may disadvantage non-shareholders and vice versa. Hence, proponents of the constituency approach often have recourse to moral or ethical arguments to justify such trade-offs. See Millon, 'Two Models of Corporate Social Responsibility', 525–526.

79 European Commission (2001), '*Green Paper: Promoting a European Framework for Corporate Social Responsibility*', COM(2001) 366 final, Brussels, 18 July 2001.

80 Ibid., 4.

stakeholders and new corporate constituencies as subjects of CSR concern. For instance, in its first CSR initiative, the Commission concentrates largely on labour rights along global supply chains.[81] In a subsequent document, the concerns of 'consumers, investors and the wider public' are canvassed,[82] and in more recent publications greater emphasis is placed on ethics, human rights and the environment.[83]

One of the Commission's most recent initiatives is on sustainable corporate governance.[84] While the initiative is still in its infancy, its prefatory document underscores the Commission's commitment to the constituency approach. It states that the aim of the initiative is for companies to further incorporate respect for a variety of stakeholder interests such as employees and the environment in decision-making, and for companies to take steps to proactively identify, inter alia, the environmental and human rights impacts of its operations and to mitigate and remediate those impacts.[85] In other words, the initiative makes clear the Commission's intention to propose legislation that will oblige companies to engage in due diligence (the prefatory document proposes a new 'due diligence duty' in respect of directors).[86] European-style CSR can thus be praised for both its responsiveness to the evolving nature of the corporation and its recognition of the corporation's diverse constituent groups.

Developments within the EU serve to strengthen the commitment across Continental Europe to the stakeholder-oriented tradition. Germany is a prototypical example of such European pluralism. The Co-determination Act (MitbestG) allows employees to elect half of the membership of the supervisory board in companies with 2,000 or more employees.[87] Meanwhile, in companies with between 500 and 2,000 employees, the employee-elected

---

[81] Ibid., 7.

[82] European Commission (2006), '*Implementing the Partnership for Growth and Jobs: Making Europe a Pole of Excellence on Corporate Social Responsibility*', COM(2006) 136 final, Brussels, 22 March 2006, at 6.

[83] European Commission (2011), '*A Renewed EU Strategy 2011–2014 for Corporate Social Responsibility*', COM(2011) 681 final, Brussels, 25 October 2011, at 6; see European Commission (2012) '*Action Plan: European Company Law and Corporate Governance – A Modern Legal Framework for more Engaged Shareholders and Sustainable Companies*', COM(2012) 740 final, Brussels, 12 December 2012.

[84] European Commission, Sustainable Corporate Governance initiative, available at: https://ec.europa.eu/info/law/better-regulation/have-your-say/initiatives/12548-Sustainable-corporate-governance; see Chapter 9 in this volume.

[85] See generally, 'Inception Impact Assessment', ibid.

[86] For a discussion of due diligence and an overview of some due diligence initiatives see, C. Villiers, 'Global Supply Chains and Sustainability: The Role of Disclosure and Due Diligence Regulation', in Sjåfjell and Bruner (eds.), *The Cambridge Handbook of Corporate Law, Corporate Governance, and Sustainability*, 551, pp. 559–565.

[87] Law on the co-determination of employees (Co-determination Act – MitbestG), p. 7.

members of the supervisory board constitute one-third of its membership.[88] A similar system of co-determination exists in Austria, Denmark, Luxembourg, Hungary and the Netherlands.[89] The idea is that the supervisory board, with its significant employee representation, would supervise the exercise by the management board of its duties, and would be responsible for the day-to-day management of the company. This is reinforced by the German Corporate Governance Code, which underscores the pluralistic understanding of the 'interests of the company'.[90] The manner in which management considers the various interests and their method for weighing the competing interests in reaching their decisions is at their discretion, but responsibility for ensuring that the 'interests of the company' viewed through a stakeholder-oriented lens is observed by management is with the supervisory board.[91] Hence, the role of the supervisory board is as the guardian of the 'interests of the company'. Another important consequence of co-determination and of the pervasiveness of the stakeholder-value concept in German corporate governance is long-termism, with the effect that 'operational' risk-taking,[92] which prioritises 'the short term wealth of the shareholders rather than the long term health of the company',[93] can be discouraged. Hence, the method for calculating executive remuneration no longer rewards short-termism exclusively but rather 'must be geared towards sustainable and long-term development of the company'.[94] It follows that the remuneration structure applicable across German listed companies is arguably a model for the forthcoming EU Sustainable Corporate Governance initiative referred to previously, which seeks to address, inter alia, the association between directors' remuneration and the company's financial

---

[88] Law on employee participation on the supervisory board (Third Participation Act – Third Party Act), p. 4.

[89] D. Millon, 'Corporate Social Responsibility and Environmental Sustainability', in Sjåfjell and Richardson (eds.), *Company Law and Sustainability*, p. 48 see Lynch Fannon, *Working Within Two Kinds of Capitalism*, pp. 108–111.

[90] Section A (I) of the German Corporate Governance Code 2019, available at: https://ecgi .global/node/7493. The Dutch Corporate Governance Code takes a similar stakeholder-value approach. See Sections II.1 and III.1 of the Dutch Corporate Governance Code, available at: https://ecgi.global/code/dutch-corporate-governance-code.

[91] A. Rühmkorf, 'Stakeholder Value versus Corporate Sustainability: Company Law and Corporate Governance in Germany' in B. Sjåfjell and C. M. Bruner (eds.), *The Cambridge Handbook of Corporate Law, Corporate Governance and Sustainability* (Cambridge University Press, 2020), pp. 232–245, 237.

[92] For discussion of 'operational' risk-taking compared with 'entrepreneurial' risk-taking in the context of reckless trading see, I. Lynch Fannon, 'Reckless Trading: Good and Bad Risk-Taking in Irish Companies' (2017) 24(1) *Commercial Law Practitioner*, 7, available at: https:// papers.ssrn.com/sol3/papers.cfm?abstract_id=2966655.

[93] J. Quinn, 'What it Means to Act in the Best Interests of the Company' (2016) 34(15) *Irish Law Times*, 218.

[94] Stock Corporation Act 1965, s. 87(1).

performance. In line with the initiative's objective that decision-making should take account of the long-term rather than short-term interests of the company, the initiative's prefatory document specifically refers to the issue of executive remuneration as a catalyst of short-termism and, therefore, indicates that a remuneration structure similar to that provided for in Germany's Stock Corporation Act should be introduced. One critique of the German remuneration structure, however, is that the relevant statutory provision seems to confine itself to rewarding economic sustainability but not environmental or social sustainability.[95] This, it is argued, would be rectified in the Commission's forthcoming initiative, which encourages sustainability in all its forms to be incorporated further into corporate governance structures.

European-style CSR can thus be praised for both its responsiveness to the evolving nature of the corporation and its recognition of the corporation's diverse constituent groups.

3.3.3 *The Experience of CSR in the US*

In contrast, Hansmann and Kraakman, in their now infamous article, exhorted the strength of the shareholder-oriented model that they argued reflected US corporate practice.[96] Hansmann and Kraakman criticised the constituency approach, which they termed the stakeholder model, on the basis that it defied the forces of example and logic.[97] They also argued for the economic superiority of the shareholder-oriented model, a claim that has been discredited by corporate scandals and financial catastrophes.[98] Hansmann and Kraakman also claimed that the shareholder-oriented model is logically superior to the stakeholder model. In support of this, they drew on the contractarian view of the firm as a nexus of contracts in which stakeholders are protected by contract.

Not only do many of Hansmann and Kraakman's reasons for labelling US corporate purpose as one of shareholder wealth-maximisation fail to withstand scrutiny,[99] and have largely been discredited by the global financial crisis, but there is also very little doctrinal basis for such a categorisation. Baumfield argues that US corporate law allows socially responsible corporate action,[100]

---

95 Rühmkorf, 'Stakeholder Value versus Corporate Sustainability', 239–240.
96 H. Hansmann and R. Kraakman, 'The End of History for Corporate Law' (2001) 89 *The Georgetown Law Journal*, 439.
97 Ibid., 449–450.
98 Ibid., 451–453.
99 For an in-depth critique of Hansmann and Kraakman's conclusions see generally, M. Welsh, P. Spender, I. Lynch Fannon and K. Hall, 'The End of the "End of History for Corporate Law"' (2014) 29 *Australian Journal of Corporate Law*, 147.
100 V. S. Baumfield, 'How Change Happens: The Benefit Corporation in the United States and Considerations for Australia' in Sjåfjell and Lynch Fannon, (eds.), *Creating Corporate Sustainability*, pp. 201–207.

despite the prevailing view in the US that the social responsibility of business is to increase its profits.[101] Drawing on the work of Easterbrook and Fischel,[102] Baumfield urged that the corporation, as a nexus of explicit and implicit contracts, can privilege social objectives over profit maximisation if the parties to those contracts so desire.[103] The US Supreme Court ostensibly followed this reasoning,[104] in *Burwell v. Hobby Lobby Stores*,[105] which held that for-profit companies were entitled to prioritise values other than exclusive profit-making once the shareholders sanctioned this course of action. In the case of *Hobby Lobby*, these values were influenced by the Christian tradition, although, as Baumfield observes, its reasoning also supports secular social objectives,[106] and can therefore be considered an endorsement of the constituency approach.

Elsewhere, the Delaware courts have described the function of management as being to 'maximise the long-run interests of the corporation's stockholders'.[107] Millon has interpreted the statement to mean that management may consider a multiplicity of interests including those of non-shareholders, provided a reciprocal benefit to shareholders will accrue in the 'long-run'.[108]

Other US cases have endorsed the constituency approach. For example, the Delaware Supreme Court has said that in defending against a hostile takeover the interests of 'constituencies other than shareholders (i.e. creditors, customers, employees, and perhaps even the community generally)' become the most important concern.[109] Not only does this seminal decision capture the spirit of the constituency approach, but its reference to the 'community generally' also encapsulates the essence of the communitarian school of thought, which considers the broader social effects of corporate activity on, inter alia, communities in which firms operate and the environment.[110]

We proffer these arguments to show that both in the EU and the US the idea that corporations are free to act in socially responsible ways is supported in many different ways, which are, at the same time, reflective of the particular political and socio economic contexts.

[101] M. Friedman, 'The Social Responsibility of Business is to Increase its Profits', *New York Times Magazine*, 13 September 1970, pp. 12–14, 12.
[102] F. H. Easterbrook and D. R. Fischel, *The Economic Structure of Corporate Law* (Cambridge, MA: Harvard University Press, 1991), p. 35.
[103] Baumfield, 'How Change Happens', p. 203.
[104] Ibid., p. 207.
[105] *Burwell v. Hobby Lobby Stores Inc*, 573 US 682, Reports 1 (2014).
[106] Baumfield, 'How Change Happens', p. 207.
[107] *Katz v. Oak Industries Inc.*, 508 Del. Ch. 873 at 879 (1986).
[108] Millon, 'Two Models of Corporate Social Responsibility', 527.
[109] *Unocal Corp. v. Mesa Petroleum Co.* 493 Del. 946 at 955 (1985).
[110] Millon, 'Crisis in Corporate Law', 1379.

3.3.4 *The Challenge of Defining CSR*

Although we can see that both in the US and the EU there is scope for interpreting CSR movements in a positive, constituency-oriented light, there is the remaining problem as to whether and if CSR is hijacked by those who are against regulation. The challenge now is that there is a blurring of the line between what is traditionally viewed as a CSR initiative and a regulatory approach.[111] The challenge is probably aggravated by removing from CSR subjects that have been viewed as being within its remit and locating them within the regulatory space. Take, for example, the EU Directive on the disclosure of non-financial and diversity information.[112] This Directive requires the boards of large companies and financial undertakings to publish information in their annual report about their environmental and human rights policies; to make anti-corruption and bribery disclosures; and to provide social and employee information.[113] Applying on a 'comply or explain' basis, the Directive mandates that the company respond to matters such as environmental and employee-related matters that heretofore belonged to the CSR field. But even though this is represented as a regulation, its regulatory effect is minimal. The effect is at a remove from the regulatory space in that it obliges the provision of information so that others can act to influence corporate behaviour. Significantly, this directive has been extensively reviewed and is now in its second iteration as a draft directive.[114] A second, companion directive has also been proposed creating a more elaborate range of obligations in the due diligence space, obliging companies and their officers to ensure compliance with a range of sustainability standards across their value chains.[115]

A similar observation can be made with respect to the Commission's *Action Plan on Sustainable Finance*,[116] launched in 2018, which treats the disclosure of environmental, social and corporate governance information as instrumental to the practice of socially responsible investment in the sense that it is undertaken to enable investors and their advisors to screen investment

---

[111] Lynch Fannon, 'The Corporate Social Responsibility Movement', 4–5.
[112] Council Directive 2013/34/EU, O.J. L 182/19 as am. by Council Directive 2014/95/EU, O.J. L 330/1.
[113] Clarke, 'The Role of Board Directors in Promoting Environmental Sustainability', 157–158.
[114] Draft Directive on Corporate Sustainability Reporting COM 2021/189; COD 2021/0104.
[115] Draft Directive on Corporate Sustainability Due Diligence 2022/71; COD 2022/0051. European Commission, Sustainable Corporate Governance Initiative; see Villiers, 'Global Supply Chains and Sustainability'.
[116] Communication from the Commission, 'Action Plan: Financing Sustainable Growth', COM (2018) 97 final.

portfolios for ethical values and social responsibility.[117] The question thus raised is whether an initiative can be presented *as a* CSR initiative if its catalyst is simply a pre-existing legal requirement. Furthermore, how effective is regulation that simply amounts to an obligation to report on CSR activities?[118]

The same phenomenon is present in the context of gender diversity on corporate boards. The EU response to the issue of gender diversity was originally through the use of voluntary gender quotas to increase female participation on boards. However, the voluntary approach has been found to be unsatisfactory, hence the introduction of the proposed Directive mandating gender quotas, which has not yet been passed.[119]

Although we applaud a growing support for constituency approaches to CSR across political divides, and an identification of CSR as a way of providing standards in a manner that can be viewed as a precursor or complement to regulation, nevertheless the **relationship between regulation and CSR must be clearly defined**. This necessitates a period of introspection about the future of CSR.[120] It offers an opportunity to consider new subjects for CSR concern.[121] The problem is a lack of harmony between binding regulation and non-binding CSR: where regulation is reactive, CSR is proactive; where regulation seeks to decrease negative externalities such as pollution or corruption, CSR aspires to increase positive externalities such as respect for the environment and human rights.

---

[117] For discussion of socially responsible investment, see B. J. Richardson, 'Financial Markets and Socially Responsible Investment', in Sjåfjell and Richardson (eds.), *Company Law and Sustainability*, p. 226. See also J. Cullen, J. Mähönen and H. Rapp Nilsen, 'Financing sustainable value creation', Chapter 8 in this volume.

[118] Lynch Fannon, 'The Corporate Social Responsibility Movement', 5.

[119] See, for example, the EU Capital Requirements Directive, which recognises the value of gender diversity to prevent instances of so-called 'groupthink'; see I. Lynch Fannon, 'A Toad We Have to Swallow': Perceptions and Participation of Women in Business and the Implications for Sustainability', in Sjåfjell and Lynch Fannon (eds.), *Creating Corporate Sustainability*, p. 114, p. 131.

[120] In the aftermath of the financial crisis, Millon called for a similar period of introspection. While the present invitation is to reflect on new targets for CSR attention, Millon invited corporate law scholars to teach and write about corporate law in pluralist terms, which, in turn, might debunk the legal myth of shareholder primacy. See Millon, 'Shareholder Primacy in the Classroom after the Financial Crisis', 191.

[121] Institutional investors are beginning to invest in projects that are unrelated to the classic targets for socially responsible investment which traditionally focused on portfolios that respect the environment (see, Richardson, 'Financial Markets and Socially Responsible Investment', pp. 234–239). For example, a London-based investment fund has agreed to finance a public-private partnership in Ireland with the goal of providing social housing in Dublin. Even though this is but one example, it is evidence of investors' appetite to champion different causes, which, in this instance, relates to the ongoing Irish housing crisis. See B. J. Whyte, 'British Investment Fund Wants to Back 20,000 Social Homes in Dublin', *The Sunday Business Post*, 19 August 2018.

3.4 MOVING ON

In Sections 2 and 3, we question whether the presentation of economies in a binary oppositional fashion and the underlying description of corporate law theory in a binary opposition of contractarianism versus communitarianism coupled with the discussion of CSR movements in a similarly binary fashion are reflective of reality. Our conclusion is that there is less reality attached to these debates than imagined. If this is so, it is also time to reconsider where new solutions might lie. If, as we describe in the Introduction, the fundamental characteristics of the corporation across jurisdictions and sectors are the same, our argument is that perhaps it is time to take a closer look at the dynamics *within* the corporation. In doing so we accept that the limited liability corporation as an engine of capitalism is here to stay, but we nevertheless present an alternative to current mindsets, theories and debates that we consider offers a potential way forward.

3.4.1 *The Ethical Shareholder*

A number of ideas are often conflated in corporate law theory. As has been observed recently by Cheffins,[122] the nexus of contracts approach does not dictate the concept of shareholder primacy. He goes on to observe that whilst 'neither agency theory nor the nexus of contracts model necessarily compels ... shareholder primacy, contractarian scholars did ... tend to ascribe pre-eminence to shareholders. Of course this theory has been discredited in recent years.'[123] Therefore, whilst we can agree that the goal of corporations is to create profits and corporate wealth, we can also assert that the structure of the corporation is such that this can be done in an ethical way to the satisfaction of shareholders who take an ethical interest in how profits are generated. One only has to think of real-world examples such as Ben and Jerry's, the Patagonia company, the popularity of CSR movements and the broader issue of sustainable investing by Green Funds to accept that this is a pragmatic reality.[124] There is nothing inherent in the basic corporate structure that requires

---

[122] B. Cheffins, 'The Team Production Model as Paradigm' (2015) 38(2) *Seattle University Law Review*, 397, 408.

[123] See the discussion relatively recently from two leading US academics decrying the politicisation of their earlier work: R. Gilson and R. Kraakman, 'Market Efficiency after the Financial Crisis: It's Still a Matter of Information Costs' (2014) 458 *Stanford Law School Working Paper Series* and 470 *Columbia Law and Economic Working Paper*, available at: https://papers.ssrn.com/sol3/papers.cfm?abstract_id=2396608.

[124] See, for example, G. Tett, 'Ethical investing has reached a tipping point' *Financial Times*, 18 June 2019, available at: www.ft.com/content/7d64d1d8-91a6-11e9-b7ea-60e35ef678d2.

that corporate wealth must be generated at the expense of the broader corporate community of stakeholders.

3.4.2 *Ethical Management*

Turning to management, corporate law theory often tends to ignore how corporate law systems support a great deal of management discretion. Bainbridge, a prolific corporate law scholar, identifies what he calls two 'basic systems of classification' that capture most of the competing theories of the firm: the shareholder primacy school and the director primacy school. Bainbridge argues that the function of corporate law is to support the latter:[125]

> In its various guises, shareholder primacy contends that shareholders are the principals on whose behalf corporate governance is organised, but also that shareholders do (and should) exercise ultimate control of the corporate enterprise. In contrast, director primacy accepts the shareholder wealth maximisation principle as the proper corporate decision-making norm, but rejects the notion that shareholders are entitled to either direct or indirect decision-making control.[126]

Bainbridge's support is enlisted for the insight that director primacy or managerial primacy is in fact the guiding principle of corporate law. But the myth of shareholder wealth maximisation supposes that all these decisions must be made for the benefit of the shareholders, when in reality this is not the case. Management discretion can be exercised to respond positively and proactively to regulation or voluntary CSR movements. Indeed, management has the discretion to act ethically. An interesting question then arises regarding our assessment of existing realities. What motivates management to cause the corporation to act in egregious ways? Going back to Apple, in an interview with the CEO of Apple shortly after the EU Commission launched its action, the CEO stated that 'Apple has always been about doing the right thing, not the easy thing'.[127]

---

[125] S. Bainbridge, 'Director Primacy: The Means and Ends of Corporate Governance' (2002–03) 97(2) *Northwestern Law Review*, 547. Marc T. Moore's contribution to the debate in this area raises these issues with a great deal of renewed clarity: see generally, M. T. Moore, *Corporate Governance in the Shadow of the State* (Oxford: Hart Publishing, 2013); see M. T. Moore, 'Private Ordering and Public Policy: The Paradoxical Foundations of Corporate Contractarianism' (2014) 34(4) *Oxford Journal of Legal Studies*, 795.

[126] Bainbridge, 'Director Primacy: The Means and Ends of Corporate Governance', ibid., 563.

[127] T. Cook, 'No Special Deal between Ireland and Apple – Tim Cook' RTÉ *Radio 1 – Drivetime*, 1 September 2016, available at: www.rte.ie/radio/radioplayer/html5/#/radio1/21046478.

In this sentence we hear a strongly worded claim to an ethical corporation. This is curious given the scale of Apple's tax avoidance as alleged by the European Commission. One is reminded of comments from Bakan, who has claimed that corporations exhibit psychopathic traits:

> [The corporation] … remains, as it was at the time of its origins as a model business institution in the middle of the nineteenth century, a legally designated 'person' designed to valorise self-interest and invalidate moral concern. Most people would find its 'personality' abhorrent, even psychopathic, in a human being, yet curiously we accept it in society's most powerful institutions.[128]

When one considers the enormous wealth of major corporations (for example, it seems that Apple Inc. has a hoarded cash pile valued at over US$190 billion as reported for the first quarter of 2021),[129] all one can see in human terms is an inability to distribute wealth amounting to singular self-interest. This inability to share its wealth even with its shareholders is extraordinary. The obvious question is who benefits from the cash hoarding? In the Apple case it seems that no one does, not the various stakeholders nor even the shareholders in the company. Not the employees. Not the public tax authorities. The tentative conclusion is that this cash hoard has all the characteristics of the creation of a power base for those who can control its distribution, namely management. And while criminologists grapple with these kinds of problems as an intrinsic part of criminal law theory, it is time that corporate law theorists addressed these issues in a clearly expressed ethical discourse.

Bakan goes on to state that '[u]nlike the human beings who inhabit it, the corporation is *singularly* self-interested and unable to feel genuine concern for others in any context'.[130] However, we would argue that the corporation cannot act in a self-interested way unless caused to do so by individuals, its shareholders, management or lenders, who themselves are motivated by self-interest.

3.4.3 *The Ethical Construction of the Corporation*

The contractarian pursuit of shareholder wealth and self-interest is the source of the communitarian opprobrium. Both schools of thought argue that their

---

[128] J. Bakan, *The Corporation: The Pathological Pursuit of Profit and Power* (New York: Free Press, 2004).

[129] See Apple Financial Reports for Q1 of 2021, www.apple.com/newsroom/pdfs/FY21%20Q1%20 Consolidated%20Financial%20Statements.pdf, 'Apple now has $195.57 billion in cash on hand, up $3.7 billion', CNBC reporting on this report, 27 January 2021, available at: www .cnbc.com/2021/01/27/apple-q1-cash-hoard-heres-how-much-apple-has-on-hand.html.

[130] Ibid., pp. 28, 56 (emphasis in original).

perspective carries an ethical imperative. This is what Goodpaster terms the 'stakeholder paradox' that recognises, in the first instance, the ethical responsibility of management to increase wealth for shareholders and, in the second, the significant moral obligations management owe to other stakeholders and third parties.[131] He explains it thus: '[e]thics seems both to forbid and to demand a strategic, profit-maximising mindset'.[132]

Parallel to the 'stakeholder paradox' is another moral dilemma triggered by the root assumptions of the contractarian school.[133] Communitarians say adherence to the ironclad logic of shareholder wealth-maximisation and its progenitor, the principal-agent relationship, 'casts the flesh and blood persons who animate the corporation in roles that conform them to corporate personhood'.[134] Accordingly, communitarians see the free market ideal and its emphasis on shareholders as creating a seemingly confrontational relationship between 'persons acting within the corporation' and 'persons acting without'. The latter act with a sense of social responsibility, whereas the 'morals of the marketplace' tend to dominate the actions of the former.[135] This explanation seems unfair and inadequate, in the sense that communitarian corporate law scholars cannot pretend to hold their noses while supporting the corporate construct.[136]

3.5 CONCLUSION

The real challenge, therefore, is to reconcile economics and ethics and to articulate a legal theory that will support an ethical corporation and the actors within that corporation. This involves an assumption, to which we subscribe, that we can recalibrate the limited liability corporation to reflect urgent modern concerns.

This is an easy theoretical aspiration, but yet we have examples mentioned already of corporations that make ethical choices. Furthermore, we have many leaders exhorting corporations to take other stakeholders into account and to act ethically. As the communitarian theory of corporate law, however underdeveloped at present, has been overtly identified with the values of 'social Europe', we might expect to find some resonance for ideas of an ethical

---

[131] K. E. Goodpaster, 'Business Ethics and Stakeholder Analysis' (1991) 1(4) *Business Ethics Quarterly*, 53, 63.
[132] Ibid.
[133] L. E. Mitchell, 'Groundwork of the Metaphysics of Corporate Law' (1993) 50(4) *Washington and Lee Law Review*, 1477.
[134] Ibid., 1481.
[135] Ibid., 1484.
[136] C. Mayer, *Firm Commitment: Why the Corporation is Failing Us and How to Fix it* (Oxford: Oxford University Press, 2013) pp. 45–49.

corporation in Catholic social theory. As a number of European states have Catholic traditions (and those that do not have other Christian traditions), it would not be surprising to find values concerning social and distributive justice derived from this tradition influencing modern thinking about corporate function. For example, while Pope Francis, albeit tentatively, supports capitalism as a means to economic and social progression, in *Evangelii Gaudium* he decries an economic system that 'tends to devour everything which stands in the way of increased profits, whatever is fragile, like the environment, is defenceless before the interests of a deified market, which becomes the only rule'.[137] Pope Francis is not alone in this kind of leadership, but we mention this as an example of a leader with a uniquely global voice.

Similarly, even very wealthy corporations and their leaders act responsively to dramatic public events. The unusually rapid development of COVID-19 vaccinations is not simply driven by profit motivation. In early 2021, we saw Twitter Inc. and Facebook acting to remove former US President Donald Trump from their social media platforms regardless of the decline in share price that ensued. Notwithstanding the perplexing questions that Donald Trump's removal from Twitter raises about the power of technology companies, their complicity in the 'insurrection' on Capitol Hill owing to their laissez-faire approach to content moderation prior to that crisis, their resistance to regulation over many years, their role in undermining the democratic process and the important civil liberties implications of this action, all of which were highlighted by the European Commissioner for the Internal Market,[138] what the recent actions of these corporations indicates for present purposes is the ability to comply with a different, non-legally binding set of norms.

Moreover, it would seem that in certain contexts, corporations may be more independent of any of their internal stakeholders (shareholders) than as yet imagined. We argue strongly against continuing the assumption, based on shaky theoretical assumptions, that the corporation itself is imbued with values that contradict ethical action as we understand it. We are optimistic that the corporation can be an actor that respects the concerns of stakeholders such as employees (as we have seen in Europe), the environment, communities and others, and that the answers lie in regulation and ethical discourse.

---

[137] Apostolic Exhortation *Evangelii Gaudium* of the Holy Father Francis to the Bishops, Clergy, consecrated persons and the lay faithful on the proclamation of the gospel in today's world (Vatican City: Vatican Press, 2013), Para. 56, p. 47.

[138] T. Breton, European Commissioner for the Internal Market, 'Capitol Hill – the 9/11 moment of social media' *Politico*, 10 January 2021, available at: www.politico.eu/article/thierry-breton-social-media-capitol-hill-riot/.

PART II

THE (UN)SUSTAINABILITY OF THE EU ECONOMIC SYSTEM

4

Fiscal Austerity and Monetary Largesse

The EU's Constitutional and Ideological Straitjacket

Andrew Johnston and Trevor Pugh

4.1 INTRODUCTION

This chapter argues that the combination of the European economic and monetary constitution with neo-liberal ideology is – or was, until the arrival of the COVID-19 pandemic – hindering the necessary move towards a more sustainable economy. Neo-liberalism insists that the role of the state should be strictly limited to creating the conditions that will allow individuals to interact and allocate resources through market transactions.[1] Spending by the state must be reined in because fiscal policy will 'almost surely make matters worse',[2] by interfering with the market's efficient allocation of resources, creating uncertainty and generating inflation.[3] National central banks (NCBs) should be independent,[4] and conduct monetary policy with an exclusive focus on ensuring price stability, as opposed to wider goals such as full employment.[5] Labour should be weakened, particularly in its collective dimension,[6] and financial markets should be structured to ensure that corporations prioritise

---

[1] D. Harvey, *A Brief History of Neoliberalism* (Oxford: Oxford University Press, 2005) pp. 64–65; P. Mirowski, *Never Let a Serious Crisis go to Waste* (London: Verso Books, 2013) pp. 53–58.

[2] M. Friedman, *Capitalism and Freedom* (Chicago: University of Chicago Press, 1962), p. 78.

[3] M. Blyth, *Austerity: The History of a Dangerous Idea* (Oxford: Oxford University Press, 2015) pp. 155–156.

[4] See, for example, R. J. Barro and D. B. Gordon, 'Rules, Discretion and Reputation in a Model of Monetary Policy' (1983) 12 *Journal of Monetary Economics*, 101–121, arguing for enforced monetary policy commitments to prevent inflation shocks; K. Rogoff, 'The Optimal Degree of Commitment to an Intermediate Monetary Target' (1985) 100 *Quarterly Journal of Economics*, 1169–1189 at 1177 arguing that conservatives, who 'place a greater weight on inflation stabilization relative to unemployment stabilization', should be appointed to head NCBs.

[5] M. Friedman, 'The Role of Monetary Policy' (1968) 58 *American Economic Review*, 1–17, 12–13. On the evolution of central bank mandates see D. Cobham, 'The Past, Present, and Future of Central Banking' (2012) 28 *Oxford Review of Economic Policy*, 729–749.

[6] Friedman, 'The Role of Monetary Policy', 8–9.

the shareholder interest.[7] The European Union (EU) Treaties conform to these neo-liberal prescriptions by imposing fiscal spending limits on Member State governments, and giving NCBs and the European Central Bank (ECB) a clear single mandate to ensure price stability.

After the global financial crisis of 2008, public sector debt ballooned. Some of this additional debt resulted from automatic stabilisers triggered by the recession and discretionary Keynesian fiscal policies pursued in the immediate aftermath of the crisis. However, much of the debt was transferred from the private sector. Member States had to borrow money to finance their bailouts of financial institutions, whilst loans made before the crisis by private sector financial institutions to private borrowers in the periphery were gradually moved onto the balance sheets of the ECB and the NCBs – and in the case of Greece, the International Monetary Fund (IMF) – further adding to the indebtedness of the peripheral Member States. The neo-liberal policy response to public debt is that it must be cut, and this was reinforced by a number of politically driven changes to EU law in 2011, which sought to activate the ineffective Stability and Growth Pact (SGP).

With further fiscal policy measures (public spending) ruled out, the primary policy response to the financial crisis was monetary policy. Central banks conducted conventional monetary policy in line with neo-liberal prescriptions, that is with great largesse, slashing interest rates to close to zero. They also launched unconventional monetary policies that probed the outer limits of their powers, actions that were accommodated by the Court of Justice of the European Union (CJEU). The net effect is that unelected central banks can intervene in financial markets to protect financial institutions and to boost asset prices, but elected governments are not permitted to intervene in the real economy to protect citizens and create more reliable demand.[8]

This combination of fiscal austerity and monetary largesse led to a number of undesirable consequences, including an ever greater polarisation of wealth distribution as asset prices rose but real wages were stagnant or falling, and increased fragility of private sector balance sheets, as households stopped deleveraging and went into debt to sustain consumption and purchase property

[7] T. Palley, 'Europe's Crisis without End: The Consequences of Neoliberalism Run Amok' (2013) *Macroeconomic Policy Institute Working Paper* 111 at 5. Friedman's work was highly influential in disseminating ideas about shareholder primacy, which were being developed in neoclassical economics at the time. See, for example, Friedman, *Capitalism and Freedom*, p. 112; M. Friedman, 'The Social Responsibility of Business is to Increase its Profits', *New York Times Magazine*, 13 September 1970, p. 17.

[8] J. P. Watkins, 'Quantitative Easing as a Means of Reducing Unemployment: A New Version of Trickle Down Economics' (2014) 48 *Journal of Economic Issues*, 431–440; T. Palley, 'Quantitative Easing: A Keynesian Critique' (2011) 70 *Investigación Económica*, 69–86 at 84.

and financial assets. In addition, smaller companies found it difficult to borrow from banks, but large listed corporations, under pressure from the shareholder primacy corporate governance system, took advantage of enormous liquidity and historic low long-term interest rates to borrow money through bond issuance, using the proceeds to finance dividends and repurchase shares. At the same time, a variety of national, supranational and international pressures operated to force indebted states to cut expenditures on welfare and other social services.

None of this suggests that the EU's economy was operating in a sustainable manner before the COVID-19 pandemic struck in early 2020. A sustainable economy may provisionally be defined as one in which the financial system is governed so as to produce stability; in which the wealth generated is distributed so that all people have sufficient income to meet their present essential consumption needs and lead satisfying lives without going into debt and prejudicing future consumption;[9] and in which sufficient resources are available to the state to provide public goods and social services for all.[10]

After the pandemic hit Europe in March 2020, the EU institutions implemented a range of far-reaching and coordinated fiscal and monetary policy measures. These were intended to protect individuals and businesses and to stabilise and stimulate the economy in the face of the losses and other disruptions, both triggered by the virus itself and arising out of the associated political responses, such as mandatory business closures and lockdowns. The actions taken in response to this state of emergency demonstrates that, if the political will is there, there is scope for the EU to intervene significantly in its economy in order to make it more sustainable. The question remains, however: once the pandemic recedes over the horizon of history, will the EU revert to its straitjacket, imposing (even more) fiscal austerity to deal with the new (enlarged) debt burdens at both EU and Member State level, whilst reverting to exclusive reliance on monetary policy to stimulate the economy? Or might the pandemic demonstrate that other policy choices are possible, and might a new form of political solidarity emerge in its aftermath, leading to a greater pooling of fiscal sovereignty and, in turn, a more sustainable economy?

The chapter proceeds as follows. Section 4.2 looks at the constitutional limitations on Member State fiscal spending, showing how more conventional Keynesian responses to the aftermath of the financial crisis were ruled out by legally binding instruments. Section 4.3 explores the scope of monetary policy available to the ECB and NCBs, and the ways in which monetary policy has been used in the aftermath of the financial crisis. This shows that constitutional limits on fiscal spending effectively forced central banks into unconventional monetary policy actions in order to deal with the crisis. The almost exclusive reliance on monetary policy to stimulate the economy has produced a number of pathologies, which have made the economy far less sustainable. These are examined in Section 4.4. Section 4.5 then looks at the way in which the EU responded to the COVID-19 emergency, uncharacteristically releasing itself from its straitjacket, at least temporarily and as an emergency measure. Section 4.6 then asks whether these recent developments indicate a change in approach on the part of the EU, heralding a shift to a new, more economically sustainable system of allocating economic resources, or whether a return to the constitutional and ideological straitjacket beckons. We fear it will be the latter, leaving economic sustainability as far away as ever.

4.2 THE CONSTITUTIONAL LIMITS ON FISCAL SPENDING

The Treaty on the Functioning of the European Union (TFEU) leaves fiscal spending largely in the hands of the Member States but provides for monetary policy to be determined at supranational level, at least for members of the Eurozone. Since national budget deficits could undermine financial and monetary stability, Member States' fiscal policies were 'placed within an agreed macroeconomic framework and [made] subject to binding procedures and rules'.[11] These provisions use a combination of market forces and legal rules to place significant limitations on the ability of Member State governments to stimulate their economies through public spending.

First, there are treaty provisions intended to ensure that fiscal spending does not become a problem in the first place. Article 120 TFEU requires Member States to coordinate their 'economic' (i.e. fiscal or public spending) policies. More detailed rules are found in the SGP. Article 121 TFEU puts in place a multilateral surveillance procedure to ensure that Member States comply with guidelines laid down. Article 126(1) TFEU imposes an obligation on Member States to 'avoid excessive government deficits' (that is, borrowing in order to spend much more than they received in taxes). Sub-articles (2)-(14) of Article 126 then establish a supranational process that ultimately allows the Council to require a Member State to reduce an excessive deficit. A deficit is excessive for

---

[11]   See Committee for the Study of Economic and Monetary Union, *Report on the Economic and Monetary Union in the European Community* (17 April 1989) (the 'Delors Report'), p. 20.

the purposes of Article 126 if it amounts to 3 per cent of gross domestic product (GDP), whilst public debt is excessive if it exceeds 60 per cent of GDP.[12] The Article 126 procedure will be triggered by a Member State crossing these thresholds unless the ratio of debt to GDP has either declined substantially and continuously and reached a level that comes close to the reference value, or the excess is 'only exceptional and temporary'.[13]

Second, these processes operate against the backdrop of rules intended to ensure that market forces operate to constrain Member State public spending. Article 123(1) TFEU prohibits central banks from providing credit to, and purchasing bonds directly from, Member State governments, so that governments have to fund their deficits by borrowing on the bond market. Article 125 TFEU complements Article 123 by prohibiting bailouts of Member States by the EU or other Member States, confirming to markets (at least until the advent of unconventional monetary policies, discussed in Section 4.3) that there would be no interference by Member States or the EU with the borrowing rates charged to Member States by the market.

The SGP came into force in 1999, and for the first couple of years only a handful of peripheral Member States were in breach, but in 2004 both France and Germany failed to bring their deficits within 3 per cent of GDP. However, action by the Council was blocked by France, Germany, Italy and the UK, a decision that the CJEU subsequently ruled unlawful.[14] The SGP was then ignored in wholesale fashion when deficits ballooned as Member States intervened in their economies to bail out banks, stabilise the financial system and stimulate their economies, with the Commission also coordinating an emergency stimulus package of €200 billion claimed to be 'in full respect of the Stability and Growth Pact' and intended to 'restore business and consumer confidence'.[15]

In May 2010, with the financial sector fully bailed out with public funds and supported by guarantees, neo-liberal orthodoxy was restored, with the Commission launching a proposal for new regulation to ensure that the SGP was adhered to in the future.[16] Enforcement of the Article 126 excessive deficit procedure has now been reinforced by the 'six-pack' (consisting of five

---

[12] Protocol (No. 12) on the Excessive Deficit Procedure OJ L 115/279-80, 9 May 2008.

[13] Article 126(2) TFEU.

[14] For the early history of the SGP, see J. Fischer, L. Jonung and M. Larch, '101 Proposals to reform the Stability and Growth Pact. Why so Many? A Survey', *European Commission Directorate-General for Economic and Financial Affairs Economic Papers*, No 267, December 2006, pp. 6–10.

[15] *European Economic Recovery Plan*, COM(2008) 800 final, 26 November 2008. See further L. Schuknecht, P. Moutot, P. Rother and J. Stark, 'The Stability and Growth Pact: Crisis and Reform', *European Central Bank Occasional Paper Series* No 129, September 2011, p. 11.

[16] See EU economic governance: the Commission delivers a comprehensive package of legislative measures, IP/10/1199, Brussels, 29 September 2010.

regulations and a directive),[17] adopted under Article 136 TFEU in November 2011, which gives each Member State a medium-term budgetary objective from which they must not deviate significantly, and makes detailed provision for enforcement against Member States that are not reducing debt sufficiently quickly towards the 60 per cent threshold.[18]

Finally, there is the Treaty on Stability, Coordination and Governance (TSCG), also known as the Fiscal Compact, which reaffirms the need for a 'balanced budget rule' to 'safeguard the stability of the Euro area as a whole'.[19] This intergovernmental agreement was agreed and signed by twenty-five Member States in 2012 (the UK and Czech Republic did not sign), and has been in force since January 2013, running in parallel with the SGP. The TSCG requires the budgets of signatory governments to be balanced or in surplus, and to converge on the medium-term objective set in the SGP.[20] Member State signatories are required to create binding and permanent national budgetary rules, preferably at constitutional level, under threat of sanction from the CJEU. Sanctions are imposed automatically when Member States deviate from the SGP,[21] although 'temporary deviations' are permitted,[22] provided that they do not 'endanger fiscal sustainability in the medium-term', in 'exceptional circumstances' where there is 'an unusual event outside the control of the Contracting Party concerned which has a major impact on the financial position of the general government or to periods of severe economic downturn as set out in the revised Stability and Growth Pact'.[23] The TSCG was then integrated into EU law by the so-called two-pack, a pair of regulations that provide rules for euro area Member States in the corrective arm of the SGP and for enhanced oversight of national budgets of euro area Member States that are threatened with financial difficulties.[24]

---

[17] See Regulations 1173–1177/2011 and Directive 2011/85/EU, OJ L 306, 23 November 2011.

[18] Commission, 'EU economic governance "six-pack" enters into force', MEMO/11/898, 12 December 2011, available at: https://ec.europa.eu/commission/presscorner/detail/en/ MEMO_11_898. In 2019, Italy was in dispute with the European Commission about its deficit, with the Commission deciding, in light of Italy's commitment to adopt measures to bring it into line with the SGP, not to propose to the Council to open an Excessive Deficit Procedure: see European Commission press release, 3 July 2019, available at: http://europa.eu/rapid/ press-release_IP-19-3569_en.htm.

[19] See preamble to Treaty on Stability, Coordination and Governance.

[20] This is subject to a permissible structural deficit of 0.5 per cent (Article 3(1)(a)), whilst signatories whose general government debt is below 60 per cent of GDP and is considered sustainable in the long term can run a structural deficit of up to 1 per cent of GDP (Article 3(1)(d)).

[21] Article 3(1)(e).

[22] Article 3(1)(c).

[23] Article 3(3)(b).

[24] See Regulations 472/2013, OJ L 140/1, 27 May 2013 and 473/2013, OJ L 140/11, 27 May 2013.

The TSCG purports to contribute to the EU's objectives of 'sustainable growth, employment, competitiveness and social cohesion'.[25] However, it is difficult to see how it can possibly achieve this. These provisions entrench fiscal austerity, and effectively prevent counter-cyclical Keynesian demand management policies, at least for those signatories whose debt is above 60 per cent of GDP (which in 2017 encompassed fourteen of the twenty-five signatories, a figure that had been reduced to eleven by 2019, as a number of Member States ran budget surpluses).[26] The result is declining welfare and social service provision, increasing economic insecurity and fewer opportunities for citizens in indebted Member States. These constraints on government spending mean that growth in many Member States will be heavily dependent on either renewed borrowing by the private sector or an improved net trade position. The former is undesirable, given high existing household and corporate debt levels, while the latter looks unlikely at present with globalisation in retreat (and, as we will see at the end of this chapter, it is likely to depend upon increasing competitiveness by cutting labour costs).

We will see in the next section that reducing interest rates so as to boost borrowing and spending by the private sector is one of the aims of unconventional monetary policy. However, where growth is driven by borrowing, it is unlikely to be sustainable because these new private sector debts must be repaid in the future. We will then see in Section 4.5 that the SGP has been temporarily suspended through activation of the general escape clause contained in both the 'six pack' and 'two pack' in order to give Member States – at least temporarily – more fiscal leeway to address the economic and social consequences of the COVID-19 pandemic.

4.3 THE BREADTH OF MONETARY POLICY

With fiscal policy massively circumscribed by the TFEU and associated instruments, monetary policy was the only way to stimulate European economies after the financial crisis. This section shows that the ECB and Bank of England (BoE) pushed their powers to their legal limits in an effort to reduce long term interest rates and inflate asset prices, in the hope that this would stimulate borrowing and spending by the private sector.

---

[25] Article 1(1).
[26] Eurostat, *Government finance statistics*, April 2018 and October 2020 (for more details, see http://ec.europa.eu/eurostat/statistics-explained/index.php/Government_finance_statistics#Government_debt.

In line with neo-liberal prescriptions, both the BoE and the ECB are given a mandate to maintain price stability.[27] In the UK, the BoE has, since independence, been given a symmetrical target of '2 per cent as measured by the 12-month increase in the Consumer Prices Index',[28] and is required to conduct monetary policy so as to target this level. In the EU, the NCBs of the Member States and the ECB together constitute the European System of Central Banks (ESCB). The ESCB's 'primary objective' is 'to maintain price stability', but, as long as this primary objective is not prejudiced, it should also contribute to achieving the EU's wider goals as set out in Article 2 TFEU.[29] One of the 'basic tasks' to be carried out through the ESCB is to 'define and implement the monetary policy of the Union'.[30] The ECB's Governing Council 'formulate[s] the monetary policy of the Union including, as appropriate, decisions relating to intermediate monetary objectives, key interest rates and the supply of reserves in the ESCB' and to 'establish the necessary guidelines for their implementation'.[31] However, the monetary policy of the EU is 'conducted' by the Eurosystem, which consists of the ECB and the NCBs of the Member States that have adopted the euro.[32]

The principal mechanism used by NCBs to hit their inflation target is control over interest rates. Both the BoE's monetary policy committee and the ECB's Governing Council set overnight interest rates at the level they consider appropriate in order for inflation to hit their target. Both the ECB and the BoE reduced interest rates dramatically in the aftermath of the financial crisis. The BoE reduced interest rates from 5.75 per cent in July 2007 to 0.5 per cent in March 2009. Rates dipped to 0.25 per cent between August 2016 and October 2017, and currently stand at 1.75 per cent. The ECB cut its refinancing rate from 3.75 per cent in October 2008 to 1 per cent in May 2009. It subsequently raised the rate as high as 1.5 per cent in July 2011, but started cutting again in November 2011, with the refinancing rate hitting zero in March 2016,

---

[27] See s11(a) of the Bank of England Act 1998 and Article 2 of Protocol (No. 4) on the Statute of the European System of Central Banks and of the European Central Bank, OJ C 326/230, 26 October 2012.

[28] s12(1) of the Bank of England Act 1998 requires the Treasury to specify annually a single inflation target. For the latest specification, see letter from Chancellor of the Exchequer to Governor of the Bank of England dated 27 October 2021, available at: www .bankofengland.co.uk/-/media/boe/files/letter/2021/october/mpc-remit-october-2021.pdf.

[29] Article 2 of the Protocol (No 4) on the Statute of the European System of Central Banks and of the European Central Bank as annexed to TFEU.

[30] Article 127(2) TFEU and Article 3 of Protocol No 4.

[31] Article 12.1, emphasis added.

[32] Article 282(1) TFEU.

and it remained there until July 2022. The ECB deposit rate is even lower, currently 0.00 per cent.[33]

Once set, the central bank has to ensure that the interest rate applies to lending and borrowing in the overnight market. Where private banks need access to liquidity in the form of reserves, they normally borrow them from other private banks overnight. Reserves are liabilities of the central bank, held in private banks' accounts at the central bank, and used to clear interbank liabilities. The central bank only enters the market and supplies reserves where, owing to shortage of reserves or other disruptions, the interbank overnight rate exceeds the base rate set by the central bank. In this situation, the central bank has to add reserves to the system in order to drive down their price, and it does this by purchasing bonds from private banks, crediting those banks' accounts with reserves. Likewise, if there is a surplus of reserves in the system, the cost of borrowing will fall below base rate, and the central bank will sell bonds in order to drain reserves from the interbank market. These activities are referred to as open market operations (OMOs), and they are a normal aspect of monetary policy.[34]

Once interest rates hit their 'lower bound', further cuts to stimulate the economy are difficult, although five NCBs (Eurozone, Japan, Sweden, Denmark and Switzerland) have been experimenting with negative interest rates in recent years. This dilemma led NCBs to engage in unconventional monetary policy, commonly referred to as quantitative easing (QE). The use of large scale asset purchases by the central bank to stimulate the economy was advocated by Friedman and Schwartz in 1963.[35] The policy was first deployed by the Bank of Japan from 2001 to 2006, whilst the US Federal Reserve launched a large QE programme in November 2008, initially focusing on the purchase of mortgage-backed securities and later extending to government bonds.[36] In 2009, the BoE responded to the financial crisis by purchasing £200 billion of

---

[33] Whereas the refinancing rate is the rate at which the ECB provides liquidity to the system, the deposit rate is more relevant, given the vast amount of excess reserves currently in the system (see following discussion).

[34] See Article 18 of the ECB Statute and Article 123(1) TFEU, which implicitly allow secondary market purchases, provided they are compatible with the other provisions of the Treaty. For the BoE's OMO, see BoE, *The Framework for the Bank of England's Operations in the Sterling Money Markets* (June 2012), p. 5.

[35] M. Friedman and A. Schwartz, 'Money and Business Cycles' (1963) 45 *The Review of Economics and Statistics*, 32–64, although it appears that Keynes, in his *Treatise on Money*, was the first economist to recognise that NCBs could stimulate the economy by intensifying their use of OMOs, albeit with doubts as to its effectiveness: see J. Kregel, 'Was Keynes's Monetary Policy À *Outrance* in the *Treatise* a Forerunner of ZIRP and QE? Did He Change his Mind in the *General Theory*?', Levy Economics Institute of Bard College Policy Note 2011/4 (2011).

[36] See Federal Open Market Committee statement, 18 March 2009, available at: www .federalreserve.gov/newsevents/pressreleases/monetary20090318a.htm.

government bonds between March and November 2009, another £175 billion between October 2011 and July 2012, and a further £60 billion of government bonds and £10 billion of corporate bonds in August 2016 following the Brexit referendum.

The ECB eventually launched its QE programme in January 2015, with the Eurosystem purchasing €60 billion per month of securities issued by the European institutions and the Member States, a programme that continued until December 2018.[37] In March 2016, the programme was increased to €80 billion per month, and was extended to include investment grade corporate bonds issued by non-bank corporations.[38] Overall, 20 per cent of the assets purchased are subject to loss-sharing in the event of a default or a loss when the QE programme is unwound.[39] The remaining 80 per cent of the securities are purchased by NCBs on their home market in proportion to the ECB's capital key, ensuring that there will be no loss sharing.[40] In effect, this means that the German central bank will purchase almost 18 per cent of the remaining bonds, whilst France will purchase 14.2 per cent. Greek and Cypriot bonds were originally excluded on the basis that they were not investment grade, although Cyprus was granted a waiver during the time its bailout programme was ongoing.

QE operates through central bank purchases of large quantities of financial assets from the private sector, using newly created reserves. The central bank's balance sheet expands, with the bonds as an asset and the reserves as a liability. The sellers of bonds may be private banks, which hold them on their balance sheets as safe, highly liquid assets, but for the most part, private banks act as conduits through which pension funds, insurance companies and other holders of bonds sell their holdings to the central bank. When a private or institutional investor sells its bonds to the central bank, the central bank adds reserves to that investor's bank's account at the central bank, and the investor's

---

[37] See Account of the monetary policy meeting of the Governing Council of the European Central Bank, 21–22 January 2015, available at: www.ecb.europa.eu/press/accounts/2015/html/mg150219.en.html.

[38] See ECB press release, 'Monetary policy decisions', 10 March 2016, available at: www.ecb.europa.eu/press/pr/date/2016/html/pr160310.en.html.

[39] Under Article 33.2 of Protocol 4 to the TEU and TFEU, any losses made by the ECB are set off against the general reserve fund, and then against income accruing in proportion to their shareholdings to the NCBs from their performance of the ESCB's monetary policy function. The Protocol is silent on the question of recapitalisation, but presumably if the ECB makes losses that exceed this income, the capital will be written down, and Member States will be required to recapitalise the ECB in line with their shareholdings.

[40] 'Public sector purchase programme (PSPP) – questions & answers', available at: www.ecb.europa.eu/mopo/implement/omt/html/pspp-qa.en.html. The ECB's current capital subscription key can be found at www.ecb.europa.eu/ecb/orga/capital/html/index.en.html.

bank credits the investor's account with a deposit, which they can either hold on to, or (more likely) use to purchase other financial assets.

The principal effect of QE is to raise asset prices. It raises the price of government bonds, and therefore lowers the yield (the effective interest rate) on those bonds. It also raises the price of other assets (such as corporate equities and bonds), as those who sold their bonds to the central bank rebalance their portfolios by purchasing other assets that they consider to be more efficient substitutes for government bonds than a deposit in a bank account.[41] House prices too are considerably higher than they would have been in the absence of QE.[42] These higher asset prices are expected to produce a number of effects on the economy.[43]

First of all, higher asset prices and lower yields should reduce 'the cost of borrowing for households and companies leading to higher consumption and investment spending', and give companies working capital, allowing them to maintain output, increasing employment and consumer spending.[44] This first channel depends on households and companies having access to – and demanding – credit in the first place.[45] Whilst larger companies can access capital markets directly by issuing bonds, households and smaller companies depend on bank lending. Smaller companies may indirectly benefit through effects on the supply chain and (unless they are net importers) because QE also causes a depreciation in the currency, potentially leading to greater external demand. However, households remain entirely dependent upon banks passing on the lower cost of funding to them.[46]

Second, higher asset prices create a wealth effect, so this should boost the spending of asset holders. Through this channel, there is more consumption

---

[41] See M. Joyce, N. McLaren and C. Young, 'Quantitative Easing in the United Kingdom: Evidence from Financial Markets on QE1 and QE2' (2012) 28 *Oxford Review of Economic Policy*, 671–701 at 693.

[42] The BoE estimates that, without QE, 'real equity prices and real house prices in 2014 would have been 25 per cent and 22 per cent lower respectively than they actually were': see P. Bunn, A. Pugh and C. Yeates, 'The Distributional Impact of Monetary Policy Easing in the UK between 2008 and 2014', *Bank of England Staff Working Paper No 720*, March 2018, p. 8.

[43] For a more detailed explanation of these mechanisms, see J. Benford, S. Berry, K. Nikolov and C. Young, 'Quantitative Easing' (2009) *Bank of England Quarterly Bulletin*, 90–100.

[44] Ibid., 93.

[45] A collapse in the demand for – rather than supply of – credit presents considerable difficulties for monetary policy. The experience of Japan in the 1990s showed that in the case of a balance sheet recession where the asset side of the balance sheet collapses, firms and individuals will attempt to avoid bankruptcy by continuing to pay off loans, but given their technically insolvent position will have no demand for new credit: see R. Koo, *The Holy Grail of Macroeconomics: Lessons from Japan's Great Recession* (Chichester: Wiley, 2008).

[46] C. Bowdler and A. Radia, 'Unconventional Monetary Policy: the Assessment' (2012) 28 *Oxford Review of Economic Policy*, 603 at 611–612.

activity as asset holders liquidate or borrow against higher priced assets to finance spending. However, the BoE recognised that there is considerable uncertainty surrounding this channel, as it depends on whether households believe the increase in asset prices will persist; if they do not, they may hold the wealth as a precautionary buffer against income shocks rather than spend it.[47]

Third, following QE, private banks have more central bank reserves (assets) and more customer deposits (liabilities). Since 'the banking system would be holding a higher level of reserves in aggregate', this 'might cause it to increase its lending to companies and households'.[48] Banks do not lend out reserves to their customers.[49] However, they need reserves when customers withdraw or transfer their deposits, so increasing their reserves means 'they should be more willing to hold a higher stock of illiquid assets in the form of loans as they have the funds to cope with the potentially higher level of payments activity'.[50] In other words, banks might be more willing to expand their balance sheets, creating deposits (liabilities repayable on demand) in return for customer promises to repay in the future (illiquid assets). However, researchers at the BoE recognised that this channel 'may be impaired, at least in the near term' because of 'the financial stresses that banks are currently facing'.[51] But they added that, even if banks do not actually increase their lending, the extra reserves should lower the interbank borrowing rate, allowing banks which face outflows of deposits to finance them more cheaply.[52]

Finally, by demonstrating that the central bank will 'do whatever it takes to meet the inflation target', QE can affect the inflation expectations of private actors, leading firms to set higher prices, raising inflation directly and perhaps leading to perceptions of an improved economic outlook, and therefore confidence.[53] There may also be 'policy signalling effects', as asset purchases may lead 'market participants to expect policy rates to remain low for longer'.[54]

Unconventional monetary policies push NCBs very close to the limits of their powers. In raising bond prices and lowering yields (making borrowing cheaper), QE certainly has the effect of reducing the cost to Member States of financing their debt, and therefore comes very close to being unlawful

---

[47] Benford et al., 'Quantitative Easing', 99.
[48] See BoE Monetary Policy Committee, Minutes of Meeting of 4 and 5 March 2009, para. 31.
[49] M McLeay, A Radia and R Thomas, 'Money Creation in the Modern Economy', (2014) *Bank of England Quarterly Bulletin* (Q1), 14 at 17.
[50] Benford et al., 'Quantitative Easing', 93.
[51] Ibid., 97.
[52] Ibid., 94.
[53] Ibid., 95.
[54] M. Joyce, M. Tong and R. Woods, 'The United Kingdom's Quantitative Easing Policy: Design, Operation and Impact' (2011) *Bank of England Quarterly Bulletin*, 200–212 at 201.

economic (fiscal) policy on the part of the ECB and unlawful finance of a deficit under Article 123(1) TFEU. However, this argument was implicitly rejected by the CJEU when it examined the legality of the ECB's July 2012 Outright Monetary Transactions (OMT) programme, a programme that has not been activated to date. Faced with soaring yields on bonds issued by peripheral Member States, the ECB announced that the Eurosystem would use its OMO power to purchase Member State bonds in secondary markets. There were no *ex ante* quantitative limits on these purchases, but access to the OMT would be restricted to Member States that have access to bond markets and are participating in a Eurozone Macroeconomic Adjustment Programme. The simple fact that the ECB stood ready to buy bonds if yields crept back up (and prices dropped) had the effect of keeping prices higher and yields at lower levels.

The legality of OMT was referred to the CJEU by the German Federal Constitutional Court,[55] which concluded that 'it is likely' that OMT 'is not covered by the mandate of the European Central Bank',[56] and 'is likely to violate' the Article 123(1) prohibition on monetary finance,[57] even if no bonds are actually purchased.[58] In its decision,[59] the CJEU ruled that, both in objective and form, OMT was a monetary policy measure within the ECB's powers. Its ultimate objective was to ensure the ability of ESCB to guarantee price stability in line with its mandate by safeguarding 'the singleness of monetary policy' and ensuring that the ECB was able to transmit monetary policy throughout the Eurozone.[60] In form, OMT amounted to a threat of large scale OMOs, which are recognised as an instrument of monetary policy under the ECB Protocol.[61] Any indirect effects on the 'stability of the Euro area', which is a matter of economic policy, would not suffice to make OMT unlawful.[62] Nor did OMT contravene Art 123(1), because it contained sufficient safeguards to ensure that that Article's objective, namely 'encourag[ing] the Member States to follow a sound budgetary policy', is not circumvented.[63]

---

[55] Bundesverfassungsgericht, 2 BvR 2728/13 vom 14.1.2014, Absatz Nr (1–105). An English translation is available online at: www.bundesverfassungsgericht.de/SharedDocs/Entscheidungen/EN/2014/01/rs20140114_2bvr272813en.html. For further discussion of this decision, see C. Gerner-Beuerle, E. Küçük and E. Schuster, 'Law Meets Economics in the German Federal Constitutional Court: Outright Monetary Transactions on Trial' (2014) 15 *German Law Journal*, 281..

[56] Ibid., para. 69.

[57] Ibid., para. 84.

[58] Ibid., para. 93.

[59] Judgment of 16 June 2015, *Gauwiler and others v Deutscher Bundestag*, C-62/14, EU:C:2015:400.

[60] Ibid., paras 47–50.

[61] Ibid., para. 54.

[62] Ibid., para. 52.

[63] Ibid., paras 100–102.

QE differs from OMT in a number of respects, including that precise details of its scope were announced in advance and that it would result in huge increases in base money and liquidity. The ECB's decision to launch a QE programme was referred to the CJEU by the German Federal Constitutional Court in July 2017.[64] Given the deferential approach of its OMT decision, it was unsurprising that the CJEU ultimately confirmed that the ECB was not acting illegally. As with OMT, indirect effects on economic stability did not turn a monetary policy measure into a measure of economic policy.[65] Perhaps most importantly, the programme was 'not selective', meaning it would 'have an impact on financial conditions across the whole of the euro area and will not meet the specific financing needs of certain Member States of that area'.[66] Uncertainty about future bond purchases meant that its impact on the need for 'sound budgetary policy' would be limited.[67] Nor was the programme disproportionate to its goal of raising inflation, and if such measures were unlawful, this 'might – in particular in the context of an economic crisis entailing a risk of deflation – represent an insurmountable obstacle to its accomplishing the task assigned to it by primary law'.[68] Finally, the programme was subject to safeguards in terms of loss-sharing, as discussed earlier.[69] If losses do occur, they are likely to arise at the level of NCBs when they unwind their bond purchases, potentially requiring the relevant national treasury to indemnify its central bank (discussed further in Section 4.4).

Overall, then, central bankers have a far broader discretion in terms of how they conduct monetary policy than national treasuries have in relation to fiscal policy. This serves to underline the extent to which the EU's monetary and economic constitution complies with neo-liberal policy prescriptions, and poses a serious threat to the sustainability of the EU's economy.

4.4 THE PATHOLOGICAL EFFECTS OF EXCLUSIVE RELIANCE ON MONETARY POLICY

The significant legal restrictions on expansionary fiscal policy contrast starkly with the light-touch policing of monetary policy by the courts. In line with the neo-liberal prescription, apart from the first year or two after the financial crisis, monetary policy has been the only permissible way to stimulate economies.

---

[64] Judgment of 11 December 2018, *Weiss and others*, C-493/17, EU:C:2018:1000.
[65] Ibid., paras 63–64.
[66] Ibid., para. 82.
[67] Ibid., para. 132.
[68] Ibid., para. 67.
[69] Ibid., paras 94–95.

A number of observations can be made about the effects of QE. Most of the focus in this section is on the UK, where the QE programme has been running for longer, and so there is more evidence about its consequences.

First, QE blurs the lines between fiscal and monetary policy,[70] because NCBs receive either explicit or implicit backing from their treasuries. The BoE has an explicit indemnity for losses arising from its QE programme from the UK Treasury,[71] and interest payments on bonds held by the central bank are remitted to the Treasury,[72] effectively relieving the Treasury of the obligation to pay interest on the bonds that are held by the central bank. These circular flows of money show that, whilst formally independent, the BoE is not entirely separate, because it is financing the Treasury's operations. Similarly, whilst the vast majority of any losses resulting from Eurozone QE are likely to fall on the NCBs, which are explicitly or implicitly backstopped against losses by national treasuries, the ECB might have to be recapitalised by the Eurozone Member States in line with their shareholdings in the event that it makes losses on its purchases that exceed its reserves. Payment by a national treasury under an indemnity would amount to public spending.[73] As such it must comply with the SGP, although it would presumably be considered an 'exceptional circumstance' outside the control of the Member State in question, given that the ECB required NCBs to purchase bonds. Whilst the possibility of such backdoor fiscal spending was not at issue before the CJEU when it considered QE, allowing it merely to note that any economic policy effects were 'indirect' and therefore insufficient to impugn the programme,[74] it does serve to highlight the wider discretion available to unelected central bankers than to elected politicians.

Second, QE in the UK may have headed off a far worse downturn,[75] but at the price of further exacerbating inequality,[76] an aspect of monetary policy

---

[70] J. Green and S. Lavery, 'The Regressive Recovery: Distribution, Inequality and State Power in Britain's Post-Crisis Political Economy' (2015) 20(6) *New Political Economy*, 894–923 at 906–907.

[71] See letter dated 29 January 2009 from the Chancellor of the Exchequer to the Governor of the Bank of England, available at: http://webarchive.nationalarchives.gov.uk/+www.hm-treasury.gov.uk/d/ck_letter_boe290109.pdf.

[72] See letter dated 9 November 2012 from the Chancellor of the Exchequer to the Governor of the Bank of England, available at: www.hm-treasury.gov.uk/d/chx_letter_091112.pdf.

[73] Cobham, 'The Past, Present, and Future of Central Banking', 741–742.

[74] *Weiss and others*, para. 63.

[75] C. Martin and C. Milas, 'Quantitative Easing: A Sceptical Survey' (2012) 28 *Oxford Review of Economic Policy*, 750–764.

[76] The BoE claimed that the UK's Gini co-efficient is lower than it would have been in the absence of QE, although it also recognised that wealthiest households and those around retirement age benefitted the most: see Bunn, Pugh and Yeates, 'The Distributional Impact of Monetary Policy Easing'.

that was little discussed before the crisis.[77] As it was intended to, QE has driven up the prices of financial and non-financial assets, such as houses,[78] benefitting households that hold those assets.[79] This has primarily boosted the wealth of the top 5 per cent of households, which hold 40 per cent of financial assets, but has also skewed distribution of benefits towards those aged over forty-five, who hold close to 80 per cent of financial assets. At the same time, rates payable on the stock of loans and deposits have fallen, benefitting debtors but disadvantaging those who hold their savings in deposit accounts.[80] Yet politicians, under the influence of neo-liberal ideology, have not sought to counter these regressive distributional effects of QE through changes to progressive taxation and redistributive fiscal spending, whilst central bankers, aware of the distributional effects of their emergency actions, have called on politicians to take such steps, albeit with relatively little publicity and even less effect.[81]

Third, in line with the doubts expressed by both Minsky and Keynes,[82] there is little evidence that QE has produced effects on the real economy, and it has been argued that 'QE, by itself, is not strong enough to spark an economic recovery.'[83] Event studies suggest that 'QE has a sizeable impact on corporate bond rates',[84] but that 'QE does not appear to have affected interest rates facing

---

[77] See G. Epstein, 'Central Banks as Agents of Economic Development' *University of Massachusetts Amherst Political Economy Research Institute Working Paper No 104*, September 2005, pp. 5–6.

[78] BoE, 'The Distributional Effects of Asset Purchases' (2012) Q3 *Quarterly Bulletin*, 254–266 at 258.

[79] Joyce, McLaren and Young, 'Quantitative Easing in the United Kingdom, 696–697. In contrast, research by McKinsey suggests that in the UK, 'household wealth may have increased by $1.1 trillion as a result of ultra-low interest rates, with an estimated 89 per cent coming from housing, 10 per cent from bonds, and 2 per cent from equity'. See McKinsey Global Institute, 'QE and Ultra-Low Interest Rates: Distributional Effects and Risks', November 2013, p. 32.

[80] BoE, 'The Distributional Effects of Asset Purchases', 258–259.

[81] The Governor of the BoE, Mark Carney, in his 2016 Report to the Treasury Committee, simply noted that 'Trade and fiscal policy continued to drag on growth', available at: www.bankofengland.co.uk/-/media/boe/files/about/people/mark-carney/mark-carney-annual-report-2016. Similarly, then President of the ECB, Mario Draghi, emphasised the limits of monetary policy, but also noted that, under the regulatory constraints discussed earlier, 'current fiscal space to support growth is limited' in many euro area Member States and that 'we should avoid the fiscal rules being stretched to a point where they lose credibility': see M Draghi, Introductory Remarks at the Portuguese Council of State, Lisbon, 7 April 2016, available from Bank for International Settlements online repository of central bankers' speeches at: www.bis.org/review/r160408a.htm.

[82] See H. Minsky, 'Comments on Friedman's and Schwartz' Money and the Business Cycles' (1963) 45 *The Review of Economics and Statistics*, 64–78 at 69–70. For Keynes, see fn.35.

[83] Martin and Milas, 'Quantitative Easing', 762. In its 2015 Annual Report, the Bank of International Settlements (BIS) concluded at 20 that 'the evidence suggests that central banks have been very successful in influencing financial markets and financial risk-taking but less so in boosting risk-taking in the real economy and hence output'.

[84] Martin and Milas, 'Quantitative Easing', 757.

small and medium enterprises and households.'[85] Whilst the yields on corporate bonds may have fallen, relatively few UK listed companies raise debt finance on the bond market and so are able to take advantage of its low, long-term interest rates.[86] Larger companies appear to have been taking advantage of low bond yields to resume their pre-crisis pattern of issuing bonds and buying back their shares. While corporate bond issuance has been buoyant, smaller companies, as well as those with more volatile earnings, have been struggling to obtain finance.[87] Likewise, in the Eurozone, where bank lending is the dominant source of corporate finance, small or medium-sized enterprises (SMEs) have faced greater difficulty than larger firms in obtaining bank finance, with considerable divergences between Member States.[88] This is regressive both in terms of sustainability and innovation, and in terms of employment, as smaller companies are the main drivers of employment growth in the EU.[89]

The wider effects of QE on employment are more uncertain. The UK's headline unemployment rate was impressive, falling from over 8 per cent in 2010–2011 to 5.7 per cent in October 2014,[90] and even dipping below 4 per cent in January 2019. Between 2010 and 2014, most Eurozone Member States had higher unemployment rates, and also saw a considerable increase in involuntary part-time unemployment.[91] Whether or not QE prevented more unemployment in the UK, it appears to have done nothing to prevent falling real wages in the UK between 2010 and 2013: by 2013, real wages were down by 8.5 per cent from their 2009 level.[92] This was in marked contrast to most countries (including the Eurozone, where QE had not yet been launched), where downwards wage adjustments slowed after 2011.[93] The more important drivers were surely the UK's neo-liberal-inspired flexible labour market policies and shareholder primacy corporate governance system.[94]

---

[85] Ibid., 758.

[86] In 2010, 141 public non-financial corporations had issued both bonds and equity to the public, while a further 116 issued only bonds: see A Pattani and G Vera, 'Going Public: UK Companies' Use of Capital Markets' (2011) *Bank of England Quarterly Bulletin* Q4, 319–330 at 322.

[87] BoE data shows that lending to SMEs declined in most of the years post-crisis and in 2018 remained slightly negative after two years of positive but weak growth: see www.bankofengland .co.uk/statistics/visual-summaries/businesses-finance-raised. See also www.ukfinance.org.uk/ wp-content/uploads/2018/10/SME-Finance-Where-are-we-nowV4.pdf.

[88] ECB, 'Survey on the Access to Finance of Enterprises in the Euro Area – October 2018 to March 2019', May 2019, para. 4.2.

[89] European Commission, 'Small and medium-sized enterprises – Key for delivering more growth and jobs. A mid-term review of Modern SME policy' COM (2007) 592 final, 4 October 2007, 3.

[90] ONS Labour Market Statistics, February 2015.

[91] OECD, *Employment Outlook 2018*, pp. 24, 35–37.

[92] ONS, *Real Wages Down by 8.5 per cent since 2009*, 5 April 2013.

[93] 'How Does the United Kingdom Compare?', OECD Employment Outlook, September 2014.

[94] For discussion of the 'neoliberal box' in which lower income households are trapped by the abandonment of full employment policies, small government, labour market flexibility and

With the monetary stimulus not reaching the economy either through increased borrowing and investment by most corporations, or through higher wages, any stimulatory effect of QE on the real economy has had to operate through the wealth effect channel, with asset owners increasing their borrowings and spending in response to rising asset prices. It seems plausible, then, to argue that QE amounts to little more than a continuation of the 'financialised demand strategy' that prevailed before the crisis,[95] which, against a backdrop of wage stagnation, relied on rising asset prices and private rather than public debt to stimulate demand in the economy.[96] Yet relying on QE to produce a wealth effect is likely to be less effective than conventional Keynesian fiscal stimulus, because increased inequality puts downwards pressure on demand, as 'poorer income groups have higher marginal propensities to consume'.[97] It may also lay the groundwork for financial instability if lower income households resume borrowing to fund consumption,[98] whilst higher income households and institutional investors take more speculative financial positions in a search for yield.[99] Finally, it is hard to see how interest rates can normalise (even in the face of recent, rapid increases in inflation) because the ongoing rise in private debt levels, encouraged by low interest rates both before and after the financial crisis, is likely to keep interest rates below the rate of inflation and require QE to continue in order prevent a major economic downturn.[100]

---

globalisation, see T. Palley, 'Financialization: What It Is and Why It Matters' (2007) *Levy Economics Institute of Bard College Working Paper No 525*, p. 22.

[95] Green and Lavery, 'The Regressive Recovery', 6.

[96] Bhaduri terms this 'a vulgar version of Keynesian demand management', which revolves around stimulating the economy with liquidity to save financial institutions in the hope that 'this will also revive aggregate demand sufficiently to save not only banks but also the real economy'. A. Bhaduri, 'What Remains of the Theory of Demand Management in a Globalizing World?' (2014) *Levy Economics Institute Public Policy Brief* No. 130.

[97] Ibid., 7.

[98] Then BoE Monetary Policy Committee member Jan Vlieghe highlighted this concern in a September 2017 speech, noting that the deleveraging of UK household balance sheets that started in 2010 appeared to end in 2016 (see J Vlieghe, 'Real interest rates and risk', speech at Business Economists' Annual Conference, London, 15 September 2017, available at: www .bankofengland.co.uk/-/media/boe/files/speech/2017/real-interest-rates-and-risk.pdf. On the drivers of increasing household debt to finance consumption, see R. Bellofiore, J. Halevi and M. Passarella, 'Minsky in the "New" Capitalism: the New Clothes of the Financial Instability Hypothesis', in D. B. Papadimitriou and L. R. Wray (eds.), *The Elgar Companion to Hyman Minsky* (Cheltenham: Edward Elgar Publishing, 2010), pp. 92–98.

[99] E Stockhammer, 'Rising Inequality as a Cause of the Present Crisis' (2015) 39 *Cambridge Journal of Economics*, 935–958.

[100] In its 2015 Annual Report, 8, the Bank for International Settlements suggests that low interest rates may not be conducive to sustainable and balanced global expansion, and that with 'too much debt, too little growth and excessively low interest rates … low rates beget lower rates'.

4.5 THE EU'S FISCAL AND MONETARY POLICY RESPONSE TO THE COVID-19 PANDEMIC

Everything changed – at least temporarily – when the pandemic hit Europe in March 2020. Fiscal policy became very expansionary, and this was complemented by the European Central Bank engaging in QE and lowering interest rates. Whilst the EU's response touched many areas beyond fiscal and monetary policy,[101] it is on those policies that we will focus here.

With national governments ordering businesses to close, it was viewed as imperative to use fiscal policy to support the economy in ways that would not be contemplated in an ordinary recession. Countries such as France, Germany and Italy added between 4.9 per cent and 8.3 per cent of GDP by way of additional spending,[102] and a range of other measures such as equity injections, loans and asset purchases were also witnessed.[103] At EU level, a further 3.8 per cent of GDP (€427.8 billion) in additional spending had been committed under a variety of programmes by early September 2020,[104] including the Corona Response Investment Initiative and the Recovery and Resilience Facility. The latter, agreed in July 2020 is composed of up to €312.5 billion in grants (as well as up to €360 billion in loans) to Member States. Member States should prepare recovery and resilience plans setting out a coherent package of reforms and investments to be implemented by 2026, of which at least 37 per cent of expenditure should be related to green investments and reforms.[105] These loans and grants are financed by the European Commission issuing bonds, the first time the EU has agreed to issue supranational debt instruments in response to an economic crisis. The Commission was authorised to do so by the Council under Article 122 TFEU.[106] Borrowing costs are low, given the EU's high credit rating, and the borrowings will either be rolled over and refinanced or paid back, either from Member State repayments of loans made to them, or, in

---

[101] See, for example, the adoption by the Commission of a Temporary Framework to enable Member States to use the full flexibility foreseen under state aid rules to support the economy in the context of the COVID-19 outbreak: Commission Communication, 'Temporary Framework for State Aid Measures to Support the Economy in the Current COVID-19 Outbreak', C(2020) 1863 final, 19 March 2020.

[102] IMF, Fiscal Monitor, 'Database of country fiscal measures in response to the COVID-19 pandemic', October 2020 at 19, available at: www.imf.org/en/Publications/FM/Issues/2020/09/30/october-2020-fiscal-monitor.

[103] Ibid.

[104] Ibid., 2.

[105] European Commission, 'Recovery and resilience facility', available at: https://ec.europa.eu/info/business-economy-euro/recovery-coronavirus/recovery-and-resilience-facility_en.

[106] 'Q&A: next generation EU – legal construction', QANDA/20/1024, available at: https://ec.europa.eu/commission/presscorner/detail/en/QANDA_20_1024.

the case of grants, out of the revenue sources in the EU's budget, including customs duties, Member State VAT contributions and other Member State contributions.[107] The effect of this is that the cost of the €312.5 billion of grants issued to Member States will be spread among the Member States in proportion to their contribution to the EU budget; as Article 122 TFEU puts it, the action is taken 'in a spirit of solidarity between Member States'.

The European Council also approved the issue of up to €100 billion in social bonds under the SURE Regulation,[108] the proceeds of which will support eighteen Member States with loans to finance public expenditure to preserve employment. By December 2020, €39.5 billion of the approved SURE bonds had been issued.[109]

As for monetary policy, the ECB was supportive, buying much of the newly issued debt, as it announced a €750 billion extension of its QE programme. The Pandemic Emergency Purchase Programme includes all asset categories eligible under the existing Asset Purchase Programme.[110] In addition, euro area banks were temporarily permitted to exclude their exposures to their central bank from their leverage ratio calculation,[111] and the banking system was supported with additional liquidity in the form of Pandemic Emergency Long Term Repo Operations.[112]

However, perhaps the most significant development was the suspension, in March 2020, of the SGP, which until then had been the primary instrument by which fiscal discipline was imposed on Member States. The Commission and Council agreed to activate the general escape clause, which was introduced as part of the six-pack in 2011 in the aftermath of the financial crisis.[113]

---

[107] European Commission, 'Recovery plan for Europe', available at: https://ec.europa.eu/info/strategy/recovery-plan-europe_en.

[108] Council Regulation (EU) 2020/672 of 19 May 2020 on the establishment of a European instrument for temporary support to mitigate unemployment risks in an emergency (SURE) following the COVID-19 outbreak, OJ L 159/1, 20 May 2020.

[109] European Commission, 'Investor presentation', December 2020, available at: https://ec.europa.eu/info/sites/info/files/about_the_european_commission/eu_budget/investor_presentation_21122020.pdf.

[110] 'Decision of 24 March 2020 on a temporary pandemic emergency purchase programme' (ECB/2020/17), OJ L 91/1, 25 March 2020.

[111] 'Decision on the temporary exclusion of certain exposures to central banks from the total exposure measure in view of the COVID-19 pandemic' (ECB/2020/44), OJ L 305/30, 21 September 2020.

[112] European Central Bank, 'ECB extends pandemic emergency longer-term financing operations', press release, 10 December 2020, available at: www.ecb.europa.eu/press/pr/date/2020/html/ecb.pr201210~8acfa5026f.en.html.

[113] European Commission, 'Communication on the activation of the general escape clause of the Stability and Growth Pact', COM (2020) 123 final, 20 March 2020; European Council, 'Statement of EU ministers of finance on the Stability and Growth Pact in light of the

That clause applies to both the preventive and corrective arms of the SGP in the event of a 'severe economic downturn for the euro area or the Union as a whole'. Member States in the preventive arm may be permitted 'temporarily to depart from the adjustment path towards the medium-term budgetary objective … provided that this does not endanger fiscal sustainability in the medium term',[114] whilst recommendations and notices given to Member States in the corrective arm may be revised, allowing them to adopt a revised fiscal trajectory.[115] The effect of this is that the 'budgetary impact of the measures taken in response to the outbreak will be excluded from the Commission's assessments of compliance with the Stability and Growth Pact'.[116]

In essence, then, the suspension of the SGP means that the additional debt issued by Member States to finance their response to the pandemic will not be taken into account in assessing whether their deficits breach the SGP. As to what should be done when the crisis has passed, it has been noted by two ECB researchers that, once the Member States' 'economies have sufficiently recovered, the important fiscal support provided during the crisis will need to be withdrawn and government debt must be reduced'.[117] It is worth noting, however, that the Recommendations issued to Member States in the preventive arm of the SGP state that they should resume a focus on 'achieving prudent medium-term fiscal positions', at least 'when economic conditions allow'.[118] The European Fiscal Board, an independent body that advises the Commission, reported in July 2020 that 'activation of the general escape clause of the SGP was fully justified; but it should have included indications on (and conditions for) exit or review …. Clarity should be offered in due course, ideally by spring 2021.'[119]

COVID-19 crisis', 23 March 2020, available at: www.consilium.europa.eu/en/press/press-releases/2020/03/23/statement-of-eu-ministers-of-finance-on-the-stability-and-growth-pact-in-light-of-the-covid-19-crisis/#.

[114] Article 9(1) of Regulation 1466/97 as amended.

[115] Articles 3(5) and 5(3) of Regulation 1467/97 as amended.

[116] European Commission, 'Communication on the activation of the general escape clause of the Stability and Growth Pact'.

[117] S Hauptmeier and N Leiner-Killinger, 'Reflections on the Stability and Growth Pact's Preventive Arm in Light of the COVID-19 Crisis' (2020) 55(5) *Intereconomics Review of European Economic Policy*, 296.

[118] See, for example, 'Recommendation for a Council Recommendation on the 2020 National Reform Programme of France and delivering a Council opinion on the 2020 Convergence Programme of France', COM(2020) 510 final, 20 May 2020. Equivalent recommendations were made to all Member States that are in the preventive arm of the Stability and Growth Pact: see European Parliament Briefing, 'Implementation of the Stability and Growth Pact under pandemic times', Economic Governance Support Unit (EGOV) PE 659.618, November 2020.

[119] European Fiscal Board, 'Assessment of the fiscal stance appropriate for the euro area in 2021', 1 July 2020, 6. For further discussion of post-crisis ways forward, including considerations

A more comprehensive review of the SGP was launched by the Commission in February 2020, noting both the danger of changes in market sentiment towards heavily indebted Member States, and that, with interest rates having hit their effective lower bound, 'the appropriate role of fiscal and economic policy in macroeconomic stabilisation should be assessed'.[120] However, the review was put on hold after the onset of the pandemic, and was only relaunched in October 2021. Whilst it is currently unclear how far and how quickly Member States will be required to reduce their pandemic-related debt, it seems clear from the documents discussed here that this is not a permanent change and a reduction will ultimately be required, entailing some combination of fiscal austerity and tax increases. Whilst the balance between these two is a political question for Member States, neo-liberal ideology would privilege cuts to public spending above tax increases. If Member States' political choices follow neo-liberal ideology, then this will further undermine economic sustainability in the EU.

4.6 CONCLUSION

In the Eurozone, as a result of the financial crisis and long before the COVID-19 pandemic, the economic and social situation in heavily indebted 'peripheral' Member States such as Greece, Italy and Spain appeared unsustainable. Similarly, growing inequality within Member States was driving the emergence of populist governments, a dynamic that was creating serious political tensions within the EU. Indeed, one need look no further than the UK, where the rampant inequality created by forty years of neo-liberalism has been further exacerbated, first by the distributional consequences of QE and fiscal austerity in the aftermath of the global financial crisis, and second by the pandemic.[121] Indeed, fiscal austerity and the inequality it deepened appears to have played an important role in the outcome of the UK's 2016 referendum on membership of the EU.[122]

Heavily indebted members of the Eurozone do not have the 'luxury' of depreciating their currency against their intra-EU trading partners, nor do

---

relating to transitionary arrangements, see European Parliament, 'When and how to deactivate the SGP general escape clause?' Economic Governance Support Unit (EGOV), Directorate-General for Internal Policies, PE 651.378, November 2020, available at: www.europarl.europa.eu/RegData/etudes/IDAN/2020/651378/IPOL_IDA(2020)651378_EN.pdf.

[120] European Commission, 'Economic Governance Review', COM (2020) 55 final, 5 February 2020, 5–6.

[121] See Institute for Fiscal Studies, 'Covid-19: the impacts of the pandemic on inequality', Briefing Note, 11 June 2020, available at: www.ifs.org.uk/publications/14879.

[122] See, for example, T Fetzer, 'Did Austerity Cause Brexit?' (2018) *University of Warwick Department of Economics Working Paper No. 1170*.

they have control over interest rates and unconventional monetary policy, so they cannot unilaterally decide to stimulate their economy in this way. They also face very significant constraints on fiscal policy as a result of the SGP. As a result, if they want to improve economic growth, they will have to engage in unilateral structural adjustment (a euphemism primarily referring to reducing the power of labour). But if this also reduces the income of labour, this will further weaken domestic demand, further undermining economic sustainability and also potentially creating further political instability.

As for what should be done, the Bank for International Settlements rightly noted the need to 'replace the debt-fuelled growth model that has acted as a political and social substitute for productivity-enhancing reforms .... Monetary policy, overburdened for far too long, must be part of the answer, but it cannot be the whole answer.'[123] However, its prescription for reform was straight out of the neo-liberal playbook, emphasising 'improving the flexibility of product and labour markets,[124] providing an environment conducive to entrepreneurship and innovation, and boosting labour force participation'.[125] In other words, further structural adjustment, and with it further social dislocation.

Others have been calling for more far-reaching reform ever since the financial crisis, with researchers at the IMF in 2013 calling for increased fiscal risk-sharing[126] and a banking union within the Eurozone to address the structural imbalances.[127] A 2018 IMF paper noted that the lack of fiscal union was an ongoing vulnerability that 'presents an existential risk that policymakers should not ignore',[128] although the same paper also noted that 'progress towards "more Europe", including in the fiscal domain, [had] stalled as the [financial] crisis ebbed'.[129] However, everything changed when the pandemic hit in 2020 and the policy playbook was, at least temporarily, replaced by something more sensible.

The EU's willingness to use emergency measures to allow fiscal policy to offset shortages in demand comes at a time when the international institutions

---

[123] Bank for International Settlements, Annual Report 2015, 9.

[124] A key part of Palley's 'neoliberal box': Palley, 'Financialization', 22.

[125] Bank for International Settlements, Annual Report 2015, 18.

[126] C. Allard et al., 'Toward a Fiscal Union for the Euro Area', IMF Staff Discussion Note, September 2013, SDN/13/09.

[127] R. Goyal et al., 'A Banking Union for the Euro Area', IMF Staff Discussion Note, February 2013, SDN/13/01.

[128] H. Berger, G. Dell'Ariccia and M. Obstfeld, 'Revisiting the Economic Case for Fiscal Union in the Euro Area', IMF Departmental Paper No 18/03, 2, available at www.imf.org/en/Publications/Departmental-Papers-Policy-Papers/Issues/2018/02/20/Revisiting-the-Economic-Case-for-Fiscal-Union-in-the-Euro-Area-45611.

[129] Ibid., p. 1.

appear to be reversing their long-standing support for neo-liberalism. The IMF suggested in 2016 that neo-liberalism may have been 'oversold' because it has 'increased inequality', which in turn undermines the 'sustainability of growth'.[130] Similarly, in 2014, the Organisation for Economic Co-operation and Development (OECD) recognised that widening income inequalities significantly curbs economic growth; that tax and transfer policies do not harm growth if they are well designed and implemented; and that countries should support lifelong skills development and learning.[131] Whilst this apparent change of approach is to be welcomed, this chapter has shown that there are significant legal, political and ideological barriers to change. Sawyer, who calls for significant income transfers between Member States (of the kind subsequently – but exceptionally – witnessed in the response to the COVID-19 pandemic) and a supranational social security system, admits that his recommendations are 'very far removed from the present policy positions, and remote from what could be viewed as politically feasible'.[132]

Whilst the pandemic has provided a space in which policies aimed at economic sustainability could be deployed on a temporary basis, it is clear that the intention of the European institutions is to return to the previous regime in due course, if not as soon as possible, and it is to be expected that there will be pressure for debt reduction once the disruption is behind us. The (limited) fiscal integration embodied in the grant component of the 2020 Recovery and Resilience Facility shows what can be done when there is political will. However, economic sustainability will require the EU to go much further than time-limited measures taken in a state of emergency. It is clear that, without constitutional change, whether loosening the constraints on public debt or providing for continuous fiscal transfers as required between Member States, and without an ideological shift away from neo-liberalism, sustainable growth within the EU will remain elusive. At present, such change looks politically implausible, yet a failure to address these issues creates the very unwelcome risk that the EU itself may break apart.

---

[130] J. D. Ostry, P. Loungani and D. Furceri, 'Neoliberalism: Oversold?' (2016) 53(2) *Finance & Development*, 38–41.

[131] OECD, 'Does Income Inequality Hurt Economic Growth?', Focus on Inequality and Growth, December 2014.

[132] M. Sawyer, 'Alternative Economic Policies for the Economic and Monetary Union' (2013) 32 *Contributions to Political Economy*, 11–27 at 11.

5

Sustainability and Eurozone 2.0

Still Impossible?

Alexandros Kyriakidis

5.1 INTRODUCTION

The Eurozone crisis in the late 2000s (hereafter 'the crisis') has undoubtedly constituted a force majeure of reforms within the Eurozone and the entire European Union (EU). The crisis was related to the broader financial crisis of 2008–2009, which began in the US during 2007–2008 and the collapse of the housing market bubble (primarily sub-prime mortgages). The EU and Member States experienced the crisis in the banking sector and then a sovereign debt overload that eventually resulted in a credit crunch. The measures assumed within the EU to counter the crisis can be broadly separated into those that were EU-wide, which include financial assistance mechanisms (e.g. the European Stability Mechanism) and enhanced coordination measures (e.g. six-pack or two-pack), and those that were specific to Member States, primarily financial assistance programmes.[1]

The EU-wide measures included legislative changes designed to address weaknesses of the EU's (mainly economic) operating framework that led to Member States being susceptible to the crisis, fundamentally altering the operating and decision-making structure of the EU and its institutions. This has led to the transformation of the Eurozone into a version 2.0. The aim of this chapter is to evaluate each of those EU-wide measures against the overarching general principles of sustainability, as presented in the relevant scholarship, focusing not on the measures' specific outcomes (many of which have not yet occurred), but rather on whether or not their foundations produce a sustainable (or at least a more sustainable) EU structure and modus operandi.

---

[1] A. Kyriakidis, 'Social Exclusion and the Eurozone Crisis Reforms: Improvement or Stalemate?', in D. Anagnostopoulou and L. Papadopoulou (eds.), *Towards an Inclusive European Citizenship* (Athens: Papazisis Publishing, 2019), pp. 60–61.

5.2 REVIEW OF SCHOLARSHIP ON SUSTAINABILITY

The meaning of sustainability is usually dependent upon the context.[2] The concept existed as early as the 1930s. Arthur Cecil Pigou noted the need of governments, acting as trustees for future, unborn generations, to act, to a certain degree, as guardians against 'rash and reckless spoliation of exhaustible natural resources of the country' (e.g. Pigouvian tax).[3] Sustainability involves not only a strong intergenerational equity element, but also a consideration towards the current living conditions of individuals. As Anand and Sen highlight, 'if one thinks that people will be deprived in the future unless different policies are followed, then one is morally obliged to ask whether people are deprived right now', and, accordingly, pursue redistributive measures to ensure non-deprivation.[4]

Beyond merely theoretical perspectives, sustainability has been most commonly utilised via the term 'sustainable development'.[5] Although as much debated as sustainability, the concept of development can be largely understood as 'a process of directed change … (embodying) both (a) the objectives of this process, and (b) the means of achieving these objectives'.[6] Sustainable development is, then, progress over time that includes sustainable objectives and the sustainable means for reaching those objectives, embodying both ecological and social considerations. In 1987, the World Commission on Environment and Development provided the definition of sustainable development that most scholars broadly agree with:[7] for development to be

---

[2]   N. L. Pollesch and V. H. Dale, 'Normalization in Sustainability Assessment: Methods and Implications' (2015) 130 *Ecological Economics*, 195–208 at 195; K. Ueda and T. Takenaka and J. Vancza and L. Monostori, 'Value Creation and Decision-Making in Sustainable Society' (2009) 58 *CIRP Annals – Manufacturing Technology*, 681–700 at 687.

[3]   S. Anand and A. Sen, 'Human Development and Economic Sustainability' (2000) 28 *World Development*, 2029–2049 at 2034.

[4]   Ibid., 2038.

[5]   S. Lele, 'Sustainable Development: A Critical Review' (1991) 19 *World Development*, 607–621 at 609.

[6]   Ibid.

[7]   Anand and Sen, 'Human Development and Economic Sustainability', 2033; B. Sjåfjell, 'Internalizing Externalities in EU Law: Why Neither Corporate Governance nor Corporate Social Responsibility Provides the Answers' (2008) 40 *George Washington International Law Review*, 977–1024 at 977; F. Figge and T. Hahn, 'The Cost of Sustainability Capital and the Creation of Sustainable Value by Companies' (2005) 9 *Journal of Industrial Ecology*, 47–58 at 48; D. Stern, 'The Capital Theory Approach to Sustainability: A Critical Appraisal' (1997) 31 *Journal of Economic Issues*, 145–173; S. L. Hart and M. B. Milstein 'Creating Sustainable Value' (2003) 17 *Academy of Management Executive*, 56–67 at 56; K. Ueda, T. Takenaka, J. Váncza and L. Monostor, 'Value Creation and Decision-Making in Sustainable Society' (2009) 58 *CIRP Annals*, 681–700 at 687.

sustainable, it has to meet 'the needs of the present without compromising the ability of future generations to meet their own needs'.[8] This definition encapsulates most key elements that are pertinent and relative for this research, not least considering that the EU also largely utilises it to monitor sustainable development (chief among them the Millennium Development Goals,[9] and the 2030 Agenda for Sustainable Development).[10]

From the relevant scholarship, the following can be considered key characteristics of sustainability and sustainable development. First, it is clear that sustainability includes a temporal element: future generations have to be accounted for in utilising present resources. However, the concept also accounts for present generations in terms of a more equitable distribution of resources. In other words, for development to be sustainable, resources have to be allocated fairly, equitably and efficiently in the present, and in a manner that ensures future generations can enjoy, at the very least, an equal standard of living. Secondly, sustainability includes social and ecological factors, aside from economic ones, which eventually contribute to more sustainable living standards for both present and future generations, for example through building human capital, such as education. Thirdly, for a system to be sustainable, it should be adequately fortified against external shocks. As sustainability implies the preservation of some form of stock (primarily capital), a sustainable system should be able to efficiently respond to an external shock by using part of it for unforeseen emergencies.[11]

---

[8] UN Secretary General, 'A/42/427, Secretary General – forty-second session. Development and international co-operation: environment – report of the World Commission on Environment and Development' (1987), available at: www.un-documents.net/a42-427.htm at 16.

[9] In September 2000, the UN's General Assembly adopted the Millennium Declaration, pursuant to which eight goals for achieving sustainable development were set (Millennium Development Goals): '(1) eradicate extreme poverty and hunger; (2) achieve universal primary education; (3) promote gender equality and empower women; (4) reduce child mortality; (5) improve maternal health; (6) combat HIV/AIDS, malaria and other diseases; (7) ensure environmental sustainability; and (8) develop a global partnership for development'. See United Nations, 'Millennium summit (6–8 September 2000)', available at: www.un.org/en/events/pastevents/millennium_summit.shtml, and also United Nations, 'Millennium declaration progress chart' (2005), available at: www.un.org/millenniumgoals/pdf/mdg2005progresschart.pdf at 1.

[10] European Commission, 'The 2030 agenda for sustainable development' (2019), available at: https://ec.europa.eu/europeaid/policies/european-development-policy/2030-agenda-sustainable-development_en; European Commission, 'The sustainable development goals' (2019),   available   at: https://ec.europa.eu/europeaid/policies/sustainable-development-goals_en. Also in United Nations, 'Resolution adopted by the General Assembly … 70/1. Transforming our world: the 2030 agenda for sustainable development' (2015), available at: www.un.org/millenniumgoals/pdf/mdg2005progresschart.pdf at 14.

[11] This resonates with the definition of sustainability presented in the introductory chapter and setting the scene for this volume, namely that of 'securing social foundations for humanity

What does this mean for the EU, and the Eurozone more specifically? While it is not the aim of this chapter to provide a list of specific indicators (the EU already uses the United Nations (UN) Sustainable Development indicators, as mentioned earlier), the aforementioned foundational elements have clear applications within the Eurozone. In terms of the first one, it is clear that policies assumed by the Eurozone and its Member States should always account for the impact on future generations. For example, this would mean consideration of the macro-economic impact of economic policies implemented (by and large the primary policies on which decision-making within the Eurozone is focused). At the same time, this should not jeopardise the equitable distribution and consumption of resources for the present economy of each Member State and the Eurozone as a whole. The second element necessitates the inclusion and measurement of factors other than economic impact. For example, ensuring the existence of a robust pension system or sufficient healthcare for citizens would be of primary importance in achieving sustainable development. The third element is the one most lacking. It necessitates a structural overhaul of the Eurozone (and the EU to a lesser degree) so as to ensure that, in the case of an impending financial crisis, for example, there is proper fortification: actions are taken to ensure that it is averted, and if, in spite of these actions, a crisis occurs, measures are in place to counter it and cushion its effects. A detailed analysis of the Eurozone crisis measures follows in order to determine whether, to what extent and in what way the above has been achieved.

5.3 OVERVIEW OF EU-WIDE CRISIS MEASURES

5.3.1 *Pre-Crisis Framework*

In relation to the provision of financial assistance, EU mechanisms for the provision of financial assistance were created as early as 1971 with the 'machinery for medium-term financial assistance' accompanied by economic policy conditionality for EU Member States with balance of payments problems.[12] This machinery was complemented by the creation of a Community Loan Mechanism,[13] accompanied by stricter conditionality, and these two

now and for the future within planetary boundaries', C. Villiers, B. Sjåfjell and G. Tsagas, 'Stimulating Value Creation in a Europe in Crisis'; see also Chapter 1 in this volume at xx.

[12] 'Council Decision 71/143/EEC setting up machinery for medium-term financial assistance' (1971) *Official Journal* L73.

[13] 'Council Regulation 682/81 adjusting the Community loan mechanism designed to support the balance of payments of Member States' (1981) *Official Journal* L73.

mechanisms were then combined into a single facility for Medium-Term Financial Assistance.[14] After the establishment of the Eurozone, this Medium-Term Financial Assistance was modified,[15] restricting its use to non-Eurozone Member States.[16]

In relation to fiscal rules and coordination of economic policies, the pre-existing EU legislation is encapsulated in primary EU law through clear stipulations that EU Member States should maintain a balanced budgetary position and avoid excessive deficits: this is to be found in Article 126 of the Treaty on the Functioning of the European Union (TFEU) and Protocol No. 12.[17] Sustainability is also referenced throughout the EU Treaties, mostly in relation to the financial situation of Member States,[18] and also including a few references to environmental and social issues (employment, growth, etc.).[19] In terms of secondary legislation, the Stability and Growth Pact (SGP) exists, consisting of (prior to the crisis) European Council Resolution 97/C 236/01,[20] together with Regulations 1466/97 and 1467/99.[21]

5.3.2 *EU-wide Crisis Measures*

In relation to the provision of financial assistance, there were three new mechanisms created, all of which provide it under strict conditionality, budgetary discipline and extensive policy monitoring. The first is the European Financial Stabilisation Mechanism (EFSM), created to provide financial

---

[14] Ibid., 1–2.

[15] 'Council Regulation 332/2002 establishing a facility providing medium-term financial assistance for Member States' balances of payments' (2002) *Official Journal* L53.

[16] Ibid., 1–2.

[17] This sets the 3 per cent GDP deficit/60 per cent GDP debt targets; in 'Consolidated versions of the Treaty on European Union and the Treaty on the Functioning of the European Union' (2012) *Official Journal* C326, 99–102 and 279–280.

[18] Ibid., 16, 96–97, 108–109.

[19] Ibid., 16, 28, 53.

[20] Includes, inter alia, the commitment by EU Member States (except those under derogation) to maintain budgetary discipline; in 'Resolution of the European Council on the Stability and Growth Pact' (1997) *Official Journal* C236.

[21] The first introduces, inter alia, the procedures and guidelines for the submission of EU Member States' Stability and Convergence programmes, and their evaluation and monitoring, and the second concerns, inter alia, the specifics of the process initiated upon violation of TFEU/ SGP deficit criteria; on the European Commission's website, available at: http://ec.europa .eu/economy_finance/economic_governance/sgp/legal_texts/index_en.htm, in Resolutions of the European Council 97/C 236/01 on the Stability and Growth Pact (1997), and 97/C 236/02 on growth and employment (1997) *Official Journal* C236, in Council Regulations (EC) No. 1466/97 on the strengthening of the surveillance of budgetary positions and the surveillance and coordination of economic policies, and (EC) No 1467/97 on speeding up and clarifying the implementation of the excessive deficit procedure (1997) *Official Journal* L209.

assistance to any EU Member States and with a lending capacity of €60 billion.[22] The other two mechanisms had the purpose of providing financial assistance only to Eurozone Member States, and were both outside the EU framework. The first was the Public Limited Company European Financial Stability Facility Société Anonyme (EFSF SA), based in Luxembourg, with a maximum capacity of €440 billion.[23] The second, currently serving as the permanent financial assistance mechanism of the Eurozone, is the European Stability Mechanism (ESM), with a total capital of €500 billion.[24] The ESM is an international, intergovernmental organisation outside the EU framework,[25] established under an international treaty (the ESM Treaty).[26]

In relation to the EU-wide measures establishing enhanced coordination between the Eurozone and the EU Member States, the first one adopted was the Euro Plus Pact (EPP) in March 2011, establishing 'a stronger economic policy coordination for competitiveness and convergence', and with participants being all the then Eurozone Member States as well as Latvia and Lithuania (which joined the Eurozone after 2011), Bulgaria, Denmark, Latvia, Lithuania, Poland and Romania; that is, twenty-three out of the then twenty-seven EU Member States (European Council 2011d, 5).[27] The second EU-wide enhanced coordination measure was the upgrade of the three existing Lamfalussy third-level committees to authorities, creating the European Bank Authority, European Insurance and Occupational Pensions Authority,

[22] Council Regulation 407/2010 establishing a European financial stabilization mechanism (2010) *Official Journal* L118, 7.

[23] EFSF Framework Agreement, 7 June 2010, in force from 2010 (consolidated version, available at: www.esm.europa.eu/sites/default/files/20111019_efsf_framework_agreement_en.pdf), 1, 7, 24; EFSF Articles of Incorporation available at: www.esm.europa.eu/sites/default/files/efsf_status_coordonnes_23avrl2014.pdf, pp. 1–2.

[24] European Council, '24/25 March 2011 conclusions' (2011), available at: www.consilium.europa.eu/uedocs/cms_Data/docs/pressdata/en/ec/120296.pdf.

[25] In order for the establishment of the ESM to be compatible with the EU framework, TFEU article 136 was amended (under Decision 2011/199/EU), adding a third paragraph to allow the Eurozone MS to 'establish a stability mechanism to be activated if indispensable to safeguard the stability of the euro area as a whole. The granting of such financial assistance … will be made subject to strict conditionality.' In Council Decision 2011/199/EU amending Article 136 of the Treaty on the Functioning of the European Union with regard to a stability mechanism for Member States whose currency is the euro (2011) *Official Journal* L91.

[26] It entered into force approximately six months after its signature on 27 September 2012, in 'Treaty establishing the European Stability Mechanism, 2 February 2012, in force 27 September 2012', Council of the European Union (2012), available at: www.esm.europa.eu/sites/default/files/20150203_-_esm_treaty_-_en.pdf, p. 1, and in the press release of the European Commission, available at: https://europa.eu/rapid/press-release_IP-08-1679_en.htm.

[27] The EPP concerns areas under national and not EU competence, and is aimed towards fostering competitiveness, employment, and contributing to the sustainability of public finances (European Council 24/25 March 2011).

European Securities and Markets Authority, and the Risk Board, established in November 2011 with augmented oversight competences.[28]

The third EU-wide measure was the six-pack, a total of five regulations (1173, 1174, 1175, 1176, and 1177/2011) and one directive (2011/85/EU), adopted during November 2011 and aimed mostly at amending, renewing and enriching the SGP.[29] The fourth measure was the Treaty on Stability, Coordination and Growth (TSCG), an international agreement signed on March 2012 (in force from January 2013) between twenty-five EU Member States and aimed at introducing stricter criteria of budgetary discipline.[30] The fifth measure was the two-pack, consisting of Regulations 472/2013 and 473/2013, concerning only Eurozone MS and 'designed to further enhance economic integration

---

[28] Regulations of the European Parliament and of the Council (EU) No 1092/2010on macroprudential oversight of the financial system and establishing a European Systemic Risk Board, (EU) No 1093/2010 establishing a European Supervisory Authority (European Banking Authority), amending Decision No 716/2009/EC and repealing Commission Decision 2009/78/EC, (EU) No 1094/2010 establishing a European Supervisory Authority (European Insurance and Occupational Pensions Authority), amending Decision No 716/2009/EC and repealing Commission Decision 2009/79/EC, and (EU) No 1095/2010 establishing a European Supervisory Authority (European Securities and Markets Authority), amending Decision No 716/2009/EC and repealing Commission Decision 2009/77/EC (2010) *Official Journal* L331.

[29] Council Directive 2011/85/EU of 8 November 2011 on requirements for budgetary frameworks of the Member States, and Regulations of the European Parliament and of the Council (EU) No 1173/2011 on the effective enforcement of budgetary surveillance in the euro area, (EU) No 1174/2011 on enforcement measures to correct excessive macro-economic imbalances in the euro area, (EU) No 1175/2011 amending Council Regulation (EC) No 1466/97 on the strengthening of the surveillance of budgetary positions and the surveillance and coordination of economic policies, (EU) No 1176 on the prevention and correction of macro-economic imbalances, and Council Regulation (EU) No 1177/2011 amending Regulation (EC) No 1467/97 on speeding up and clarifying the implementation of the excessive deficit procedure(2011) Official Journal L306. Directive 2011/85/EU aims, inter alia, at delineating the process of rules for budgetary frameworks of EU Member States, Regulation 1173/2011 concerns the budgetary surveillance of Eurozone MS, Regulation 1174/2011 also concerns only Eurozone MS and the correction of macro-economic imbalances within the Eurozone, Regulation 1176/2011 concerns all EU Member States, and aims at correcting macro-economic imbalances that occur within the EU, Regulation 1175/2011 is the first main SGP revision, and amends Regulation 1466/97, broadly provisioning 'more stringent surveillance' of the Stability Programmes submitted by EU Member States, and Regulation 1177/2011 is the second main SGP revision that amends Regulation 1467/97 pertaining to the Excessive Deficit Procedure and introducing similar provisions to Regulation 1175/2011 in terms of monitoring.

[30] Treaty on Stability, Coordination and Governance in the Economic and Monetary Union, Brussels, 1 February 2012, in force January 2013, available at: www.consilium .europa.eu/media/20399/stootscg26_en12.pdf; P. Novak, 'Article 136 TFEU, ESM, Fiscal Stability Treaty – ratification requirements and present situation in the Member States' (2013), available at: www.europarl.europa.eu/meetdocs/2009_2014/documents/afco/dv/2013-06-12_pe462455-v16_ /2013-06-12_pe462455-v16_en.pdf.

and convergence amongst euro area Member States'.[31] Finally, the sixth EU-wide measure was the Banking Union, decided in principle during late-June 2012 and established during 2013–2015.[32]

5.4 ANALYSIS OF SUSTAINABILITY OF EU-WIDE CRISIS MEASURES

Given the aforementioned outline of the scholarship relevant to sustainability and sustainable development, there are two main issues to be examined across the EU framework, whether pre- or post-crisis. The first is the austerity-based approach towards responding to the crisis. There are questions to be raised in terms of how this impacts the preserved stock as well as

[31] Memo of the European Commission, available at http://europa.eu/rapid/press-release_MEMO-13-457_en.htm. Regulations of the European Parliament and the Council (EU) No 472/2013 on the strengthening of economic and budgetary surveillance of Member States in the euro area experiencing or threatened with serious difficulties with respect to their financial stability, and (EU) 473/2013 on common provisions for monitoring and assessing draft budgetary plans and ensuring the correction of excessive deficit of the Member States in the euro area (20134) *Official Journal* L140. The first one focuses, inter alia, on enhanced budgetary surveillance of Eurozone MS under financial stress or already under a financial assistance programme or simply when 'threatened with serious financial difficulties', while the second concerns the supranational evaluation, by the European Commission and Eurogroup, of Eurozone Member State national budgets before their enactment by relevant national provisions.

[32] Consisting of the Single Supervisory Mechanism, the Single Resolution Mechanism, and the Single Rulebook, in Communication from the Commission to the European Parliament and the Council: A Roadmap towards a Banking Union (2012), available at: https://eur-lex.europa.eu/legal-content/EN/TXT/PDF/?uri=CELEX:52012DC0510&from=EN, pp. 1 and 7–10. Also in Council Regulation (EU) No 1024/2013 conferring specific tasks on the European Central Bank concerning policies relating to the prudential supervision of credit institutions and Regulation (EU) No 1022/2013 of the European Parliament and of the Council amending Regulation (EU) No 1093/2010 establishing a European Supervisory Authority (European Banking Authority) as regards the conferral of specific tasks on the European Central Bank pursuant to Council Regulation (EU) No 1024/2013(2013) *Official Journal* L287, Directives of the European Parliament and of the Council 2013/36/EU on access to the activity of credit institutions and the prudential supervision of credit institutions and investment firms, amending Directive 2002/87/EC and repealing Directives 2006/48/EC and 2006/49/EC (2013) *Official Journal* L176, and 2014/59/EU establishing a framework for the recovery and resolution of credit institutions and investment firms and amending Council Directive 82/891/EEC, and Directives 2001/24/EC, 2002/47/EC, 2004/25/EC, 2005/56/EC, 2007/36/EC, 2011/35/EU, 2012/30/EU and 2013/36/EU, and Regulations (EU) No 1093/2010 and (EU) No 648/2012, of the European Parliament and of the Council (2014) *Official Journal* L173, and 2014/49/EU on deposit guarantee schemes (2014) *Official Journal* L173, and Regulations of the European Parliament and of the Council (EU) No 575/2013 on prudential requirements for credit institutions and investment firms and amending Regulation (EU) No 648/2012 (2013) *Official Journal* L176, (EU) No 806/2014 establishing uniform rules and a uniform procedure for the resolution of credit institutions and certain investment firms in the framework of a Single Resolution Mechanism and a Single Resolution Fund and amending Regulation (EU) No 1093/2010 (2014) *Official Journal* L225.

the economic and societal factors of current generations (thus, by extension, impacting the development of human value in future generations). The second issue is the delegation of decision-making authority from politically based to technocratic-founded supranational institutions. Even if it is accepted that an ordoliberal direction of the EU is one that promotes sustainability,[33] there are concerns raised in terms of better coordination and increased political and economic integration. This would contribute better preparedness against external shocks (such as the crisis, for example), as well as to a more coherent and less differentiated development for all Member States. It would also provide for maximising utilisation of resources in the short term, and better coordinating development into long-term sustainability.

5.4.1 Pre-Crisis Framework Sustainability

The first question to be addressed is whether the EU operated in a sustainable manner before the crisis. The preventive part of the SGP did include provisions relevant to sustainable growth, particularly in relation to output and employment, to be achieved through 'the objective of sound government finances' as well as in relation to 'sustainable exchange rate stability', to be achieved by 'lasting convergence of economic fundamentals'. In addition, it was suggested that stability and convergence programmes submitted by Member States provide 'an essential basis ... for strong sustainable growth conducive to employment creation'.[34]

However, these provisions yielded a number of problems and were often not entirely implemented. First, the intensely ordoliberal foundations of the Eurozone, originating primarily with Germany, created several problems. Germany, with a very strong ordoliberal tradition, was only willing to participate in the Economic and Monetary Union provided that this tradition was not compromised.[35] Hence, it exerted substantial influence in its design, primarily

[33] Ordoliberalism was developed during the 1930s by Walter Eucken, Franz Böhm and Hans Grossmann-Doerth in Germany. It proposes a more regulated approach to the laissez-faire economics of liberalism, with the state actively pursuing the maintenance of a free market economy by being limited but able to intervene where that is necessary (e.g. monopolies): G. Schnyder and M. Siems, 'The Ordoliberal Variety of Neoliberalism' in S. J. Konzelmann and M. Fovargue-Davies (eds.), *Banking Systems in the Crisis: The Faces of Liberal Capitalism* (Abingdon: Routledge, 2013), p. 3; R. Sally, 'Ordoliberalism and the Social Market: Classical Political Economy from Germany' (1996) 2 *New Political Economy*, 233–257.

[34] Council Regulations 1466/97 and 1467/97.

[35] G. Majone, 'Rethinking European Integration After the Debt Crisis' (2012) 3/2012 *The European Institution University College of London Working Paper*, 10, available at: www.ucl.ac.uk/european-institute/analysis-publications/publications/WP3.pdf.

in succeeding to ensure that the concept of 'sound money' was a key commitment,[36] undertaken by all Member States in relation to their finances.[37] However, the strict implementation of ordoliberalism within the Economic and Monetary Union has, it has been argued, produced adverse results.[38]

Sound public finances ensure a better financial situation for a country, thus leading to improved financial and also overall sustainability. However, budgetary indiscipline is not the only problem leading to economic difficulties.[39] Economic booms on the periphery of the Eurozone, which were often accompanied by cheap capital inflows by banks in more economically powerful Eurozone Member States (Germany, France, etc.) inevitably led to a loss of competitiveness. The governments of the periphery Eurozone Member States had little ability to restore this, as Eurozone participation had removed fiscal policy alternatives that would otherwise have been available to them.[40] This effect was further intensified by the fact that within the ordo-liberal-oriented environment, the primary focus was placed on price stability, which was misaligned with the economic and socio-political traditions of the periphery Member States.[41] This resulted in trade imbalances and growth disequilibria, further weakening the import-led, deficit-expanding economy of the periphery Eurozone Member States vis-à-vis the export-led, highly competitive economies of the core Eurozone Member States.[42] Therefore, the application of this model and the construction of the Eurozone, and more generally the EU around it, seems to have fostered extensive imbalances that eventually led to the creation of a system that is essentially unsustainable. While there has been legislative focus on sustainability, the system parameters established not only did not provide for its development, but also potentially hindered it.

---

[36] This is enshrined as an obligation in Article 119(3) of the TFEU, where it is stipulated that EU Member States are to maintain 'sound public finances'.

[37] G. Strange, 'The Euro, Social Democracy and International Monetary Power: A Critique of New Constitutionalism' (2011) *Globalizations*, 9, 257–272 at 261.

[38] A. Regan, 'The Political Economy of Social Pacts in the EMU: Irish Liberal Market Corporatism in Crisis' (2012) 17 *New Political Economy*, 465–491 at 473.

[39] Ibid., p. 479.

[40] F. Scharpf, 'Monetary Union, Fiscal Crisis and the Preemption of Democracy' (2011) 11/11, *Max Planck Institute for The Study of Societies MPIfG Discussion Paper* 16–8; P. Tsoukala, 'Narratives of the European Crisis and the Future of (Social)Europe' (2013) 48 *Texas International Law Journal*, 241–266 at 249.

[41] Regan, 'The Political Economy of Social Pacts in the EMU: Irish Liberal Market Corporatism in Crisis', 470–472; E. Mourlon-Druol 'Don't Blame the Euro: Historical Reflections on the Roots of the Eurozone Crisis' (2014) 37 *West European Politics*, 1282–1296 at 1283–1284.

[42] M. Otero-Iglesias, 'Stateless Euro: The Euro Crisis and the Revenge of the Chartalist Theory of Money' (2014) *Journal of Common Market Studies*, 1–16 at 1.

Even if it is argued that the SGP did provide for sustainability in the form of economic policy convergence, it was often not implemented, particularly in regard to more economically powerful Member States, further reinforcing the existence and continuation of imbalances and thus harming sustainability. For example, in 2005, France and Germany pushed for more relaxed SGP criteria and, while they had qualified for an Excessive Deficit Procedure, they, unlike other Eurozone Member States (e.g. Portugal), were successful in halting the process.[43] Given the aforementioned observations, the pre-crisis EU framework was mostly unsustainable. It seemed to ascribe to ordoliberal foundations, which proved to further reinforce, instead of eliminating, imbalances and disequilibria across the Eurozone. In addition, delegation to technocratic institutions, towards an, ideally, more objective and uniform application of rules, was minimal, with most of the decision-making authority retained in political intergovernmental actors. This led to the misapplication of or even nonconformity with the established rules.

5.4.2 *Sustainability of EU-wide Crisis Measures*

Although references to sustainability throughout the EU-wide crisis measures have somewhat increased compared with the pre-crisis environment, their application falls short of expectations. References to sustainability almost exclusively concern public finance and debt of Member States,[44] with only a few references to growth and employment that are of a general nature.[45]

The more encouraging reference by far is in the EPP, which states its main aim as increasing competitiveness, which 'will help the EU grow fast and more sustainably in the medium and long term'.[46] Sustainability here is addressed

---

[43] C. De La Porte and E. Hanke, 'A New Era of European Integration? Governance of Labour Market and Social Policy Since the Sovereign Debt Crisis' (2015) 13 *Comparative European Politics Studies*, 8–28; Majone, 'Rethinking European Integration After the Debt Crisis'; A. Annett, M. Estevão, H. Faruqee, X. Debrun, J.-J. Hallaert, 'International Monetary Fund: Euro Area Policies' (2004) No 04/235 *IMF Country Report*, available at: www.imf.org/external/pubs/ft/scr/2004/cr04235.pdf, at 86–89.

[44] Recital 25 and Article 9(2)(d) of Directive 2011/5/EU; Recitals 1 and 3 of Regulation 1174/2011; Recitals 1, 3, 9, 17, 21, 22 and Articles 1(5), 1(6), 1(8), 1(9), 1(10), 1(12), 1(13) of Regulation 1175/2011; Recital 1 of Regulation 1176/2011, Recital 18 and Articles 2, 6, 7, 14 of Regulation 472/2013; Recital 2, 17, 24, 27, 32 and Articles 5(2)(c), 6(4), 9(2) of Regulation 473/2013; Recital 7 of Regulation 407/2010; Recitals 1, 3, 6, 12, 16, 17, 20, and Articles 1(2)(c), 1(4)(c), 1(6) of Regulation 1177/2011; Articles 2(1)(a) and 2(3), of the EFSF Framework Agreement; Articles 4(4) and 13(1)(b) of the ESM Treaty; Articles 3(1) and 9 of the TSCG.

[45] For example, see Article 1 of the TSCG, provisioning the adoption of rules supporting the EU's 'objectives for sustainable growth, employment, competitiveness and social cohesion'.

[46] European Council 24/25 March 2011, 13.

primarily in relation to public finances, with a particular focus on social welfare. However, considering the essentially voluntary nature of the EPP, its implementation has been far from full, with few, if any, examples (between 2011 and 2016 only Ireland had a separate document for EPP commitments, and only for a few years).[47] This is unsurprising because of the salience of related policies for national governments.

In terms of the ordoliberal foundations of the Eurozone (and more broadly the EU), austerity-based politics surged throughout the crisis. All three financial-assistance mechanisms established (EFSM, EFSF SA, ESM), included strict policy conditionality that accompanied any provision of assistance. The policies included were geared towards increased austerity and further ordoliberalisation. This is also evident from the participation of the International Monetary Fund (IMF), culminating in its now permanent involvement in the ESM.[48] The strict application of austerity policies has caused considerable damage to the sustainable development of those Member States in which they are employed. First, it is worth highlighting that sustainability is referenced minimally across the three mechanisms, and is focused exclusively on either public finances or debt. Hence, a broader conceptualisation of socio-political or ecological sustainability is entirely absent, which is surprising given the considerable impact of the assistance programmes on those issues. Secondly, the implementation of austerity in a pro-cyclical manner (e.g. wage cuts during a recession) may result in a Sisyphean situation: more austerity leads to more lending, which leads to an increase in the state's already sizeable debt and so on. For example, Greece, the first Eurozone Member State to request financial assistance, lost 25.5 per cent of its gross domestic product (GDP) between 2008 and 2013.[49] Even when related to debt sustainability, there is still an adverse effect, with the debt (as a percentage of GDP) of all Member States under financial assistance programmes spiralling upwards after the programmes to unsustainable levels (especially in the long term).[50]

---

[47] For example in Republic of Ireland, 'Euro plus pact commitments made by Ireland in May 2011: update as of April 2013' (2013), available at: http://ec.europa.eu/europe2020/pdf/nd/europact2013_ireland_en.pdf.

[48] A. Kyriakidis, 'Input or Output? Evaluation of the EU Democratic Deficit Approaches after the Eurozone Crisis' (2016), in D. Anagnostopoulou, I. Papadopoulos and L. Papadopoulou (eds.), *The EU at a Crossroads: Challenges and Perspectives* (Cambridge: Cambridge Scholars Publishing, 2016), pp. 212–234 at 218–219.

[49] According to Eurostat statistics, available at: https://appsso.eurostat.ec.europa.eu/nui/show .do?dataset=nama_10_gdp&lang=en.

[50] Increase from the year before each Member State's Memorandum of Understanding until 2015: Greece 40 per cent, Ireland 52 per cent, Portugal 34 per cent, Spain 43 per cent, Cyprus 66 per cent (Eurostat statistics available at: http://ec.europa.eu/eurostat/tgm/table.do?tab=tabl e&init=1&language=en&pcode=tsdde410&plugin=1).

The conclusions in relation to enhanced coordination EU-wide crisis measures are similar. The six-pack, the SGP's reinforcement, further strengthens provisions relating to budgetary discipline and sound finances. Chapter 4 of Directive 2011/85/EU introduces the three-year Medium-Term Budgetary Framework as an integral part of the SGP: it stipulates that specific numerical values should exist within the EU Member States' national budgets to ensure compliance with the deficit/debt targets. Chapter 3 of Regulation 1173/2011, among others, calls for new and stricter sanctions within the Eurozone in case of deficit/debt violations. Articles 3 and 4 of Regulation 1174/2011 introduce fines for macro-economic imbalances within the Eurozone.

Regulation 1176/2011 (Article 5), aiming to correct macro-economic imbalances that occur within the entire EU, establishes surveillance that includes possible missions 'to Member States by the Commission, in liaison with the European Central Bank'. The Regulation (Chapter 3) also introduces the 'excessive imbalance procedure', under which the EU Member State concerned must provide a plan and timetable of the implementation of relevant Council of Ministers recommendations. Article 1(3) of Regulation 1175/2011 introduces the concept of the European Semester, through which the Council of Ministers surveys and reviews how EU Member States apply the broad economic guidelines and what measures are taken to prevent macro-economic imbalances. Regulation 1177/2011 (Article 1) introduces similar provisions in terms of monitoring.

Similar new provisions are also included in the two-pack. Regulation 472/2013 (especially articles 2–3) introduces the process of enhanced surveillance, to be applied to Eurozone Member States under financial assistance or simply when 'threatened with serious financial difficulties'. The process involves the preparation of a Macroeconomic Adjustment Programme by the Member State concerned, and surveillance is conducted by the European Commission, the European Central Bank and the IMF.

Regulation 473/2013 (Chapters 3 and 4) introduces the evaluation by the European Commission and the Eurogroup of Eurozone Member States' national budgets before their national enactment. If discrepancies or non-compliance with obligations (e.g. SGP) are found, the Member State concerned needs to modify the budget and then re-submit it. In addition, the Regulation (Article 8) provisions that Eurozone Member States are to 'report ex ante on their public debt issuance plans to the Eurogroup and the Commission'. This Regulation also introduces (Article 9) the Economic Partnership Programme, to be submitted by a Eurozone Member State that runs an excessive deficit (Member States under Programmes of Regulation 472/2013 are exempted).

Finally, the TSCG includes provisions that aim at further enhancing the ordoliberal structure of the Eurozone, which are in addition to the existing

EU framework, such as *ex ante* reporting on debt issuance (Article 6) and discussion among all Eurozone Member States of major economic reforms to be undertaken by one of them (Article 11). The TSCG also provides for specific limits for when a budget of a Member State is to be considered balanced (maximum 0.5 per cent GDP structural deficit) and for a specific 1/20 rate per year reduction of the debt if it is in excess of 60 per cent GDP, going beyond what is referenced within the EU Treaties (Articles 1–3, 5). Perhaps the most important provision relating to ordoliberal reinforcement is the obligation (Article 3) undertaken by participating Member States to introduce a correction mechanism to be activated automatically when divergence from medium-term budgetary targets is observed, to be established through 'provisions of binding force and permanent character, preferably constitutional'.

All these elements demonstrate the considerable reinforcement of the ordoliberal foundations of both the Eurozone and EU, introducing many additional, and mostly novel, processes in relation to budgetary discipline. This framework may further adversely impact sustainable development, prolonging disequilibria and imbalances. Budgetary discipline and enhanced coordination now take place in a much stricter framework and include many more new processes than the previous version of the SGP. However, insistence on budgetary discipline can cause considerable imbalances and, by extension, incur adverse consequences in relation to medium- and long-term sustainability. This also makes fortification against external shocks unsustainable, in that it is, essentially, uneven: Member States that fit this model are very well prepared, while Member States for which this model is not well fitted to their socio-political and economic traditions may actually be made even weaker.

In terms of the delegation to and increase in the decision-making authority of supranational technocratic institutions vis-à-vis political, intergovernmental actors, this could be indicative of a more equal, objective and consistent application of the relevant provisions, and thus foster sustainable development. The European Commission in particular has acquired considerably more decision-making authority through the crisis measures regarding the enforcement of rules of budgetary monitoring and discipline. In particular, mostly in relation to the six-pack, there is a widespread introduction of reverse qualified majority voting for European Commission acts. These acts, mainly concerning breaches of SGP obligations, including interest and non-interest-bearing deposits and fines, as well as corrective actions, are considered automatically adopted unless a blocking majority is formed in the Council of Ministers.[51] Obviously, it is much more difficult to form a blocking majority than to form a

---

[51] Regulations 1173/2011, 1174/2011, 1176/2011.

minority opposition under regular qualified majority voting, and hence many of the European Commission's acts should now be enacted much more easily than before. Furthermore, the European Commission has also acquired the ability to conduct in-depth and enhanced surveillance reviews and on-site missions in EU Member States that are in breach of SGP obligations,[52] in many cases even when an EU Member State is merely at risk of being affected by macro-economic imbalances.

However, while in theory the more objective and accurate application of the rules by the European Commission, as opposed to the politically based Council of Ministers, would lead to an increase in sustainable development for the Eurozone and EU, in reality there have been rather modest changes compared with the pre-crisis SGP framework. An example is the case of Spain and Portugal during the summer of 2016, when the Council of Ministers decided that they qualified for an SGP obligation violation (Excessive Deficit Procedure).[53] In this case, according to the six-pack, the European Commission had to impose a fine that applies automatically unless a majority is achieved in the Council of Ministers. However, in what seemed to repeat the 2005 France/Germany situation, the European Commission eventually decided not to impose the fine.[54] There were reports that then German Finance Minister Wolfgang Schäuble, being a supporter of intergovernmental authority over supranational technocracy and also eager to avoid a political situation that might result in the centre-right Spanish government being out of office, actively lobbied against the imposition of a fine prior to the Commission's college meeting.[55] In effect, this, similarly to 2005, undermined the new, reinforced SGP rules.

A similar surge to the authority of the Commission is observed across the two-pack. Through the process of enhanced surveillance of Regulation 472/2013 (Articles 2–3), the Commission (along with the European Central Bank and IMF) can conduct on-site monitoring of Eurozone Member States in relation to measures to be assumed and/or the Macroeconomic Adjustment Programme. In Regulation 473/2013 (Article 7), it is provisioned that Eurozone Member States must submit their budgetary plans to the European Commission for evaluation before they become binding at the national level, and it can request modifications. In other words, the European Commission

---

[52] Ibid. and Regulation 1175/2011.

[53] Press release of the European Commission, available at: https://europa.eu/rapid/press-release_IP-16-2625_el.htm.

[54] The Commission's argument was that 'both Member States have submitted a reasoned request to cancel the fine …' (ibid.).

[55] F. Eder, 'Wolfgang Schäuble Bails Out Spain, Portugal', *Politico*, 27 July 2016.

can now directly influence the budget of Eurozone Member States, even before national elected representatives adopt it. Furthermore, the European Commission is responsible (Article 9) for monitoring compliance with the Partnership program that is submitted by Eurozone Member States, and this includes the structural reforms necessary to correct an excessive deficit.

The aforementioned provisions of the two-pack seem to promote sustainability through better economic policy coordination between Eurozone Member States. However, there are issues to be raised in terms of the budgetary supranational oversight process established by Regulation 473/2013, since the budget is a key national policy area in which multiple national civil and institutional stakeholders are involved. As such, the overview of the budgetary plan by supranational actors, even before the national representative assembly of each Member State enacts it, reduces the input of these stakeholders and thus could create considerable problems for sustainable development.

Increase in the decision-making capacity of supranational technocratic actors is not confined to the Commission. Another example is the European Supervisory Authorities, which, after their upgrade are able to, inter alia, set supervisory standards, manage cooperation with and between national supervisors, adopt decisions that are binding to individual institutions, license EU-wide institutions and so on, thereby providing better coordination and cooperation between the different national processes and institutions.[56] In this case, there seems to be some improvement and enhanced coordination and more centralised and cohesive decision-making relevant to financial supervision, which can both improve the operation of the financial sector across the EU (thus reducing disequilibria) and also better shield it from external shocks, thus improving sustainability.

Similar augmenting in the decision-making capacity of technocratic, supranational institutions occurs in the Banking Union where, through the Single Supervisory Mechanism, the European Central Bank assumes a greater role in supervising banks as the primary relevant regulation, 1024/2013, 'confers on the ECB specific tasks concerning policies relating to the prudential supervision of credit institutions', thus making supervision more centralised and supranational (Article 1). The Single Resolution Mechanism assumes the responsibility for the resolution of financially failed banks of Member States from the national level, and the Single Rulebook, inter alia, establishes capital requirements.[57]

---

[56] Report of the High-Level Group on Financial Supervision in the EU, pp. 47–49, 57, available at: https://ec.europa.eu/economy_finance/publications/pages/publication14527_en.pdf.

[57] References as in fn.45.

5.5 CONCLUSION

This chapter has evaluated the sustainability of the new structure of the Eurozone/EU created after the financial crisis. The EU-wide measures assumed during the crisis were imposed to address several weaknesses in the EU's operating framework, thus better shielding it from outside shocks, as well as gearing its development to a more sustainable direction. Sustainability, as a concept, lacks a comprehensive definition across the relevant literature. However, scholars do seem to agree to some of its foundational characteristics, primarily focused on sustainable development. The first one is the temporal element; that is, that future generations need to be taken into consideration when utilising resources in the present. The aim is to provide for an equitable and adequate distribution of resources in the present, while ensuring that they will also be able to be enjoyed in the future. The second one is the need to include socio-political and ecological factors in the evaluation of sustainability, and not just confining it to economic indicators. Exclusive focus on economics might disregard the contribution of other factors to more sustainable living standards for both present and future generations. The third one is the ability of a system that can adequately respond to external shocks, which primarily implies the existence of a capital stock that could potentially be used in unforeseen circumstances.

The evaluation of the EU-wide crisis measures in relation to their sustainability has yielded mixed to negative results. The pre-crisis EU and Eurozone operating framework, with strong ordoliberal foundations, weak technocratic institutions and few references to sustainability, harboured extensive imbalances and created disequilibria across the entirety of the EU, and especially between Eurozone Member States. The new, modified operating framework has introduced some improvements to this process, but overall sustainability still remains unachieved. The references to sustainability have increased, albeit they are still mostly confined to financial issues, and thus they lack the consideration of broader socio-political and ecological perspectives, as required for true sustainability to be achieved. This is concurrent with a substantial reinforcement of the ordoliberal foundations of the EU across the measures implemented, with a particular focus on Eurozone Member States. This system, which has definitely been the primary cause for extensive imbalances across the Eurozone, and EU, has been modified to include even more rules for even stricter budgetary discipline, with enhanced sanctions upon non-compliance.

In addition, financial assistance, when provided, is accompanied by austerity policies that not only do not further sustainability in the Member States where they are implemented, but also potentially severely harm it. Lastly, in relation to technocratic, supranational authority, the considerable increase in its decision-making capacity, especially in relation to the implementation of rules and the contribution to a more coordinated policy-making process, could arguably provide for a more sustainable environment that is less prone to shocks. However, the implementation of the provisions has fallen considerably short of the desired level of objectivity and uniformity in rule-enforcement.

So where do we stand? The measures assumed during the Eurozone crisis definitely have elements that can further sustainable development within the Eurozone. Consider, for example, the creation of a Eurozone-targeted financial assistance mechanism (increased fortification), the evaluation of the macro-economic effect of policies through the Excessive Imbalance Procedure (EIP) or the enhanced coordination of pension systems through the European Insurance and Occupational Pensions Authority (EIOPA). However, these measures are still heavily influenced by particular presuppositions of a specific economic paradigm, and thus, while advantageous in principle, they can be quite detrimental in practice (e.g. the EIP, if applied with strict fiscal discipline in mind, can result in adverse consequences for the economy).

So, in order to improve sustainability within the Eurozone, additional steps are needed. First, there needs to be a decoupling of the admittedly improved (sustainability-wise) crisis measures and implementation in accordance with particular ideological assumptions (ordoliberalism). Secondly, while technocratic institutions have been considerably reinforced, they still fall short of complete independence, and thus having a meaningful impact on policies, while at the same time lack democratic oversight. Simplification of the operating framework of all the different institutions and actors involved in the policy-making process, as well as their legal and regulatory frameworks, would make their impact considerably quicker and stronger, and would also improve democratic oversight. In conclusion, while the EU-wide measures assumed in light of the Eurozone crisis offer some improvements in terms of sustainability, compared with the previous status quo, overall there is still some way to go before a truly sustainable Eurozone operating framework is achieved. However, moves are on the right track.

6

The Economic Adjustment Programmes
of Greece (2010–2018): Why Failure?

Panagiotis Liargovas and Voula Kratimenou

6.1 INTRODUCTION

From May 2010 until August 2018, Greece was under the so-called economic adjustment programmes. The first one was agreed between Greece and the troika: the European Commission, the European Central Bank (ECB) and the International Monetary Fund (IMF), on 2 May 2010. It was accompanied with a three-year €110 billion loan to Greece (which was deprived from the private capital markets) in order to avoid a sovereign default. The loan was conditional on the implementation of austerity measures to restore the fiscal balance and privatisation of government assets to keep the debt pile sustainable, as well as implementation of structural reforms to improve competitiveness and growth prospects. In October 2011, Eurozone leaders consequently agreed to offer a second €130 billion loan to Greece, conditional not only on the implementation of another austerity package (combined with the continued demands for privatisation and structural reforms outlined in the first programme), but also on a restructuring of all Greek public debt held by private creditors. In August 2015, a third programme was agreed, offering Greece an additional €86 billion loan. In 2018, the third programme was concluded. Does this delay reflect the failure of economic adjustment programmes in the case of Greece?

Yes, although we recognise that the answer is rather complex for a number of reasons. First, economic adjustment programmes are based on forecasts that might change owing to external shocks. However, this does not mean that these programmes fail. Moreover, programme parameters are often subject to renegotiation. Hence, initial conditions are very likely to change. Furthermore, not all policy decisions taken by a country result from the economic adjustment programme; that is, national authorities often decide to implement policies that are not compatible or consistent with the programme. In addition, programme success is contingent on implementation by national authorities. If the government is unable or unwilling to fully implement the programme, this does not necessarily mean that the programme itself was defective. Finally, programme outcomes are affected by spillovers from other countries. For example, a possible recession in the Eurozone has a negative effect on the Greek economy.

This chapter is structured as follows: Section 6.2 compares some key macro-economic indicators of Greece in 2008 (one year before the crisis) and in 2013, which was the first year with some positive economic signs. But the social crisis in 2013 was at its nadir. Unemployment rate surged to 27.3 per cent and people at risk of poverty or social exclusion surged to 35.7 per cent. Section 6.3 discusses the period 2015–2018, at the beginning of which the Greek economy deteriorated again and an additional economic adjustment programme was implemented. Section 6.3 also offers some explanations as to why Greece went through all these economic adjustment programmes for such a long period. Finally, Section 6.4 offers some concluding remarks regarding the factors that might have affected the outcome of the fiscal austerity measures announced in 2010, 2011 and 2015 in Greece.

6.2 GREECE 2008 VERSUS GREECE 2013

What were the fundamentals of the Greek economy in 2008 (Table 6.1 and Figure 6.1)? The country recorded rather disappointing performance in fiscal management (fiscal deficit of around 10 per cent of gross domestic product (GDP)). There was also a huge deficit in the Current Account balance of around 15 per cent of GDP. On the other hand, Greece's unemployment rate was at a record low (7.7 per cent). GDP per capita was at a record high, reaching €21,000. A completely different picture appears in 2013. GDP per capita had fallen to €16,500, unemployment had skyrocketed to 27.3 per cent and people at risk of poverty or social exclusion had reached 35.7 per cent. At the same time, the fiscal situation was improved considerably with positive primary and current account balances. By the end of 2013, Greece was no longer the country with the highest deficits in the Eurozone. It had improved its position in the most important fiscal indicators.[1]

The fiscal adjustment contributed to the reduction in uncertainty and the improvement in both the business climate and the country's position in the international rankings,[2] but at the same time the long-term prospects for

---

[1]   According to Eurostat data.
[2]   See, for example, Doing Business, 'Doing Business, 2014: Understanding Regulations for Small and Medium-Size Enterprises' (2014), 11th edition *Doing Business series*, World Bank and IFC.

TABLE 6.1 *Fiscal and social indicators in Greece, 2008 and 2013*

Variables	2008	2013
General government primary balance*	−4.8	0.8
General government balance*	−10	−3.2
current account balance*	−15	0.7
inflation**	4.2	−0.9
General government gross debt*	113	175
People at risk of poverty or social exclusion	28.1	35.7
unemployment rate ***	7.7	27.3
GDP per capita****	21,000	16,500

Note: *% GDP, ** per cent change, average consumer prices, # percentage of total population, *** per cent of total labour force, **** current market prices in €.
Source: IMF World Economic Outlook database, October 2014, Eurostat (published data)

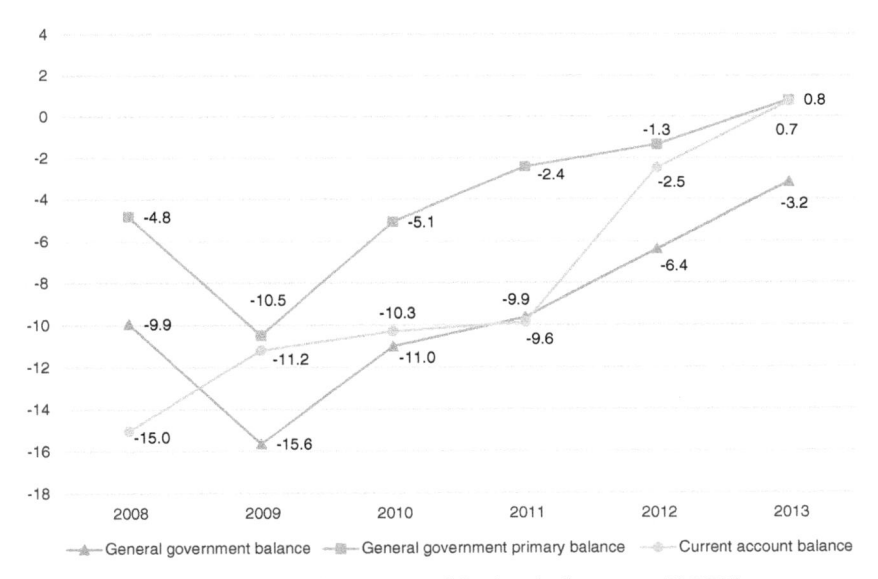

FIGURE 6.1 *The achievements of the fiscal adjustment (%GDP).*

recovery weakened owing to widening social inequality and unemployment that soared to unprecedented levels. Other uncertainties were related to political stability. The interim report of the Bank of Greece for monetary policy stated that the political climate, which showed elements of polarisation, created problems in a period during which a broad political consensus was required.[3]

3 Bank of Greece, 'Monetary Policy', interim report, December 2013.

The mixed picture of 2013 was repeated in 2014. According to Greek National Accounts, in 2014, GDP growth was positive at 0.8 per cent for the first time since 2008. Moreover, the latest figures provided by the Hellenic Statistical Authority (ELSTAT) showed that the number of employed persons increased by 1 per cent in July compared with June, while the number of the unemployed fell by 0.9 per cent. This development was based on (1) the substantial increase in tourism, as reflected in the approximately 30 per cent increase in arrivals; (2) the stabilisation of private consumption, which was enhanced by the increase of employment in the private sector of the economy; (3) the small rise in investment in fixed capital; and (4) the successful implementation of the 2014 budget, which led to a high primary surplus.

Moreover, some reforms, especially in the labour market, had begun to bear fruit. Finally, several measures had improved the international competitiveness of the Greek economy. In particular, among the 144 countries, Greece was ranked 81st in 2014, compared to 91st position a year earlier.[4]

In contrast to the developments noted here, a number of indicators for social justice (e.g. youth unemployment, poverty, inequality, extreme poverty of several groups) indicated that the macro-economic equilibrium that had been achieved was fragile.[5] These problems would threaten any economic progress.

The discussion here poses two questions: First, can a growth model with high consumption, low unemployment and increasing deficits be sustainable over time? Secondly, and by the same token, can a growth model with a balanced fiscal situation alongside social imbalances be sustainable over time? Based on the Greek experience, the answer is negative in both cases.

6.2.1 Recession again, in 2015, and a Third Economic Adjustment Programme

Greece's economy deteriorated as the country returned to a recessionary trend in the first half of 2015. There were many reasons for this development. First, the national elections and then the non-agreement with the Institutions (the troika) eventually affected businesses' investment decisions, as well as consumption. Additionally, the combination of lean liquidity by a bank financing tool, Emergency Liquidity Assistance, and the increased

---

[4] See the World Economic Forum report on competitiveness, available at: http://reports.weforum.org/global-competitiveness-report-2014-2015/.pdf.

[5] See Parliamentary Budget Office, 'Quarterly Report', Hellenic Parliament, Athens, various issues.

deposits outflow from Greek banks exacerbated the situation. Business closures continued and unemployment started to rise again, while tourism was also threatened.[6] In sum, uncertainty was the main reason that led the country back to recession.

The economic situation was aggravated owing to the government's withdrawal from negotiations, the expiration of the second economic adjustment programme, the discontinuation of loans repayment to the IMF, capital controls and a referendum on 5 July 2015.[7] The country seemed to be moving towards a chaotic default. As recognised by the prime minister, Alexis Tsipras, in a parliamentary speech on 15 July 2015,[8] the country faced a dilemma: whether to accept a new agreement with its EU partners (as eventually happened on 12 July 2015),[9] or go bankrupt and leave the Eurozone, detached from EU solidarity mechanisms.

Finally, an agreement was made between the Greek government and the European Stability Mechanism for a new loan. This agreement, despite the political difficulties, was – from a prosperity point of view – preferable to the continuation of uncertain conditions or a possible chaotic default. The August 2015 agreement secured Greece's financial needs for the next three years, thus offering time to ease the recession and take measures that would lead to a path of economic development.

The third economic adjustment programme (like the preceding ones) was a broad and basically liberal programme for Greek economy modernisation and reform; this encompassed the policies of the social state, which was fully opposed to the change of legacy structures and traditional clientelistic attitudes, and held incompatible views about the world and the country.[10] The paradigm that was incorporated by the new programme was characterised by fiscal equilibrium, healthy market competition and lessening state size via privatisations and other measures, all aimed at restoring the country to sustainable development paces. At the same time, however, it called for a better state, capable of coping with environmental challenges (initiatives including waste recycling and forest maps), of rationalising social policy through new

---

[6] Ibid.

[7] The referendum was to decide whether Greece should accept the agreement imposed by the country's European creditors or not.

[8] See 'Proceedings of plenary meeting of Parliament 15 July 2015', available at: www .hellenicparliament.gr.

[9] See *Euro Summit Statement*, Brussels, 12 July 2015.

[10] See P. Kazakos, 'Stabilization and Reform in a Statist Regime, 1974–2011', in P. Liargovas (ed.), *Greece, Economics, Political and Social Issues* (New York: Nova Science Publishers, 2001), pp. 11–32.

solidarity institutions, of making justice more functional and public admin-istration more effective and of optimising the quality of its services (health, etc.).[11] Not overlooking trade-off issues, we note that the paradigm seeks to balance the economic goal of growth through open markets with social and environmental goals presupposing an active and effective state, which is also effective against individual interests. However, several segments of the politi-cal world, as well as social groups defending their traditional sets of interests, were not convinced by the programme's relevance and correctness, and there-fore did not embrace it. According to the majority of surveys, over 67 per cent of citizens held the view that the third economic adjustment programme pointed in the wrong direction.[12]

On 16 June 2016, Greece and the EU institutions concluded a 'Supplemental Memorandum of Understanding (MoU)', following adoption by the Hellenic Parliament of a series of preconditions and prior obligations, as well as adop-tion by the government of relevant ministerial decisions for concluding the first assessment/review. In October 2016, the prime minister announced an upcoming swift completion of the second review within three weeks, thus sending an optimistic message both to businesses and employees. But it was not achieved. Relations with the partners were aggravated, resulting in tech-nical staff-representatives from the institutions departing from Greece, thus prolonging the timescale for the second review.

Delays, combined with negative feelings forming within the IMF over its participation and involvement in the Greek programme, threatened to mini-mise the actual economic benefits. Obviously, the political leadership – to its degree of authority – found it hard to convince various political and social parties about the need to take the necessary measures and legislative initiatives that were to be adopted upon completion of the programme implementa-tion agreement. In other words, for Greece the economic cost of delays and postponements in review processes proved greater than the potential benefits. The most visible, and simplest, indicator of economic cost was the difference between expected growth rates for 2017 and 2018 and those that were actually achieved.[13]

On 21 August 2018, the third economic adjustment programme was completed, bringing an end to nine years of international support and

[11] See Parliamentary Budget Office, *April–June Quarterly Report* (2016), Hellenic Parliament, Athens.

[12] See www.protothema.gr/greece/article/818688/dimoskopisi-9-stous-10-pisteuoun-oti-oi-politikes-litotitas-tha-sunehistoun/.

[13] In 2017, 1.4 per cent instead of 2.7 per cent, and in 2018, 1.9 per cent instead of 2.4 per cent. These data come from ELSTAT and the state budgets for 2017 and 2018.

demonstrating that the recipe had at last borne fruit. However, the programme had heavy and largely unexpected economic and social costs. The Greek economy had undergone a severe depression, a depression that has few historical parallels: since 2009 the country had lost more than a quarter of its real economic output, with dire social consequences. A study by the Athens-based think-tank DiaNeosis found that in 2015, 15 per cent of the population earned below the extreme poverty threshold.[14] In 2009, that number did not exceed 2.2 per cent.

6.3 THE LONG PROCESS OF RECOVERY: WHAT WENT WRONG?

The previous section highlighted the main difficulties that Greece faced in achieving both macro-economic and social stability. In this section, we try to explain what went wrong in Greece's fiscal adjustment programmes by looking at the academic and empirical literature.

6.3.1 *Extremely Frontloaded Austerity*

Until recently, the dominant perception was that austerity should be the priority of economic policy; that is, the rapid elimination of fiscal deficits and therefore the implementation of a tight income policy. Austerity aims at reducing the public debt.[15] This choice is based on a theoretical background: fiscal adjustment induces a fall in real interest rates owing to lower budget deficits. Increased investment and consumption affect positively aggregated demand. Fiscal adjustment (through expenditure cuts and/or tax increases) also has favourable expectation and credibility effects since it is a strong signal to international capital markets; it increases the authorities' solvency and, as a consequence, reduces the yield on government bonds. This effect reinforces the fall in real interest rates, induces positive demand effects and creates very favourable conditions for growth. In addition, fiscal consolidation reduces uncertainty about future fiscal policy, therefore reducing precautionary savings and further increasing aggregate demand.

The extremely front-loaded austerity was the basic requirement in order for Greece to take financial assistance from its international partners. However, there are counter-arguments too: according to the negative Keynesian effects,

---

[14] See www.dianeosis.org/wp-content/uploads/2018/11/social_mobility_report_final_161118.pdf.

[15] See, for example, A. Alesina and S. Ardagna, 'Tales of Fiscal Adjustment' (1998) 27 *Economic Policy*, 489–545, F. Heylen and G. Everaert, and M. Larch and A. Turrini, 'Received Wisdom and Beyond: Lessons from Fiscal Consolidation in the EU', (2011) 217:1 *National Institute Economic Review*, R1–R18.

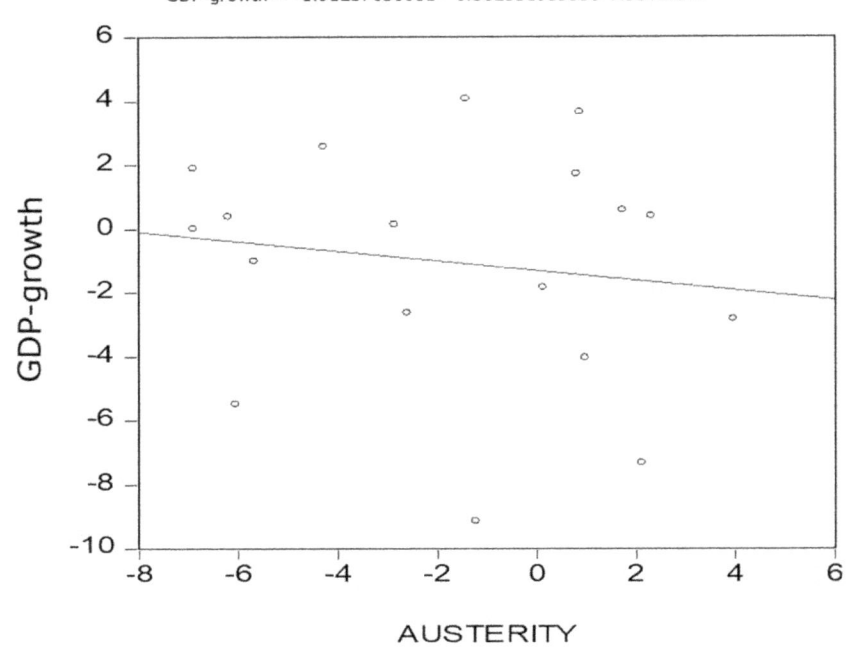

FIGURE 6.2 *Austerity and GDP growth (2010–12). Source: Liargovas and Kratimenou (2016)*

austerity decelerates growth and may also be completely ineffective above a critical threshold. Expenditure cuts or tax increases reduce aggregate demand and public revenue, leading to a vicious cycle. The fall in demand might occur either directly, owing to the decline in government consumption and investment, or indirectly, owing to the decline in private consumption and investment. Evidence from Greece and other countries (Portugal, Italy, Ireland, Spain and Germany) shows that the more severe the austerity, the deeper was the recession in the economy (Figure 6.2) and the larger was the subsequent increase in the debt-to-GDP ratios (Figure 6.3).[16] Recession then led to explosive public debt dynamics (Figure 6.4).

Austerity in the first economic adjustment programme focused on wages and pension cuts. However, in the second and third economic adjustment

[16] See P. De Grauwe and J. Yuemei, 'The legacy of austerity in the Eurozone' (2013), available at: www.ceps.eu/system/files/PGD_YJ%20Austerity.pdf, and V. Kratimenou and P. Liargovas, 'Fiscal Policy Mix and Macroeconomic Performance: Evidence from the EU Member States', paper presented at I.CO.D.ECON (International Conference of Development and Economy), Thessaloniki, June 2016.

FIGURE 6.3 *Austerity and debt to GDP (2008–14). Source: Liargovas and Kratimenou (2016)*

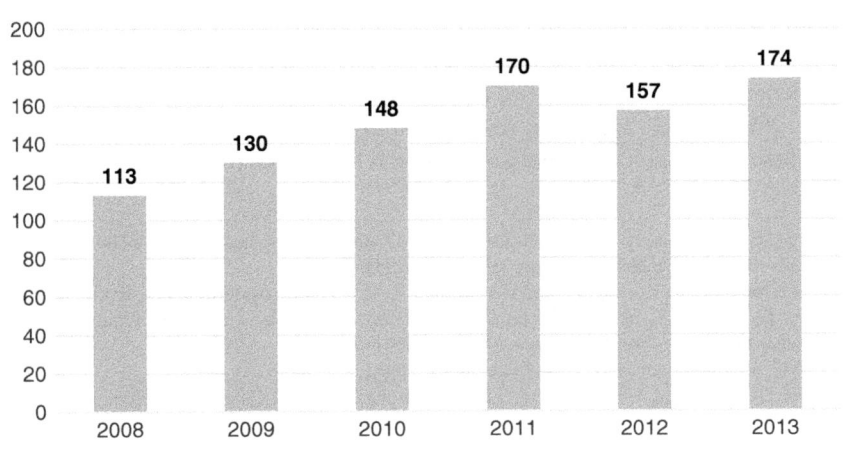

FIGURE 6.4 *Debt as percentage of GDP.*

programmes it took the form of increased taxation (tax-based austerity). In April 2017, at the Eurogroup of Malta, an agreement was reached that extended austerity through further tax increases and pension cuts until 2020.[17] Recent empirical research has shown that fiscal austerity effectiveness is affected by three factors: duration, openness of the economy and institutional quality.[18] In general, austerity is effective in the long term in open economies with high-quality institutions. In other words, austerity programmes may be effective in some specific cases but fail in others that have different characteristics. Greece is one of these latter cases. Its institutions are weak or dysfunctional and its exports base is narrow.[19] Greece was then in an 'austerity trap', where the constant tax increases and expenditure cuts reduced the GDP and increased debt. These two problems (low quality of Institutions and the narrow export base) can only be resolved through reforms; however, reforms needed time to bear fruit, even if they were implemented in a coherent way.

Empirical studies have offered one more argument to explain why austerity led to a much deeper recession than originally projected (Figure 6.5 and Figure 6.6): the models that estimated or predicted the impact of austerity policies on GDP and unemployment used much smaller multipliers, and this led to the underestimation of the consequences of the austerity measures on economic activity.[20] Note that fiscal multipliers show the impact of 1 percentage point of fiscal adjustment (e.g. salary cuts) on GDP. The IMF was the first to recognise that it had underestimated fiscal multipliers and therefore the consequences of the austerity measures on Greece's GDP.[21] As a result, it was believed by a number of researchers that the austerity required by the IMF was ineffective or even self-defeating.[22] This debate affected the political environment concerning the implementation of austerity measures. However, in 2013 further austerity measures could not be easily implemented, owing to the prolonged recession and unemployment that they brought to the Greek economy (Figure 6.5). Moreover, severe austerity could not be socially approved (strikes and protests were very frequent) and it favoured the rise of nationalism

[17] See. Eurogroup President Jeroen Dijsselbloem's statement, 7 April 2017, available at: www.consilium.europa.eu/en/meetings/eurogroup/2017/04/07/.
[18] See, for example, P. Liargovas and V. Kratimenou, 'When Does Austerity Work? Evidence from the EU' (2018), 18 *The Jean Monnet Papers on Political Economy*, University of Peloponnese.
[19] According to the World Economic Forum (2017) index.
[20] IMF, *World Economic Outlook*, October 2012, pp. 41ff.
[21] See. T. Pusch and A. Rannenberg, 'Fiscal Spending Multiplier Calculations based on Input–Output Tables – with an Application to EU Members' (2011), 1/2011 *IWH Discussion Papers*, pp. 6–10.
[22] See O. Blanchard and D. Leigh, 'Growth Forecast Errors and Fiscal Multipliers' (2013) 103(3) *The American Economic Review*, 117–120.

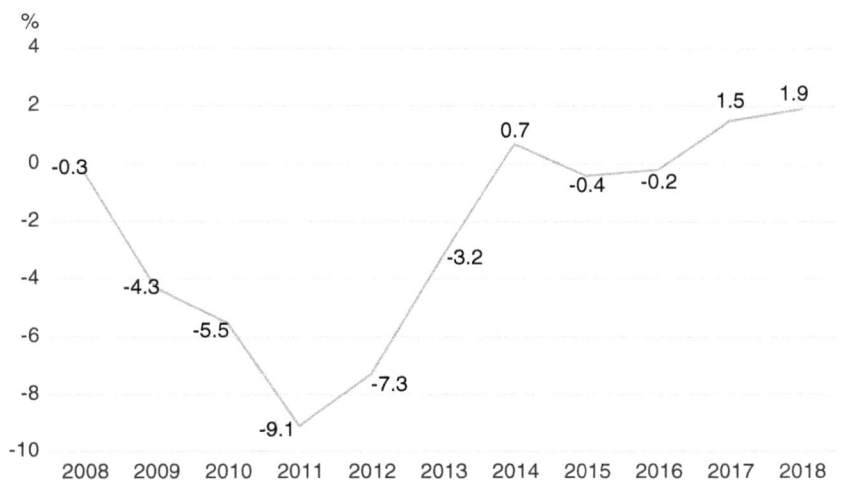

FIGURE 6.5 *Greece's real GDP growth rates, 2008–2018.*

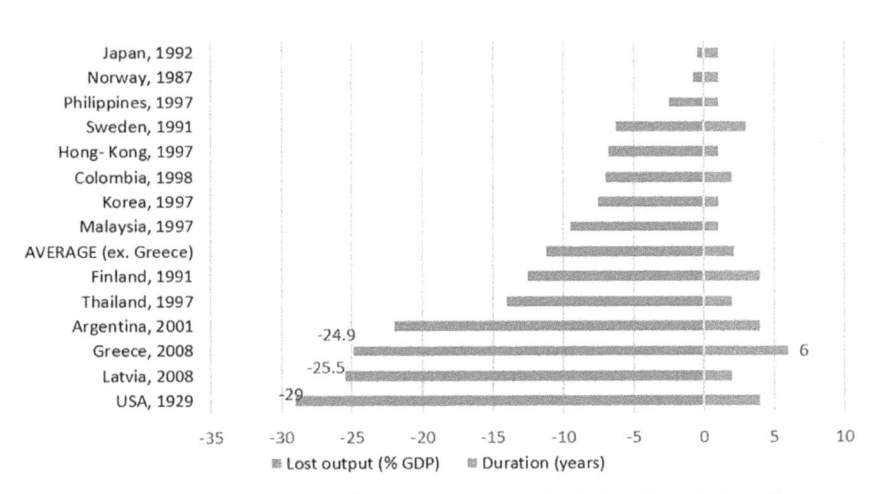

FIGURE 6.6 *Economic crises and lost output. Source: IMF, Reinhart & Rogoff (2009), Budget Introductory Report 2012 and 2013, ELSTAT (published data)*

(e.g. the far right Golden Dawn party), which threatened the European integration process.

Turning to more expansionary (Keynesian) policies seems quite attractive. This argument is based on economic theory and evidence from the Great Depression in 1929–1932. But Greece was unable to use expansionary policies because of high accumulated public deficits. Therefore, although expansionary policies are attractive, they have many problems as well. Among others, they ignore the question of debt, shift the burden of solution to future generations and certainly underestimate the required reforms. Besides, the expansionary policy during the pre-crisis period, 2007–2009, did not prevent the recession.

6.3.2 *The Role of Expectations*

According to the academic literature, expectations play a crucial role in the effectiveness of fiscal adjustment programmes.[23] Since 1975, in Greece there have been two large-scale fiscal adjustment periods. The most recent one was in 2010–2018, consisting of three individual programmes that took place according to the Memoranda signed by Greece in order to achieve fiscal sustainability, restore competitiveness and return to the international markets. It was an adjustment in the general government's deficit of about 13 percentage points of GDP (from -15.6 per cent in 2009 to 2.3 per cent in 2016). The other large-scale economic adjustment programmes had taken place during the period 1990–1999. At that time, the deficit from 15.9 per cent of GDP in 1990 dropped to 3.2 per cent in 1999. That period was accompanied by significant primary surpluses (and indeed was sustainable for a nine-year period). The adjustment was then enforced by the Maastricht criteria on the way to Economic and Monetary Union.

These two economic adjustment programmes have some similarities and one key difference, which is their effect on GDP. They are both almost of the same size and have almost the same duration. They both started with a rather high deficit ratio (the 2009 figures were worse, but in any case they were both well above the critical limits). Both of these adjustments were based mainly on the efforts to increase revenue rather than on a permanent reduction of expenditures, which is believed to be a better policy.

The critical difference, however, was the impact of these two adjustment programmes on the country's GDP. The latter caused a great depression and as a result it caused an unprecedented rise in unemployment and an increase in the debt-to-GDP ratio. Negative expectations for the future developments of the Greek economy were also created. In contrast, the period 1990–1999 differs considerably, since the adjustment effort was accompanied by significant growth rates, which allowed the achievement of sustainable primary surpluses and the decrease of the debt ratio (achieved after 1996). Cumulatively, according to the World Bank, the Greek GDP was increased

---

[23] F. Giavazzi and M. Pagano, 'Can Severe Fiscal Contractions be Expansionary? Tales of Two Small European Countries' (1990) 3372 *NBER Working Papers*, pp. 1–36.

by almost 20 per cent in the period 1990–1999. Therefore, the view that a de facto fiscal adjustment causes a recession seems to be disputed, at least in this case. Of course, the measures taken during a fiscal adjustment programme can cause a fall in GDP (to a greater or lesser extent), but there existed other factors that determined the developments. Expectations seem to have played that crucial role.

During the period of convergence before the adoption of the euro, the Maastricht criteria were a reliable anchor for the economic policy of Greece. Governments had been convinced that they must implement the necessary measures with consistency, continuity, credibility (the three c's of the fiscal policy) and devotion. Therefore, positive expectations were created. The belief was that the Greek economy would eventually enter the euro area and, as a result, interest rates would fall significantly and the country would have a sustainable budget (owing to the rules of the Stability and Growth Pact) and credible monetary policy (owing to the ECB). Theoretically, the positive role of expectations on GDP is based on the idea that fiscal consolidation – if it is believed to be long-lasting – implies a permanent reduction in future taxes on households and firms.[24] Therefore, consumers and businesses will leave their current private spending unaffected even if a current increase in taxes or a current reduction in transfers reduces their current disposable income. In addition, fiscal consolidation reduces uncertainty about future fiscal policy.[25] As a result, precautionary savings will be reduced and aggregate demand will be further supported.

The adjustment policy initiated in 2010 was very different, though, as the memorandum of understanding completely failed to be a reliable anchor for the Greek economy. The reversals in the presentation and implementation of the programme, the governmental hesitation, the lack of ownership of reforms, the negative international reports, the careless statements of government officials abroad,[26] the defects of the first Memorandum (with excessive front-loaded austerity measures) and the unstable environment of the Eurozone were some of the factors that embedded uncertainty in the Greek economy, leading to a negative outlook. They formed negative expectations, which in turn caused consumer and investor uncertainty and, eventually, a great recession in the Greek economy.

[24]   This is also called 'Ricardian equivalence' effect.
[25]   O. Blanchard, *'Comment on Giavazzi and Pagano'*, in S. Fischer (ed.), *NBER Macroeconomics Annual* (Cambridge, MA: MIT Press, 1990), pp. 111–116.
[26]   T. Barber, 'Greece admits it is riddled with corruption', *Financial Times*, 21 December 2009, available at: www.ft.com/content/54f4983e-e637-11de-bcbe-00144feab49a.

6.3.3 *Policy Mix*

Should there be expenditure cuts or tax increases to reduce fiscal deficits? The answer can be given both from a theoretical and an empirical point of view.[27] Consolidation programmes that rely mainly on government consumption cuts and social transfer cuts have a high probability of success; that is, a high probability of generating strong economic growth and reducing the debt ratio. Programmes that rely mainly on tax rises and government investment cuts, on the other hand, are expected to fail. The theoretical arguments come from so-called supply-side economics, which was very popular in the 1980s, especially in the US, and known as 'Reaganomics'. They are still very popular and influential, being promoted by the press (e.g. the *Wall Street Journal*) and relevant studies.[28] The founders of this theory are the American economists Robert Mundel and Arthur Laffer.

According to supply-side economics, it is better to cut expenditure because tax increases bring more public revenue and more available liquidity, and therefore government officials tend to spend more. In contrast, expenditure cuts do not offer liquidity to public officials. They create positive credibility effects on supply and demand because governments appear to be decisive in bringing down public deficits debt. Therefore, the risk premium will fall. Furthermore, tax increases create incentives to consume more and work less – and also to evade taxes more. Let's think of a woman who has to choose between leisure and labour. Leisure increases her happiness, but labour gives her income. When the labour tax-rate is low, labour supply increases and disposable income increases as well. As the labour tax-rate increases, labour supply decreases because the disposable income decreases too. In this case, it is very likely that the individual will choose leisure or may decide to work in the so called grey economy. This is known as the Laffer curve. It shows that there is a threshold beyond which any increase in tax coefficients is inefficient and leads to lower tax revenues. Finally, tax increases create disincentives for investments, which can boost growth.

There is also significant empirical research that points out that expenditure cuts are growth friendly.[29] They indicate that cuts in public expenditures

[27] A. Alesina and R. Perotti, 'Fiscal Expansions and Adjustments in OECD Countries' (1995) 10:21 *Economic Policy*, 205–248. See also A. Alesina and R. Perotti, 'Fiscal Adjustments in OECD Countries: Composition and Macroeconomic Effects' (1996) 5730 *NBER Working Paper*.

[28] IMF, 'Will it Hurt? Macroeconomic Effects of Fiscal Consolidation', *World Economic Outlook, October 2010: Recovery, Risk, and Rebalancing* (2010), chapter 3, pp. 93–123.

[29] See, for example, A. Alesina, and S. Ardagna, 'Large Changes in Fiscal Policies: Taxes versus Spending' (2009) 15438 *NBER Working Paper*.

reduce production costs and therefore favour the activities of the private sector, boost growth and reduce the fiscal deficit. In this context, it is crucial to specify the expenditures that should be cut. The answer is related to the efficiency of public expenditure. The government should cut those expenditures with low efficiency (bureaucracy, procurement costs, etc.), something that did not happen in Greece. According to Arin and colleagues, corruption appears to play an important role in the choice of the policy mix (tax increases rather than expenditures cuts).[30] Corruption also discourages healthy entrepreneurship, is a disincentive for foreign direct investments and tends to undermine societal cohesion. Furthermore, corruption had a negative impact on macroeconomic performance and decelerated growth. According to Kaufmann, reducing corruption could also reduce the fiscal deficit by 4 or even more percentage points.[31]

However, apart from corruption, there is one more factor that seems to have played an important role in the choice between expenditure cuts or tax increases: rent-seeking behaviour by state actors.[32]

Therefore, countries with poor and corrupted political structures tend to prefer tax increases in economic adjustment programmes.[33]

According to the literature,[34] the optimal mix in a successful fiscal adjustment programme should involve reliable cuts in primary expenditure (at a share of more than 70 per cent of the total measures, excluding public investment), while increases in revenue should not exceed 30 per cent of total measures (including revenues from tackling tax evasion).The Greek fiscal adjustment was not sufficiently based on permanent cuts to primary expenditure (Figure 6.7), with the notable exception of 2010 and 2013. In the depression years of 2011 and 2012 (a cumulative loss of 15.5 per cent of GDP), only 45 per cent and 49 per cent respectively were on the expenditures side.

[30] P. Arin, V. Chmelarova, E. Feess and A. Wohlschlegel, 'Why Are Corrupted Countries Less Successful in Consolidating their Budgets?' (2011) 95 *Journal of Public Economics*, 521–530.

[31] D. Kaufmann, 'Can Corruption Adversely Affect Public Finances in Industrialized Countries?' (April 2010) *The Brookings Institution*.

[32] For such an explanation see A. Huliaras and D. Sotiropoulos, 'The Crisis in Greece: The Semi-Rentier State Hypothesis' (2018) 120 *GreeSE Paper Hellenic Observatory Discussion Papers on Greece and Southeast Europe*, LSE, available at: http://eprints.lse.ac.uk/87077/1/GreeSE-120.pdf.

[33] This is probably the reason why privatisations always lagged behind the programme; there was arguably enough tolerance towards corruption in the Tax Administration and other public entities. See A. Drazen, 'The Political Economy of Delayed Reform' (1996) 1:1 *The Journal of Policy Reform*, 25–46.

[34] See A. Bassanini and R. Duval, 'Unemployment, Institutions and Reform Complementarities: Re-assessing the Aggregate Evidence for OECD Countries' (2009) 25(1) *Oxford Review of Economic Policy*, 40–59.

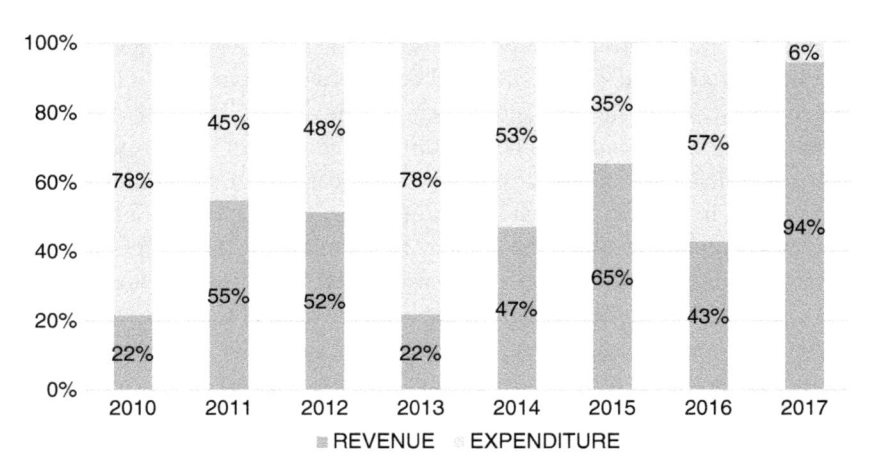

FIGURE 6.7 *Policy mix per year: Cuts in primary expenditure vs increases in revenue. (% of total measures).*

6.3.4 *Inefficient Institutions*

According to Acemoglu and Robinson, the good quality of domestic institutions and governance contribute significantly not only to economic growth in general, but also to the successful implementation of adjustment programmes.[35] Rapanos and Kaplanoglou made a comparative study on the Greek and the Cypriot economic adjustment programmes. Using several indicators, they showed that the prolonged economic crisis in Greece is due to the low quality of domestic institutions and bad governance.[36] On the other hand, it is very likely that good governance and high-quality institutions have helped the economy of Cyprus return to growth earlier than Greece. The authors believe that Greece had much worse institutions and governance both before and during the crisis.

In order to compare the institutional performance of Greece, Ireland and Portugal, we use the indicators of institutional quality from the World Economic Forum (WEF) and the Global Competitiveness Report 2014–2015.[37] Institutional quality is a broad concept that captures law, individual rights and high-quality government regulation and services. The reports used

[35] D. Acemoglu and J. Robinson, 'The Role of Institutions in Growth and Development' (2010) 1(2) *Review of Economics and Institutions*, 2–33.
[36] V. Rapanos and G. Kaplanoglou, 'Governance, Growth and the Recent Economic Crisis: The Case of Greece and Cyprus' (2014), 8:1 *Cyprus Economic Policy Review*, 3–34.
[37] Global Competitiveness Report 2014–2015, available at: https://reports.weforum.org/global-competitiveness-report-2014-2015/.

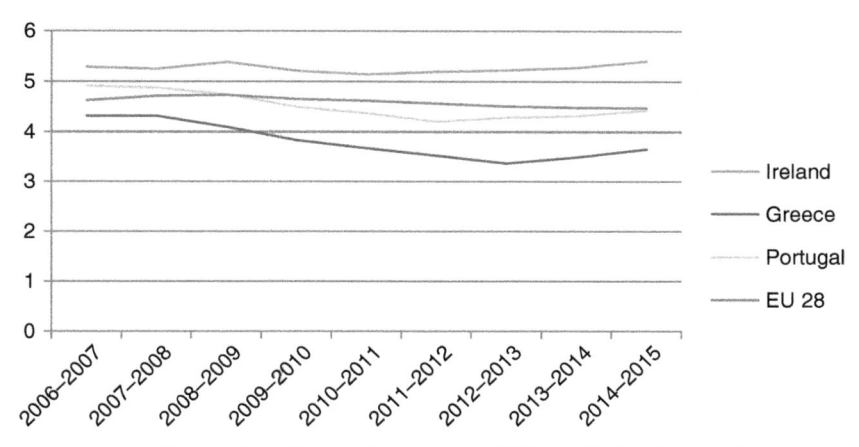

FIGURE 6.8 *Quality of Institutions. Source: WEF published data and own calculations*

analyse the performance of 144 countries according to specific criteria, providing an extended evaluation of global competitiveness that has the scope to create the necessary knowledge platform for public dialogue on this issue. According to the WEF's definition, 'Competitiveness is defined as the set of institutions, policies and factors that determine the level of productivity of a country. The level of productivity, in turn, sets the level of prosperity that can be earned by an economy.' The progress of the institutional quality indicator in Greece, Ireland, Portugal and EU-28 average is depicted in Figure 6.8.

We observe both the comparatively low institutional quality of Greece and its deteriorating trend. The prolonged negotiations between Greece and the European and international creditors on various economic issues and reforms highlighted the problems of formal and informal governance institutions in Greece.[38] Institutions could mitigate the negative social effects of fiscal consolidation. For example, the Minimum Guaranteed Income, which is a safety net protecting vulnerable social groups, was established only after strong pressure from Greece's European partners in 2012. This institutional problem in Greece is probably associated with the established system of social rules that form social behaviour, not only restricting but also enabling actions and

[38] See D. Acemoglou and J. A. Robinson, *Why Nations Fail, The Origins of Power, Prosperity, and Poverty* (New York: Crown Business, 2012). The authors distinguish two types of politico-economic regimes. Here we are interested in those called 'inclusive'. The economic institutions ensure property rights, the rule of law and public services that ensure a general framework for economic activity providing opportunities to everyone. Such financial institutions boost growth, productivity and welfare and promote technological progress and education. It can be argued that in several sectors Greece (more or less) deviated from that model.

cooperation among members of a society that would have not existed otherwise.[39] Values such as trust, respect for others, the sense that success depends on an individual's effort, are some parts of this social behaviour. Hence, it is a rather hard task to change them, especially in a short period. Therefore, beliefs affect the way that institutions work within modern society. Politics, education, justice and public administration are major areas for testing this hypothesis. [40]

But besides domestic institutions, the Eurozone was not ready to cope with the crisis. This found Europe unprepared, without a satisfactory 'immunity' from economic crises— there was only the Stability and Growth Pact. The euro was a significant institutional innovation, but like any other innovation it was not complete from the very beginning. It was like the first cars that were invented many years ago: they didn't have high safety standards (e g. seatbelts, airbags) to protect the driver. Accidents were rare because few cars were on the streets; but when they started to become common, manufacturers developed security systems and the state regulated the issuance of driving licences. The euro was created without 'airbags' or other safety standards to protect countries from debt crises. Accidents could happen owing to inappropriate behaviour or external factors. And accidents did happen. In 2012, Europe created mechanisms and rules (the six-pack and two-pack), but this was rather late because the crisis had already severely affected a number of European member states (e.g. Greece, Portugal, Ireland and Cyprus).[41]

6.3.5 *Fairness*

About one and a half months after Greece's fiscal consolidation programme, in the summer of 2010, the IMF's Chief Economist Olivier Blanchard and Carlo Cottarelli set out 'Ten Commandments' for fiscal consolidation in advanced economies. Commandment VI states that 'You shall be fair. To be sustainable over time, the fiscal adjustment should be equitable.'[42] Based on this 'commandment', Rapanos, Kaplanoglu and Bardakas undertook research on the relationship between fairness and effectiveness in fiscal adjustment programmes.[43] They tried to examine whether fairness is necessary for the

---

[39] See G. M. Hodgson, 'What Are Institutions?' (2006) 40(1) *Journal of Economic Issues*, 1–25.

[40] See, for example, P. Liargovas, P. Evangelopoulos and V. Kouyia, 'Institutions, Growth and the Recent Economic Crisis: The EU Case' (2017) 13(1–2) *Review of Applied Economics*, 55–66.

[41] Y. Varoufakis, *And the Weak Suffer What They Must? Europe's Crisis and America's Economic Future* (London: The Bodley Head, 2016), 38–249.

[42] See O. Blanchard and C. Cottarelli, 'Ten Commandments for Fiscal Adjustment in Advanced Economies', *IMFBlog*, 24 June 2010, available at: https://blogs.imf.org/2010/06/24/ten-commandments-for-fiscal-adjustment-in-advanced-economies/.

[43] V. Rapanos, G. Kaplanoglou and I. Bardakas, 'Does Fairness Matter for the Success of Fiscal Consolidation?' (2015) 68(2) *Kyklos*, 197–219.

success of these programmes. In their detailed research, they used data of twenty-nine members of the Organisation for Economic Co-operation and Development (OECD) for forty years. They showed that Blanchard's and Cottarelli's VI commandment is right: distribution of the burdens should be fair and the disadvantaged groups of the society should be protected in order for an adjustment programme to be successful.

In another study, Ball and colleagues found that on average a consolidation of 1 per cent of GDP increases the long-term unemployment rate by 0.6 of a percentage point and raises by 1.5 per cent within five years the Gini measure of income inequality.[44] They also found that both expenditure- and tax-based fiscal consolidations at national level have typically raised inequality for a panel of OECD countries, even if the distributional effects of spending-based adjustments tends to be larger relative to tax-based adjustments.

Furthermore, Rawdanowicz and colleagues presented empirical evidence on the impact of consolidation on equity by comparing the evolution of income inequality and poverty during the ten largest and most protracted past consolidation episodes in OECD countries.[45] They found that in about half of the analysed cases, the Gini index for disposable income increased, potentially reflecting both increasing dispersion of market income and less redistribution of taxes and transfers. In the other half of the episodes, the net Gini index was unchanged or even declined.

More recently, Agnello and Sousa have analysed a panel of eighteen industrialised countries.[46] Their results support the view that inequality generally increases during periods of fiscal consolidation. This seems to be especially the case for periods driven by spending cuts, whereas tax hikes seem to have a redistributing effect.

There are two typical cases of successful implementation of such programmes, in Sweden and in Finland. Sweden had to implement an adjustment programme between 1994 and 1997, after a banking crisis in 1990.[47] It reduced significantly the budget deficit, but on the other hand it provided for cuts in the Value Added Tax of foods. Finland adopted an ambitious

[44] See L. Ball, D. Furceri, D. Leigh, and P. Loungani, 'The Distributional Effects of Fiscal Austerity' (2013) 129 *UN-DESA Working Paper*. The Gini index is a measure of distributional inequalities. A country that scores 0.0 on the Gini scale has perfect equality in income distribution. The higher the number over 0.0, the higher the inequality; a score of 1.0 (or 100) indicates total inequality, where only one person obtains all the income.

[45] L. Rawdanowicz, E. Wurzel and A. K. Christensen, 'The Equity Implications of Fiscal Consolidation' (2013) 1013 *OECD Economics Department Working Papers*.

[46] L. Agnello and R. Sousa, 'How does fiscal consolidation impact on income inequality?' (2014) 60(4) *Review of Income and Wealth*, 702–726.

[47] See M. Flodén, 'A Role Model for the Conduct of Fiscal Policy? Experiences for Sweden' (2012) 9095 *CEPR Discussion Paper*.

adjustment programme, after an economic and banking crisis in the early 1990s, which was considered quite successful as well.[48] Despite extensive cuts in several expenditures, transfers to the disadvantaged groups of the society increased by almost 14 per cent on an annual basis.

Were the Greek programmes fair? The answer in short is no.[49] Greece ranks as the worst-performing country in terms of social justice in comparison with all the twenty-eight EU Member States in all six dimensions that compose the social justice index (Figure 6.9).[50] Greece has a score of 3.66, when the EU average is 5.75.

6.3.6 *Exports*

Exports (as a percentage of GDP) and the openness of the economy in general are strongly believed to be crucial for the success of an adjustment programme as well. Between 2011 and 2013, exports increased by 8.18 per cent in Spain, 10.3 per cent in Portugal and 6.1 per cent in Ireland, while in Greece they increased hardly at all, by 1.5 per cent (Figure 6.10). If the performance of Greek exports had been the same as that of Portugal, the recession would also have been over much quicker, income would be 8–10 per cent higher and, with all the expenditure restraint, the budget would actually be in surplus. According to Daniel Gros, the experience of Greece and Portugal since 2010 has been exactly the opposite: In Portugal entrepreneurs found new markets abroad when the domestic market collapsed as austerity was implemented. During the boom years the biggest market for Portugal had been Spain, but this market also sagged at the same time as Portugal needed exports most. But Portuguese exporters found new markets, for example Angola, which boomed with high oil prices until 2014.[51]

Monastiriotis has observed that focusing on the implementation of austerity measures in order to achieve debt sustainability is rather problematic in countries with a low degree of openness.[52] He examined the relationship between

---

[48] See H. Blöchliger, D. Ho Song and D. Sutherland, 'Fiscal Consolidation. Part 4. Case Studies of Large Fiscal Consolidation Episodes' (2012) 935 *OECD Economics Department Working Papers*, 21–22.

[49] See Parliamentary Budget Office, 'Fiscal Adjustment: How Fair is the Distribution of the Burdens?' (2014) Hellenic Parliament, Athens.

[50] Poverty prevention, intergenerational justice, health, social cohesion and non-discrimination, labour market access, equitable education.

[51] D. Gros, 'The mystery of the missing Greek exports', *Capital.gr English*, 22 April 2016, available at: http://english.capital.gr/News.asp?id=2413559.

[52] V. Monastiriotis, '(When) Does Austerity Work? On the Conditional Link between Fiscal Austerity and Debt Sustainability' (2014) 8:1 *Cyprus Economic Policy Review*, 71–92.

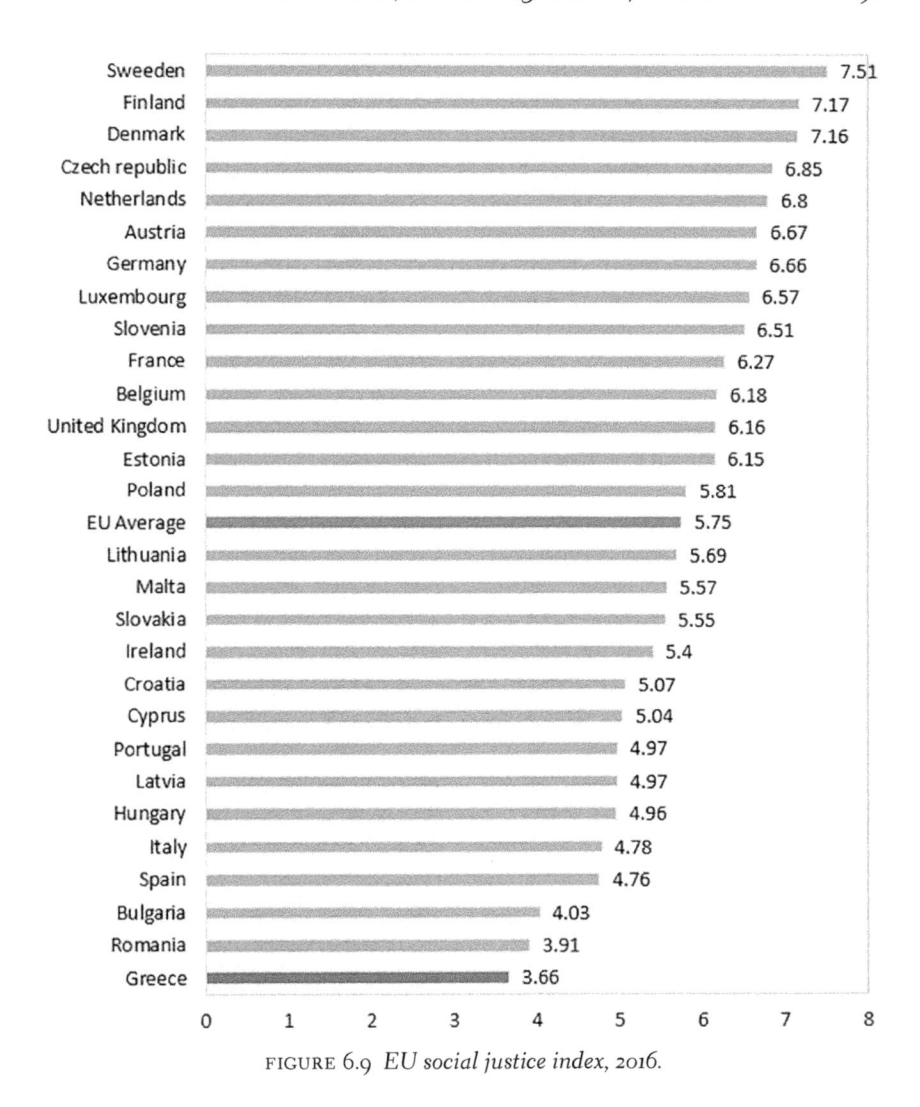

FIGURE 6.9 *EU social justice index, 2016.*

openness and austerity in two groups of countries with high and low degree of openness over the period 2008–2012. He found that in the high openness group the relationship between austerity and growth turns out to be totally insignificant. In contrast, in the more closed economies this relationship is clearly negative and very significant statistically. For this group of countries, 1 percentage point of fiscal consolidation is associated with a drop in GDP growth of 3.5 percentage points. This value is over twice as high as those reported by Wolf, and also by Krugman (2012), which exerted a significant

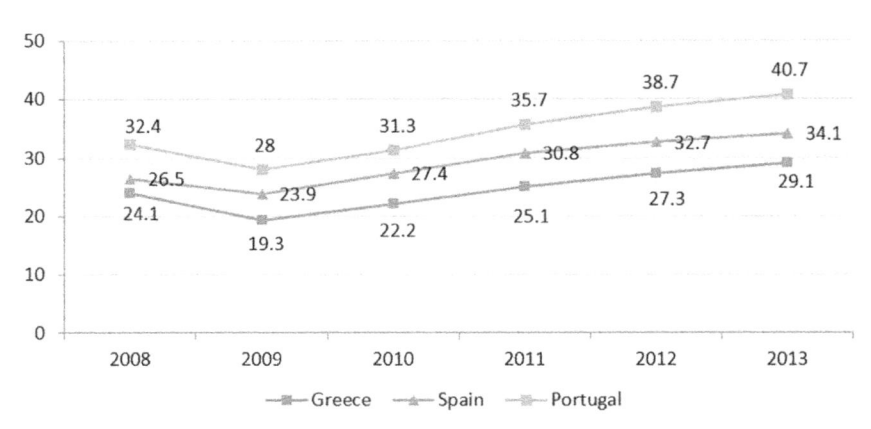

FIGURE 6.10 *Exports of goods and services (% of GDP).*

influence on the emergence of the 'austerity doesn't work' narrative that was also evident in the case of Greece.[53]

6.4 CONCLUDING REMARKS

This chapter has evaluated factors that might have affected the success or failure of the fiscal austerity measures announced in 2010, 2011 and 2015 in Greece. Based on the academic literature, we identified in particular six factors that are likely to be of significance. These are the size of austerity, expectations, the policy mix, the country's institutional setting, fairness and the degree of openness of the country.

Our analysis has shown that there are non-Keynesian effects, which may be associated not only with tax increases at high levels of government indebtedness or other macro-economic variables, but also with strong institutions, expectations, fairness and the openness of the economy. Austerity programmes that can work well in specific cases may fail to work well when every country imposes austerity at the same time, without taking into account the weaknesses and peculiarities of the economy. Austerity measures may be expansionary in particular cases, where policy is sufficiently effective, but they can have devastating effects in other cases, where the quality of government and the export base are significantly weaker. In this respect, when concerning the countries in the Eurozone that seem to have been locked into an 'austerity trap', the lesson drawn from our

53   See http://blogs.ft.com/martin-wolf-exchange/2012/04/27/the-impact-of-fiscal-austerity-in-the-eurozone/; M. Wolf, 'The sad record of fiscal austerity', *Financial Times*, 26 February 2013, available at: www.ft.com/content/73219452-7f49-11e2-89ed-00144feabdc0; P. Krugman, 'Austerity and growth, again', *New York Times*, 24 April 2012.

analysis is not that this has been the outcome of a 'wrong recipe', but rather the outcome of a potentially good recipe being applied in environments that were not suited to, or capable of, executing the recipe correctly. In countries with a weak economic base, institutional capacities and policy effectiveness, austerity leads to worse economic outcomes and no gains in terms of GDP growth.

Therefore, supporters of rescue packages in the Eurozone will have to shift their attention to the question about how to implement the austerity measures, and not on whether they will be applied. The two factors mentioned (exports and institutions) are slow-moving, in the sense that they cannot be changed instantaneously from administrative or political decisions of policy makers. Policy actions should be more specific in order to produce less undesirable fiscal consolidation programmes and less recessionary austerity.

So what are the lessons learned in the case of Greece? First, the country needs to increase its export base. Open economies (economies that are export oriented) may generate significant gains from austerity programmes owing to internal devaluation (wage decline). As wages decrease, export-oriented businesses become more competitive and can increase their exports. Subsequently, exports lead to economic growth. This is what happened in Portugal, but not in Greece. Secondly, Greece should improve the quality of its institutions. Countries with strong institutions (e.g. Cyprus) can be more successful in absorbing crises' shocks. This is valid not only in the case of economic crises but also in other cases, such as the COVID-19 pandemic. Conditions in society and in the economy could be better if the state had developed strong institutions (minimum guaranteed income, land-use plan, fiscal transparency, stable tax system) before the economic crisis. Greek policy makers should reverse the policy mix from tax-based austerity to an expenditure-based one. Austerity programmes that can be effective in specific cases may fail in others that have different characteristics. In countries with a weak economic base, with limited institutional abilities and political ineffectiveness, austerity leads to worse economic outcomes and does not contribute to GDP growth. Greece is one of these cases. Accordingly, what the country still needs is a radical change of incentive and disincentive systems, in the rules of the game and its institutions as well. Only in this way will it be possible to overcome practices that impede growth, favour corruption and make possible rent-seeking behaviour, all of which undermines society.

7

Shareholder Activism

A Driver or an Obstacle to Sustainable Value Creation?

Jukka Mähönen[*]

7.1 INTRODUCTION

There are, in a modern listed public company, two dominant types of share-holders: the active marginal trader who sets market price often through using algorithmic trading,[1] and the activist (or potential activist) institutional investor,[2] who exerts pressure on company governance.[3] Pressure can take a number of forms. These range from shareholder dialogue and temporary voting blocks of investors with relatively small shareholdings, to full takeovers. Between these two are found hedge fund activism and proxy fights.[4] Share ownership has, at the same time, not been concentrated solely by shareholders owning larger blocks of shares, but also by the use of different classes of shares that grant multiple

[*] This chapter is based on research of the Sustainable Market Actors for Responsible Trade (SMART) research project, funded by the European Union (EU) under the Horizon 2020 programme, grant agreement 693642.

[1] See, for example, T. C. W. Lin, 'The New Investor', (2013) 60 *UCLA Law Review*, 678–735.

[2] By 'institutional investors', I mean institutions investing others' savings on their behalf ('money managers'). Typical institutional investors are public and private pension funds and companies, insurance companies and other joint investment properties such as civil law foundations and sovereign wealth funds, as well as hedge funds. E. B. Rock, 'Institutional Investors in Corporate Governance', in J. N. Gordon and W.-G. Ringe (eds.), *The Oxford Handbook of Corporate Law and Governance* (Oxford: Oxford University Press, 2018), pp. 363–386, 364. Institutional investors hold 41 per cent of the global market capitalisation of listed companies; A. De La Cruz, A. Medina and Y. Tang, 'Owners of the World's Listed Companies' (2019), OECD Capital Market Series, pp. 1–41, 5, available at: www.oecd.org/corporate/owners-of-the-worlds-listed-companies.htm.

[3] L. E. Strine, Jr., 'Can We Do Better by Ordinary Investors? A Pragmatic Reaction to the Dueling Ideological Mythologists of Corporate Law' (2014) 114 (2) *Columbia Law Review*, 449–502, 452 fn 6.

[4] M. R. Denes, J. M. Karpoff and V. B. McWilliams, 'Thirty Years of Shareholder Activism: A Survey of Empirical Research' (2017) 44 *Journal of Corporate Finance*, 405–424, 405–406.

voting rights and by the issue of no voting shares to the public.[5] Concentrated share ownership is widespread around the world, including in Europe, the Nordic countries and Italy.[6] For example, close to two-thirds of all listed companies in the Nordic area have at least one shareholder who controls more than 20 per cent of total votes. Around one-fifth of companies in the Nordic countries are also under the absolute control of a single shareholder.[7] Forms of control, however, vary from country to country, and from institutional investors such as pension funds to founders, states, sovereign wealth funds, families and foundations that act more as direct shareholders.[8] There is considerable heterogeneity in the ecosystem. The two dominant types of shareholder still, however, prevail.

The investments themselves have, at the same time, become more short-sighted than previously. In the US, for example, the shareholder base of public companies turns almost fully over each year,[9] the average holding period for institutional investors being a mere eight months.[10] There are unfortunately no comparable results for Europe, most European research being conducted using US data. The EU High-Level Expert Group on Sustainable Finance (HLEG), which was established by the European Commission, urged in its Final Report that the European Commission and European Supervisory Authorities establish globally consistent data on portfolio turnover.[11] In its

5 A. H. Choi, 'Concentrated Ownership and Long-Term Shareholder Value' (2018) 8 (1) *Harvard Business Law Review*, 53–99; J. G. Hill, 'Good Activist/Bad Activist: The Rise of International Stewardship Codes' (2018) 41 *Seattle University Law Review*, 497–524; K. M. Kahle and R. M. Stulz, 'Is the US Public Corporation in Trouble?' (2017) 31 *Journal of Economic Perspectives*, 67–88.

6 Choi, 'Concentrated Ownership', 63–65; J. Cullen and J. Mähönen, 'Taming Unsustainable Finance: The Perils of Modern Risk Management', in B. Sjåfjell and C. Bruner (eds.), *The Cambridge Handbook of Corporate Law, Corporate Governance and Sustainability* (Cambridge: Cambridge University Press, 2019), p. 100–113; J. Mähönen and G. Johnsen, 'Law, Culture and Sustainability: Corporate Governance in the Nordic Countries', in Sjåfjell and Bruner (eds.), *The Cambridge Handbook of Corporate Law, Corporate Governance and Sustainability*, pp. 218–231.

7 P. Lekvall (ed.), *The Nordic Corporate Governance Model* (Stockholm: SNS Förlag, 2014), p. 23.

8 As an example of the Nordic area, see in Norway J. Mähönen, B. Sjåfjell and M. Mee, 'Stewardship Norwegian-Style: Fragmented and State-Dominated (but Not Without Potential?)', in D. Katelouzou and D. W. Puchniak (eds.), *Global Shareholder Stewardship* (Cambridge: Cambridge University Press, 2022), pp. 174–191.

9 L. E. Strine, Jr., 'One Fundamental Corporate Governance Question We Face: Can Corporations Be Managed for the Long Term Unless Their Powerful Electorates Also Act and Think Long Term?' (2010) 66:1 *The Business Lawyer*, 1–26, 17.

10 M. W. Roberge, J. C. Flaherty, Jr., R. M. Almeida, Jr. and A. C. Boyd, 'Lengthening the Investment Time Horizon' (2014), *MFS White Paper Series*, 1–6, available at: https://conferences.pionline.com/uploads/conference_admin/mfse_time_wp_12_13.pdf.

11 EU High-Level Expert Group on Sustainable Finance, 'Financing a sustainable European economy: final report 2018', 1–99, 48, available at: https://ec.europa.eu/info/sites/info/files/180131-sustainable-finance-final-report_en.pdf.

February 2019 call for advice to the European Supervisory Authorities (ESAs), the European Commission urged the ESAs to collect evidence of the exertion of undue short-term pressure on corporations by the financial sector.[12] The turnover ratios for both equities and bonds are, according to the ESAs' December 2019 responses, quite stable and relatively low for example in the insurance sector.[13] Short-termism in holding periods was also not seen as being a problem among banks.[14] The ESAs, however, recognised in their responses the short-termism issue among other financial sector undertakings, particularly the two dimensions of short-termism – short-termism of investors and the short-termism of investments. Long holding periods do not necessarily correlate with long-termism in the investments themselves,[15] the potential differences in the investment horizons of institutional shareholders being undermined by the short-term nature of investments. Some institutional investors, such as pension funds, *might* have longer-term investment horizons than for example mutual funds, pension funds in principle supporting sustainable investments.[16] This, however, appears not to play a significant role, owing to US-domiciled institutional investors accounting for 65 per cent of global institutional investor holdings.[17] This major capital market shift, which Gilson and Gordon have labelled 'agency capitalism', has important implications for both investor 'activism' and regulation.[18]

---

[12] European Commission, 'Call for advice to the European Supervisory Authorities to collect evidence of undue short-term pressure from the financial sector on corporations' (1 February 2019), available at: https://ec.europa.eu/info/sites/info/files/business_economy_euro/banking_ and_finance/documents/190201-call-for-advice-to-esas-short-term-pressure_en.pdf. The ESAs include the European Banking Authority (EBA), the European Securities and Markets Authority (ESMA) and the European Insurance and Occupational Pensions Authority (EIOPA).

[13] EIOPA, 'Potential undue short-term pressure from financial markets on corporates: Investigation on European insurance and occupational pension sectors: Search for evidence' (18 December 2019), available at: www.eiopa.europa.eu/content/potential-undue-short-term-pressure-financial-markets_en.

[14] EBA, 'EBA Report on undue short-term pressure from the financial sector on corporations' (18 December 2019), available at: https://eba.europa.eu/file/461440/down-.

[15] European Securities and Markets Authority, 'Report: undue short-term pressure on corporations' (18 December 2019), 1–164, 20–21, available at: www.esma.europa.eu/press-news/ esma-news/esma-proposes-strengthened-rules-address-undue-short-termism-in-securities.

[16] T. Jain and D. Jamali, 'Looking Inside the Black Box: The Effect of Corporate Governance on Corporate Social Responsibility' (2016) 24 (3) *Corporate Governance: An International Review*, 253–273, 260.

[17] De La Cruz, Medina and Tang, 'Owners of the World's Listed Companies', 9.

[18] R. J. Gilson and J. N. Gordon, 'Agency Capitalism: Further Implications of Equity Intermediation' in J. G. Hill and R. S. Thomas (eds.), *Research Handbook on Shareholder Power* (Cheltenham: Edward Elgar Publishing, 2015), pp. 32–52, 32–33; Hill, 'Good Activist/ Bad Activist', 500.

Modern capital markets are ruled by intermediaries in the extended investment supply chains. There is therefore a disconnect between the individual ultimate beneficiaries of these chains, such as pension fund customers whose funds are managed by institutional investors, and the productive firms in which the institutional investors invest.[19] The investment chain places the focus on the institutional investors and other investment intermediaries. The ultimate beneficiaries are therefore not able to directly influence the practices of the firms in which they invest.[20]

Even more important is what Mark Carney, the Governor of the Bank of England, characterises as the 'tragedy of the horizon',[21] and the inability to manage the risks from this which 'fall beyond the traditional horizons of most actors – imposing a cost on future generations that the current generation has no direct incentive to fix'.[22] For example, the rise of increasing passive index investing, led by the 'Big Three' (BlackRock, Vanguard and State Street), threatens to further undermine this investment model. Capital providers investing in the entire equity market or a subsection of it through exchange-traded funds or index trackers chase short-term returns. This is likely to lead to monodimensionality in portfolio allocation, money managers allocating capital to corporations that are likely to provide superior short-term returns. These factors overwhelm sustainability considerations through money managers disregarding environmental, social and governance (ESG) investment principles.[23]

A major proportion of the ultimate beneficiaries of institutional investors are 'forced capitalists'.[24] An example of forced capitalism is employees being enrolled in an employer-provided pension plan, in which investments are made by both the employee and the employer via an intermediary in a

---

[19] In this article I use the concept 'productive firms' or 'productive corporations' to differentiate between these target corporations and the corporations investing in them. The term for dichotomy managers of productive corporations, 'money managers', is used for instance in Strine, 'Can We Do Better', 451.

[20] V. Harper Ho, 'Risk-Related Activism: The Business Case for Monitoring Nonfinancial Risk' (2016) 41 *The Journal of Corporate Law*, 647–706, 677.

[21] M. Carney, 'Breaking the Tragedy of the Horizon – Climate Change and Financial Stability', speech given at Lloyd's of London, 29 September 2015; see Cullen and Mähönen, 'Taming Unsustainable Finance', p. 104.

[22] Cullen and Mähönen, 'Taming Unsustainable Finance', p. 104.

[23] Ibid.; compare, however, with M. Condon, 'Externalities and the Common Owner' (2020) 95:1 *Washington Law Review*, 1–81, that claims that universal institutional investors have an incentive to internalise their intra-portfolio negative externalities by activism against unsustainable businesses.

[24] A concept coined by L. E. Strine, Jr, 'Toward Common Sense and Common Ground? Reflections on the Shared Interests of Managers and Labor in a More Rational System of Corporate Governance' (2007) 33 (1) *The Journal of Corporation Law*, 1–26, 4.

pension fund or a pension insurance company. In forced capitalism, employers directly or indirectly select the intermediary.[25] Most ordinary ultimate beneficiaries therefore have little choice but to invest in the market indirectly. Their economic security is based on their ability to sell their labour, such forced capitalists therefore having no interest in quarter-to-quarter earnings or in beating the market for quick bursts of cash at the expense of sustainable growth. Their asset managers do, however, have an interest in this.[26]

In Europe, a positive view of shareholder engagement underpinned a number of recommendations of the 2012 UK *Kay Review*. This review was established to examine the impact of activity in UK equity markets on the long-term performance and governance of UK listed companies.[27] There have been no legislative responses to the Review. The HLEG, which was established by the European Commission, also emphasised in its Final Report the dominance of short-termism. The report stated that:

> [t]here is much evidence of the strong short-term pressures that corporate management experiences. A 2005 survey shows that 78% of executives feel pressure to sacrifice long-term value to meet earnings targets. A more recent McKinsey and Canada Pension Plan Investment Board (CPPIB) survey of over 1,000 board members and executives finds that 86% believe that if they had a longer time horizon to make business decisions, this would positively affect corporate performance in a number of ways, including strengthening financial returns and increasing innovation.[28]

The HLEG Final Report stressed that sustainability and long-term orientation required a number of supporting strategies. This includes a sufficient number of investors who, in their relations with the companies they invest in, support a focus on long-term value creation and long-term research. Companies should also focus more strongly on issues and metrics that are relevant to the longer-term success of the business.

Institutional shareholders, despite these problems, have continuously been seen to be important in corporate governance. Shareholder 'empowerment'

---

[25] The Economist, 'Reinventing the Deal: America's Startups are Changing What it Means to Own a Company', *The Economist*, 24 October 2015, from the print edition, available at: www.economist.com/news/briefing/21676760-americas-startups-are-changing-what-it-means-own-company-reinventing-deal.

[26] Strine, 'Toward Common Sense', 4.

[27] J. Kay, 'The Kay review of UK equity markets and long-term decision making', Final Report, July 2012, 1–122, available at: https://assets.publishing.service.gov.uk/government/uploads/system/uploads/attachment_data/file/253454/bis-12-917-kay-review-of-equity-markets-final-report.pdf.

[28] High-Level Expert Group, Final Report, 47 (footnotes omitted).

has been an important part of this new trend, this involving a policy shift that makes corporate managers accountable to shareholders as 'owners' of the company.[29] Corporate boards should therefore, according to this policy thinking, be 'independent' and focus on monitoring the company on behalf of the shareholders as opposed to managing it independently. Shareholders should also 'engage' with companies on issues ranging from strategy to corporate responsibility, which are mandated to the board by law.[30]

Corporate governance regulation also reflects the new stewardship trend, shareholder engagement and empowerment policies from the early 1990s that are being increasingly embedded in corporate governance codes, listing rules, company legislation, EU directives and transnational regulatory standards.[31] The influence of this trend has become even stronger after and in response to the global financial crisis of 2008–2009. This is despite doubts that the crisis was due to the shareholder empowerment trend. We see this in particular in the 2017 reform of the 2007 Shareholders' Rights Directive (SHRD I),[32] a number of European jurisdictions also seeing the emergence of specific stewardship codes. The 2017 amended Shareholders' Rights Directive (SHRD II)[33] includes elements found in previous stewardship codes, such as a requirement that institutional investors publicly disclose their policy for integrating shareholder engagement in their investment strategies or provide an explanation of why they have chosen not to do so ('comply or explain').[34]

Encouraging shareholders to act as 'stewards' is, according to the arguments behind the codes and stewardship regulation such as SHRD II, a way forward not only towards better corporate governance in the mainstream

---

[29] 'Owners', as we do not know any jurisdiction in which the shareholders of a limited liability company are recognised as its owners under property law. Shareholders own shares that entitle their holders to rights and duties in a company. From a property rights perspective, a company owns its assets and owes its responsibilities. B. Sjåfjell, A. Johnston, L. Anker-Sørensen and D. Millon, 'Shareholder Primacy: The Main Barrier to Sustainable Companies', in B. Sjåfjell and B.J. Richardson (eds.), *Company Law and Sustainability: Legal Barriers and Opportunities* (Cambridge: Cambridge University Press, 2015), pp. 79–147, 80.

[30] S. Deakin, 'Against Shareholder Empowerment', in J. Williamson, C. Driver and P. Kenway (eds.) *Beyond Shareholder Value: The Reasons and Choices for Corporate Governance Reform* (London: Trades Union Congress, July 2014), pp. 36–40, 36.

[31] Deakin, 'Against Shareholder Empowerment', p. 36.

[32] Directive 2007/36/EC of the European Parliament and of the Council of 11 July 2007 on the exercise of certain rights of shareholders in listed companies, OJ L 184, 14.7.2007, 17.

[33] Directive (EU) 2017/828 of the European Parliament and of the Council of 17 May 2017 amending Directive 2007/36/EC as regards the encouragement of long-term shareholder engagement, OJ L 132, 20.5.2017, 1.

[34] EY, 'Q&A on Stewardship Codes' (August 2017) 2, available at: www.ey.com/Publication/vwLUAssets/ey-stewardship-codes-august-2017/$FILE/ey-stewardship-codes-august-2017.pdf.

economics-focused sense, but also towards more sustainable and responsible companies in terms of the environmental and social challenges we as a global community face.

Shareholders play a crucial role in promoting better governance of companies according to the European Commission's Company Law Action Plan of 2018, which is the Commission's response to the HLEG Final Report. This is furthermore a role that is in the interests of shareholders and the company.[35] The Commission's proposal to amend SHRD I, which was approved in 2017 as SHRD II, more specifically promoted an 'effective and sustainable shareholder engagement' as a cornerstone of listed companies' corporate governance model.[36] This, however, depends on checks and balances between the different organs and different stakeholders.[37]

The stewardship concept reflected in SHRD II is widely connected to institutional investors, and refers to the actions that asset managers can take to enhance the value of the companies that they invest in on behalf of their beneficiaries. The nature of stewardship varies, however, from jurisdiction to jurisdiction based on shareholder structures. In the Nordic region (which is similar to many Asian jurisdictions), the role of states, sovereign holding companies and wealth funds, other public market actors such as public pension funds, families, family controlled investment companies and family based foundations is significant compared with (other) national and international institutional investors.[38]

The EU approach is, however, based on an agency theory idea of all shareholders being principals of the company,[39] and particularly in relation to the board and the management.[40] This approach is not, however, based

[35] Communication from the European Commission to the European Parliament, the Council, the European Economic and Social Committee and the Committee of the Regions, Action Plan: European Company Law and Corporate Governance – A Modern Legal Framework for More Engaged Shareholders and Sustainable Companies. COM(2012) 740 final, 3 ('Company Law Action Plan').

[36] European Commission, Proposal for a directive of the European Parliament and of the Council amending Directive 2007/36/EC as regards the encouragement of long-term shareholder engagement and Directive 2013/34/EU as regards certain elements of the corporate governance statement, COM(2014) 213 final ('Commission Proposal'), 12.

[37] Commission Proposal, 12.

[38] See Mähönen, Sjåfjell and Mee., 'Stewardship Norwegian-Style'; G. Goto, A. K. Koh and D. W. Puchniak, 'Diversity of Shareholder Stewardship in Asia: Faux Convergence' (2020) 53 *Vanderbilt Journal of Transnational Law*, 829–880.

[39] A. A. Alchian and H. Demsetz, 'Production, Information Costs, and Economic Organization' (1972) 62 (5) *The American Economic Review*, 777–795; M. C. Jensen and W. H. Meckling, Theory of the Firm: Managerial Behavior, Agency Costs and Ownership Structure' (1976) 3 *Journal of Financial Economics*, 305–360.

[40] W. W. Bratton and M. L. Wachter, 'The Case Against Shareholder Empowerment', (2010) 158 *University of Pennsylvania Law Review*, 653–728, 662.

on European nor Member States' company law.[41] The shareholder empowerment movement is generally inspired by three phenomena: (1) changing investment practices and especially institutional investor drive, spearheaded by aggressive hedge funds; (2) the emergence of shareholder proxy advisory services that concentrate investor voice; and (3) the creation of complex financial instruments that are capable of decoupling, which separate voting rights from economic interests, and as key developments in the strengthening of shareholder power.[42] Activist investors are deemed to be benevolent champions for the other non-controlling shareholders.[43]

Complicating this picture is the representation of both types of equity investors, marginal traders and institutional investors, by a group of agents that can be called 'money managers' or 'asset managers'. Corporate life means life with these money managers for actors involved with listed companies, whether they are board members, management or other employees. The 'owners' that managers and board members of productive firms deal with are largely anonymous,[44] as they are represented by the money managers buying and selling securities. Money managers furthermore operate to achieve a balance between quarterly results that keep corporate management sharp and long-term investments that keep the companies growing.[45] Most corporate literature is, however, focused on the duties of corporate managers and board member towards these 'owners'.[46]

Financial intermediaries, owing to institutional shareholder complexity, are now at the centre of corporate ownership and of debate. This further reflects how the capital of forced capitalists is put to work and how the mountain of shares owned for their benefit is used to influence the management of listed companies; this is no longer determined by the forced capitalists or the board members of the productive companies, but by these intermediaries, or to be exact their money managers.[47] As stated in the *G20/OECD Principles*

[41] Sjåfjell et al., 'Shareholder Primacy: The Main Barrier to Sustainable Companies', p. 79.

[42] I. Anabtawi and L. A. Stout, 'Fiduciary Duties for Activist Shareholders' (2008) 60 *Stanford Law Review*, 1255–1308, 1280–1281; V. Harper Ho, '"Enlightened Shareholder Value": Corporate Governance Beyond the Shareholder-Stakeholder Divide' (2010) 36 *The Journal of Corporation Law*, 59–112, 66.

[43] Generally, see R. J. Gilson, 'Controlling Shareholders and Corporate Governance: Complicating the Comparative Taxonomy' (2006) 119:6 *Harvard Law Review*, 1641–1679.

[44] In the legal sense, shareholders of course do not own the company they have invested in. They own shares that bring rights and duties in the company.

[45] The Economist, 'Reinventing the Company: Entrepreneurs are Redesigning the Basic Building Block of Capitalism', *The Economist*, 24 October 2015, from the print edition, available at: www.economist.com/news/leaders/21676767-entrepreneurs-are-redesigning-basic-building-block-capitalism-reinventing-company?frsc=dg%7Cd..

[46] See, for instance, Strine, 'One Fundamental'.

[47] Strine, 'Toward Common Sense', 4–5.

of Corporate Governance, the real world of corporate governance and ownership is therefore no longer characterised by a straight and uncompromised
relationship between the performance of the company and the income of the
ultimate beneficiaries of shareholdings.[48]

There has also been a normative change. The increasing power of institutional investors searching worldwide for investment opportunities has been
accompanied by their vocal calls for effective governance. Firms seeking to
obtain capital in international securities markets will therefore be compelled
to adjust their governance practices to meet the expectations of potential
activist institutional investors. Pressures from foreign institutional investors to
improve standards of behaviour, financial reporting, board accountability and
shareholder activism have furthermore stimulated the development of codes
of good governance.[49] A primary example of these are the 'stewardship codes'
modelled by the *UK Stewardship Codes*.[50] The perceived shift in the corporate
governance role of corporate shareholders, 'stewardship', is therefore due to
the change in controlling structures from dispersed shareholdings to more
concentrated ones of institutional shareholders.[51]

These conflicting interests, short-termism and regulation, all impose costs
and externalities. Money managers, however, reductively focus on equity
returns. They therefore turn a blind eye to any consideration of the externality
effects or the larger economic outcomes upon the economy for its citizens.[52]
End-user investors such as employees, saving for retirement benefits, depend
on their portfolios' ability to generate sustainable long-term growth. Short-
term bubbles in equity prices caused by money managers therefore come at
the expense of their need for more durable and higher long-term growth, and
so the need for sustainability. The system of forced capitalism is counterpro-
ductive for its ultimate beneficiaries, but also for society as a whole. Further
empowering money managers with short-term holding periods will subject
employees to lower long-term growth and job creation, to wreckage from corporate failures owing to excessive risk taking and debt, and the collateral harm

---

[48] OECD, *G20/OECD Principles of Corporate Governance* (Paris: OECD Publishing, 2015),
     p. 29, available at: http://dx.doi.org/10.1787/9789264236882-en.
[49] R. V. Aguilera and A. Cuervo-Cazurra, 'Codes of Good Governance Worldwide: What Is the
     Trigger?' (2004) 25 (3) *Organization Studies*, 415–443, 430.
[50] Financial Reporting Council, The UK Stewardship Code, July 2010; Financial Reporting
     Council, The UK Stewardship Code, September 2012; Financial Reporting Council, The
     UK Stewardship Code 2020; see Hill, 'Good Activist/Bad Activist'. On stewardship codes
     generally see Katelouzou and Puchniak (eds.), *Global Shareholder Stewardship* (Cambridge:
     Cambridge University Press, 2022).
[51] Hill, 'Good Activist/Bad Activist', 499.
[52] Strine, 'Can We Do Better', 461.

caused when corporations face strong incentives to cut regulatory corners in order to maximise short-term profits.[53]

The fundamental question about shareholder activism is whether it creates societal value, measured as value in the target company and in society as a whole.[54] Yet, paradoxically, the institutional investors in Europe are seen as being an increasingly active force for sustainable finance. The HLEG urged, in its Interim report, a more 'active responsible ownership', and use of corporate governance and stewardship codes (e.g. the UK Stewardship Code) as tools to increase sustainability in the investment community, by making institutional shareholders more effective in holding firms to account.[55] The HLEG also proposed, as a recommendation, the development of 'a set of European stewardship principles (building on established principles) that incorporate active ownership and long-term value creation'.[56]

The purpose of this chapter is to focus on the activism of institutional investors and the impact of that activism on both the target productive companies and their ultimate beneficiaries, and how they could be incentivised to more sustainable behaviour in their activism. The focus is on the EU. However, the markets for institutional investors are global. A broader perspective including, for example, North America and Asia is therefore taken. The most important impact of institutional activism is arguably normative, causing changes in corporate governance. Specific attention is therefore given to governance questions.

The structure of the remainder of the chapter is as follows. In Section 7.2 I discuss the nature of shareholder activism in general, in both the US and in Europe. In Section 7.3 I discuss the possibilities for activism for sustainability, and particularly how law should respond to the challenge from activists for sustainability. The chapter ends with conclusions in Section 7.4.

7.2 AGE OF ACTIVISM: THE VOYAGE ACROSS THE ATLANTIC

Shareholder activism has its roots in the hostile 'corporate raiders' of the 1980s.[57] The picture has, however, become more colourful, more critical and more robust, as has the idea of the purpose of a listed company and the agency relationships prevailing in it. Globalisation and the rapid growth in

---

[53] Ibid., 459.
[54] Denes, Karpoff and McWilliams, 'Thirty Years of Shareholder Activism', 409.
[55] HLEG Interim Report, p. 26 (using the French, German and Dutch codes as positive examples).
[56] Ibid., p. 61.
[57] See, for example, P. H. Eddey, 'Corporate Raiders and Takeover Targets' (1991) 18 *Journal of Business Finance & Accounting*, 151–171.

international financial markets increased the presence of US-style institutional investors all over the world. Institutional investors such as pension funds have become important capital providers, particularly in equity markets that otherwise struggle to provide sufficiently accessible capital. The presence of Anglo-American institutional investors in the global equity market therefore acted as a catalyst for the worldwide diffusion of corporate governance practices.[58] Pension funds and other institutional investors, especially hedge funds and mutual funds, have changed the behaviour of especially 'independent' board members to one in which they are more willing to compromise with the short-term interest of activists, than stand on principle for a company's long-term interest. This change has been facilitated by withhold campaigns, proxy contests, proposals to eliminate takeover defences, proposals to increase shareholder power in key areas of corporate decision-making and campaigns to change corporate business plans.[59] These tactics also include letter writing, litigation and publicity campaigns, as well as dialogue with corporate management or the board, asking questions at general meetings and filing formal shareholder proposals.[60]

Activists ultimately also affect the law. For example US corporate law makes corporate managers accountable to only one constituency (the shareholders), this accountability being tightened because market developments have concentrated voting power in the hands of institutional investors and because information technology innovations have made communication and joint action among shareholders easier.[61] The idea of the sole purpose of a US public corporation being to maximise financial gain for its shareholders is not new.[62] However, the concept of 'shareholder primacy' has, through activism, come to be widely accepted among practitioners. Activism therefore represents, in practice and in law, a new and radical shift from the passive, dispersed and faceless individual shareholders described by Adolf Berle and Gardiner Means.[63]

Institutional investors have, through the power provided by forced capitalism, been able to challenge the managers and board members of the

---

[58] Aguilera and Cuervo-Cazurra, 'Codes of Good Governance', 430.
[59] L. E. Strine, Jr., 'Making It Easier for Directors to "Do the Right Thing"?' (2014) 4 *Harvard Business Law Review*, 235–254, 239.
[60] R. V. Aguilera, K. Desender, M. K. Bednar and J. H. Lee, 'Connecting the Dots: Bringing External Corporate Governance into the Corporate Governance Puzzle' (2015) 9 (1) *The Academy of Management Annals*, 483–573, 535.
[61] Strine, 'Making It Easier', 241–242.
[62] See *Dodge v. Ford Motor Company*, 170 NW 668 (Mich 1919).
[63] A. A. Berle and G. C. Means, *The Modern Corporation and Private Property* (New York: The Macmillan Company, 1932).

companies they invest in on a variety of issues. This includes urging firms to make structural changes to their boards and redesign firm voting procedures. Leading US institutional investors such as the California Public Employees' Retirement System (CalPERS), for example, believe that 'good governance is good business', and therefore by default creates shareholder value. CalPERS had, as early as 1996, established a specific corporate governance office to pressure domestic and international firms to adopt shareholder-friendly proposals and other measures designed to improve share performance.[64] The rise of institutional investors has therefore not been caused by market forces alone. US regulation was also an important force in urging, for example, pension funds in particular to activism. The Employee Retirement Income Security Act of 1974 and similar state regulation (such as the California Constitution for CalPERS) set a mandatory trust structure for most private pension and retirement accounts through a 'prudent investor standard', requiring fiduciaries to act exclusively and solely in the interests of the fund's beneficiaries.[65] This exclusive and mandatory focus on the financial benefits obtained for beneficiaries distinguishes US pension law from that in the UK and Europe, which is more tolerant of non-financial investment factors such as ESG.[66]

Not all institutional investors nor their activism are, however, similar. Shareholder activism is a more recent phenomenon in Europe than in the US,[67] and European regulation of pension funds and companies is also more tolerant of ESG investing than the US equivalent. For example, Norwegian domestic institutional investors have long been interested in activism,[68] and investor engagement in Sweden, owing to shareholder friendly corporate governance, has in recent years led to both domestic activism and foreign activism towards management. Nordic activism, which is based on dialogue with boards rather than confrontation, is 'softer' and more long term oriented than for example in the US.[69] Shareholder activism is also generally viewed

---

[64] Aguilera and Cuervo-Cazurra, 'Codes of Good Governance Worldwide', 430.

[65] See M. M. Schanzenbach and R. H. Sitkoff, 'Reconciling Fiduciary Duty and Social Conscience: The Law and Economics of ESG Investing by a Trustee' (2020) 72 *Stanford Law Review*, 381–454, 384, 394.

[66] Schanzenbach and Sitkoff, 'Reconciling', 3, 15–16. According to Schanzenbach and Sitkoff (pp. 15–16), the US position reflects a 'paternalistic public policy of protecting the financial security of a retired worker against poor spending and investment decisions by her younger self'.

[67] D. Katelouzou, 'Worldwide Hedge Fund Activism: Dimensions and Legal Determinants' (2015) 17 (3) *University of Pennsylvania Journal of Business Law*, 789–860, 791–792.

[68] B. Scholtens and R. Sievänen, 'Drivers of Socially Responsible Investing: A Case Study of Four Nordic Countries' (2013) 115 *Journal of Business Ethics*, 605–616.

[69] See Mähönen and Johnsen, 'Law, Culture and Sustainability'; Mähönen, Sjåfjell and Mee, 'Stewardship Norwegian-Style'.

in Europe in a far more positive light than in the US, as illustrated by the European Commission's desire to increase shareholders' say in European listed companies and by a neutral attitude towards hedge funds and proxy advisors working with them. According to the EU 2012 Company Law Action Plan, an effective corporate governance framework is of crucial importance, and so is the shareholders' role in the promotion of corporate governance, which can have a positive effect on both the company's and its shareholders' interests.[70] In the 2014 European Commission proposal for amending SHRD I with SHRD II, the Commission iterated that effective and sustainable shareholder engagement is one of the cornerstones of listed companies' corporate governance model.[71] It also iterated that effective shareholder control is a prerequisite for sound corporate governance, and should therefore be facilitated and encouraged.[72]

7.3 ACTIVISM FOR SUSTAINABILITY

7.3.1 *How to Regulate Investors to Sustainability?*

Is there then hope for sustainable shareholder activism as the EU HLEG for example claims, or is it a mission impossible? The stewardship trend sends a mixed message, as the Danish example shows. In January 2016 the Danish Minister of Business and Growth requested that the Danish Committee on Corporate Governance, which is responsible for the Danish Corporate Governance Codes,[73] drafted a stewardship code 'in order to encourage the kind of stewardship in Danish listed companies that is beneficial to their value creation'.[74] The Code, published in November 2017, consists of seven principles: engagement policy, monitoring and dialogue, escalation,[75] collaboration with other investors, voting policy, conflicts of interest and reporting. The aim of the Stewardship Code is, according to the Danish Committee on Corporate Governance, similar to that of its Corporate Governance Code and

---

[70] European Commission, Company Law Action Plan, 3.
[71] Commission Proposal, 12; see in detail K. Reynisson, 'Related Party Transactions: Analysis of Proposed Article 9c of Shareholders' Rights Directive' (2016) 13 (5) *European Company Law*, 175–182.
[72] Para. 3 of the Preamble of the Commission Proposal.
[73] The Committee on Corporate Governance, Recommendations for corporate governance 2005–2020, available at: https://corporategovernance.dk/recommendations-corporate-governance.
[74] The Committee on Corporate Governance, Stewardship Code (November 2016) (Danish Stewardship Code), 3, available at: https://corporategovernance.dk/stewardship-code.
[75] 'Escalation' means enlarging stewardship activities beyond regular monitoring and dialogue; Danish Stewardship Code, 8.

is 'to promote the companies' long-term value creation and thereby contribute to maximising long-term return for investors'. Therefore the Codes 'are mutually reinforcing in serving a common purpose'.[76] Birkmose and Madsen consider that it would be better, instead of working with two parallel codes, to seek a closer integration between the duties of the institutional investors and asset managers and the duties of the boards of the investee companies. SHRD II is, however, unlikely to have much effect on Danish stewardship owing to the many parallels with the existing Stewardship Code.[77] The Danish Corporate Governance Code was revised in 2020 to reflect the implementation of SHRD in Denmark. Unlike the previous codes, the 2020 Code is based on sustainability and long-term value creation as a company's purpose.[78]

There is, however, no one single type of activist shareholder, despite the focus in the international discussion on short-term-focused activists such as hedge funds. The focus in the more positive European discussion is on money managers, though. Action 7 of the European Commission Action Plan *Financing Sustainable Growth* states that EU law requires institutional investors and asset managers to act in the best interest of their end-investors or beneficiaries. Institutional investors and asset managers do not systematically consider sustainability factors and risks in the investment process, nor do they sufficiently disclose to their clients whether and how they consider these sustainability factors in their decision-making. As the Commission stated, end-investors may not therefore receive the full information they require to be able to take into account sustainability-related issues in their investment decisions. Investors therefore, and as a result of this, do not take the impact of sustainability risks sufficiently into account when assessing the performance of their investments over time.[79]

The investment motives and horizons of institutional investors may, despite possible fiduciary duties and disclosure rules, differ materially.[80] They can vary widely from 'fearless defenders of long-term investors to short-term profit maximisation seekers to social activists with non-financial agendas'.[81] There are two key motivations for engaging in activism. Financial motivation (to

---

[76] Danish Stewardship Code, 3.

[77] H. S. Birkmose and M. B. Madsen, 'The Danish Stewardship Code – The Past, the Present and the Future', in Katelouzou and Puchniak (eds.), *Global Shareholder Stewardship* (Cambridge: Cambridge University Press, 2022), pp. 150–173, 173.

[78] Danish Committee on Corporate Governance, Danish Recommendations on Corporate Governance (2 December 2020), 3, 7, available at: https://corporategovernance.dk/sites/default/files/media/anbefalinger_for_god_selskabsledelse_engelsk.pdf.

[79] European Commission, Action Plan, 8.

[80] J. C. Coffee and D. Palia, 'The Wolf at the Door: The Impact of Hedge Fund Activism on Corporate Governance' (2016) 1 (1) *Annals of Corporate Governance*, 1–94.

[81] Aguilera et al., 'Connecting the Dots', 534–535.

increase shareholder value) and social motivation (such as to divest from conflict zones and adopt corporate social responsibility practices). What is clear, however, is that activists such as hedge funds have contributed to a fundamental change in the division of powers between corporate organs in listed companies. This is particularly so in the US, where board selection has traditionally been staggered to prevent sudden policy changes. It is also so where the board has been vested with general competence in material and fundamental decisions, such as in the People's Republic of China or the Nordic countries, but not in, for example, the UK. The UK abandoned a management-centric governance model in the mid-twentieth century, opting for a US-style shareholder-centrist model of director accountability to shareholders, as explicitly shown in the changes from 1948 to 2006 in the Companies Acts.[82] The corporate governance environment has simultaneously changed decisively in the US since the 1980s, owing to the activism of shareholders such as hedge funds. This has narrowed the board's competence and expanded the competence of the annual general meeting, in particular in board member selection and in major corporate transactions.[83] The role of shareholders in non-Anglo-American jurisdictions has, however, also strengthened owing to legislative actions such as SHRD II in the EU or influential control-holders in the Nordic countries, China and other Asian countries.

The key to the differences between ESG and non-ESG investing is therefore regulation, and whether it is restrictive, permissible or mandatory for sustainable finance. Three alternatives are proposed: increasing shareholder rights, increasing disclosure and reforming company law in a more fundamental way.

7.3.2 *Increasing Shareholders' Rights?*

Those hoping for greater institutional investor commitment to sustainable finance have contributed to empowerment projects such as the stewardship codes or to the EU SHRD II.[84] These projects are, however, unlikely to achieve success, because they do not truly create incentives to act in accordance with them for institutional investors.[85] On the contrary, passive investors eagerly ally with activists who have the opportunity to, through shareholder

[82] A. Johnston, 'Market-Led Sustainability through Information Disclosure: The UK Approach', in Sjåfjell and Bruner (eds.), *The Cambridge Handbook of Corporate Law, Corporate Governance and Sustainability*, pp. 204–217, 205–206.

[83] Strine, 'One Fundamental', 13–16; Coffee and Palia, 'The Wolf at the Door', 18 and 100.

[84] See Rock, 'Institutional Investors', pp. 15–17.

[85] Gilson and Gordon, 'The Agency Costs of Agency Capitalism' (2013) 113 (4) *Columbia Law Review*, 863–927, 888; Rock, 'Institutional Investors', p. 13.

empowerment, achieve a short-term abnormal return through a promise of dividends and share buy-backs. Passive investors can therefore quickly ignore the lip service they have paid to long-term return development.[86] An exception might be public institutional investors, whose management remuneration is moderate and is not tied to the institutional investor's income.[87] However, as stated in the UK Stewardship Code, the core goal of stewardship or active ownership is, at the end of the day, the 'enhancing and protecting … [of] value for the ultimate beneficiary or client'.[88] The stewardship codes, in that sense, enhance short-term activism. The same applies in a clearer way to, for example, the Danish stewardship code.

No matter how attractive the idea is in theory, efforts to increase shareholders' rights are a risk to a company's interests where active shareholders' interests differ and there is no evidence of their positive impact on the company's long-term value. The ideal situation is where efforts to increase shareholders' rights do not discourage those investors who wish the company well and who want to create added value, and also where bad corporate raiders and seekers of sub-optimal returns can be prevented from gaining control through acquisitions. This is, however, unfortunately impossible.[89] The examples show that the first area to suffer from activists' attacks on corporate management is the long-term corporate interest.[90]

There is furthermore a counter-effect. The focus when analysing in detail the European regulation for encouraging a more long-term engagement of shareholders is solely on shareholder identification, the transmission of information, the facilitation of the exercise of shareholders' rights and the oversight of executive remuneration policies.[91] SHRD II gives the right to listed companies to identify their shareholders and requires intermediaries to cooperate in that identification process. It also aims to improve the listed companies' communication with their shareholders, in particular the transmission of information along the chain of intermediaries, and requires intermediaries to facilitate the exercise of shareholder rights. The Commission Implementing Regulation even aims to prevent the diverging implementation of the provisions of the Directive.[92]

---

[86] See Katelouzou, 'Worldwide Hedge Fund Activism', 792 and the examples therein.

[87] Gilson and Gordon, 'The Agency Costs of Agency Capitalism', 889.

[88] UK Stewardship Code, 6.

[89] L. Enriques and M. Gatti, 'Creeping Acquisitions in Europe: Enabling Companies to Be Better Safe than Sorry' (2014) 15 (1) *Journal of Corporate Law Studies*, 55–101.

[90] See Coffee and Palia, 'The Wolf at the Door', 5–6 and 9–10.

[91] See European Commission, Company Law Action Plan, 7–11.

[92] See preamble of the Commission Implementing Regulation (EU) 2018/1212 of 3 September 2018 laying down minimum requirements implementing the provisions of Directive 2007/36/

7.3.3 *Disclosure Only or Something More?*

Repealing prohibiting regulation and just facilitating and mandating investors to participate in active sustainable investing seems not to be enough, however, because there are no market incentives. The Action Plan builds upon recommendations presented by the HLEG Final report and (unlike the European Commission's Company Law Action Plan) is cautiously (re)taking a more regulatory path. The Action Plan has three main objectives: reorient capital flows towards sustainable investment to achieve sustainable and inclusive growth; manage financial risks stemming from climate change, environmental degradation and social issues; and foster transparency and long-termism in financial and economic activity.[93]

The Commission emphasises, in particular, that current EU rules on the duty of institutional investors and asset managers to consider sustainability factors and risks in investment decision processes, are not sufficiently clear nor consistent across sectors (see section 7.3.1).[94] The Commission, to tackle this problem, proposed Action 7 to clarify institutional investors' and asset managers' duties in relation to sustainability considerations, subject to the outcome of an impact assessment. The proposal will aim to explicitly require institutional investors and asset managers to integrate sustainability considerations in investment decision-making processes, as well as increasing transparency towards end-investors on how they integrate such sustainability factors in their investment decisions, in particular their exposure to sustainability risks.[95]

As a first step, the Commission in May 2018 issued its proposal for a regulation for the disclosure obligations for institutional investors and asset managers of how they integrate ESG factors in their investment decision-making risk processes. Requirements to do so as part of their duty towards investors and beneficiaries will be further specified through delegated acts.[96] The Regulation was issued in November 2019, and entered into force in March 2021.[97] The Disclosure Regulation applies to 'financial

---

EC of the European Parliament and of the Council as regards shareholder identification, the transmission of information and the facilitation of the exercise of shareholders rights, OJ L 223, 4.9.2018, 1.

[93] European Commission, Action Plan, 2.

[94] Ibid., 8.

[95] Ibid., 8–9.

[96] European Commission, Proposal for a Regulation of the European Parliament and of the Council on disclosures relating to sustainable investments and sustainability risks and amending Directive (EU) 2016/2341, COM(2018) 354 final.

[97] Regulation (EU) 2019/2088 of the European Parliament and of the Council of 27 November 2019 on sustainability-related disclosures in the financial services sector, PE/87/2019/REV/1, OJ L 317, 9.12.2019, 1.

market participants'[98] and 'financial advisers'.[99] The Regulation adds directly applicable disclosure requirements to sectoral legislation such as the UCITS Directive,[100] the AIFM Directive, the MiFID II Directive, the Solvency II Directive,[101] and the IDD Directive.[102]

Financial market participants and financial advisors must, according to the Regulation, disclose on their websites information on their policies on the integration of sustainability risks in their investment decision-making processes. If they consider the principal adverse impacts of investment decisions on sustainability factors, or if they employ more than 500 people, then they

[98] The definition of financial market participant in Article 1(1)–(10) of the Disclosure Regulation includes:
- insurance undertakings that make available an insurance-based investment product (IBIP)
- investment firms as defined in Article 4(1)(1) of Directive 2014/65/EU of the European Parliament and of the Council of 15 May 2014 on markets in financial instruments and amending Directive 2002/92/EC and Directive 2011/61/EU, OJ L 173, 12.6.2014, 349 (MiFiD II Directive), which provides portfolio management
- institutions for occupational retirement provision
- manufacturers of a pension product
- alternative investment fund managers (AIFMs)
- pan-European Personal Pension Product providers
- managers of a qualifying venture capital fund registered in accordance with Article 15 of Regulation (EU) No 345/2013 of the European Parliament and of the Council of 17 April 2013 on European venture capital funds, OJ L 115, 25.4.2013, 1 (EuVECA Regulation)
- managers of qualifying social entrepreneurship funds registered in accordance with Article 15 of Regulation (EU) No 346/2013 of the European Parliament and of the Council of 17 April 2013 on European social entrepreneurship funds, OJ L 115, 25.4.2013, 18 (EuSEF Regulation]
- management companies of undertakings for collective investment in transferable securities (UCITs)
- credit institutions that provide portfolio management.

[99] The definition of financial adviser in Article 1(11) of the Disclosure Regulation includes:
- insurance intermediaries that provide insurance advice on IBIPs
- insurance undertakings that provide insurance advice on IBIPs
- credit institutions that provide investment advice
- investment firms that provide investment advice
- AIFMs that provide investment advice in accordance with Article 6(4)(b)(i) of Directive 2011/61/EU of the European Parliament and of the Council of 8 June 2011 on Alternative Investment Fund Managers and amending Directives 2003/41/EC and 2009/65/EC and Regulations (EC) No 1060/2009 and (EU) No 1095/2010, OJ L 174, 1.7.2011,1 (AIFM Directive)
- UCITS management companies that provide investment advice in accordance with Article 6(3)(b)(i) of the MiFiD II Directive.

[100] Directive 2009/65/EC of the European Parliament and of the Council of 13 July 2009 on the coordination of laws, regulations and administrative provisions relating to undertakings for collective investment in transferable securities (UCITS), OJ L 302 17.11.2009, 32.

[101] Directive 2009/138/EC of the European Parliament and of the Council of 25 November 2009 on the taking-up and pursuit of the business of Insurance and Reinsurance (Solvency II), OJ L 335, 17.12.2009, 1.

[102] Directive (EU) 2016/97 of the European Parliament and of the Council of 20 January 2016 on insurance distribution (recast), OJ L 26, 2.2.2016, 19.

are to provide a statement of due diligence policies for these principal adverse impacts. If they do not consider any adverse impacts of investment decisions on sustainability factors, then clear reasons are to be given for not doing so and, where relevant, it is to be clearly stated whether and when they intend to consider such adverse impacts. Information is also to be provided on how their remuneration policies are consistent with the integration of sustainability risks.

Financial market participants and financial advisors must also disclose, as part of their pre-contractual disclosure obligations, the manner in which sustainability risks are integrated into their investment decisions. This disclosure is to include the result of the assessment of the likely impacts of sustainability risks on the returns of their funds or portfolios. If sustainability risks are deemed not to be relevant, then a clear and concise explanation of why not is to be given. If principal adverse impacts of investment decisions on sustainability factors are considered, or if they employ more than 500 people, then a clear and reasoned explanation of whether and how that fund or portfolio considers principal adverse impacts on sustainability factors is to be provided within three years of the entry into force of the Disclosure Regulation, for each fund or portfolio that they offer. A statement on principal adverse impacts on sustainability factors is to be provided in periodic reports. If the adverse impacts of investment decisions on sustainability factors are not considered, then a statement that the asset manager does not consider the adverse impacts of investment decisions on sustainability factors, and a reasoned explanation for not doing so, are to be provided.

The Disclosure Regulation is an important step. Market transparency is also an important corporate governance aim, as it is considered to be able to bring reputational benefits for companies and more legitimacy in the eyes of stakeholders and society as a whole.[103] The enhancement of transparency and shareholder engagement, according to the Company Law Action Plan, go hand in hand.[104]

Transparency rules are important. They do, however, contain risks for sustainability. The Commission recognised the importance in the Action Plan of ensuring that accounting standards do not directly or indirectly discourage sustainable and long-term investments. Greater flexibility in the endorsement of international financial reporting standards is therefore required to allow specific adjustments that would be more conducive to long-term investment.[105]

---

[103] Para. 5 of the Preamble of the Commission Recommendation of 9 April 2014 on the quality of corporate governance reporting ('comply or explain') 2014/208/E, OJ L 109, 12.4.2014, 43; K. Reynisson, 'Related Party Transactions', 176.

[104] European Commission, Company Law Action Plan, 3, 4.

[105] European Commission, Communication from the Commission to the European Parliament, the European Council, the Council, the European Central Bank, the European Economic

The Commission emphasised an appropriate balance between flexibility and the standardisation of disclosure necessary to generate the data needed for investment decisions, through endorsing the so called Non-Financial Reporting Directive.[106] This allows the disclosure of material information on key environmental, social and governance aspects and on how risks stemming from them are managed in a 'flexible manner'.[107] The main problem, however, is that sustainability in these reports has remained biased owing to a lack of a true sustainability basis in the reports. The meanings of sustainability, corporate social responsibility and related terms are ambiguous, and companies are therefore often uncertain how to define and implement sustainability.[108]

7.3.4 *Harder Line: Should Company Law Respond to the Activists?*

One can turn, as the third alternative, to the target companies and their regulation as an answer to the potential activist threat. Contrary to the belief of the international corporate governance community, the effectiveness and the credibility of the corporate governance framework and company oversight cannot depend solely on the willingness and ability of institutional investors to make informed use of their shareholder rights, and to effectively exercise their ownership functions in the companies in which they invest.[109] If our conclusion is that shareholder primacy activists (or shareholders in general) in a free-market mostly create harm and only by chance create good for sustainable value creation, then preventing the devastating impact of activists through company law is difficult as the attempt itself may cause companies more harm than good. The starting point as such is simple. We should protect the 'good' activists from the 'evil' activists, because the 'evil' activists may also infect the 'good' investors. This is, of course, only a defensive victory. As long as shareholders have (and this is one of the main axioms of company law)

---

and Social Committee and the Committee of the Regions: Action Plan: Financing Sustainable Growth (8.3.2018, COM/2018/097 final), p. 10, available at: https://eur-lex.europa .eu/legal-content/EN/TXT/?uri=CELEX:52018DC0097#footnoteref34.

[106] Directive 2014/95/EU of the European Parliament and of the Council of 22 October 2014 amending Directive 2013/34/EU as regards disclosure of non-financial and diversity information by certain large undertakings and groups, OJ L 330, 15.11.2014, p. 1–9.

[107] European Commission, Proposal for a Directive of the European Parliament and of the Council amending Council Directives 78/660/EEC and 83/349/EEC as regards disclosure of non-financial and diversity information by certain large companies and groups, COM(2013) 207 final, 6.

[108] N. E. Landrum and B. Ohsowski, 'Identifying Worldviews on Corporate Sustainability: A Content Analysis of Corporate Sustainability Reports' (2018) 27 *Business Strategy and the Environment*, 128–151, 130.

[109] Cf. G20/OECD Principles of Corporate Governance, 30.

the last word on board composition, then activists cannot be prevented from sooner or later shortening the planning horizons of companies, so preventing them from long-term investment and curbing companies' commitment to research and development.[110]

It is, however, possible to slow them by using company law. European company law is still board oriented, despite the shareholder primacy drive and being strengthened by EU regulation (foremost SHRD II). Activists' entry cannot be prevented in a free market. The price they must pay for influence should, however, not be too low. The best interests of the ultimate beneficiaries are served by empowering a strong central authority (the board) to make business decisions and not by interfering with its unconflicted judgements.[111] The best way to ensure that corporations generate sustainable wealth for diversified shareholders is therefore to give the boards and managers a strong hand to take and manage risks and implement business strategies, without the constant disruption of shifting short-term market sentiments and without fearing displacement of themselves or those strategies by shareholders.[112]

The Action Plan can be seen to be a cautious step in this direction. Corporate governance can, according to the Commission, 'significantly contribute to a more sustainable economy, allowing companies to take the strategic steps necessary to develop new technologies, to strengthen business models and to improve performance. This would in turn improve their risk management practices and competitiveness, thus creating jobs and spurring innovation.'[113] The Commission promises in Action 10 to assess the possible need to require corporate boards to develop and disclose a sustainability strategy, including appropriate due diligence throughout the supply chain, and measurable sustainability targets, and the possible need to clarify the rules according to which directors are expected to act in the company's long-term interest. The Commission invited the ESAs to collect evidence of undue short-term pressure from capital markets on corporations, and to consider any necessary further steps based on such evidence. The Commission more specifically invited ESMA to collect information on undue short-termism in capital markets, including portfolio turnover and equity holding periods by asset managers, and whether there are any practices in capital markets that generate undue short-term pressure in the real economy.

---

[110] Coffee and Palia, 'The Wolf at the Door', 105.
[111] K. J. Arrow, 'Scale Returns in Communication and Elite Control of Organizations' (1991) 7 *The Journal of Law, Economics & Organization*, 1–6, 6; Bratton and Wachter, 'The Case Against', 660; Strine, 'Can We Do Better', 455 fn.19.
[112] Strine, 'Can We Do Better', 455, 457.
[113] European Commission, Action Plan, 11.

In February 2019 the Commission invited ESAs to each develop a report that presents initial evidence of potential pressures from the financial sector on corporations to prioritise near-term shareholder interests over the long-term growth of the firm. Qualitative sources and relevant literature should be complemented in the evidence gathering and, where feasible, by quantitative evidence such as data from public and commercial databases. The Commission also expected the ESAs to engage with the most relevant stakeholders, to develop the requested report. The request aimed at providing a pragmatic approach towards delivery of the report, the deadline for this being the end of 2019.[114]

EBA, EIOPA and ESMA advice was published on 18 December 2019.[115] ESMA recommended improvements in issuers' ESG disclosures by developing European regulation and international harmonisation of disclosure frameworks, and by enhancing institutional investor engagement, for example by a review of SHRD II and of whether it effectively encourages long-term engagement. The EBA highlighted the need to promote long-term approaches, a robust regulatory prudential framework as a pre-condition for long-term investments and the disclosure of long-term risks and opportunities. The EIOPA recommended long-term performance benchmarks.

The market for shareholders' corporate influence should be in balance with the wide competence of the board and its business judgement. The control and representation of the corporation should therefore be a part of the board's competence, not the shareholders'. The board also enjoys broad discretion under existing law to consider its best business judgement in fulfilling the company's interests. These legal firewalls protect a strong board from its shareholders, although the shareholder empowerment movement tends to compel

---

[114] European Commission, Cover letter to the call for advice to the European Supervisory Authorities to collect evidence of undue short-term pressure from the financial sector on corporations, 1 February 2019, available at: https://ec.europa.eu/info/sites/info/files/business_economy_euro/banking_and_finance/documents/190201-call-for-advice-to-esas-short-term-pressure-cover-letter_en.pdf.

[115] The European Securities and Markets Authority (ESMA), 'Report: undue short-term pressure on corporations', ESMA30-22-762 (18 December 2019), available at: www.esma.europa.eu/press-news/esma-news/esma-proposes-strengthened-rules-address-undue-short-termism-in-securities; European Banking Authority (EBA), EBA report on undue short-term pressure from the financial sector on corporations (18 December 2019), available at: https://eba.europa.eu/eba-calls-banks-consider-long-term-horizons-their-strategies-and-business-activities; European Insurance and Occupational Pensions Authority (EIOPA), Advice: Potential undue short-term pressure from financial markets on corporates: Investigation on European insurance and occupational pension sectors: Search for evidence, Year-end 2018, EIOPA-BOS-19-537 (18 December 2019), available at: www.eiopa.europa.eu/content/potential-undue-short-term-pressure-financial-markets_en.

the board to focus solely on shareholder wealth maximisation.[116] The law is, however, behind the board. Most jurisdictions in Europe also follow a 'business judgment rule', guiding the courts not to second-guess the management's business decisions.[117] Shareholder centrism is a 'market norm' or social norm, not a legal rule.[118]

The heterogeneity of shareholder (and general stakeholder) interests makes centralised decision-making by the board more, not less, essential to the efficient sustainable management of the firm.[119] This is especially important in those jurisdictions that have (so far) followed 'enlightened shareholder value' models, such as the UK,[120] and Finland.[121] This emphasises long-term shareholder value and the requirement that the board considers the effects of their decisions on 'extended stakeholder constituencies'.[122] The board should on the other hand know the business, and should keep the management on a short leash. Chief executive officers (CEOs) and management who are insulated from shareholder pressure and who do not receive high-power pay are less prone to engage in risk-taking.[123] Conversely, equity-based pay, and so greater shareholder orientation, and greater risk-taking in financial firms tend to associate with the run-up to a financial crisis.[124] This requires insiders on the board.

The strategy chosen by the Commission has, however, contrary to this approach of strengthening the role of the board, primarily been the opposite of this, as seen in the SHRD II. The control rights of institutional investors and asset managers over the corporate assets have been enhanced, to allow them a

[116] Harper Ho, '"Enlightened Shareholder Value"', 61.

[117] Sjåfjell et al., 'Shareholder Primacy', 96; B. Sjåfjell, J. T. Mähönen, A. Johnston and J. Cullen, 'Obstacles to Sustainable Global Business. Towards EU Policy Coherence for Sustainable Development' (2019) 2019–02 *University of Oslo Faculty of Law Research Paper*, 1–106, 32–34, available at SSRN: https://ssrn.com/abstract=3354401.

[118] C. M. Bruner, 'Conceptions of Corporate Purpose in Post-Crisis Financial Firms' (2013) 36 *Seattle University Law Review*, 527–561, 530, 532.

[119] Harper Ho, '"Enlightened Shareholder Value"', 69, referring to S. M. Bainbridge, 'The Case for Limited Shareholder Voting Rights' (2006) 53 *UCLA Law Review*, 601–636.

[120] For instance section 172 of the UK Companies Act of 2006, c. 46.

[121] J. Mähönen, 'Finland: Corporate Governance: Nordic Tradition with American Spices', in A. Fleckner and K. Hopt (eds.), *Comparative Corporate Governance: A Functional and International Analysis* (Cambridge: Cambridge University Press, 2013), pp. 393–443.

[122] Harper Ho, '"Enlightened Shareholder Value"', 79.

[123] L. A. Bebchuk and H. Spamann, 'Regulating Bankers' Pay' (2010) 98 *Georgetown Law Journal*, 247, 262; C. M. Bruner, 'Conceptions', 552.

[124] S. Deakin, 'The Corporation as Commons: Rethinking Property Rights, Governance and Sustainability in the Business Enterprise' (2012) 37 (2) *Queen's Law Journal*, 339–381, 341–343, 379; Bruner, 'Conceptions', 552. As an example, banks receiving bailout funds in the US had more 'independent' boards, larger boards, more outside board memberships and greater incentive pay for CEOs. See R. B. Adams, 'Governance and the Financial Crisis' (2009) 248/2009 *ECGI – Finance Working Paper*, 1–22, 13, available at SSRN: https://ssrn.com/abstract=1398583.

greater ability to protect their investments.[125] The most important aspect is that the focus has been on non-national institutional investors and asset managers, and their engagement.[126] In the same way, the G20/OECD Principles urge engagement, such as a continuing dialogue between institutional investors and companies.[127] On the other hand, there is clear concern in the February 2019 call about the prevailing corporate culture that focuses on near-term performance at the expense of the mid- to long-term objectives, the influence of activist shareholder engagement that is focused on short-term profit extraction, and short-term market pressure incentivising under-investment in long-term value drivers including innovation and human capital.[128]

7.4 CONCLUSIONS

The European examples illustrate that there is little future in activating passivists to sustainability without hard law. Passivists are the underdog in the free markets. Activist short-term investors are always able to engage in hedging strategies that limit their exposure if their preferred strategies for the corporation do not turn out to be sound.[129] They can always use derivatives and other financial innovations to decouple their voting power from their economic interest.[130] Other institutional investors are also of little help without strong regulation.[131] Public employee pension funds are furthermore vulnerable to being used as a vehicle for advancing political/social goals that are unrelated to shareholder interests in general.[132] The state as a market actor might, however, be in a different position. State actions are governed not only by market rationality and corporate law, but also by public law considerations. The state investor's governance structure is regulated by constitutional and administrative law, and its actions are governed by judicial review.[133] Strong state market actors such as Norway are, in this sense, either directly as a shareholder in

---

[125] Commission Proposal 5; K. Reynisson, 'Related Party Transactions', 177.

[126] Commission Proposal, 3; K. Reynisson, 'Related Party Transactions', 177.

[127] G20/OECD Principles of Corporate Governance, 30.

[128] European Commission, Call for Advice, 2.

[129] Strine, 'Can We Do Better', 455–456.

[130] H. T. C. Hu and B. Black, 'The New Vote Buying: Empty Voting and Hidden (Morphable) Ownership' (2006) 79 *Southern California Law Review*, 811–908, 828–835; L. Anker-Sørensen, *Corporate Groups and Shadow Business Practices* (Cambridge: Cambridge University Press, 2022).

[131] Strine, 'Can We Do Better', 456.

[132] S. M. Bainbridge, *Corporate Governance After the Financial Crisis* (Oxford: Oxford University Press, 2012), pp. 243–251.

[133] M. Kahan and E. B. Rock: 'When the Government is the Controlling Shareholder' (2011) 89 *Texas Law Review*, 1293–1364, 1298; S. Davidoff Solomon and D. Zaring, 'After the Deal: Fannie, Freddie, and the Financial Crisis Aftermath' (2015) 95 *Boston University Law Review*, 371–426, 389.

state-owned enterprises or indirectly through sovereign wealth funds important drivers of sustainability. They also, however, have a drive to act as an index fund for maximising the benefits of their ultimate beneficiaries, the people.[134]

At the end of the day, the demands of money managers and their advocates for additional rights will compromise the ability of corporations to pursue the most profitable courses of action for those whose money is ultimately at stake, end-user investors. The board is, under the threat of a transfer of corporate influence, tempted to maintain its position by maximising the distributable funds at the expense of the company's going concern value, so sacrificing a solid balance sheet, capital investments, research, development and ultimately jobs.[135]

How then, in practice, can companies be defended from activists? The typical defence tactics mentioned include aggressively challenging the activists' short-term economic plans, electing shareholder-friendly board members based on the board's proposal and propagating the idea that activist board membership damages the interests of the company.[136] Even if the other shareholders react positively to activism, that activists exist may be enough to encourage the board to perform better, without reserving seats on the board for them.

One strategy is to make shareholder activism more transparent. In Europe, the Transparency Directive requires disclosure of major shareholdings when the proportion of voting rights reaches, exceeds, or falls below eight triggering thresholds ranging between 5 and 75 per cent.[137] The Member States remain

---

[134] See, for instance, Mähönen and Johnsen, 'Law, Culture and Sustainability'.

[135] M. Lipton, 'Empiricism and Experience; Activism and Short-Termism; the Real World of Business', *Harvard Law School Forum on Corporate Governance*, 28 October 2013, available at: https://corpgov.law.harvard.edu/2013/10/28/empiricism-and-experience-activism-and-short-termism-the-real-world-of-business/.

[136] R. Blackden, S. Foley and E. Crooks, 'Nelson Peltz fails to win board seats at DuPont' *Financial Times*, 13 May 2015, available at: www.ft.com/content/e57afdbe-f97b-11e4-ae65-00144feab7de.

[137] Directive 2004/109/EC of the European Parliament and of the Council of 15 December 2004 on the harmonisation of transparency requirements in relation to information about issuers whose securities are admitted to trading on a regulated market and amending directive 2001/34/ EC, L 390, 31.12.2004, 38, as amended by Directive 2013/50/EU of the European Parliament and of the Council of 22 October 2013 amending Directive 2004/109/EC of the European Parliament and of the Council on the harmonisation of transparency requirements in relation to information about issuers whose securities are admitted to trading on a regulated market, Directive 2003/71/EC of the European Parliament and of the Council on the prospectus to be published when securities are offered to the public or admitted to trading and Commission Directive 2007/14/EC laying down detailed rules for the implementation of certain provisions of Directive 2004/109/EC, OJ L 294, 6.11.2013, 13.

free to adopt further thresholds, including lower ones, such as a 3 per cent threshold in Italy and the Netherlands or a 2 per cent threshold in Portugal.[138] Reducing the flagging thresholds and tightening the deadlines for flagging enables 'an activist attack' to be detected as early as possible.[139] Shareholders can also be required to vote in their own name, not anonymously through proxy advisors.[140] For example, the Finnish Companies Act prohibits anonymous voting.[141] Other tools include making derivative arrangements transparent, requiring institutional investors to make their investment policies public, and tightening 'act in concert' regulation. These are just a few examples.[142]

These methods do not prevent shareholder activism, but make it less attractive. They are, however, not very popular in the present regulatory atmosphere. For example, the European Commission's attitude to these issues illustrates well that even where it proposes making proxy advisors' actions more transparent,[143] this does not address the material problems associated with them.[144]

The third and the only long-term feasible alternative is to set both the productive companies' and also the institutional investors' boards specific fiduciary duties to act in the best interest of their end-investors and ultimate beneficiaries, as suggested by the HLEG in its Final Report in January 2018 and endorsed by the European Commission in its Action Plan on sustainable finance in March 2018. As emphasised in the Action Plan, several pieces of EU legislation already require institutional investors and asset managers to act in the best interest of their end-investors/beneficiaries.[145] To tackle these problems, the Commission suggested Actions 7 and 10, fostering sustainable corporate governance, attenuating short-termism in capital markets and clarifying institutional investors' and asset managers' duties. The Disclosure Regulation, implementing Action 7, is the first step on this path. The real challenge is, however, the Commission's ambitious sustainable corporate governance initiative, which aims to improve

---

[138] European Securities and Markets Authority, Practical Guide National rules on Directive notifications of major holdings under the Transparency, ESMA31-67-535, 15 June 2022, available at: www .esma.europa.eu/sites/default/files/library/practical_guide_major_holdings_notifications_ under_transparency_directive.pdf.

[139] Katelouzou, 'Worldwide Hedge Fund Activism', 809–811.

[140] Ibid., 811.

[141] See § 5:6(2) second sentence of the Finnish Companies Act.

[142] Katelouzou, 'Worldwide Hedge Fund Activism', 811–818.

[143] See Article 3 i(1) of the Commission Proposal.

[144] See, however, Coffee and Palia, 'The Wolf at the Door', 95–96, in which they make similar types of transparency proposals as the Commission in its proposal.

[145] The Solvency II Directive, the IORP Directive (Directive (EU) 2016/2341 of the European Parliament and of the Council of 14 December 2016 on the activities and supervision of institutions for occupational retirement provision (IORPs), OJ L 354, 23.12.2016, 37), the UCITS Directive, the AIFM Directive and the MiFID II Directive.

the overall EU regulatory framework on company law and corporate governance. This can enable companies to focus on long-term sustainable value creation rather than short-term benefits. It also aims to better align the interests of companies, their shareholders, managers, stakeholders and society, and help companies to better manage sustainability-related matters in their own operations and value chains in, for example, terms of social and human rights, climate change and the environment.[146] The key issues are the definition of company purpose and board duties, including due diligence duties, in the Company Law Directive,[147] and shareholders' rights in SHRD II.

Traditional company law should not, however, be ignored. Shareholder-centred corporate governance legislation, which was previously promoted by the Commission, appeals to activists. Minority protection rules in European company law in particular play a key role in curbing corporate control opportunism.[148] It is difficult to weaken the most typical influence-enhancing tools used by the activist without undermining the essence of effective governance.[149] This is because of the minority's right to convene an extraordinary general meeting and the right to bring a matter before the general meeting.[150] These tools are also used by activists urging companies to sustainability.[151] More recent inventions, such as the independence requirements for board members that create obstacles for insider information and are so crucial for independent decision-making, nomination committees consisting of major shareholders instead of board members,[152] veto rights over issues that belong to the board's competence, compulsory cumulative voting when selecting board members or a qualified minority's right to appoint board members, are not governance standards that are so crucial that they could justify undermining the board's competence and capability.[153]

---

[146] European Commission, Sustainable corporate governance, available at: https://ec.europa.eu/info/law/better-regulation/have-your-say/initiatives/12548-Sustainable-corporate-governance.

[147] Directive (EU) 2017/1132 of the European Parliament and of the Council of 14 June 2017 relating to certain aspects of company law. OJ L 169, 30.6.2017, 46.

[148] See, for instance Mähönen, 'Finland'; Mähönen and Johnsen, 'Law, Culture and Sustainability'.

[149] Katelouzou, 'Worldwide Shareholder Activism', 821–823.

[150] Seemingly, minority derivative suits seem not to have significance for activists, as private benefits from these are small even in countries in which shareholders have the right to compensation of indirect damage; see ibid., 826–826.

[151] See for instance ShareAction, 'Voting matters 2020: are asset managers using their proxy votes for action on climate and social issues?' (2020), available at: https://shareaction.org/wp-content/uploads/2020/11/Voting-Matters-2020.pdf.

[152] Swedish companies are presumably attractive targets for activists for this reason; see Katelouzou, 'Worldwide Shareholder Activism', 825–826.

[153] Ibid., 824–826.

These paths are, however, difficult. The relationship between heterogeneous activist shareholders and governments is complicated and, at the corporate level, novel. On the other hand, index investors tend to resist activism.[154] Activists have traditionally tried to influence regulatory policy to make it more investor friendly and to make their investments, based on the hope of the adoption of a particular government policy. Activists may seek favourable regulatory treatment, as have investors who have purchased failed banks from government receivers in the past.[155] On the other hand, more and more activism against unsustainable businesses can also be seen among institutional investors.[156] At the end of the day, the problem of corporate law is whether institutional investor and asset manager engagement contributes to long-term sustainability of public companies, or just increases their attractiveness for short-term profit maximising.

Ultimately, however, corporate governance is about value choices – whether it is more efficient, from the point of view of shareholders, to focus on corporate added value to dividends and share buy-backs or investments and future added value; and whether this can be achieved without taking a position on which alternative would be more effective from a more general societal point of view. At the end of the day, the answer lies not in shareholders but in the boards of both financial and productive firms. What, therefore, is the boards' opportunity to ensure a sustainable business model? The only efficient way to ensure sustainability may therefore be hard law on corporate purpose and board duties – and not reliance solely on shareholders.[157]

---

[154] See ShareAction, 'Voting matters 2020'.

[155] Davidoff Solomon and Zaring, 'After the Deal', 422–423.

[156] ShareAction, 'Voting matters 2020'; Condon, 'Externalities and the Common Owner'.

[157] See the reform proposals of the Sustainable Market Actors for Responsible Trade (SMART) project, B. Sjåfjell, J. Mähönen, T. Novitz, C. Gammage and H. Ahlström, 'Securing the Future of European Business: SMART Reform Proposals' (2020) 2020–11 *University of Oslo Faculty of Law Research Paper*, 20–08 *Nordic & European Company Law Working Paper*, 1–88, available at SSRN: https://ssrn.com/abstract=3595048; B. Sjåfjell and G. Tsagas, 'Integrating Sustainable Value Creation in Corporate Governance: Company Law, Corporate Governance Codes and the Constitution of the Company', Chapter 9 in this volume.

PART III

WAYS FORWARD IN THE PROMOTION OF VALUE CREATION

8

Financing Sustainable Value Creation

Jay Cullen, Jukka Mähönen and Heidi Rapp Nilsen[*]

8.1 INTRODUCTION

European financial markets provide the credit and financing required for businesses and the public sector in the European Union (EU)/European Economic Area (EEA) and beyond. Addressing the contribution of EU financial markets to unsustainable business practices is therefore vital to realising the EU's commitments on sustainable value creation, as expressed for instance in the European Green Deal from December 2019,[1] and the subsequent European Green Deal Investment Plan.[2] Additionally, the EU has committed to implementing the United Nations Sustainable Development Goals (SDGs), including the complete decarbonising of its economy by 2050.[3]

Realising these objectives requires rapid and meaningful policy interventions, including the introduction of heightened monitoring and regulation of financial markets and their contribution to environmental degradation – and channelling investments into projects creating sustainable value. The World Economic Forum estimates that \$44 trillion of economic value creation – over half of gross world product in 2020 – is moderately or highly dependent

[*] This chapter is based on research by the Sustainable Market Actors for Responsible Trade (SMART) research project, funded by the European Union under the Horizon 2020 programme, grant agreement 693642.

[1] European Commission, Communication from the Commission to the European Parliament, the European Council, the Council, the European Economic and Social Committee and the Committee of the Regions: The European Green Deal, 11.12.2019, COM(2019) 640 final.

[2] European Commission, Communication from the Commission to the European Parliament, the European Council, the Council, the European Economic and Social Committee and the Committee of the Regions: Sustainable Europe Investment Plan, European Green Deal Investment Plan, 14.1.2020, COM(2020) 21 final, available at: https://ec.europa.eu/commission/presscorner/api/files/attachment/860462/Commission%20Communication%20on%20the%20European%20Green%20Deal%20Investment%20Plan_EN.pdf.pdf.

[3] European Commission, Reflection Paper: Towards a Sustainable Europe by 2030, 30.1.2019, COM(2019) 22 final.

on nature.[4] The recent UK Dasgupta Review of the Economics of Biodiversity has highlighted the need for a fundamental shift in course in relation to mitigating damage to natural resources from the activities of the financial system.[5] The risks of unsustainable business therefore have significant macro-economic and societal implications, a point noted by the EU's High-Level Expert Group on Sustainable Finance in 2018, when it argued that:

> Natural capital has typically not been included in the past in standard economic production functions, largely because it was widely thought that it could be taken for granted. This is no longer the case. Even though it is critical for virtually all kinds of production, and most of the SDGs are either directly concerned with or strongly dependent on natural capital, natural capital continues to be degraded … It is essential to halt the destruction of natural capital and instead manage it within boundaries that maintain the resilience and stability of natural ecosystems, and allow for resources to renew … The externalities generated by the misuse of natural capital are dangerously high …[6]

The Commission's programme relies in general upon private markets to deliver change, and applies tried-and-trusted mechanisms in order to assist in the scaling-up of sustainable finance markets and secure financial stability. Such mechanisms are designed to provide higher levels of information, standardisation and transparency to private actors. The thinking goes that increasing information flows to investors and allowing them to compare products and instruments on a case-by-case basis will spur investment in these asset classes, in particular by large institutional investors who have complained in the past that green financial product markets, such as those for green bonds, have been too opaque and prone to 'greenwashing'. To this end, the EU has been proactive in facilitating the introduction of new financial products with green credentials, taking a lead in developing such markets.

On the surface, much progress appears to have been made. The January 2020 European Green Deal Investment Plan, also referred to as Sustainable Europe Investment Plan,[7] is the investment pillar of the December 2019

4 World Economic Forum, 'Nature Risk Rising: Why the Crisis Engulfing Nature Matters for Business and the Economy' (January 2020) *New Nature Economy series*, 88, available at: www3.weforum.org/docs/WEF_New_Nature_Economy_Report_2020.pdf.

5 The Economics of Biodiversity: the Dasgupta Review (February 2021), available at: https://assets.publishing.service.gov.uk/government/uploads/system/uploads/attachment_data/file/962785/The_Economics_of_Biodiversity_The_Dasgupta_Review_Full_Report.pdf.

6 EU's High-Level Expert Group on Sustainable Finance, 'Financing a Sustainable European Economy: Final Report 2018' (2018), p. 88.

7 European Commission, Communication from the Commission to the European Parliament, the European Council, the Council, the European Economic and Social Committee and

European Green Deal,[8] and is designed to contribute to the emergence of new, clean energy and circular economy industries. Moreover, the EU's Sustainable Finance Initiative, launched in 2018 with the Commission Action Plan, promised to 'connect finance with the specific needs of the European and global economy to the benefit of the planet and our society'.[9] The EU has made progress regarding its adoption in principle of the Sustainable Finance Initiative to prevent greenwashing of financial products, so that in future their merits can be reliably ascertained. Further, the development of consultative processes and an expert group speaks of a genuine commitment to deliver, which may be realised in the present EU Parliament and the Commission. A Taxonomy of sustainable activities, developed by the Commission and the EU Technical Expert Group on Sustainable Finance, has recently been adopted,[10] in addition to the introduction of mandatory disclosure requirements of sustainability risk management by institutional investors,[11] and rules on how indices used as the basis for sustainable investment products are benchmarked.[12] These are the three crucial pillars of the Sustainable Finance

---

the Committee of the Regions: Sustainable Europe Investment Plan, European Green Deal Investment Plan, 14.1.2020, COM(2020) 21 final.

[8] European Commission, Communication from the Commission to the European Parliament, the European Council, the Council, the European Economic and Social Committee and the Committee of the Regions: The European Green Deal, 11.12.2019, COM/2019/640 final.

[9] European Commission, Communication from the Commission to the European Parliament, the European Council, the Council, the European Economic and Social Committee and the Committee of the Regions: Action Plan: Financing Sustainable Growth, COM/2018/097 final p. 2.

[10] Regulation (EU) 2020/852 of the European Parliament and of the Council of 18 June 2020 on the establishment of a framework to facilitate sustainable investment, and amending Regulation (EU) 2019/2088, PE/20/2020/INIT, OJ L 198, 22.6.2020, pp. 13–43.

[11] Regulation (EU) 2019/2088 of the European Parliament and of the Council of 27 November 2019 on sustainability-related disclosures in the financial services sector, PE/87/2019/REV/1, OJ L 317, 9.12.2019, pp. 1–16.

[12] Regulation (EU) 2016/1011 of the European Parliament and of the Council of 8 June 2016 on indices used as benchmarks in financial instruments and financial contracts or to measure the performance of investment funds and amending Directives 2008/48/EC and 2014/17/EU and Regulation (EU) No 596/2014, OJ L 171, 29.6.2016, pp. 1–65, as amended by Regulation (EU) 2019/2089 of the European Parliament and of the Council of 27 November 2019 amending Regulation (EU) 2016/1011 as regards EU Climate Transition Benchmarks, EU Paris-aligned Benchmarks and sustainability-related disclosures for benchmarks, PE/90/2019/REV/1, OJ L 317, 9.12.2019, pp. 17–27 and Regulation (EU) 2021/168 of the European Parliament and of the Council of 10 February 2021 amending Regulation (EU) 2016/1011 as regards the exemption of certain third-country spot foreign exchange benchmarks and the designation of replacements for certain benchmarks in cessation, and amending Regulation (EU) No 648/2012, OJ L 49, 12.2.2021, pp. 6–17.

Initiative, together with a Commission-planned EU Green Bond Standard and labels for green financial products.[13]

Moreover, in relation to the financing of unsustainable business activities, the EU has recognised the vital importance of integrating sustainable finance into the Capital Markets Union framework.[14] Much regulatory attention in the sphere of finance has been captured by accelerating the contribution of capital markets to these developments. The post-financial crisis environment has also provided fertile ground for challenging the model of central bankers as passive agents concerned only with price and financial stability.[15] If central banks are to assist in tackling the issue of sustainable value creation, arguably there must be a more nuanced treatment of their role(s) and independence. Most notably, the Bank of England,[16] De Nederlandsche Bank,[17] and also the European Central Bank (ECB),[18] have argued recently that the role of central banks must be interpreted more broadly, specifically to include climate and environmental risks into their respective financial system monitoring tools. Moreover, the UK government recently amended the Bank of England mandate to ensure its monetary policy operations are 'environmentally sustainable and consistent with the transition to a net zero economy'.[19]

[13] European Commission, Ecofriendly investment – EU standard for 'green bonds', available at: https://ec.europa.eu/info/law/better-regulation/have-your-say/initiatives/12447-EU-Standard-for-Green-Bond-.

[14] European Commission, Communication from the Commission to the European Parliament, the European Council, the Council, the European Economic and Social Committee and the Committee of the Regions: A Capital Markets Union for people and businesses-new action plan, 24.9.2020, COM/2020/590 final.

[15] E. Balls, J. Howat and A. Stansbury, 'Central Bank Independence Revisited: After the Financial Crisis, What Should a Model Central Bank Look Like?' (2018), 87 *Harvard-Kennedy School M-RCBG Associate Working Paper Series*, available at: www.hks.harvard.edu/sites/default/files/centers/mrcbg/working.papers/x87_final.pdf.

[16] S. Breeden, 'Avoiding the Storm: Climate Change and the Financial System', Speech at the Official Monetary & Financial Institutions Forum, London, 15 April 2019.

[17] F. Elderson, 'Climate crisis requires urgent action by financial sector and financial supervisors', Opening statement Frank Elderson at the Banco de España Climate Change Conference Madrid, 11 December 2019, De Nederlandsche Bank, available at: www.dnb.nl/binaries/Cc_tcm46-386494.pdf.

[18] European Parliament, 'New ECB boss quizzed for the first time by Economic Affairs Committee' (2019), available at: www.europarl.europa.eu/news/en/press-room/20191202IPR67811/new-ecb-boss-quizzed-for-the-first-time-by-economic-affairs-committee.

[19] Bank of England, 'MPC remit statement and letter and FPC remit letter' (London: Bank of England, 2021), available at: www.bankofengland.co.uk/news/2021/march/mpc-remit-statement-and-letter-and-fpc-remit-letter.

Yet patterns of investment in unsustainable projects – routinely funded by large EU banks – have not been addressed sufficiently by EU financial regulators, in spite of the introduction of the Sustainable Finance Initiative. The Initiative lacks a systematic integration of sustainability factors in the actions proposed, limiting focus on selected environmental issues, especially climate change. Research suggests that banks and other financial institutions continue to routinely fund unsustainable businesses and projects, in spite of commitments to sustainable value creation by financial institutions.[20] As an example of this, recent research reveals that, despite the commitments made by nations in the 2015 Paris Climate Accord, the world's biggest sixty banks have since then provided $3.8 trillion of financing for fossil fuel companies.[21]

What we argue in this chapter, therefore, is for a fundamental recalibration of what is required of financial system participants in preventing the funding of activities that cause damage to the environment and thereby to necessary premises for securing a social foundation of humanity. Our focus in the analysis is at EU level but the principles we discuss may be applied to almost any jurisdiction. Financial regulators and central banks must evaluate such potential for damage and assess the systemic extent of financial risks. The main weaknesses of current approaches are (1) a reliance on the existing incentive structures for private actors in financial markets that prioritise information disclosure as a regulatory technique; (2) the reticence of the EU to reform its regulatory structures and policies with regard to financial markets; and (3) a continued adherence to the principle of market neutrality in relation to both monetary policy and bank regulation. Further factors hindering development in this field are the EU's financial structure and budget rules, which prevent sustained deficit spending absent extraordinary circumstances, although discussion of this is beyond the scope of this chapter.[22] This makes it difficult for states to commit funds to financing the sustainable investments needed to address climate change and other challenges threatening planetary boundaries and the foundations for social order.

The chapter proceeds as follows. In Section 8.2 we discuss some of the legislative and regulatory initiatives to emerge at the EU level in the field of disclosure and sustainable finance, before discussion why such measures

[20] M.A. Urban and D. Wójcík, 'Dirty Banking: Probing the Gap in Sustainable Finance' (2019) 11(6) *Sustainability*, 1745.

[21] BankTrack, 'Banking on climate chaos: fossil fuel finance report card 2021' (2021), available at: www.banktrack.org/article/new_report_world_s_60_largest_banks_have_poured_3_8_ trillion_into_fossil_fuels_since_paris_agreement_climate_groups_sound_alarm_as_financ-ing_for_fossil_fuel_expansion_continues_to_rise.

[22] A. Johnston and T. Pugh, 'Fiscal Austerity and Monetary Largesse: The EU's Constitutional and Ideological Straitjacket', Chapter 4 in this volume.

are likely to be limited in impact. In Section 8.3, we consider ways in which policies can be introduced in the context of financial regulation, in particular to mobilise financial resources to reduce the potential for investment in unsustainable activities. Section 8.4 concludes. Throughout, we make recommendations for reform.

8.2 INFORMATION DISCLOSURE IN THE CONTEXT OF SUSTAINABILITY

8.2.1 *The Disclosure Regulation and Taxonomy Regulation*

The Disclosure Regulation, which came into force in March 2021, requires manufacturers of financial products, financial market participants and financial advisers to make disclosures with regard to their approach to sustainable investment. They must also disclose whether they consider negative externalities on environment and social justice of their investment decisions or advice, and, if so, how this is reflected at the product level.[23] In particular, fund managers must disclose the manner in which sustainability risks are integrated into investment decisions and the results of the assessment of the likely impacts of sustainability risks on the returns of the relevant funds, or if not deemed relevant, the reasons why. Where relevant, advisory processes and transparency as regards financial products that target sustainable investments must also be disclosed. The expectation is that by requiring the disclosure of standardised information by market participants concerning sustainability, investors will discriminate in favour of sustainable investments where appropriate, thereby increasing capital flows to more sustainable products.

Working in tandem with the Disclosure Regulation, the EU Taxonomy, based on the Taxonomy Regulation,[24] is a tool to help investors and companies identify environmentally friendly and in future socially friendly economic activities. Article 1 of the Taxonomy Regulation establishes the criteria for determining the degree of environmental sustainability of an investment. To this end, the Commission started a review of the so called Non-Financial Reporting Directive, Article 19a of the Accounting

---

[23] Regulation (EU) 2019/2088 of the European Parliament and of the Council of 27 November 2019 on sustainability-related disclosures in the financial services sector (Text with EEA relevance), PE/87/2019/REV/1, OJ L 317, 9.12.2019, pp. 1–16.

[24] Regulation (EU) 2020/852 of the European Parliament and of the Council of 18 June 2020 on the establishment of a framework to facilitate sustainable investment, and amending Regulation (EU) 2019/2088 OJ L 198, 22.6.2020, pp. 13–43.

Directive,[25] to determine how companies ought to report their compliance with the provisions of the Taxonomy Regulation. As the first step towards a new European corporate sustainability reporting regime, the European Financial Reporting Advisory Group prepared in March 2021 a roadmap for the development of a comprehensive set of EU sustainability reporting standards, necessary to meet the political ambition and urgent timetable of the European Green Deal, followed by the Commission proposal for a Corporate Sustainability Reporting Directive in April 2021,[26] to be finalised in Summer 2022. In preparing the standards based on the Directive it is also necessary to ensure consistency of reporting rules in Disclosure Regulation, Accounting Directive and Taxonomy Regulation.[27] A comprehensive reporting framework is also necessary for the requirements of the legislation on sustainable corporate governance and due diligence proposed by the Commission in February 2022 and discussed now in the European Parliament and the Council.[28] Additionally, to ensure appropriate management of environmental risks and mitigation opportunities, and reduce related transaction costs, the Commission will also support businesses and other stakeholders in 'developing standardised natural capital accounting practices within the EU and internationally'.[29]

The Taxonomy Regulation was originally designed to expand climate change mitigating economic activities and to improve the environmental performance of securities and bond issuers. The scope shall, however, be enlarged by the end of 2021.[30] The Commission will also explore how the

---

[25] Directive 2013/34/EU of the European Parliament and of the Council of 26 June 2013 on the annual financial statements, consolidated financial statements and related reports of certain types of undertakings, amending Directive 2006/43/EC of the European Parliament and of the Council and repealing Council Directives 78/660/EEC and 83/349/EEC, as amended by Directive 2014/95/EU of the European Parliament and of the Council of 22 October 2014 amending Directive 2013/34/EU as regards disclosure of non-financial and diversity information by certain large undertakings and groups, OJ L 330, 15.11.2014, pp. 1–9.

[26] Proposal for a Directive of the European Parliament and of the Council, amending Directive 2013/34/EU, Directive 2004/109/EC, Directive 2006/43/EC and Regulation (EU) No 537/2014, as regards corporate sustainability reporting, COM(2021) 189 final.

[27] European Commission, Reports on development of EU sustainability reporting standards, available at: https://ec.europa.eu/info/publications/210308-efrag-reports_en.

[28] European Commission, Proposal for a Directive of the European Parliament and of the Council, on Corporate Sustainability Due Diligence and amending Directive (EU) 2019/1937. COM(2022) 71 final.

[29] European Commission, Communication from the Commission to the European Parliament, the European Council, the Council, the European Economic and Social Committee and the Committee of the Regions: The European Green Deal, Brussels, 11.12.2019 COM(2019) 640 p. 17.

[30] See EU Technical Expert Group on Sustainable Finance: Final Report of the Technical Expert Group on Sustainable Finance, March 2020, p. 51.

Taxonomy can be used in the context of the European Green Deal by the public sector.[31]

For an action to meet the definition of an 'environmentally sustainable economic activity' (Article 2) and thus be considered Taxonomy-eligible, it must:

1. contribute substantially to one or more of the environmental objectives;
2. do no significant harm to any other environmental objective;
3. comply with minimum social safeguards (under the draft regulation, these are defined as ILO core labour conventions[32]); and
4. comply with the technical screening criteria being developed.

The technical criteria for these additional activities are being developed by the EU Technical Expert Group on Sustainable Finance.[33] According to the Regulation the criteria should take into account the life cycle of the products and services provided by that economic activity, including evidence from existing life-cycle assessments, notably by considering their production, use and end-of-life, in addition to the environmental impacts of the economic activity itself.[34]

In their analysis, the Technical Expert Group focused mainly on bond and equity markets but investments in private equity, real estate funds and private securitised loans could also be subject to the regulation if the resulting funds are marketed as green. Under the Taxonomy Regulation, financial market participants, when offering financial products as environmentally sustainable investments or as investments having similar characteristics, will be required to disclose how the product in question meets certain sustainability criteria.[35] The Taxonomy will also form as said the basis of a European green bond standard that is being developed from the summer of 2021 when the Commission published its proposal for a Regulation on European green bonds.[36] According to the present plans, to qualify as a green bond, 100 per cent of the bond will

---

[31] European Commission, The European Green Deal Investment Plan and Just Transition Mechanism explained, 14 January 2020, available at: https://ec.europa.eu/info/publications/200114-european-green-deal-investment-plan_en.

[32] See ILO Labour standards, available at: www.ilo.org/global/standards/lang--en/index.htm.

[33] High-Level Expert Group, Final Report.

[34] Preamble 11 of Taxonomy Regulation.

[35] Article 4(2) of Taxonomy Regulation.

[36] European Commission, Proposal for a Regulation of the European Parliament and of the Council on European green bonds, COM(2021) 391 final ('Commission Proposal'), see also European Commission, Communication from the Commission to the European Parliament, the European Council, the Council, the European Economic and Social Committee and the Committee of the Regions: Sustainable Europe Investment Plan, European Green Deal Investment Plan, 14.1.2020, COM(2020) p. 21; European Commission, Ecofriendly investment – EU standard for 'green bonds', available at: https://ec.europa.eu/info/law/better-regulation/have-your-say/initiatives/12447-EU-Standard-for-Green-Bond-.

need to be Taxonomy-aligned.[37] This is designed to provide more granular information to would-be investors and to limit the potential for greenwashing of particular investment products.

8.2.2 *Disclosure of Environmental and Social Risks by Financial Institutions*

At present, sustainability assessments are often routinely conducted by banks and other financial institutions where any potential issues are identified during the due diligence stages of granting loans or engaging in project finance. Such internal due diligence processes are designed to evaluate the financial risks and opportunities of the investment, the compliance risk of the investment and the reputational risk of the investment.[38] Moreover, in the EU there are requirements under prudential supervision that require banks to assess risks in their credit decision-making processes. In tandem, there are industry-generated guidelines for financial institutions to consider in their financing programmes. We now briefly consider them.

8.2.2.1 The Capital Requirements Regulation

The third pillar (Disclosure and Market Discipline) under the Capital Requirements Regulation (CRR),[39] which regulates EU banks' capital and liquidity positions, has arguably received most recent attention in the literature on financial markets concerning environmentally related systemic risks. Pillar 3 concerns the development of a set of disclosure requirements that allow investors and other market participants to view and assess relevant information about bank's balance sheets and business models, including information on investments, capital and forward-looking risks, particularly those of a systemic character. In the EU, the European Banking Authority (EBA) has been mandated by the recent reform to the CRR to require large financial institutions with publicly listed issuances to disclose information on environmental, social and governance (ESG) risks, physical risks and transition risks as defined in the report referred to in Article 98 of the Capital Requirements

---

37 Article 6(1) of the Commission Proposal.
38 W. Warmerdam and J. W. van Gelder, 'EU-Regulatory Reform concerning EU Investments in Non-EU Agribusiness', Report produced by Profundo for FERN, Friends of the Earth Europe and Global Witness, November 2017.
39 Regulation (EU) No 575/2013 of the European Parliament and of the Council of 26 June 2013 on prudential requirements for credit institutions and investment firms and amending Regulation (EU) No 648/2012: [2013] OJ L176/1 (CRR).

Directive (CRD).[40] In this context, Article 434a of the CRR includes a mandate to the EBA according to which the EBA shall develop a technical standard implementing the disclosure requirements on ESG risks.[41]

8.2.2.2 The Financial Stability Board Taskforce on Climate-Related Disclosures

In this vein, banks and securities firms (as well as insurers) are also encouraged to develop and use a comprehensive sustainability disclosure framework developed by the Financial Stability Board (FSB) created under the auspices of the FSB Task Force on Climate-Related Disclosures (TFCD).[42] This framework 'develop[s] voluntary, consistent climate-related financial disclosures that would be useful to investors, lenders, and insurance underwriters in understanding material risks'.[43] The TFCD framework addresses two key categories of risk stemming from climate change and environmental damage: transition risk and physical impacts of climate change. This is founded on the recognition that climate impacts will exert stress on both the income streams and balance sheets companies, as losses mount and assets are revalued.

The TFCD recommends that all organisations with public debt or equity implement its recommendations and report in their annual filings on compliance, in order that investors, creditors and the public are as informed as possible regarding the climate risks involved in each business.[44] Importantly, the TFCD also contains specific recommendations for disclosure by banks and other financial institutions, to supplement the guidance proposed for all sectors. The FSB notes that financial sector disclosures would assist investors and regulators in at least two key ways:

1. 'foster an early assessment of [climate-related] risks [to] facilitate market discipline'; and
2. 'provide a source of data that can be analysed at a systemic level, to facilitate authorities' assessments of the materiality of any risks posed by climate change to the financial sector, and the channels through which this is most likely to be transmitted'.[45]

---

[40] Directive 2013/36/EU of the European Parliament and of the Council of 26 June 2013 on access to the activity of credit institutions and the prudential supervision of credit institutions and investment firms, amending Directive 2002/87/EC and repealing Directives 2006/48/EC and 2006/49/EC, [2013] OJ L 176/338 (CRD).

[41] European Banking Authority, Draft Implementing Standards on prudential disclosures on ESG risks in accordance with Article 449a CRR, Consultation Paper EBA/CP/2021/06.

[42] Task Force on Climate-Related Disclosures, 'Final Report: Recommendations of the Task Force on Climate-Related Financial Disclosures', June 2017 (TFCD).

[43] See TFCD, p. iii.

[44] TFCD p. 17.

[45] Ibid.

Because banks are exposed to climate-related ESG risk and opportunities via their lending activities and own operations, the FSB recognises the importance of these institutions to dampening the financing of high-ESG-risk projects. In particular, exposures to large fossil-fuel producers, or carbon-intensive manufacturers, might 'present risks that merit disclosure or discussion in a bank's financial filings'.[46] Banks should also provide the amount and percentage of carbon-related assets relative to total assets as well as the amount of lending and other financing connected with climate-related opportunities'. The TFCD has also recently updated its scenario analysis to account for potential stressors on the financial system in the event of climate-related losses.[47]

The TFCD disclosure requirements are certainly consistent with the disclosure and market discipline considerations espoused under Pillar 3 of the CRR. The requirements under the FSB Disclosure Framework in Pillar 3 would provide a lever to enhance disclosure in these areas to support enhanced information collection and disclosure.[48] The risks disclosed by these institutions could thereby be evaluated by investors and regulators to determine the banking system's contribution to financing of high-ESG-risk activities.

8.2.2.3 Other Guidelines on Sustainable Banking

In addition to the limited sustainability criteria included in Pillar 2 and Pillar 3 and the TFCD, there are other guidelines for banks and financial institutions to follow in relation to sustainable investment. These guidelines include:

1. the Equator Principles (the IFC's Performance Standards on Environmental and Social Sustainability), arguably the globally recognised good practice in dealing with environmental and social risk management;[49]
2. guidelines issued by the United Nations Principles for Responsible Banking:[50] this is an initiative of the United Nations Environment Program Finance Initiative (UNEP FI) in collaboration with the banking sector; and
3. the Organisation for Economic Co-operation and Development (OECD) Guidelines for Multinational Enterprises, together with compliance guidance aimed specifically at financial institutions.[51]

[46] Task Force on Climate-Related Disclosures, 'Implementing the Recommendations of the Task Force on Climate-related Financial Disclosures', June 2017, Annex 23.

[47] Climate Financial Risk Forum, 'Climate Financial Risk Forum Guide 2020: Scenario Analysis Chapter', June 2020.

[48] In some countries such as France, all potential ESG risk exposures as they relate to financial performance and soundness must be publicly disclosed by listed companies and financial institutions. See Conseil d'Etat Decree, Regulation, Article 225.

[49] See 'The equator principles', available at: https://equator-principles.com.

[50] See 'Principles for responsible banking', available at: www.unepfi.org/banking/bankingprinciples/. The Principles aim to ensure the banking industry is aligned with the UN Sustainable Development Goals (SDGs) and the Paris Climate Agreement.

[51] See 'Guidelines for multinational enterprises', available at: www.oecd.org/corporate/mne/.

The principles espoused by the various groups overlap considerably and place considerable emphasis on similar considerations.

The European Disclosure Regulation requires the integration of sustainability risks in financial market participants' investment decision-making processes. Many of those requirements remain non-binding in relation to ensuring that the sustainability credentials of investments and compliance with sustainability principles are assured. Specific requirements include pre-contractual disclosures, disclosures on websites and disclosures in periodic reports in relation to financial products. The Regulation suggests that financial market participants and financial advisers should consider the due diligence guidance for responsible business conduct developed by the OECD,[52] and/or the United Nations-supported Principles for Responsible Investment (PRI).[53] For reasons of space, in the brief analysis that follows, we concentrate only on the OECD Guidelines, which are designed to work explicitly to promote the SDGs.[54]

The OECD's Guidelines for Multinational Enterprises, together with compliance guidance aimed specifically at financial institutions,[55] outline the recommended steps in the due diligence process and may be summarised as:

1. embed Responsible Business Conduct (RBC) into policies and management systems;
2. identify actual and potential adverse RBC impacts;
3. cease, prevent and mitigate such impacts;
4. track implementation and results;
5. communicate how impacts are addressed; and
6. provide for or cooperate in remediation when appropriate.

The Guidelines are comprehensive and extend to the entire lifecycle of projects, including recommendations on post-completion due diligence. Under the Disclosure Regulation, banks will be under an obligation under EU law to incorporate due diligence guidelines into their risk management frameworks. The Regulation imposes transparency rules for financial institutions on the

---

[52] Organisation for Economic Co-operation and Development, 'OECD Due Diligence Guidance for Responsible Business Conduct' (OECD 2018).

[53] See 'Principles for responsible investment', available at: www.unpri.org/.

[54] Organisation for Economic Co-operation and Development, 'Responsible Business Conduct and the Sustainable Development Goals', available at: https://mneguidelines.oecd.org/RBC-and-the-sustainable-development-goals.pdf.

[55] Organisation for Economic Co-operation and Development, 'Due Diligence for Responsible Corporate Lending and Securities Underwriting: Key considerations for banks implementing the OECD Guidelines for Multinational Enterprises' (OECD, 2019).

integration of sustainability risks and impacts in their processes and financial products, including reporting on adherence to internationally recognised standards for due diligence. It seeks to harmonise existing provisions on disclosures to investors in relation to sustainability-related disclosures by imposing requirements on so-called financial market participants (e.g. alternative investment fund managers (AIFMs) and undertakings for the collective investments in transferable securities (UCITs) management companies and investment firms carrying out portfolio management) and financial advisers (firms authorised under Markets in Financial Instruments Directive(MiFID) to give investment advice and credit institutions) in relation to financial products.[56]

8.2.3 *Mandatory Due Diligence for Sustainability Risks*

All these initiatives are not only more or less voluntary but also limited to climate change, ignoring a comprehensive approach to financial risks rising from environmentally and socially unsustainable activities. Instead, regulation should be more comprehensive and science-based.[57]

Although laudable for contributing to awareness-raising of the significance of climate change for business and finance, the OECD and other sustainability-based guidelines have shortcomings when analysed from a holistic sustainability perspective. Such guidelines suffer from several major limitations that restrict their efficiency in risk management, the most serious of which are:

1. The guidelines are not mandatory, with a system of self-assessment and reporting acting as the principal mechanisms for compliance assessment. There is therefore usually no recourse in law for aggrieved parties unless local legal provisions have been breached specifically by the institution concerned.

2. The guidelines that are used vary considerably between institutions, in both coverage and depth, and the resulting patchwork of guidelines reduces comparability and standardisation.

3. The due diligence guidelines on sustainability are often proprietary and not disclosed to external parties. Moreover, even where sustainability risk management exists, it does not penetrate core internal processes.[58]

---

[56] Directive 2014/65/EU of the European Parliament and of the Council of 15 May 2014 on markets in financial instruments and amending Directive 2002/92/EC and Directive 2011/61/EU, [2014] OJ L 173/349.

[57] B. Sjåfjell, 'The Financial Risks of Unsustainability: A Research Agenda' (29 June 2020), 2020–18 *University of Oslo Faculty of Law Research Paper*, 21–05 *Nordic & European Company Law Working Paper*, available at SSRN: https://ssrn.com/abstract=3637969.

[58] T. Anagnostopoulos, A. Skouloudis, N. Khan and K. Evangelinos, 'Incorporating Sustainability Considerations into Lending Decisions and the Management of Bad Loans: Evidence from Greece' (2018) 10(12) *Sustainability*, 4728.

Instead, we contend that by making compliance with sustainability principles mandatory, some of the potential damage that arises from transgression of certain planetary boundaries and risk(s) to social stability would be internalised.

As the recommendations contained in these guidelines are not legally enforceable, any punishment or sanction for failure to comply with the relevant guidelines currently comes from the market. Yet past experience demonstrates that market pressure is insufficient in multiple dimensions to alleviate financial institutions' proclivity to funding unsustainable activities. The lack of an effective enforcement mechanism, coupled with difficulties in litigating against large, complex multinational enterprises, means that many financial institutions and other corporations do not incorporate sustainability risks into their strategic decision-making.[59]

As noted earlier, despite the commitments made by nations in the 2015 Paris Climate Accord, recent research reveals that since then the world's biggest sixty banks have provided trillions in financing for fossil fuel companies.[60] Research suggests that financial institution behaviour is largely unchanged by compliance with relevant sustainability guidelines.[61] For example, in the case of the Equator Principles, research suggests that they are mainly adopted because of reputational benefits and risk management and that they do not create significant changes in project financing institutions.[62]

Financial institutions would be under a positive compliance obligation to demonstrate, where required, how they have mitigated or prevented particular ESG and sustainability risks from materialising in particular projects. A proper sustainability assessment is in the interest of the financial institution itself: if it could be determined that a financial institution, after having conducted a sustainability assessment, funded or continued to fund activities with high-ESG risks, this would provide a much greater degree of certainty in legal proceedings concerning the relevant standard for compliance

[59] B. Sjåfjell, J. Mähönen, T. Novitz, C. Gammage and H. Ahlstrom, 'Securing the Future of European Business: SMART Reform Proposals' (March 2020), 2020–11 *University of Oslo Faculty of Law Research Paper*, 20–08 *Nordic & European Company Law Working Paper*, available at SSRN: https://ssrn.com/abstract=3595048.

[60] BankTrack, 'Banking on climate chaos: fossil fuel finance report card 2021', available at: www.ran.org/wp-content/uploads/2021/03/Banking-on-Climate-Chaos-2021.pdf.

[61] S. Heim, 'Why banks need to plug gaps in the Equator Principles to prevent community conflict', *Reuters Events*, 10 September 2019, available at: www.ethicalcorp.com/why-banks-need-plug-gaps-equator-principles-prevent-community-conflict.

[62] UNEP Inquiry and Centre for International Governance Innovation, 'The Equator Principles: Do They Make Banks More Sustainable?', February 2016; C. Volk, 'ESG Trends in the Banking Sector', PRI & SSF Networking Lunch on Sustainable Investment, Zurich, 25 November 2014 (Sustainalytics 2014).

and attendant liability. If a sustainability due diligence has not been carried out in accordance with the proposed EU law and harm has occurred, there should be a presumption of liability for the undertaking and its board members. This ought to apply to any commercial loans, commercial credit facilities (other than overdrafts), syndicated loans or project finance agreements that are subject to a mandatory due diligence assessment before they are agreed.[63] There ought to be a presumption that these requirements are applicable to all such loans, credit facilities or project finance agreement(s); however, the financial institution may rebut this presumption for certain categories of project, namely those projects deemed as projects covered by the existing Taxonomy. The relevant financial institution's credit committee should be required to make a recommendation to the board of directors based upon the due diligence assessment.

Conversely, if due diligence has been carried out and assured by external experts as proposed as a duty, this may serve as a defence for the undertaking and its board. This will increase the legal certainty for European business, while providing better access to justice for affected workers and communities. The introduction of a mandatory sustainability due diligence process would allow investors and other interested parties to apply specific standards to the lending and credit decisions of financial institutions. Such a standard would also provide a benchmark for any litigation relating to the role of a financial institution, or group of financial institutions, in financing activities that are damaging from ESG perspectives. Such litigation actions are, at present, often based upon voluntary filings made by corporations relating to their ESG practices.[64]

8.3 MOBILISING THE FINANCIAL SYSTEM TO SECURE SUSTAINABILITY

8.3.1 *Capital Market Finance and the Banking System*

A fundamental factor underpinning the EU's Capital Markets Union project is facilitating growth to 'strengthen Europe's economy and stimulate

---

[63] J. Cullen, J. Mähönen and H. R. Nilsen, 'Financing the Transition to Sustainability: SMART Reform Proposals' (May 2020), 2020–10 *University of Oslo Faculty of Law Research Paper*, 20–09 *Nordic & European Company Law Working Paper*, 60, available at SSRN: https://ssrn .com/abstract=3594433.

[64] D. Woodcock, A. S. Kotte and J. D. Guynn, 'Managing Legal Risks from ESG Disclosures', Harvard Law School Forum on Corporate Governance, 12 August 2019, available at: https:// corpgov.law.harvard.edu/2019/08/12/managing-legal-risks-from-esg-disclosures/.

investment to create jobs',[65] making the EU economy more competitive. Whilst other jurisdictions such as the US, China and Japan have developed deep capital markets, investment beyond the banking system within the EU – with the exception of France – remains relatively underdeveloped.[66] The EU, for example in relation to the US, lags behind in terms of financial development and financial depth; in spite of the EU economy being similar in size to the US economy, its equity markets are only half the size, and its debt markets less than a third of the size, of equivalent US markets.

In turn, any reforms to EU capital markets and the launch of market-based finance initiatives to promote sustainable finance – for example, via the Capital Markets Union – are likely to be more limited in impact. Indicatively, domestic bank credit in the Eurozone in 2012 amounted to 255 per cent of GDP, compared with around 90 per cent in the US.[67] Because banks are by far the largest source of financial capital in the EU, the effects of their lending policies are magnified. Special lessons therefore apply to the EU because of its financial structure.

8.3.2 *Central Bank Policies*

Central bank policy stances and the regulation of banking systems can influence the costs of financing for all manner of projects, notwithstanding the primary source of credit. So, for example, central bank policies will exert pressure on yields and interest rates across multiple financial product lines, no matter whether such credit originates from the banking system or not. For this reason, we argue that focusing on central bank policies and bank regulation – rather than on private capital markets – is likely to be much more effective in realising a future in which sustainable activities may access funding more easily and unsustainable activities are less profitable.

With regard to the ECB, in common with most central banks in the world, it is primarily charged with maintaining price stability (i.e. inflation targeting),[68] consistent with Article 3(3) of the Treaty on the Functioning of the European Union (TFEU), which aims for 'the sustainable development of Europe based on balanced economic growth ... and a high level of protection and improvement of the quality of the environment'. Moreover, Article

---

[65] European Commission, Questions and Answers on the Mid-Term Review of the Capital Markets Union Action Plan, Brussels, 8 June 2017, available at: http://europa.eu/rapid/press-release_MEMO-17-1528_en.htm.

[66] M. Ferreira, D. Mendes and J. C. Pereira, 'Non-Bank Financing of European Non-Financial Firms' (July 2016), *European Federation of Financial Analysts Societies*, available at: https://effas.net/pdf/Nova_SBE_EFFAs_Non_Bank_Financing_EU_12102016.pdf.

[67] See European Central Bank, 'Report on Financial Structures' (ECB, October 2013).

[68] Article 127 TFEU.

11 TFEU provides that ' [e]nvironmental protection requirements must be integrated into the definition and implementation of the Union's policies and activities, in particular with a view to promoting sustainable development'.[69]

Sustainability considerations are material factors in determining both economic growth and improving the social market economy and the quality of the environment. As noted by Dirk Schoenmaker, this leaves room for 'the greening' of monetary policy.[70] In other words, the ECB may use its mandate to support the financing of sustainable investments, where this does not conflict with its primary objective of maintaining price stability.

8.3.3 Amending the ECB Collateral Framework to Reflect Sustainability Risks

Supporting the financing of sustainable investments could be operationalised by the ECB through incorporating risks to sustainability into its strategy and operations via the use of monetary policy, which is one of the central bank's most potent tools. The ECB is empowered under the ECB Statute to provide funding for commercial banks where required.[71] In doing so, it requires the borrowing bank to post collateral – marketable securities – in exchange for central bank reserves. There are two channels through which tilting the ECB's monetary policy portfolio could operate: through collateral asset eligibility and via the margins charged on collateral when accepted in exchange for reserves.

8.3.3.1 Collateral Eligibility

The collateral framework determines the eligibility of financial assets for these facilities, making them extremely potent tools in determining liquidity and portfolio selection at commercial banks. The ECB currently includes corporate bonds with high credit ratings in its monetary policy programmes.[72] Assets that are eligible for central bank refinancing operations become more attractive for the commercial banking system to hold, which increases demand for them; there is evidence of a disproportionate jump in the price of eligible assets after the introduction of these corporate bond purchase programmes.[73]

---

[69] Article 127 TFEU.

[70] D. Schoenmaker, 'Greening EU Monetary Policy' (19 February 2019), 2 *Bruegel Working Paper*, available at: www.bruegel.org/wp-content/uploads/2019/02/Greening-monetary-policy.pdf.

[71] See Article 18 of Protocol (No 4) on the Statute of the European System of Central Banks and of the ECB, OJ C 326, 26.10.2012, p. 230.

[72] This is known as the Corporate Sector Purchase Programme.

[73] R. A. De Santis, A. Geis, A. Juskaite and L. Vaz Cruz, 'The Impact of the Corporate Sector Purchase Programme on Corporate Bond Markets and the Financing of Euro Area Non-Financial Corporations' (2018), 3 *ECB Economic Bulletin*, 66.

This has two main consequences: first, the assets become more liquid because financial institutions and investors are more likely to purchase them; and second, it reduces the cost of financing, lowering the yield that originators must offer to fund those assets. In turn, eligible assets become more attractive to investors. Accepting assets as collateral that are sustainable will be a central part of this process. Importantly, the effects of such a reform would be reflexive, in that this will not only make it cheaper to finance sustainable projects, but also presumably sustainable assets will grow as a proportion of the financial asset universe. These reforms would also be justifiable on the basis that research indicates that the ECB's collateral portfolio held via monetary policy and other programmes is tilted away from sustainable investment. The ECB's collateral framework is supposed to reflect – to the extent it is possible – the market portfolio, yet conventional asset purchase operations have tended to favour high-carbon assets for investment purposes.[74]

The design and implementation of this would naturally require detailed analysis of the potential size of the market for the purchase of such bonds, as well as an assessment of what constitutes a sustainable asset. Transparency concerning the composition of such purchases would be needed, but there are strong motivations for expanding the current collateral framework to encompass certain ESG-friendly assets, which would allow central banks to revise their purchasing strategy to account for sustainability risks and financial stability implications. Such a reform would therefore dovetail with the Taxonomy, which would provide high-level guidance for the inclusion of certain collateral assets in the collateral framework on more favourable terms than they currently enjoy.

There have been parallel initiatives developed by other central banks, most notably the People's Bank of China, which includes green bonds in its collateral frameworks and gives lending priority to banks holding green bonds. The People's Bank of China accepts lower-rated green bonds for its Medium-Term Lending Facility, through which banks are able to exchange collateral assets for central bank liquidity.[75]

8.3.3.2 Collateral Haircuts

The collateral posted in these liquidity operations has a higher market value than the reserves it is being used to secure; the difference in value is known

[74] J. Cullen, '"Economically inefficient and legally untenable": constitutional limitations on the introduction of central bank digital currencies in the EU' (2022), 23, *Journal of Banking Regulation*, 31.

[75] Sustainable Banking Network, 'Creating Green Bond Markets – Insights, Innovations, and Tools from Emerging Markets', October 2018.

as the 'haircut'. For example, where. A financial institution pledges collateral with a market value of €1 million, and the haircut assigned to the asset is 20 per cent, the financial institution will receive €800,000 in cash. The function of this over-collateralisation is to guard against sudden falls in asset values if the repo counterparty has to liquidate its position. These haircuts are applied to collateral on a differential basis: the riskier the asset pledged as collateral, the larger the haircut demanded. There is strong evidence that the parameters applied to assets in collateral frameworks reduce bond yields, reduce interest rates on loans underpinning the relevant assets and increase credit availability in the asset class concerned.[76]

The Eurozone collateral framework is governed generally by the ECB Treaty but there are specific guidelines in place on the haircuts applied to eligible collateral.[77] The haircuts applied are then a function of the assets' features. Currently, the ECB's framework does not discriminate between collateral assets, irrespective of the environmental impact of the activities that the relevant assets are financing. This provides no disincentives for lending for unsustainable purposes, and the ECB risks capital allocation contributing to activities that damage the environment or contribute to climate change and other sustainability related problems. Collateral policy, in turn, will influence the asset portfolio choices of private commercial banks and other central bank counterparties. Banks prefer to hold assets that are more favourably treated for liquidity and refinancing purposes, which will itself encourage more bank-financed loans and green bond issuance by the private sector.[78]

The effectiveness of the programme increases relative to the responsiveness of sustainable investment to changes in bond yields.[79] This suggests that if a central bank credibly commits to supporting sustainable lending, the benefits of such programmes are much amplified. The greater the effectiveness of the programme, the higher is the responsiveness of sustainable investment to changes in bond yields. In Schoenmaker's model, investment volumes in

---

[76] C. Cahn, A. Duquerroy and W. Mullins, 'Unconventional Monetary Policy and Bank Lending Relationships', 659 *Banque de France Working Paper*; J.-S Mésonnier, C. O'Donnell and O. Toutain, 'The Interest of Being Eligible', 636 *Banque de France Working Paper*.

[77] European Central Bank, Guideline (EU) 2016/65 of the European Central Bank of 18 November 2015 on the valuation haircuts applied in the implementation of the Eurosystem monetary policy framework (ECB/2015/35).

[78] See B. Kuepper, T. Steinweg and G. Thoumi, 'Sustainable Banking Initiatives: Regulators' Role in Halting Deforestation' (July 2017), *Chain Reaction Research*, 3.

[79] Y. Dafermos, M. Nikolaidi and G. Galanis, 'Climate Change, Financial Stability and Monetary Policy' (September 2017), 1712 *Post Keynesian Economics Study Group Working Paper (PKSG)*, available at: www.postkeynesian.net/downloads/working-papers/PKWP1712.pdf.

non-sustainable covered bonds fall by up to 4 per cent, and up to 10 per cent in non-sustainable asset-backed securities, with credit spreads increasing for these asset classes by 1.75bp and 3.5bp respectively.[80]

Such unsustainable assets could have haircuts applied that are punitive or be excluded altogether from the ECB's eligible collateral for monetary policy. At present, the ECB's collateral framework and haircut regime are supportive of unsustainable sectors,[81] a practice that needs to discontinue over the upcoming years by disincentivising measures. The ECB's collateral framework criteria are based on current credit rating agency analytics, but there are alternative credit scoring approaches that incorporate risks attached to unsustainable assets; for example, the metrics used by Carbon Analytics that incorporate transition risk found that eight issuers would fall out of the ECB's investment grade criteria and hence no longer be eligible for its monetary policy programmes, representing almost 5 per cent of the issuers analysed.[82]

Enlargement of the Taxonomy to other assets as planned by the Technical Expert Group would assist central banks in this matter, allowing the ECB to either exclude assets from particular bank refinancing programmes or to adjust haircuts on unsustainable assets upwards where appropriate, and depending upon their sustainability characteristics. Any adjustment of the haircuts must be dynamic and allow the ECB some time period to identify any potential externalities and minimise transition risk.

8.3.4 *Bank Regulation*

In the absence of a shift away from a 'business-as-usual' approach, there are policy levers available to European regulators that could be used to influence the flow of credit to ventures that qualify as unsustainable. A proportionate principles-based response to such lending, in line with the parameters set out by the Commission, would be to reprice the funding of such activities to reflect externalities created.[83] In particular these levers coalesce around the

---

[80] Schoenmaker, 'Greening EU Monetary Policy', p. 17.

[81] Y. Dafermos, D. Gabor, M. Nikolaidi, A. Pawloff and F. van Lerven, 'Greening The Eurosystem Collateral Framework: How To Decarbonise ECB's Monetary Policy' (March 2021), *New Economics*, available at: https://neweconomics.org/2021/03/greening-the-eurosystem-collateral-framework.

[82] P. Monnin, 'Integrating Climate Risks into Credit Risk Assessment – Current Methodologies and the Case of Central Banks Corporate Bond Purchases' (2018), Discussion Note 2018/4 *Council on Economic Policies*.

[83] J. Cullen, 'After HLEG: EU Banks, Climate Change Abatement and the Precautionary Principle' (2018) 20 *Cambridge Yearbook of European Legal Studies*, 61–87.

capital requirements relevant to specific asset classes, which may be used to modulate the costs of credit provision, dependent on the requirement applied.

Such capital requirements are already set for all EU credit institutions at the European level under the CRR.[84] The EU recently signalled that approaches to mitigating climate risk under the CRD may be considered. Preparatory work in this field is being undertaken into the feasibility of lowering capital requirements against certain 'green assets',[85] which, it is claimed, are excessively high under the current asset risk-weighting regime.[86]

On this basis, the new CRR includes a new mandate that requires the EBA to assess whether to introduce a dedicated prudential treatment of exposures in the case of assets or activities substantially associated with environmental and/or social objectives.[87]

There is a precedent for the principle underpinning such reforms to risk-weighted capital requirements: lending to EU small and medium sized enterprises (SMEs) is currently accorded preferential capital treatment under the SME supporting factor introduced in 2014 under the CRR. Similar preferential treatment for infrastructure projects is found in EU insurance company regulation.[88] Indeed, the Commission has explicitly stated that capital requirements may be subject to 'targeted adjustments in order to reflect EU specificities and broader policy considerations'.[89] The levels of any reductions under such a supporting scheme for sustainable assets would be modelled on the discounts for small SME investments under Article 501 of CRR1, currently comprising a capital reduction of 23.81 per cent for banks' exposures to small firms for investments below €1.5 million.

---

[84] Directive 2013/36/EU of the European Parliament and of the Council of 26 June 2013 on access to the activity of credit institutions and the prudential supervision of credit institutions and investment firms, amending Directive 2002/87/EC and repealing Directives 2006/48/EC and 2006/49/EC: [2013] OJ L176/338.

[85] J. Brunsden, 'Brussels Looks at Easing Bank Capital Rules to Spur Green Investment', *Financial Times*, 10 January 2018, available at: www.ft.com/content/40df2780-e708-11e7-97e2-916d 4fbacoda.

[86] High-Level Expert Group, Final Report, p. 32.

[87] Article 501c of CRR.

[88] Commission Delegated Regulation (EU) 2017/1542 of 8 June 2017 amending Delegated Regulation (EU) 2015/35 concerning the calculation of regulatory capital requirements for certain categories of assets held by insurance and reinsurance undertakings (infrastructure corporates): [2017] OJ L236/14.

[89] Regulation of the European Parliament and of the Council amending Regulation (EU) No 575/2013 as regards the leverage ratio, the net stable funding ratio, requirements for own funds and eligible liabilities, counterparty credit risk, market risk, exposures to central counterparties, exposures to collective investment undertakings, large exposures, reporting and disclosure requirements, and amending Regulation (EU) No 648/2012, COM (2016) 850, p. 3.

8.3.5 *Introducing a Harmful Activities Factor to Reflect Sustainability Risks*

Although the Commission and EBA have indicated they may pursue a sustainability supporting factor, there are important objections to this approach. The first is that sustainable investments, whilst perhaps more desirable from a public policy standpoint than unsustainable investments, are no more creditworthy than unsustainable assets.[90] Anything green can include financial risks as technical risks and managements risks and general uncertainty risks. It is much easier to add the disincentivising factors for unsustainable investments and increase capital requirements accordingly.

The second is that research indicates that incentivising loan origination in this way would produce marginal results; banks will simply price loans less aggressively in the event that capital requirements are lowered. According to researchers at the University of Cambridge, regulatory capital requirements as currently set forth in Basel III's Pillar 1 approach play 'at most a marginal role in influencing a bank's decision to provide specialised lending on project finance for environmentally sustainable economic activities such as renewable energy infrastructure projects',[91] with other factors including political and economic riskiness having much more prominent roles. In line with this, there is little evidence that the SME supporting factor has been effective in either lowering borrowing costs or increasing access to finance for SMEs.[92] In contrast, what the introduction of the SME supporting factor *did* lead to was a reduction in aggregate EU bank capital of over €12 billion, undermining financial stability.[93] Equally undesirable consequences in relation to a sustainability supporting factor cannot be discounted.

The plans to propose an incentive-generative 'green supporting factor' are therefore inadequate. Instead a comprehensive harmful activities factor should be introduced. A harmful activities factor was mooted already by the High-Level Expert Group on Sustainable Finance in its Interim Report, where it argued that a '"brown-penalising" factor, raising capital requirements towards sectors with strong sustainability risks, would yield a constellation in

---

[90] S. Matikainen, 'Green Doesn't Mean Risk-Free: Why We Should Be Cautious About a Green Supporting Factor in the EU', *Grantham Research Institute on Climate Change and the Environment*, 18 December 2017, available at: www.lse.ac.uk/GranthamInstitute/news/eu-green-supporting-factor-bank-risk.

[91] University of Cambridge Institute for Sustainability Leadership and UNEP Finance Initiative, 'Stability and Sustainability in Banking Reform: Are Environmental Risks Missing in Basel III?' (CISL & UNEP FI, 2014).

[92] European Banking Authority, Report on SMEs and SME Supporting Factor, EBA/Op/2016/04 (23 March 2016).

[93] Ibid.

which risk and policy considerations go in the same direction [as rewarding green projects]'.[94]

It is unclear why the original High-Level Expert Group initiative was abandoned. As noted, the evidence suggests that altering capital requirements downward (e.g. under a sustainability supporting factor) would likely have a negligible effect on banks' decisions on whether to make specific loans. Indeed, research indicates that the estimated effect is a reduction in capital requirements associated with a green supporting factor of around €2–8 billion. In absolute terms and even under an expanded application, the total 'capital savings' related to the introduction of a green supporting factor would likely be significantly lower than those identified in response to the SME supporting factor, estimated by the EBA in 2016 at about €12 billion.

In contrast, higher harmful activities factor risk-weighted capital requirements are known to disincentivise lending, including when targeted at particular asset classes.[95] Powers to amend lending in this way are already afforded to bank regulators under the CRR; such an option provides regulators with a flexible, targeted tool with which to funnel credit away from particular sectors, and thus decrease financial flows to such projects by up to 8 per cent.[96]

By raising the capital requirements on certain unsustainable assets, banks would have to fund such assets with a greater proportion of capital (shareholder funds), thereby raising banks' cost of funding. Such a regulatory change is likely to mean banks will charge higher rates for particular asset forms. It also would avoid the potential avenue for banks to use the mooted sustainability supporting factor to subsidise funding for unsustainable assets. In the absence of any portfolio restrictions operating in tandem with such a sustainability supporting factor, there is substantial moral hazard embedded in any preferential prudential treatment for sustainable assets, as such assets may be used to cross-subsidise the origination of credit for greenhouse gas-intensive purposes and other unsustainable activities. Assuming a similar capital adjustment than for the green supporting factor (15–25 per cent), the simulated effects are in the ranges of €8–13 billion additional capital requirements for a limited application and €14–22 billion for an expanded application. Even stronger

---

[94] EU's High-Level Expert Group on Sustainable Finance, 'Financing a Sustainable European Economy: Interim Report, July 2017' (2017), p. 32; compare High-Level Expert Group, Final Report, p. 31.

[95] H. Fraisse, M. Lé and D. Thesmar, 'The Real Effects of Bank Capital Requirements' (June 2017), 47 *European Systemic Risk Board Working Paper Series* (ESRB).

[96] J. Thomä and K. Gibhardt, 'Quantifying the potential impact of a green supporting factor or brown penalty on European banks and lending' (2019) 27(3) *Journal of Financial Regulation and Compliance*, 380–394.

adjustments, such as 50 per cent, could lead to a €27–44 billion penalty. The main reason behind the stronger effect is the larger universe of high carbon assets compared with sustainable assets on which such a penalty would be applied.[97] This will produce two socially desirable outcomes: increased (rather than lower) loss absorbing capacity at financial institutions; and the internalisation of at least some of the costs of environmental degradation.

8.4 CONCLUSION

In this chapter we have called for a fundamental recalibration of the role and duties of financial system participants to enable sustainable value creation and prevent funding of unsustainable activities causing damage to the ecosystem and to the social foundation of humanity. We have suggested that European financial regulators and central banks must focus their regulation and supervision in evaluating the financial risks of unsustainability. According to our analysis the main weaknesses of current sustainable finance approaches have been threefold: (1) a reliance on traditional incentive structures for private actors in financial markets that prioritise information disclosure as a regulatory technique, (2) the reticence of the EU to reform its regulatory structures and policies with regard to financial markets, and (3) a continued adherence to the principle of market neutrality in relation to both monetary policy and bank regulation.

Our proposals for reform are based on a holistic approach to financial risks of unsustainability, ranging from requirements set on central bank policies and bank regulation on funding decisions and capital requirements to more comprehensive reporting requirements, and strict duties of due diligence set to financial institutions, requiring a positive compliance obligation to assess and demonstrate how they have mitigated or prevented sustainability risks from materialising.

---

[97] Ibid.

9

Integrating Sustainable Value Creation in Corporate Governance

Company Law, Corporate Governance Codes and the Constitution of the Company

*Beate Sjåfjell and Georgina Tsagas**

9.1 INTRODUCTION

In the time since the financial crisis of 2008–2009 we have seen progressive shifts and changes in the European Union (EU) Commission's approach towards the relationship between company law and sustainability. In 2021 this has culminated in a tentative willingness to adopt a policy that not only endorses sustainability but also includes it as an integral part of a corporation's corporate governance. This is supported in the European Green Deal of 2019,[1] and also the EU Commission's Communication on the (COVID-19) Recovery Plan of 2020.[2] The EU Green Deal's ambition that 'sustainability should be further embedded into the corporate governance framework', is followed up directly by the Commission's Sustainable Corporate Governance initiative.[3]

Prior to the more recent work of the EU on sustainable corporate governance, a defining initiative for business sustainability at an international level

* This chapter draws on research conducted under the Sustainable Market Actors for Responsible Trade (SMART) research project, funded by the European Union's Horizon 2020 Research and Innovation Programme, Grant Agreement No. 693642. Our warmest thanks to the SMART team as a whole for inspiring discussions and to research assistant Madeleine Østenstad for her invaluable assistance with this chapter.

[1] European Commission, Communication from the Commission to the European Parliament, the European Council, the Council, the European Economic and Social Committee and the Committee of the Regions: The European Green Deal, 11.12.2019, COM/2019/640 final.

[2] Europe's moment: Repair and Prepare for the Next Generation COM/2020/456 final.

[3] European Commission, the European Green Deal, section 2.2.1, and see the European Commission's recently concluded public consultation on the topic, available at: www .ec.europa.eu/info/law/better-regulation/have-your-say/initiatives/12548-Sustainable-corporate-governance. The legislative proposal is now expected in the first quarter of 2022.

was the United Nations (UN) adoption of the Sustainable Development Goals (SDGs) in 2015,[4] which made clear that the question was no longer whether corporations should act in a sustainable way, but rather *how* this could be effectively achieved. Together with the Organisation of Economic Co-operation and Development (OECD) Guidelines for Multinational Enterprises,[5] and the UN Guiding Principles for Business and Human Rights,[6] the SDGs have contributed to a shift in social norms as concerns society's expectations of business and expectations within business as regards their role in society. A barrier to exploring various effective and practical options within this context is that scholarly work bridging the gap between the polarised positions of shareholder primacy advocates versus stakeholder protection advocates within the sphere of company law is limited. In 2008, Aras and Crowther highlighted how little work had been undertaken to explore the relationship between corporate governance and sustainability, in spite of these being two fundamental concepts that are linked to each other.[7] As, for example, Elkington pointed out in 2006, corporate governance is fundamentally about questions such as what business is for and in whose interests companies should be run, and how.[8] The first two questions have been the centre of academic discussion for decades,[9] and sustainability, company law and corporate governance have increasingly become the topic of research and debate.[10] The recent EU and international

---

4 UN, UN General Assembly resolution 70/1, *Transforming Our World: The 2030 Agenda for Sustainable Development*, A/RES/70/1 (25 September 2015, available at: www.un.org/en/development/desa/population/migration/generalassembly/docs/globalcompact/A_RES_70_1_E.pdf.

5 The Organisation for Economic Co-operation and Development (OECD), 'Guidelines for multinational enterprises' (2011), available at: www.oecd.org/corporate/mne/.

6 UN, *Guiding Principles on Business and Human Rights*, Implementing the United Nations 'Protect, Respect and Remedy' Framework (2011), 15–17, available at: www.ohchr.org/documents/publications/guidingprinciplesbusinesshr_en.pdf.

7 G. Aras and D. Crowther, 'Governance and Sustainability: An Investigation into the Relationship between Corporate Governance and Corporate Sustainability' (2008), 46, 3 *Management Decision*, 433–448, DOI: https://doi.org/10.1108/00251740810863870.

8 J. Elkington 'Governance for Sustainability' (November 2006) 14, 6 *Corporate Governance*, 522–529, DOI: https://doi.org/10.1111/j.1467-8683.2006.00527.x.

9 The debate on the stakeholder/shareholder divide originates in the debate between E. Dodd and A. Berle; see E. Dodd, 'For Whom are Corporate Managers Trustees?' (1932) 45 *Harvard Law Review*, 1145, 1162–1163. A. Berle 'For Whom Are Corporate Managers Trustees: A Note', (1932) 45 *Harvard Law Review*, 1365–1372 at 1367. The fallacy of this dichotomy and its lacking connection with company law proper, is the topic of a contribution by Sjåfjell together with Jukka Mähönen, B. Sjåfjell and J. Mähönen, 'Corporate Purpose and the Misleading Shareholder vs Stakeholder Dichotomy', *Bond Law Review*, forthcoming 2022.

10 Discussions of the unsustainability of business and criticism of the prevailing shareholder primacy theory has long roots, including progressive company law scholarship from the 1990s onwards: L. E. Mitchell (ed.), *Progressive Corporate Law* (Boulder, CO: Westview Press, 1995); I. Lynch Fannon, *Working Within Two Kinds of Capitalism* (Oxford: Hart Publishing, 2003); K. Greenfield, *The Failure of Corporate Law: Fundamental Flaws and Progressive*

initiatives may be interpreted as an acknowledgement that the mainstream principal–agent model,[11] which has informed much of the corporate governance debate for decades, constitutes an anachronistic view of the company that should be rejected.[12] This is in line with the ever clearer call over the last decade from academia, civil society and increasingly also from policymakers and business itself.[13] The EU's Sustainable Corporate Governance initiative is

Possibilities (Chicago: University of Chicago Press, 2008), and more recent contributions: L. E. Talbot 'Why Shareholders Shouldn't Vote: A Marxist-Progressive Critique of Shareholder Empowerment', (2013) 76(5) *The Modern Law Review*, 791–816; C. Mayer, *Firm Commitment: Why the Corporation Is Failing Us and How to Restore Trust in It* (Oxford: Oxford University Press, 2013); L. A. Stout, *The Shareholder Value Myth: How Putting Shareholders First Harms Investors, Corporations, and the Public* (San Francisco: Berrett-Koehler Publishers, 2012), B. Sjåfjell and B. J. Richardson, *Company Law and Sustainability: Legal Barriers and Opportunities* (Cambridge: Cambridge University Press, 2015); B. Sjåfjell and C. M. Bruner (eds.), *Cambridge Handbook of Corporate Law, Corporate Governance and Sustainability* (Cambridge: Cambridge University Press, 2019).

[11]　E. Fama, 'Agency Problems and the Theory of the Firm' (1980) 88(2) *Journal of Political Economy*, 288, E. F. Fama and M. C. Jensen 'Separation of Ownership and Control' (1983) 26 *Journal of Law and Economics*, 301, M. Jensen and W. Meckling 'Theory of the Firm: Managerial Behaviour, Agency Costs, and Ownership Structure', (1976) 3 *Journal of Financial Economics*, 305.

[12]　T. Clarke, 'The Contest on Corporate Purpose: Why Lynn Stout was Right and Milton Friedman was Wrong' (2020) 10 *Accounting, Economics, and Law: A Convivium*; B. Sjåfjell, 'Redefining Agency Theory to Internalize Environmental Product Externalities: A Tentative Proposal Based on Life Cycle Thinking', in E. Maitre-Ekern, C. Dalhammar and H. C. Bugge (eds.), *Preventing Environmental Damage from Products*, (Cambridge: Cambridge University Press, 2018), pp. 101–124.

[13]　J. Kay, 'Theories of the Firm' (2018) 25 *International Journal of the Economics of Business* 11–17; L. A. Stout, J. P. Robé, P. Ireland, S. Deakin, K. Greenfield, A. Johnston, H. Schepel, M. M. Blair, L. E. Talbot, A. J. Dignam, J. Dine, D. Millon, B. Sjåfjell, C. Villiers, C. A. Williams, M. Koutsias, A. Pendleton, G. F. Davis, M. Galanis, D. Chandler, A.R. Keay, M. T. Moore, J. Du Plessis, A. J. Bather, B. L. Lefler, C. Bradshaw, C. M. Bruner, T. W. Joo, D. J. H. Greenwood, T. Clarke, L. Johnson, F. Mulazzi, M. Lipton, C. Liao, R. Johnson, A. Alon-Beck, G. Markel, W. Currie, F. Partnoy, L. F. Peklar, A. Di Miceli da Silveira, O. Sitbon, C. González-Cantón, J.P. Chanteau, A. R. F. Donaggio, I.M. Esser, G. North, S. A. Gramitto Ricci, R. Tomasic, R. G. Pillay, C. O'Kelly, C. Keating, H. C. Willmott, J. Veldman and P. Morrow, *The Modern Corporation Statement on Company Law* (6 October 2016), available at SSRN: https://ssrn.com/abstract=2848833; A. Johnston, J. Veldman, R. G. Eccles, S. Deakin, J. Davis, M.L. Djelic, K. Pistor, B. Segrestin, C. A. Williams, D. Millon, P. Ireland, B. Sjåfjell, C. M. Bruner, L. E. Talbot, H. C. Willmott, C. Villiers, C. Liao, B. Valiorgue, J. Glynos, T. L. Sayre, B. Morgan, R. Wartzman, P. Sikka, F. Gregor, D. C. Jacobs, R. Gill, R. Brown, V. Bavoso, N. Lancastle, J. Matthaei, S. Taylor, U. Larsson-Olaison, J. Cullen, A. J. Dignam, T. W. Joo, C. O'Kelly, C. Keating, R. Tomasic, S. Lilley, K. Tennent, K. Robson, W. Maley, I. H. Y. Chiu, E. McGaughey, C. Rees, N. Boeger, A. Leaver, M. T. Moore, L. Paape, A. D. Meyer, M. Palazzi, N. Kaul, J. F. Espinosa-Cristia, T. Kuhn, D. J. Cooper, S. Soederberg, A. Jansson, S. Watson, O. Sitbon, J. Loughrey, D. Collison, M. McCulloch, M. McCulloch, N. Samanta, D. J. H. Greenwood, G. F. Thompson, A. R. Keay, A. Contu, A. Rühmkorf, R. Hull, I.M. Esser, and N. Chabrak, *Corporate Governance for Sustainability* (11 December 2019), available at SSRN: https://ssrn.com/abstract=3502101.

a much-delayed but natural next step after the EU's paradigm shift in its definition of the relationship between business and society in 2011.[14] The question of *how* to follow through with corporate governance for sustainability is the crucial question.

Although the SDGs, adopted for 'the future of humanity and of our planet', call on business to contribute to solving these pressing challenges of continued unsustainability,[15] business remains in aggregate a driver of the current convergence of crises. At the heart of the problem of unsustainable business, we find the social norm of *shareholder primacy*, a systemically entrenched barrier to the contribution of business to sustainability. Denoting shareholder primacy as a barrier of such significance is a short form for a complex mix of perceived market signals and economic incentives, informed by path-dependent corporate governance assumptions and postulates from legal/economic theories.[16] A proper analysis of company law shows that the aim of any legislation allowing for companies to exist and become a dominant form of business is based on the assumption that this is positive for society. The idea is that companies create value, for themselves, for their employees, their business partners, their local communities and the broader society.

There is no company law in any jurisdiction that promotes companies as a business form based on the assumption that this will maximise returns to shareholders to the detriment of society. Yet that is frequently the consequence. Shareholder primacy, combined with a lack of understanding of the scope that the law gives the board, has given rise to legal myths inspired by law and economics postulates, dictating that the board and senior managers are the 'agents' of the shareholders and must maximise returns to shareholders as measured by

---

[14] European Commission, Communication from the Commission to the European Parliament, the Council, the European Economic and Social Committee and the Committee of the Regions: A renewed EU strategy 2011–14 for Corporate Social Responsibility, 25.10.2011, COM(2011) 681 final.

[15] United Nations, *The 2030 Agenda for Sustainable Development*.

[16] B. Sjåfjell, A. Johnston, L. Anker-Sørensen and D. Millon, 'Shareholder Primacy: The Main Barrier to Sustainable Companies', in B. Sjåfjell and B. J. Richardson (eds.), *Company Law and Sustainability: Legal Barriers and Opportunities*, (Cambridge: Cambridge University Press, 2015), pp. 79–147. Shareholder primacy should be distinguished from the legal norm denoted *shareholder value*, which we find notably in the UK. In earlier work, David Millon uses 'radical' and 'traditional' shareholder primacy to distinguish between the social norm and the legal norm; D. Millon, 'Radical Shareholder Primacy' (2013) 10, *University of St. Thomas Law Journal*, 1013. On UK law, see A. Johnston, 'Market-Led Sustainability through Information Disclosure: The UK Approach', in Sjåfjell and Bruner (eds.), *Cambridge Handbook of Corporate Law*, pp. 204–217. That this distinction is often not made is symptomatic of the dominance of the shareholder primacy thinking, conflating what is seen as practice and what still dominant legal-economic theories describe as efficient, with what company law actually sets out; Sjåfjell et al., 'Shareholder Primacy', pp. 79–147.

the current share price.[17] At the same time, capital markets, with reliance on strict financial reporting, function to funnel and exacerbate the shareholder primacy drive, supported by securities regulation and stock exchange rules that have as their primary aim to protect investors.[18] The normative impact of the shareholder primacy drive goes beyond the listed corporations, and is exacerbated by the chasm between corporate law's approach to corporate groups and the dominance and practice of such groups,[19] and the extensive use of global value chains and other non-equity modes of control,[20] allowing for an intensified externalisation of environmental, social and economic costs.

Aligned with this volume's theme of sustainable value creation, this chapter discusses how to integrate sustainable value creation in future regulation for European business. In doing so, it targets key sources of corporate governance of companies based in the EU: company law, corporate governance codes and corporate documents, notably the companies' constitution. Currently, all of these, law, codes and constitutions, tend mainly to limit themselves to regulating the relationship between the board, senior management and shareholders, making minimal reference to the existence of crucial contributions by other involved parties and affected interests comprising the business. Potentially laws, codes and constitutions can be remodelled in order to integrate sustainability into the governance of business, ensuring also engagement with involved parties and affected interests.

The chapter is structured as follows. Section 9.2 analyses the emerging concept in company law and corporate governance of sustainable value creation. In Section 9.3, we turn to the potential of securing sustainable value creation in Europe through company law reform, discussing what that may entail. In Section 9.4 we discuss how sustainable value creation could be integrated more fully into corporate governance codes, which could be envisaged as a support for a law reform or as an alternative way to promote sustainable

[17] Along with that of shareholders owning corporations, which they as a matter of corporate law clearly do not; see, for example, P. Ireland, 'Company Law and the Myth of Shareholder Ownership' (1999) 62 *Modern Law Review*, 32; L. Talbot, *Critical Company Law*, 2nd ed. (London: Routledge, 2015).

[18] J. Cullen *and* J. Mähönen, 'Taming Unsustainable Finance: The Perils of Modern Risk Management', in Sjåfjell and Bruner (eds.), *Cambridge Handbook of Corporate Law*, pp. 100–113; C. M. Bruner, 'Corporate Governance Reform in a Time of Crisis', (2011) 36 *Journal of Corporation Law*, 309.

[19] B. Clarke and L. Anker-Sørensen, 'The EU as a Potential Norm Creator for Sustainable Corporate Groups', in Sjåfjell and Bruner (eds.), *Cambridge Handbook of Corporate Law*, pp. 190–203.

[20] J. Salminen, 'Sustainability and the Move from Corporate Governance to Governance through Contract', in Sjåfjell and Bruner (eds.), *Cambridge Handbook of Corporate Law*, pp. 57–70.

business while waiting for legislative reform. Section 9.5 explores how the potential of integrating sustainable value creation in company constitutions can contribute to shifting business towards sustainability. Section 9.6 briefly outlines concluding reflections.

9.2 SUSTAINABLE VALUE CREATION AS AN EMERGING CONCEPT

We position and interpret the emerging concept of sustainable value creation within the research-based concept of sustainability outlined in Chapter 1 in this volume.[21] This entails that the creation of sustainable value must be interpreted as activity that engages with the goal of securing social foundations for humanity now and for the future,[22] and does it in a way that contributes to bringing and keeping global society within planetary boundaries.[23]

Interpreting sustainable value creation as an activity within planetary boundaries has potential significance on three interconnected levels: first, and most importantly, it brings to the forefront that there are ecological limits (conversely, that being perceived as 'environmentally friendly' while not respecting those limits is totally inadequate). Secondly, it highlights the complex interactions between planet-level environmental processes, recognising for example that climate change, however topical (and difficult to mitigate), is only one aspect of the convergence of crises we are heading towards. Thirdly, it continuously reminds us that state-of-the-art natural science must inform our decisions on a work-in-progress-basis, encompassing the uncertainty and complexity of the global challenges.

Engaging with the goal of securing social foundations for humanity now and for the future requires translation into the governance of business. It encompasses issues such as fair treatment of employees as well as of workers

---

[21] C. Villiers, B. Sjåfjell and G. Tsagas, 'Stimulating Value Creation in a Europe in Crisis', Chapter 1 in this volume. This section draws on the analysis in B. Sjåfjell, T. Häyhä, and S. Cornell, 'A Research-Based Approach to the UN Sustainable Development Goals. A Prerequisite to Sustainable Business and Finance' (2020) 2020–02 *University of Oslo Faculty of Law Research Paper*; B. Sjåfjell, 'How Company Law has Failed Human Rights – and What to do About it' (2020) 5, 2, *Business and Human Rights Journal*, 179–199.

[22] K. Raworth, 'A safe and just space for humanity: can we live within the doughnut?' (2012) 8, *Oxfam Discussion Papers*; M. Leach, K. Raworth and J. Rockström, 'Between Social and Planetary Boundaries: Navigating Pathways in the Safe and Just Space for Humanity', *World Social Science Report 2013* (Paris: OECD Publishing, 2013), pp. 84–90.

[23] J. Rockström et al., 'Planetary Boundaries: Exploring the Safe Operating Space for Humanity' (2009) 14 *Ecology and Society*; W. Steffen, K. Richardson, J. Rockström, S. E. Cornell, I. Fetzer, E. M. Bennett, R. Biggs, S. R. Carpenter, W. de Vries, C. A. de Wit, C. Folke, D. Gerten, J. Heinke, G. M. Mace, L. M. Persson, V. Ramanathan, B. Reyers and S. Sörlin, 'Planetary Boundaries: Guiding Human Development on a Changing Planet' (2015) 347 *Science*.

and local communities across global value chains, with respect for international human rights and core ILO conventions as a minimum, ensuring a 'living wage' and safe working conditions. This further entails supporting democratic political processes and as a minimum not undermining these through engaging in corporate capture of regulatory processes. It also entails contributing to the economic basis of the societies in which the business interacts by not engaging in so-called aggressive tax planning and outright evasion.[24]

Turning to the UN Guiding Principles for Business and Human Rights (UNGPs),[25] we see that 'internationally recognised human rights' as the 'benchmarks against which other social actors assess the human rights impacts of business enterprises',[26] refer as a minimum to those expressed in the International Bill of Human Rights. These include the Universal Declaration of Human Rights and its main instruments of codification: the International Covenant on Civil and Political Rights and the International Covenant on Economic, Social and Cultural Rights,[27] as well as the principles concerning fundamental rights set out in the eight International Labour Organization (ILO) core conventions, set out in the ILO's Declaration on Fundamental Principles and Rights at Work 1998.[28]

An emphasis on vulnerability arguably resonates with the Commentary to the UNGPs Principle 12, which emphasises that business 'may need to consider additional standards'. These concern, according to the Commentary, the human rights of 'specific groups or populations that require particular attention', elaborated on in UN instruments regarding the 'rights of indigenous peoples; women; national or ethnic, religious and linguistic minorities; children; persons with disabilities; and migrant workers and their families'.[29] The elimination of

---

[24] Sjåfjell, 'How Company Law has Failed Human Rights', p. 179.

[25] United Nations, Guiding Principles on Business and Human Rights, Principle 12.

[26] United Nations, Guiding Principles on Business and Human Rights, Principle 12, Commentary.

[27] Ibid.

[28] Ibid., Commentary. These eight conventions are: Convention 87 and 98 on freedom of association and collective bargaining (1948 and 1949); Conventions 29 and 105 on the elimination of all forms of forced and compulsory labour (1930 and 1957); ILO Convention 138 on the minimum age for admission to employment (1973); ILO Conventions 100 and 111 on the elimination of discrimination in respect of employment and occupation (1957 and 1958); and the 1999 ILO Convention 182 on the worst forms of child labour. These have been criticised as merely promoting 'civil and political rights (and even just a selection of these), while moving away from insistence on broader socio-economic entitlements', T. Novitz, 'Past and Future Work at the International Labour Organization', (2020) 17 *International Organizations Law Review*, 10.

[29] United Nations, Guiding Principles on Business and Human Rights, Principle 12, Commentary. Moreover, in cases of armed conflict, the Commentary emphasises that business should respect the 'standards of international humanitarian law', ibid.

discrimination in respect of employment and occupation, whether on the basis of gender, race, age, disability or migrant status, is crucial.[30]

As an intrinsic element of transitioning towards sustainable value creation, the following must be included: participatory aspects of the social foundations,[31] of workers, regardless of their labour law status, and of affected communities, including indigenous peoples, and ensuring that all affected are fully involved.[32] And yet we must avoid merely replacing the 'shareholder' in shareholder primacy with 'stakeholder'.[33] While involving affected communities, trade unions and civil society is crucial, a mere canvassing of 'stakeholder interests' and giving priority to the ones that make themselves heard the most is insufficient. The backdrop must always be the interconnected complexities and the vulnerability of the often unrepresented groups (whether invisible workers deep in the global value chains, indigenous communities or future generations),[34] and the aim of a sustainable future within planetary boundaries.

9.3 SECURING SUSTAINABLE VALUE CREATION THROUGH COMPANY LAW REFORM

9.3.1 *Including Company Law in the Regulatory Tool Box*

Company law is crucial to business and to the governance of business. Company law provides the dominant legal form of the company for organising business, and it sets out the organisation and the structure for the

---

[30] See the International Labour Organization, ILO Declaration on Fundamental Principles and Rights at Work and its Follow-up, 18 June 1998, art. II(d), SDG 8 targets (including SDG target 8.8 concerning migrant workers); the International Convention on the Protection of Migrant Workers and their Families, New York, 18 December 1990, in force 1 July 2003, A/RES/45/158, and the 2019 ILO Centenary Declaration, including Art. II(A)(xvi) concerning decent work for migrant workers.

[31] T. Novitz, 'Engagement with Sustainability at the International Labour Organization and Wider Implications for Collective Worker Voice' (2020) 159 *International Labour Review*, 463. Concerning some of the challenges involved, see also I. Scoones, 'The Politics of Sustainability and Development'(2016) 41 *Annual Review of Environment and Resources*, 293.

[32] As indeed is envisaged by SDG 16.

[33] See, for example, B. Sjåfjell and J. Mähönen, 'Corporate Purpose and the Misleading Shareholder vs Stakeholder Dichotomy' (21 February 2022). University of Oslo Faculty of Law Research Paper No. 2022-43, Available at SSRN: https://ssrn.com/abstract=4039565 or https://dx.doi.org/10.2139/ssrn.4039565. See also M. Ventoruzzo, 'On "Prosperity" by Colin Mayer: Brief Critical Remarks on the (Legal) Relevance of announcing a Multi-Stakeholders 'Corporate Purpose', (2020) 3546139 *Bocconi Legal Studies Research Paper*, available at SSRN: https://ssrn.com/abstract=3546139.

[34] L. J. Kotzé, 'The Anthropocene, Earth System Vulnerability and Socio-Ecological Injustice in an Age of Human Rights' (2019) 62 *Journal of Human Rights and the Environment*, 73–75.

decision-making in companies with the board in a key role. As the European Commission has observed, boards have a 'vital part to play in the development of responsible companies'.[35] The EU has in its Sustainable Finance Initiative, in Action 10 of its Action Plan, indicated that it sees a role for legislative intervention in the rules concerning corporate boards.[36] In the Commission's Sustainable Corporate Governance initiative, the environmental and notably climate change focus of the Sustainable Finance Initiative is merged with the push for mandatory human rights due diligence, informed by the UN Guiding Principles and supported by the European Parliament and a range of national legislative initiatives.[37]

As one amongst several sources in the preparation of the Commission's Sustainable Governance Initiative, the 'Study on Directors' Corporate Governance Duties and Sustainable Corporate Governance' prepared by Ernst and Young for the European Commission (EY report),[38] advocates company law reform, notably of the duties of the board, to integrate sustainability concerns. The Commission's Inception Assessment unleashed a storm of response, much of it negative,[39] attempting to drown out the calls for mandatory sustainability regulation of European business from scholars and business alike.[40] Much of the response has concentrated on the EY report, seemingly disregarding that this is one source only of what the Commission is drawing on. In that light, one may be tempted to see this as a straw man for the opposition, reacting more

---

[35] European Commission, Green Paper: The EU corporate governance framework, 05.04.2011, COM(2011) 164 final, 5.

[36] European Commission, Communication from the Commission to the European Parliament, the European Council, the Council, the European Central Bank, the European Economic and Social Committee and the Committee of the Regions, Action Plan: Financing Sustainable Growth, 08.03.2018, COM(2018) 97 final, 11.

[37] Lise Smit et al. for the European Commission, Study on due diligence requirements through the supply chain, final report, 20.2.2020, available at: https://op.europa.eu/sv/publication-detail/-/publication/8baoa8fd-4c83-11ea-b8b7-01aa75ed71a1/language-en; MEPs: Hold companies accountable for harm caused to people and planet', 27 January 2021, available at: www.europarl.europa.eu/news/en/press-room/20210122IPR96215/meps-hold-companies-accountable-for-harm-caused-to-people-and-planet; and, for example, M. Krajewski, K. Tonstad, and F. Wohltmann, 'Mandatory Human Rights Due Diligence in Germany and Norway: Stepping, or Striding, in the Same Direction?' (2021) 6 *Business and Human Rights Journal* 550–558; C. Bright, 'Hardening Soft Law: The Implementation of Human Rights Due Diligence Requirements in Domestic Legislation', in M. Buscemi, N. Lazzerini, L. Magi and D. Russo (eds.), *Legal Sources in Business and Human Rights*, (Leiden: Brill Nijhoff, 2020), pp. 218–247.

[38] European Commission, 'Study on Directors' Duties and Sustainable Corporate Governance': final report, 29.07.2020 DOI: 10.2838/472901.

[39] See, for example, J. O. Jacke, L. S. Sorensen, J. Hakamies, O. E. Almlid, A. Aas and S. Hannesson, 'Letter: Brussels' sustainable corporate governance plan is flawed', (23 April 2021) *Financial Times online*, available at: www.ft.com/content/a2ab26b3-c9fc-4f33-a4bf-96a6e136f890.

[40] See, for example, Johnston et al., *Corporate Governance for Sustainability*.

to the idea of change and less to the content of that which may be proposed (remembering that the Commission at the time of writing had not yet presented its proposal for a sustainable corporate governance legislative initiative). This may be illustrated by the minimal discussion and hardly any reference by the opposition to the report by Lise Smit and colleagues, which strongly underlined the need for mandatory due diligence requirements and showed that over 70 per cent of businesses support mandatory legislation in this area.[41] The Commission has since carried out a public consultation, which shows a much more nuanced and positive response, and strong support for change.[42]

Amongst the more nuanced responses, critiquing the EY report's recommendations and providing their own suggestions on how corporate governance can become more sustainable, Florian Möslein and Karsten Engsig Sørensen call for a cautious and subtle regulatory approach.[43] However, their proposals, based on the premise that 'nudging' of business has not been tried out sufficiently, refer to procedural regulatory instruments that have been tried and tested for some time, offering little progress towards securing the contribution of business to a more sustainable future. These include sustainability reporting requirements, a requirement for human rights and environmental due diligence, encouraging boards to make more balanced business decisions, where sustainability impacts are included, requiring the board to consult stakeholders before making material decisions and promoting the certification of sustainable companies.[44] Most of the identified initiatives have been gradually set into place over some time.

Notably, the EU's sustainability reporting requirements, under the unfortunately named 'non-financial' reporting directive of 2014,[45] has been empirically proven to have very limited effects.[46] This is unsurprising, in light of

---

[41] European Commission, Study on due diligence requirements through the supply chain.

[42] See, for example, the overview of the response available at: www.ey.com/en_pl/law/insights-from-public-consultations-on-the-eu-sustainable-corporate-governance-initiative. See also, for example, this from civil society and practice together: 'Joint statement on sustainable corporate governance', Accountancy Europe, 8 June 2021, available at: www.accountancyeurope.eu/good-governance-sustainability/joint-statement-on-sustainable-corporate-governance/.

[43] See F. Möslein and K. Engsig Sørensen, 'Sustainable Corporate Governance: A Way Forward' (4 January 2021) 21–03, *Nordic & European Company Law Working Paper*, Forthcoming in 583/2021 *European Company Law, European Corporate Governance Institute – Law Working Paper*, available at SSRN: https://ssrn.com/abstract=3761711.

[44] Ibid., pp. 2–3.

[45] Directive 2014/95/EU of the European Parliament and of the Council of 22 October 2014 amending Directive 2013/34/EU as regards disclosure of non-financial and diversity information by certain large undertakings and groups.

[46] The Alliance for Corporate Transparency, '2019 research report. An analysis of the sustainability reports of 1000 companies pursuant to the EU Non-Financial Reporting Directive' (2019), available at: www.allianceforcorporatetransparency.org/.

previous multijurisdictional comparative analyses of various sustainability reporting regimes conducted by Charlotte Villiers and Jukka Mähönen.[47] The Commission's proposal for a reform of this directive, through a more ambitious and appropriately named Corporate Sustainability Reporting Directive,[48] is a major step forward.[49] Yet it requires a connection with hard-core company law to realise its potential. Only via effective company law reform, including its hard law elements, will there be a basis for realising the full potential of initiatives that embed sustainable value creation at their core.

Nor are due diligence norms a new idea. Since 2011, the UNGPs, *Implementing the United Nations 'Protect, Respect and Remedy' Framework*, have provided that in order for businesses to meet their responsibility to respect human rights, business enterprises should express their commitment to meet this responsibility through a statement of policy that has the following characteristics: that the statement:

(a) Is approved at the most senior level of the business enterprise; (b) Is informed by relevant internal and/or external expertise; (c) Stipulates the enterprise's human rights expectations of personnel, business partners and other parties directly linked to its operations, products or services; (d) Is publicly available and communicated internally and externally to all personnel, business partners and other relevant parties; (e) Is reflected in operational policies and procedures necessary to embed it throughout the business enterprise.[50]

The report by Lise Smit et al. for the Commission on due diligence brings out very clearly the insufficiency of relying on 'soft law' norms such as the UNGPs, and concludes with a clear call for mandatory requirements in hard law.

---

[47] C. Villiers and J. Mähönen, 'Accounting, Auditing and Reporting: Supporting or Obstructing the Sustainable Companies Objective?', in B. Sjåfjell and B. J. Richardson (eds.), Company Law and Sustainability: Legal Barriers and Opportunities, (Cambridge: Cambridge University Press, 2015), 175–225. See also the comprehensive analysis in J. Mähönen, 'Comprehensive Approach to Relevant and Reliable Reporting in Europe: A Dream Impossible?' (2020) 12 *Sustainability*, 5277.

[48] See the proposal for a new Corporate Sustainability Reporting Directive (21 April 2021), available at: www.ec.europa.eu/info/business-economy-euro/company-reporting-and-auditing/company-reporting/corporate-sustainability-reporting_en.

[49] D. Monciardini and J. Mähönen, 'Goodbye, non-financial reporting! A first look at the EU proposal for corporate sustainability reporting' (27 April 2021) *Blogging for Sustainability*, available at: www.jus.uio.no/english/research/areas/companies/blog/companies-markets-and-sustainability/2021/goodbye-non-financial-reporting–monciardini-mahonen.html www.jus.uio.no/english/research/areas/companies/blog/companies-markets-and-sustainability/2021/goodbye-non-financial-reporting–monciardini-mahonen.html.

[50] United Nations, Guiding Principles on Business and Human Rights, pp. 15–17.

It is company law reform that is required to connect the pieces and move forwards.[51] The Commission's initiative brings into the spotlight and raises awareness of the need for a regulatory framework for boards to define and integrate sustainability impacts and opportunities into the corporate strategy – following appropriate procedures to build on existing corporate governance mechanisms, and to ensure that companies take measures to address their adverse sustainability impacts. In that context, we summarise here a research-based reform proposal for securing European companies' sustainable value creation within planetary boundaries through company law reform.[52]

9.3.2 *Company Law Reform to Provide a Level Playing Field for Sustainable Value Creation*

This research-based company law reform proposal suggests that EU law should set out sustainable value creation within planetary boundaries as an overarching purpose for European companies (or more broadly 'undertakings'), in a new chapter of the EU Company Law Directive of 2017.[53] The creation of 'sustainable value' in a company law reform requires definition. We propose that it should be defined as creating value for the undertaking, while respecting the rights of its members, investors, employees and other contractual parties, and promoting good governance, decent work and equality, and the human rights of its workers and affected communities and peoples. Further, a legislative reform integrating the recognition of planetary boundaries cannot be satisfied with regulating the protection of the hitherto identified nine boundaries.[54]

---

[51] That the social norm of shareholder primacy has been allowed to develop as a barrier to sustainable business because of weaknesses in company law is amply demonstrated through multi-jurisdictional analyses of company law: see Sjåfjell et al., 'Shareholder Primacy', and C.M. Bruner and B. Sjåfjell, 'Corporate Law, Corporate Governance and the Pursuit of Sustainability', in Sjåfjell and Bruner (eds), *Cambridge Handbook of Corporate Law*, pp. 713–720. For earlier contributions criticising shareholder primacy, see n.10.

[52] This Section draws on several contributions during and following the SMART Project, including B. Sjåfjell, J. Mähönen, T. Novitz, C. Gammage, and H. Ahlström, 'Securing the Future of European Business: SMART Reform Proposals' (2020) 2020–11 *University of Oslo Faculty of Law Research Paper*, 20–08 *Nordic & European Company Law Working Paper*; B. Sjåfjell, 'Reforming EU Company Law to Secure the Future of European Business' (2021) 18, *European Company and Financial Law Review*, 190–217.

[53] Directive (EU) 2017/1132 of the European Parliament and of the Council of 14 June 2017 relating to certain aspects of company law (Company Law Directive of 2017).

[54] Or the 'limits of our planet', as formulated in the Environment Action Programme to 2020, Decision No 1386/2013/EU of the European Parliament and of the Council of 20 November 2013 on a General Union Environment Action Programme to 2020 'Living well, within the limits of our planet', OJ L 354, (28 December 2013), 171–200. The EU 7th Environmental Action Programme to 2020 (7th EAP) was adopted in 2013, available at: www.eea.europa.eu/policy-documents/7th-environmental-action-programme. The proposed 8th EAP, to guide

Rather, the concept of planetary boundaries itself needs to be included, as a general clause, to be interpreted in light of the science as it develops. Planetary boundaries should there be defined as scientifically recognised processes that regulate the stability and resilience of the Earth system within which humanity can continue to develop and thrive for generations to come.[55]

This overarching purpose of sustainable value creation within planetary boundaries should be operationalised through a redefinition of the duties of the board, outlining this in a way that provides legal certainty for undertakings. To clarify a key concept of European company law, which has become somewhat clouded through the influence of the shareholder primacy drive, it should be set out in EU company legislation that the core duty of the board is to promote the interests of the company. This operationalisation would not entail a harmonisation of the definition of the interests of the company in EU company law. Rather, it would draw up the boundaries within which the board shall promote the interests of the company. Developing an understanding of what the interests of the specific company entail in a specific instance should remain with the board to define, within the scope of national legislation, articles of association and existing contracts and commitments.[56]

The duty of the board to promote the interests of the undertaking in a way that contributes to the overarching corporate purpose should be set out as ensuring that the operations and activities of the business create sustainable value and contribute to global society staying within planetary boundaries. Encompassing respect for human rights, ensuring decent working conditions and promoting good governance should be key aspects of sustainable value creation. Contributing to ensuring that global society stays within planetary boundaries should entail complying with the most ambitious politically adopted targets at EU or relevant Member State level, and – within the scope of the business of the undertaking – protecting and regenerating natural resources and processes, and avoiding, or reducing as far as possible, contributions to the transgression of currently identified planetary boundaries.[57]

European environmental policy to 2030, explicitly mentions the planetary boundaries, available at: www.ec.europa.eu/environment/pdf/8EAP/2020/10/8EAP-draft.pdf. See further Sjåfjell et al., 'A Research-Based Approach to the UN Sustainable Development Goals. A Prerequisite to Sustainable Business', section 2.

55 Sjåfjell et al., 'SMART Reform Proposals', section 6.2.1.
56 Ibid.
57 Biodiversity loss in all ecosystems, including oceans; freshwater pollution and scarcity; land system change, including change in regional vegetation; greenhouse gas emissions; atmospheric aerosol emissions; chemical pollution including synthetic organic pollutants, heavy metal compounds and radioactive materials; and the introduction of novel entities including microplastics and nanomaterials; ozone depletion; nitrogen and phosphorus

A legislative reform should specify that the board is to ensure that the business model of the undertaking is in line with the overarching purpose, developing and publishing a strategy that integrates the purpose throughout the business, including in the internal control and risk management systems.[58] Further, it should define clearly the sustainability assessment – including sustainability due diligence – that the board must ensure is undertaken, to identify ongoing negative sustainability impacts and principal risks of future negative sustainability impacts. The due diligence process should be set out so as to encompass consultative processes for engagement with local communities, including indigenous peoples and other groups and persons affected by the operations and activities of the business, encompassing, as relevant in the specific case, workers, subcontractors, local or national interest groups and community representatives. This would ensure a meaningful engagement with what may be denoted the stakeholders of the business.

Follow-up of the due diligence process should also be stipulated, where identified lack of legal compliance should be rectified immediately. For other identified sustainability impacts and risks, an ambitious continuous improvement process should be drawn up under the leadership of the board. The ambitious continuous improvement plan should include qualitative and quantitative Key Performance Indicators where appropriate. EU rules should also provide for external verification that the due diligence process is undertaken in accordance with the rules, and annual reporting on this should be audited. Together this would provide a good basis for legal certainty for the board that it is following up in this area as it should and also provide a level playing field in the sense that the board would know that other undertakings were subject to the same rules.[59]

Further, such a process would provide legal certainty for the undertaking as concerns its sustainability impacts, mitigating effectively the risks of unsustainability. As Lise Smit and Claire Bright point out, it is important that due diligence does not act as a safe harbour; that is, that affected parties cannot file a lawsuit against the undertaking or its board and that it must not devolve into a box-ticking exercise.[60] However, compliance with a thoughtfully formulated

---

pollution; and ocean acidification. See further Sjåfjell et al., 'SMART Reform Proposals', section 6.2.1.

[58] This resonates with existing requirements in the Non-Financial Reporting Directive as well as with the proposal in the Action Plan for sustainable finance, Action 10.

[59] Sjåfjell et al., 'SMART Reform Proposals', section 6.2.1.

[60] L. Smit and C. Bright, 'The concept of a "safe harbor" and mandatory human rights due diligence' (December 2020) 1 *CEDIS Working Papers*, available at: www.cedis.fd.unl.pt/wp-content/uploads/2020/12/CEDIS_working-paper_the-concept-of-safe-harbour.pdf.

mandatory sustainability due diligence regime would serve as a defence for the undertaking and its board. This will increase the legal certainty for European business, while providing better access to justice for affected workers and communities.

9.4 INTEGRATING SUSTAINABLE VALUE CREATION IN CORPORATE GOVERNANCE CODES

There is no EU harmonisation of corporate governance codes. Harmonisation has been based on a presumption of convergence of the contents of the corporate codes,[61] which has been perceived as progress.[62] Without an assessment of the quality of the content of the codes, and of the influence of codes on business and financial market trends, the EU endorsed the codes through EU-wide codification of the 'comply or explain' mechanism in 2006.[63] Together with the inclusion of corporate governance codes in the listing requirement of stock exchanges, this has given increased legitimacy and weight to the codes. They are therefore a significant soft law instrument.[64]

---

[61] The perception of convergence has been challenged inter alia by Cison et al., concluding that they 'fail to find evidence of an unchecked thematic convergence towards an Anglo-Saxon model of corporate governance, with some code themes converging to UK practices while others diverge', J. E Cison, S. P. Ferris, A. J. Kammel and G. Noronha 'European Corporate Governance: A Thematic Analysis of National Codes of Governance' (2012) 18 *European Financial Management*, 620–648.

[62] The European Commission concluded in COM(2003) 284 final section 3.1 that there was no need for a joint EU corporate governance code, as the codes, as opposed to company law, showed a 'remarkable degree of convergence' with reference to 'Comparative Study of Corporate Governance Codes Relevant to the European Union and its Member States' (European Commission, January 2002), where the 'growing interest in corporate governance codes' is explained as a reflection of the understanding that 'equity investors, whether foreign or domestic, are considering the quality of corporate governance along with financial performance and other factors when deciding whether to invest in a company', p. 2. The relevance of the OECD code was also emphasised.

[63] Directive 2006/46/EC of the European Parliament and of the Council (14 June 2006).

[64] Together with stewardship codes, which increasingly are becoming significant on the investor side, see D. Katelouzou and D. W. Puchniak, 'Global Shareholder Stewardship: Complexities, Challenges, and Possibilities', in D. Katelouzou and D. W. Puchniak (eds), *Global Shareholder Stewardship* (Cambridge: Cambridge University Press, forthcoming), available as working paper at SSRN: https://ssrn.com/abstract=3872579. See generally regarding the potential of shareholder activism to contribute to sustainable value creation. J. Mähönen, 'Shareholder Activism: Driver or Obstacle for Sustainable Value Creation?', Chapter 7 in this volume.

9.4.1 *From Shareholders through Stakeholders to Sustainability?*

Although originally and still to great extent the proponents of shareholder primacy,[65] corporate governance codes in Europe are increasingly including the concept of sustainable value creation. This is combined with, in some cases, an increased inclusion of stakeholders – while in other cases we see a shift from an undefined reference to 'stakeholders' to inclusion of sustainable value creation.

A historical overview of how key codes have evolved over time shows a tentatively more progressive approach towards a support of sustainable corporate governance. Since the 1990s, corporate governance codes have begun to be developed in various countries and have been issued from stock exchanges, corporations, institutional investors or institutes of directors with the support of governments and international organisations.[66] The proposal of the OECD in 1998 was to develop global guidelines on corporate governance and encourage states to introduce such guidelines, which was key to the gradual development of corporate governance codes worldwide.[67] Most codes at that time addressed regulation of the relationship between boards, senior managers and shareholders with the objective of safeguarding shareholders' rights, following the UK example, but a few did recognise the interests of stakeholders, including but not limited to shareholders. King I, the Corporate Governance Code of South Africa, for example, in 1994, was arguably the first and certainly most well-known Code to embrace this approach.[68] The OECD Principles have not remained static, however. Specifically, and in relation to sustainability, updates in 2015 have come to 'embrace the shared understanding that a high level of transparency, accountability, board oversight, and respect for the rights of shareholders and role of key stakeholders is part of the foundation of a well-functioning corporate governance system'.[69]

---

[65] For example, B. Sjåfjell, 'When the Solution Becomes the Problem: The Triple Failure of Corporate Governance Codes', in J. J. du Plessis and C. K. Low (eds.), *Corporate Governance Codes for the 21st Century*, (Cham: Springer International Publishing, 2017), pp. 23–55.

[66] B. Tricker, *Corporate Governance: Principles, Policies and Practices*, 2nd ed. (Oxford: Oxford University Press, 2012), p. 14.

[67] Ibid.

[68] King I Report, South Africa, Code (1994), available at: https://ecgi.global/code/king-i-report.

[69] OECD, *G20/OECD Principles of Corporate Governance*, (Paris: OECD Publishing, 2015), available at: http://dx.doi.org/10.1787/9789264236882-en. For a critical analysis leading up to the 2015 version, see P. Morrow and A. Johnston, 'Commentary on the OECD Principles of Corporate Governance' (14 January 2015), 2015–09, *University of Oslo Faculty of Law Research Paper*, 15–12 *Nordic & European Company Law Working Paper*, available at SSRN: https://ssrn.com/abstract=2549570.

Existing literature has studied the relationship between corporate social responsibility (CSR) and corporate governance codes of EU Member States. One study, dated 2005, provides an empirical analysis of twenty-two European corporate governance codes showing that the predominant majority of them are orientated towards stakeholders and the company.[70] The study stresses, among other things, the importance of corporate ethical standards, of dialogue with interested parties and of social and environmental responsibility.[71] Another study, dated 2013, provides comparative work on the topic and compares the sections that could be identified as stakeholder friendly in EU Member States' corporate governance codes, focusing on those that are seen to integrate CSR into corporate governance. This study concludes that, while recognising that there are positive exceptions, corporate governance codes are on the whole informed by and support the shareholder primacy drive; the corporate governance codes referred to still facilitate and support a system that is based on the externalisation of environmental and social costs of business.[72]

From a legal perspective the topic has in recent years been addressed by the present authors in their separate works. In 2017, Sjåfjell identified the failure of corporate governance codes to promote sustainability objectives in business, concluding that attempts at introducing CSR language into codes has been generally superficial, and not designed to achieve the internalisation of externalities that is urgently required if business and finance are to work towards becoming more sustainable, in the economic, environmental and social sense.[73] Tsagas took the discussion a step further in 2020, by advocating reform of the corporate governance codes of EU Member States in a uniform manner by including a section on the 'Relations with Stakeholders as Part of the Board's Responsibility' in them.[74] In the present joint work we build further on the idea of reform of corporate governance codes to promote sustainable value creation.

---

[70] J. Wieland, 'Corporate Governance, Values Management, and Standards: A European Perspective' (2005) 44 (1) *Business & Society*, 74–93.

[71] Ibid.

[72] D. G. Szabo and K. Engsig Sørensen, 'Integrating Corporate Social Responsibility in Corporate Governance Codes in the EU' (2013) 24 (6) *European Business Law Review*, 781–828.

[73] B. Sjåfjell, 'When the Solution Becomes the Problem: The Triple Failure of Corporate Governance Codes', in du Plessis and Low (eds.), *Corporate Governance Codes for the 21st Century*, pp. 23–55.

[74] G. Tsagas, 'A Proposal for Reform of EU Member States' Corporate Governance Codes in Support of Sustainability' (25 May 2020), 12, 10 *Sustainability* 2020, 4328, part of the Special Issue 'Corporate Sustainability Reforms: Securing Market Actors' Contribution to Global Sustainability'.

9.4.2 *The Emerging Inclusion of Sustainable Value Creation in Codes*

Following up on the proposal to reform company law in Section 9.3, and recognising the risks entailed by shifting focus from shareholders to a general reference to 'stakeholders', we suggest that the focus should be on 'sustainable value creation' rather than on stakeholders as such. The inclusion of interested and affected parties of the business of the company (which may be denoted 'stakeholders') should on a harmonised level primarily be ensured through open and participatory processes in sustainability due diligence, as a key tool for the board's integration of sustainable value creation in the strategies of the company.

Such recommendations can find support in some of the more progressive corporate governance codes of EU Member States. This resonates for example with the Austrian Corporate Governance Code of 2021, which has as its objective ensuring a system that promotes 'sustainable, long-term value', which is acknowledged as the best objective to serve the need of 'all parties whose well-being depend on the success of the enterprise'.[75] Indeed, recently revised codes provide a number of examples of inclusion of sustainable value creation. The French Corporate Governance Code states that the board is at all times to act in the 'corporate interest', and endeavours to promote 'long-term value creation by considering the social and environmental aspects of its activities'.[76] The board should also be informed about important aspects of the company, including social and environmental responsibility, and should regularly review social and environmental risks.[77]

Similarly, Germany and Belgium have adopted initiatives that encourage sustainable corporate governance. The 2020 Belgian Code on Corporate Governance,[78] for example, emphasises that the board should pursue 'sustainable value creation' through strategy, effective, responsible and ethical leadership and monitoring performance.[79] The Code's emphasis on sustainable value creation has implications for remuneration policy and provides higher standards in terms of diversity and non-financial reporting with the intention of it being less formalistic than its predecessor and to allow companies to

---

[75] Austrian Code of Corporate Governance (2021), Preamble, available at: https://ecgi.global/sites/default/files/codes/documents/austria_corporate-governance-code-012021.pdf.

[76] French Corporate Governance Code of Listed Corporations (2020), available at: https://ecgi.global/sites/default/files/codes/documents/200210_afep_medef_code_revision_2020_en_0.pdf, principle 1.1.

[77] French Corporate Governance Code of Listed Corporations, principle 1.4 and 1.5.

[78] Belgian Code on Corporate Governance (2020), available at: www.corporategovernance-committee.be/sites/default/files/generated/files/page/2020_belgian_code_on_corporate_governance.pdf.

[79] Ibid., section 2.1.

better address their specific circumstances.[80] The foreword further states that the revision was an opportunity to place more emphasis on 'sustainable value creation', involving an 'explicit focus on the long term, on responsible behaviour at all levels of the company and on the permanent consideration of the legitimate interests of stakeholders'.[81] We see here that the 'legitimate interests of stakeholders', which was also a goal of the revised Code to highlight,[82] is regarded as an element of sustainable value creation rather than a goal in its own right.

Similarly, the German Corporate Governance Code emphasises the obligations for the Management Board and Supervisory Board to take into account interests of shareholders, workforce and stakeholders 'to ensure the continued existence of the enterprise and its *sustainable value creation* (the enterprise's best interests)'.[83] Potential impacts from both social and environmental impacts have to be identified and addressed by the boards in corporate strategy and operating decisions.[84] In 2011, Germany adopted the Sustainability Code, which is an internationally applicable reporting standard for topics relating to sustainability following a comprehensive preliminary review process together with stakeholders.[85]

Along the same lines, the Danish Corporate Governance Code, in its revised version of 2020, emphasises that it is essential for a company's 'value creation' to consider sustainability in a broad sense (economic, environmental, employee and social society sustainability), with 'stakeholders' as recognised elements of the value creation.[86] Notably, the Danish Code also engages with the issue of the purpose of the company, setting out that it should be 'the company's overall aim for long-term value creation, which the company delivers to its shareholders, other stakeholders and society'.[87]

Other interesting examples of progressive corporate governance codes include the Dutch Code. This sets out for the two-tier system of Dutch company law

[80] Stibbe, 'New Belgian Corporate Governance Code 2020 for listed companies presented today' available at: www.stibbe.com/en/news/2019/may/new-belgian-corporate-governance-code-2020-for-listed-companies-presented-today.

[81] Belgian Code of Corporate Governance (2020) foreword, 3.

[82] Ibid., section 2.2.

[83] German Corporate Governance Code 2019, foreword (emphasis added), available at: https://ecgi.global/sites/default/files/codes/documents/191216_german_corporate_governance_code.pdf.

[84] Ibid.

[85] The German Council for Sustainable Development, The Sustainability Code (2011) available at: www.nachhaltigkeitsrat.de/en/projects/the-sustainability-code/?cn-reloaded=1.

[86] Danish Recommendations on Corporate Governance (2020), Introduction, available at: https://corporategovernance.dk/sites/default/files/media/anbefalinger_for_god_selskabsledelse_engelsk.pdf.

[87] Ibid.

that the Management Board is to focus on 'long-term value creation' for the company and the Supervisory Board is to monitor this. The Code's explanatory notes further explain that board members are expected to act in a sustainable manner and acknowledges that long-term sustainability is the key consideration when determining strategy and making decisions. It is stated that a sufficient level of awareness of the wider context in which the company operates contributes to continuing success and that this is therefore in line with the company's interests. The Management Board has to develop a view on long-term value creation and formulate a strategy in line with this, and when doing so attention must be paid to any aspect that is relevant to the company such as 'the environment, social and employee-related matters, the chain within which the enterprise operates, respect for human rights, and fighting corruption and bribery'.[88] The new elements that were added after it was subject to a revision in 2016 showcase a greater emphasis on long-term value creation and risk management, and culture is introduced as a new element.[89]

On the other hand, there are a number of European corporate governance codes, also recently revised, that do not mention sustainable value creation, value creation or sustainability, and remain very shareholder focused. The Finnish Corporate Governance Code in its 2020 revision is one example.[90]

The UK is an interesting example here, in spite of its departure from the EU, with its long history of corporate governance codes.[91] Its current version of the UK Corporate Governance Code (2018) uses the word 'sustainable' several times in the context of defining a 'successful company', where the board's role is to promote 'long-term sustainable success of the company'.[92] The UK Code now directly engages with corporate purpose, stating that the board should 'establish the company's purpose, values and strategy, and satisfy itself that these and its culture are aligned',[93] which could have been a powerful incentive for integrating sustainability if its purpose were defined, for example, as 'sustainable value creation'.[94] Rather, and in spite of moving towards an

---

[88] The Dutch Corporate Governance Code (2016), Principle 1.1, available at: www.mccg.nl/download/?id=3367.

[89] Ibid., Principle 1.1.1.

[90] Finnish Corporate Governance Code (2020), available at: https://ecgi.global/sites/default/files/codes/documents/corporate-governance-code-2020.pdf.

[91] Starting with the Cadbury Report and the UK's first Corporate Governance Code in 1992, see an overview of the history at: www.frc.org.uk/directors/corporate-governance-and-stewardship/uk-corporate-governance-code/history-of-the-uk-corporate-governance-code.

[92] UK Corporate Governance Code 2018, Principle A, available at: https://ecgi.global/sites/default/files/codes/documents/2018-uk-corporate-governance-code-final.pdf.

[93] Ibid., Principle B.

[94] Noting also that remuneration is connected to purpose, ibid., Principle P.

inclusion of some reference to 'stakeholders',[95] and a reference to successful companies contributing also to 'wider society', the emphasis is firmly on the shareholders, for whom the successful company is to generate value.[96]

A number of the other codes that have moved in the direction of including sustainable value creation still connect this directly to being for shareholders, even in contradiction to the pluralistic approach of the company laws of several European jurisdictions. An example here is the Norwegian corporate governance code, which has promoted and reinforced shareholder primacy. In its most recent reform of 2021, it has shifted away from a general reference to stakeholders as part of the wave of inclusion of broader interests in codes, and more specifically sets out sustainable value creation as a core element.[97] Yet its recommendations remain firmly shareholder-focused.[98]

Sustainability aspects are increasingly included in the risk management sections of codes. This is a crucial step, as a full realisation and integration of the risks of unsustainability into governance is a potential game changer. As Kaen suggested in his research in 2016, risk management needs to go beyond the narrow understanding provided by finance scholars pointing to the need to support broad public policy objectives. These are objectives beyond the immediate interests of the shareholders of the company and beyond a narrow financial objective of shareholder wealth maximisation.[99] Yet, while corporate and financial risks of unsustainability are an important driver for the increasing business and investor interest in shifting towards more sustainable business, it is crucial to recognise the limits of the business case for sustainability, especially in the narrow way that it is still perceived by business and finance.[100] A business case approach cannot be allowed to set the boundaries for the fundamental

[95] Ibid., for example Principle D, which states that the board should ensure 'effective engagement with, and encourage participation from' not only shareholders, but also stakeholders.
[96] Ibid., Principle A.
[97] The Norwegian Code of Practice for Corporate Governance (2021), available at: https://nues.no/eierstyring-og-selskapsledelse-engelsk/.
[98] Which the company should create sustainable value for, ibid, Section 2.
[99] F. R. Kaen, 'Risk Management, Corporate Governance and the Public Corporation', in M. Frenkel, M. Rudolf and U. Hommel (eds.), *Risk Management* (Berlin/Heidelberg: Springer, 2005), pp. 423–436.
[100] G. de los Reyes and M. Scholz, 'The Limits of the Business Case for Sustainability: Don't Count on "Creating Shared Value" to Extinguish Corporate Destruction' (2019) 221 *Journal of Cleaner Production*, 785–794; M. Bowman, 'The Limitations of Business Case Logic for Societal Benefit & Implications for Corporate Law: A Case Study of 'Climate Friendly' Banks' (2014), available at SSRN: https://ssrn.com/abstract=2489116. B. Sjåfjell, 'The Financial Risks of Unsustainability: A Research Agenda' (29 June 2020). 2020–18 *University of Oslo Faculty of Law Research Paper*, 21–05 *Nordic & European Company Law Working Paper*, available at SSRN: https://ssrn.com/abstract=3637969.

transformation that needs to take place. This is why redefining corporate purpose as an overarching aim for the company is a crucial part of our reform proposal (as presented in Section 9.3.2), and for our further discussions.

9.4.3 *Integrating Sustainability through Further Revision of Corporate Governance Codes*

In alignment with the recommendations relating to company law reform as referred to in Section 9.3.2 and drawing on what we may refer to as third generation corporate governance codes with their increasing inclusion of sustainable value creation, corporate culture and comprehensive risk management,[101] we suggest that further revisions of corporate governance codes should be undertaken. In this work, more systematic inclusion of sustainability, drawing on sustainability research, should be included. Thereunder, they should expressly set out sustainable value creation within planetary boundaries as the recommended overarching purpose for all companies, with 'sustainable value' and 'planetary boundaries' defined as suggested in the law reform proposal.[102]

Revised Codes should further set out that the duty of the board is to ensure the interests of the company in such a way as to position this concept within the overarching purpose and outline that this is to be integrated in the company's life-cycle-based business model, including strategies and risk management. Clearly spelling out the duties of the board would both internally, in the company, and externally, in its relationship with its current and future investors, mitigate pressures towards maximisation of returns to shareholders while at the same time clarifying the basis for evaluating the board's work. The provisions on board duties could, for example, be formulated like this:

> The board shall promote the interests of the company. This should be done in such a way as to achieve sustainable value creation, ensuring that the business model is in line with the company's overarching purpose and developing and publishing a strategy that enables the achievement of the overarching purpose. The board should work to ensure that the operations and activities of the company, including the full life of its products, processes and services, contribute to global society by staying within planetary boundaries.
>
> The board's integration of the overarching purpose should be based on a sustainability assessment of the business of the company – including sustainability due diligence – to identify ongoing negative sustainability impacts and principal risks of future negative sustainability impacts.

---

[101] Sjåfjell et al., 'SMART Reform Proposals', Section 6.3.1.
[102] See the beginning of Section 9.3.2.

We distinguish here between 'shall', which reflects legal requirements, and 'should', which may be seen as wholly or partly going beyond the requirements of the law regulating the company. This entails, for example for sustainability due diligence, that, in line with increasing legislation in this area, elements of a full sustainability due diligence may be mandated while the Code can recommend a full inclusion of all sustainability aspects, in line with a research-based definition of sustainable value creation and planetary boundaries.

Corporate governance codes that keep the reference to stakeholders should clearly define the term 'stakeholder', which should include employees, clients, creditors, the communities which they operate in or affect, suppliers, the environment and vulnerable groups of people. This should be connected with sustainability due diligence as a key tool for integrating sustainability into governance, including risk management. It should be spelled out in the Codes, unless this is already done in relevant legislative requirements, that the due diligence process should encompass consultative processes for engagement with local communities, including indigenous peoples and other groups and persons affected by the operations and activities of the business, encompassing as relevant in the specific case workers, subcontractors, local or national interest groups and community representatives.

Through such reforms, corporate governance codes can pave the way for integrating sustainability fully into corporate governance – whether by supporting sustainability legislation or by showing the way forward for legislators, as the Codes have been seen to do in other corporate governance contexts.

9.5 THE COMPANY CONSTITUTION AND ITS POTENTIAL TO CREATE SUSTAINABLE VALUE

The individual company will need to integrate sustainability into its governance, whether that is a result of effective legislative reform in Europe or of compliance with corporate governance codes that are revised to promote sustainability, or in the absence of either and rather in recognition of the business and financial risks of continued unsustainability.[103] To integrate sustainability into governance, it is regarded as crucial to set the tone from the top.

As Bishop correctly identifies (in a related context of achieving equality), the company constitution, also referred to as 'articles of association',[104] is a

---

[103] P. W. Keys, V. Galaz, M. Dyer, N. Matthews, C. Folke, M. Nyström, and S. E. Cornell, 'Anthropocene Risk' (2019) 2 *Nature Sustainability*, 667–673; Sjåfjell, 'The Financial Risks of Unsustainability'.

[104] A company's constitution normally constitutes a legal requirement to be set in place on and for a company's incorporation. The corporate constitution, as is the term commonly accepted

key document in terms of integrating a sustainability-oriented purpose in the governance of the company: 'The corporate world is recognising the need to use the articles of association to embed policy: they are the only legally binding company document that defines the company's decision-making process and purpose. Conversely, policy documents are not legally binding on the company, its members or its stakeholders'.[105]

Ideally, therefore, an overarching goal of sustainable value creation within planetary boundaries should be set out in the company's constitution. In this section, we discuss how the constitution can be used by the individual company and by national or regional policy-makers as a basis for integrating sustainability.

9.5.1 *Setting the Tone from the Top: Sustainable Value Creation as Overarching Objective*

The most authoritative way of setting the tone from the top in a specific company would be for the general meeting of shareholders to adopt a change of the constitution. The majority required according to the relevant company law will normally be a qualified majority of two-thirds of the shareholders,[106] which means that changing or removing the inclusion of 'sustainable value creation' in the constitution will require the same kind of qualified majority. It would accordingly bind future general meetings (unless and until the constitution is changed) as well as the board and senior management of the company. It would be a powerful signal to the outside world including potential investors. As noted elsewhere in work co-authored by Sjåfjell and Maria Jesus Munoz-Torres, it could serve to 'mitigate the compartmentalisation between different levels of law, various regulatory fields and between hard law and evolving duties drawn from competing social norms to the shareholder primacy model'.[107]

---

in EU Member States, is referred to as the articles of association in the UK and the charter with the company's bylaws in the USA.

[105] R. C. Bishop 'Company law: How to embed equality of opportunity into your company's articles of association' (17 March 2021) *Bloomsbury Professional Law*, available at: https://law .bloomsburyprofessional.com/blog/company-law-how-to-embed-equality-of-opportunity-into-your-companys-articles-of-association.

[106] For example, formulated as two-thirds of the votes cast and the votes present, see www .dsw-info.de/fileadmin/Redaktion/Dokumente/PDF/Publikationen/Shareholders_ Meeting_Europe-web.pdf.

[107] B. Sjåfjell and M. J. Munoz-Torres, 'The Horse before the Cart: A Sustainable Governance Model for Meaningful Sustainability Reporting' (26 April 2019), 2019–04 *University of Oslo Faculty of Law Research Paper*, 19–09 *Nordic & European Company Law Working Paper*, 6, available at SSRN: https://ssrn.com/abstract=3378473.

This can be done by introducing a purpose provision in the constitution, for example formulated like this: 'The overarching purpose of the company is to create sustainable value by [concrete area of business] within planetary boundaries.' The board's duties could further be set out in the constitution, to establish how this is to be followed up and signalling to existing and future investors, employees and society more broadly, that the overarching purpose is integrated into the decision-making of the company. As with the proposed company law reform and the suggestion for revision of corporate governance codes discussed earlier, such a clear setting out of the duties of the board would mitigate pressures towards maximisation of returns to shareholders while clarifying the basis for evaluating the board's work.

As the planetary boundaries framework is not easily operationalised on an individual company's level, the 'within planetary boundaries' should be qualified by a link to global society. To connect with the best practice guidelines, which now increasingly are becoming mandatory legislative requirements, sustainability assessment through sustainability due diligence should also be explicitly included. The due diligence process should in the constitution itself be explicitly linked to best practice standards or legislative requirements. As in Sections 9.3.2 and 9.4.3, the process should thereby encompass consultative processes for engagement with local communities, including indigenous peoples and other groups and persons affected by the operations and activities of the business, encompassing as relevant in the specific case, workers, subcontractors, local or national interest groups and community representatives, as a way of meaningful engagement with the stakeholders of the business.

This could, depending on the governance structure of the relevant company and along the lines as suggested for Corporate Governance Code, be formulated like this:

> The board shall promote the interests of the company through sustainable value creation, ensuring that the business model is in line with the company's overarching purpose and developing and publishing a strategy that enables the achievement of the overarching purpose. The board shall work to ensure that the operations and activities of the company, including the full life of its products, processes and services, contribute to global society by staying within planetary boundaries.
>
> The board's integration of the overarching purpose shall be based on a sustainability assessment of the business of the company – including sustainability due diligence – to identify ongoing negative sustainability impacts and principal risks of future negative sustainability impacts.

The benefit of doing this directly in the constitution of the company, rather than in the corporate governance codes, is that the constitution could explicitly set out board duties for the specific company, without the need for regard to the distinction of what follows from mandatory legislation and what is recommended best practice.

The further detailing of what is entailed by sustainable value creation and planetary boundaries could be done through reference to external sources or within the constitution itself.[108]

In some cases it may not be perceived as feasible to secure the commitment of the general meeting. The constitution may have a more vaguely formulated provision that provides similar support to the board and the senior management, or the controlling shareholder may have set out elsewhere that such a purpose is what motivates their investment. Raising the issue on the general meeting may then, in some cases, be seen as a precarious rocking of the boat. The second best way of setting the tone from the top, would then be the commitment of the board and senior management to a similarly formulated purpose and implementation.

9.5.2 *A Model Constitution for Sustainable Value Creation*

In the UK,[109] Model Articles of Association are set in place with the objective of constituting a set of default rules that assist companies in defining the company's purpose and laying out how basic processes relating to governance are to be realised within the organisation. It is customary for founding shareholders in UK companies to tailor the Model Articles of Association to fit their requirements. Equally, it is common for companies to adopt the template Model Articles of Association as provided by state regulation without tailored modification. Representative types of clauses that may be found in a company's constitution may relate to the powers and duties of board members, the number of members admitted to the board at any given time, the number of meetings to be held within each calendar year, the process for resigning or appointing directors, the authorised share capital, the division of the share capital into shares, the classes of shares that the company possesses, share rights in respect of dividends, pre-emptive rights, if any, and share voting rights, to name a few.

On the premise that 'default rules' matter,[110] a way forward could be that each EU Member State includes a template or default rules promoting

---

[108] See Section 9.3.2 for suggested definitions.
[109] And in a few jurisdictions building on UK law, such as Hong Kong.
[110] B. McDonnell, 'Sticky Defaults and Altering Rules in Corporate Law' (2007) 60 *SMU Law Review*, 383, available at https://scholarship.law.umn.edu/faculty_articles/166.

sustainable corporate governance in companies' constitutions. The EU Company Law Directive of 2017, which sets out the compulsory information that is to be provided in the statutes or instruments of incorporation of public limited liability companies or other related documents, includes minimum requirements to be included in the constitution.[111] These provisions neither mandate nor prevent the inclusion of a sustainability-oriented purpose in the constitution of the company, nor do they restrict the possibility of including election processes to ensure sustainability-knowledgeable board members or various forms of stakeholder engage in the governance of the company.

While such default rules by their nature would not be mandatory for companies to include in their constitution, companies that decide to opt out of including sustainability – that is, rejecting the default formulations in the relevant jurisdiction – would make themselves vulnerable to criticism. Over time, as sustainability objectives continue to be advocated in the EU at several levels and in various areas of regulation, companies not aligning with these objectives may – or hopefully will – be perceived as outsiders in markets increasingly attempting to gear themselves towards contributing to achieving sustainability. The boards' company law duty to act in accordance with the constitution of the company would then function as potential enforcement of the company's specific commitments to sustainable value creation in their constitutions.

9.6 CONCLUSION

Legislative reform of company law is needed to integrate sustainability into the corporate governance of European globalised business. Voluntary action and the emerging integration of aspects of sustainability into corporate governance codes is insufficient. Yet corporate governance codes that support sustainable value creation and integration of sustainability into risk management can play a role in strengthening the legislative reform and developing best practices. Accordingly, while we wait for hard law legislation on these issues, and for further reinforcement of future sustainability legislation, revision of corporate governance codes and, for the individual company, inclusion of sustainability in their constitution represent possibilities for change.

The reform proposals in this chapter draw on commonly agreed upon sustainability goals and sustainability research. In hard law, they would increase legal certainty for business, clarifying what the boundaries of legitimate business activities are and what societal expectations of business are. Followed

---

[111] Company Law Directive of 2017, Article 3.

up by clearly defined rules for sustainability assessment, notably including mandatory sustainability due diligence, risk management would be improved, as would legal certainty in the sense of better knowing the extent of the vulnerabilities of the business. This would give the sustainability-oriented businesses in Europe, of which there undoubtedly are many, a competitive advantage over unsustainable business.

We see an increasing role for transdisciplinary collaboration between academia, business, civil society and policy makers, to work together to contribute to the transformation to sustainability. We hope that this chapter can inspire similar discussions also in other parts of the world. The less sustainability-oriented and well enforced hard law we have – or the longer it takes to get into place – the stronger is the need for new and innovative ways of integrating sustainability into corporate governance.

The Contribution of Social Enterprises to Value Creation in Europe

The Case of Dopper BV in the Netherlands

*Tineke Lambooy, Henk Kievit, Aikaterini Argyrou,
Robert Jan Blomme and Olivera Vuletic*

'The bottle is the message' (slogan of Dopper BV)

10.1 INTRODUCTION

10.1.1 *Current Challenges in Europe*

Europe is exposed to multiple crises – financial, political and social – as well as severe environmental problems. The latter includes the contamination of major water resources (oceans, lakes, rivers) from litter and plastic,[1] and the lack of access to clean drinking water for many people.[2] This is worse in rural areas than in urban areas.[3] The European Commission (Commission) notes that marine litter, annually, results in aggregate costs of up to €630 million for the European Union (EU) spent in coastal and beach cleaning.[4]

---

[1] See the EU funded project 'Tracking Of Plastic in Our Seas (TOPIOS)', available at: http://topios.org/. According to TOPIOS the estimated amount of plastic in the Atlantic Ocean is 5 million tonnes, of which 99 per cent is currently untraceable.

[2] In 2015, of the 912 million people living in Europe, 14 million do not use a basic drinking water source, World Health Organization, Regional Office for Europe, 'Water and sanitation are still a luxury for millions of Europeans', available at: www.euro.who.int/en/health-topics/environment-and-health/water-and-sanitation/water-and-sanitation.

[3] Ibid.

[4] European Commission, 'Our Oceans, Seas and Coasts' http://ec.europa.eu/environment/marine/good-environmental-status/descriptor-10/index_en.htm. The EU supports various research initiatives, developed by various organisations and institutions to promote technology that minimises the use and the waste and maximises the recycling of litter and plastic. E.g. the EU funded project PlastiCircle http://plasticircle.eu/, which develops processes to increase the rates of recycling of plastic in the value chain. See also SuperCleanQ, available at: https://

The ecological crisis in Europe shows that the public sector – the EU and national governments – struggle to adequately address such issues.[5]

The Commission, in its European Strategy for Plastics in a Circular Economy of 2018, notes that: 'Europe, citizens, government and industry [must] support more sustainable and safer consumption and production patterns for plastics. This provides a fertile ground for *social innovation and entrepreneurship*, creating a wealth of opportunities for all Europeans.'[6] In the European Green Deal of 2019, the Commission stressed the urgency to transform the EU's economy 'for a sustainable future', by, among other steps, increasing the value given to protecting and restoring natural ecosystems, promoting the sustainable use of resources and encouraging businesses to offer, and to allow consumers to choose, reusable, durable and repairable products.[7]

10.1.2 *The Role of Social Entrepreneurship in Responding to Societal Challenges*

This approach resonates with the Commission's Communication of 2011, entitled the 'Social Business Initiative', which defines a social enterprise as:

An operator in the social economy whose main objective is to have a social impact rather than make a profit for [its] owners or shareholders. It operates by providing goods and services for the market *in an entrepreneurial and*

---

cordis.europa.eu/project/id/285889, an EU funded project with the objective to develop quality assessment tools for the valorisation of recycled plastics.

[5] The Netherlands, for instance, aspires to reduce the plastic waste from the oceans and to enhance the recycling of plastic at national level, while promoting the efficient design, use and re-use of plastic materials in the value chain. Several agreements, for example the Raamovereenkomst Verpakkingen II 2013–2022 [Dutch Agreement on Packaging] and/or the Value chain Agreement on Plastic Cycles, have been executed between the Dutch government and the packaging and plastic industry. See the report of the Dutch Government, 'A Circular Economy in the Netherlands by 2050 Government-wide Programme for a Circular Economy' (14 September 2016) 49–51, available at: www.government.nl/documents/policy-notes/2016/09/14/a-circular-economy-in-the-netherlands-by-2050.

[6] European Commission, 'Communication from the Commission to the European Parliament, the Council, the European Economic and Social Committee and the Committee of the Regions, A European Strategy for Plastics in a Circular Economy', COM/2018/028 final 16.1.2018.

[7] European Commission, 'A European Strategy for Plastics in a Circular Economy'(emphasis added), 5. See also European Commission Statement, 'Circular Economy: Commission welcomes European Parliament adoption of new rules on single–use plastics to reduce marine litter' Brussels, 27 March 2019, available at: http://europa.eu/rapid/press-release_STATEMENT-19-1873_en.htm. European Commission, 'The European Green Deal', COM (2019) 640 final, p. 2, available at: https://eur-lex.europa.eu/legal-content/EN/TXT/?qid=15964 43911913&uri=CELEX:52019DC0640#document2.

innovative fashion and uses its profits primarily to achieve social objectives. It is managed in an open and responsible manner and, in particular, involves employees, consumers and stakeholders affected by its commercial activities.[8]

In the Commission's Communication,[9] social enterprises are recognised as entities that can play a role in adding value to the EU's objectives for a 'highly competitive social market',[10] which is 'not only to establish an internal market but is also to work for the sustainable development of Europe, [...] aiming at full employment and social progress, and [...] solidarity between generations'.[11] Particularly, social enterprises can contribute to the social progress and the environmental protection by enhancing, for example, access to clean water for citizens and supporting the fight against the contamination of major water resources from litter and plastic.[12] Such a contribution also strengthens solidarity between generations as it provides future generations with reliable drinking water sources and oceans, lakes and rivers that are free from plastic and other litter.[13]

10.1.3 *Stakeholders' Involvement by Social Entrepreneurs*

The Commission's definition of a social enterprise also highlights the important characteristic of stakeholders' involvement. In pursuit of their societal aspirations, social enterprises employ inclusive and participatory governance models, which involve stakeholders and the affected society.[14] In the Commission's

---

[8] European Commission Communication from the Commission to the European Parliament, the Council, the European Economic and Social Committee and the Committee of the Regions, 'Social Business Initiative', Brussels 25 October 2011 COM (2011) 682 final, at 2 and 3, available at: https://ec.europa.eu/growth/sectors/social-economy/enterprises_en.

[9] Communication, 'Social Business Initiative', 2.

[10] Art. 3(3) of the Treaty of the European Union (TEU) states: 'The Union shall establish an internal market. It shall work for the sustainable development of Europe based on balanced economic growth and price stability, *a highly competitive social market economy*, aiming at full employment and social progress, and a high level of protection and improvement of the quality of the environment. It shall promote ... solidarity among Member States' (emphasis added). Although there is scholarship that explains policy-related barriers to such an achievement in F. W. Scharpf, 'The Asymmetry of European Integration, or Why the EU Cannot Be a "Social Market Economy"' (2010) 8 *Socio-Economic Review*, 211–250. See also the development of the 'social market economy concept' in R. H. Hasse, H. Schneider and K. Weigelt (eds.), *Social Market Economy History, Principles and Implementation: From A to Z* (Johannesburg: Konrad-Adenauer-Stiftung, 2008), pp. 393–416.

[11] Ibid. See also: Judgment of 21 December 2016, *AGET Iraklis*, C-201/15, EU:C:2016:972, paragraph 76 and Judgment of 11 December 2007, *International Transport Workers' Federation and Finnish Seamen's Union*, C-438/05, EU:C:2007:772, para. 78.

[12] Social economy in the EU; see http://ec.europa.eu/growth/sectors/social-economy_en.

[13] Communication, 'Social Business Initiative', 3.

[14] A. Argyrou, T. Lambooy, R.J. Blomme and H. Kievit, 'Unravelling the Participation of Stakeholders in the Governance Models of Social Enterprises in Greece' (2017) 17(4)

definition, the feature of participatory governance that characterises a social enterprise is key. Participatory and inclusive governance is a type of corporate governance that allows internal and external stakeholders to influence and participate in the decision-making process.[15] It is a way to ensure that the societal objectives of a social enterprise are safeguarded.[16]

Giving stakeholders a role and a voice in governance might entail participation in a social enterprise's 'multi-stakeholder ownership' scheme,[17] but does not per se need to be based on capital ownership.[18] Stakeholder influence on the business decisions of a social enterprise can be provided for in a mandatory way in the law, where a tailor-made legal form for social enterprises exists in a jurisdiction. However, it can also be organised on a voluntary basis, as this chapter will demonstrate, while we discuss also the importance and the relevance of a supportive legal and institutional environment for social enterprises. The discussion in this chapter contributes to the theoretical elaborations in scholarship concerning the development of effective and appropriate participatory governance structures for social enterprises, which allow for the participation of multiple types of stakeholders (i.e. those who are involved in either environmental or social goals or in both types of goals at the same time).[19]

Corporate Governance: The International Journal of Business in Society, 661–677 at 661–662. A. Argyrou, *Social Enterprises in the EU: Law Promoting Stakeholder Participation in Social Enterprises* (Deventer: Wolters Kluwer, 2018) pp. 1–314.

[15]   T. E. Lambooy and A. Argyrou, 'Improving the Legal Environment for Social Entrepreneurship in Europe' (2014) 11(2) *European Company Law*, 71–76.

[16]   L. Timmerman, M. De Jongh and A. Schild, 'The Rise of the Social Enterprise: How Social Enterprises Are Changing Company Law Worldwide', in S. Muller et al. (eds.), *Law of the Future and the Future of Law* (Oslo: Torkel Opsahl Academic ePublisher, 2011), pp. 305–319 at 313; F. Cafaggi and P. Iamiceli, 'New Frontiers in the Legal Structure and Legislation of Social Enterprises in Europe: A Comparative Analysis', in: A. Noya (ed.), *The Changing Boundaries of Social Enterprises* (Paris: OECD Publishing, 2009), pp. 25–86 at 28.

[17]   J. Defourny and M. Nyssens, 'Conceptions of Social Enterprises and Social Entrepreneurship in Europe and the United States: Convergences and Divergences' (2010) 1(1) *Journal of Social Entrepreneurship* 32–53 at 37; G. Galera and C. Borzaga, 'Social Enterprise: An International Overview of Its Conceptual Evolution and Legal Implementation' (2009) 5(3) *Social Entrepreneurship Journal*, 210–228 at 217.

[18]   C. Travaglini, F. Bandini and K. Mancinone, 'An Analysis of Social Enterprises Governance Models Through a Comparative Study of the Legislation of Eleven Countries' (2009) *Alma Mater Studiorum AMS ACTA*, 1–23; J. Defourny and M. Nyssens, 'Defining Social Enterprise', in M. Nyssens (ed.), *Social Enterprise: At the Crossroads of Market, Public Policies and Civil Society* (London: Routledge, 2006), pp. 3–26 at 5–6.

[19]   For example, B. Doherty, H. Haugh and F. Lyon, 'Social Enterprises as Hybrid Organizations: A Review and Research Agenda' (2014) 16(4) *International Journal of Management Reviews*, 417–436; J. Larner and C. Mason, 'Beyond Box-Ticking: A Study of Stakeholder Involvement in Social Enterprise Governance' (2014) 14 *Corporate Governance*, 181–196; C. Mason and B. Doherty, 'A Fair Trade-Off? Paradoxes in the Governance of Fair-Trade Social Enterprises' (2016) 136 *Journal of Business Ethics*, 451–469.

10.1.3.1 Research Subject of this Chapter

The Commission's approach, stipulating that social enterprises can contribute to resolving contemporary societal crises, has gained resonance in academia and with other policy makers. The idea of developing favourable and enabling legal environments is increasingly gaining support.[20] We show in this chapter that social enterprises, at the intersection of the private and public sector, can contribute to economic development and simultaneously to resolving societal problems and thereby contributing to mitigating broader societal (social and environmental) crises.

Since around 2010, a growing number of social enterprises in the Netherlands have aimed to address societal challenges, and they are met with public enthusiasm. Job applicants compete to work for them, consumers and companies buy their products and government agencies and representatives give them a podium at political and other public gatherings.[21] Paradoxically, social enterprises have emerged in the Netherlands without tailor-made legislation for social enterprises.

To gain insight into the mechanisms that stimulate and enable participatory governance structures in the early stages of a social enterprise, we have chosen Dopper as a case study, in the first years of its development. Dopper is a Dutch social enterprise that has grown substantially since its founding. It aims to provide solutions to the ecological crisis of plastic waste and – at the same time – the social crisis of lack of access to clean drinking water. Dopper contributes to the EU policy objectives that aim to tackle marine pollution from plastic waste in various ways: first, through developing an innovative business model and product that offers a viable alternative to disposable plastics and promotes a sustainable consumption pattern; and secondly, through executing concrete actions aimed at plastics waste prevention.[22] Dopper originates

---

[20] A. Fici, 'A European statute for social and solidarity-based enterprise' (2017) Policy Department for Citizens' Rights and Constitutional Affairs, available at: www.europarl .europa.eu/supporting-analyses. European Commission, 'A Map of Social Enterprises and their Ecosystems in Europe: Synthesis Report' (European Union, 2015) 52, available at: https:// euricse.eu/wp-content/uploads/2015/11/Synthesis-report-FINAL.pdf; European Parliament, 'Report on Social Entrepreneurship and Social Innovation in Combating Unemployment (2014/2236 (INI))' (Committee on Employment and Social Affairs, 30 July 2015) see www .europarl.europa.eu. A. Fici, 'Recognition and Legal Forms of Social Enterprise in Europe: A Critical Analysis from a Comparative Law Perspective' (2016) 27(5) *European Business Law Review*, 664; C. Liao, 'Limits to Corporate Reform and Alternative Legal Structures', in B. Sjåfjell and B. Richardson (eds.), *Company Law and Sustainability: Legal Barriers and Opportunities* (Cambridge: Cambridge University Press, 2015), pp. 274–311 at 275.

[21] Dopper was contracted by the Dutch government to provide their reusable water bottles for all EU delegates who participated in the EU meetings in June 2016, hosted by the Dutch government during its EU presidency.

[22] Commission, 'A European Strategy for Plastics in a Circular Economy', 6.

in, and operates from, the Netherlands, an EU country that is also severely exposed to the ecological crises that currently torment Europe, among which are loss of biodiversity and ecosystems services, plastic waste, a poor air and soil quality owing to discharged chemicals, and climate change.[23]

This social enterprise was selected because it has a societal objective that addresses ecological and social challenges by contributing to the reduction of plastic waste on the streets, and in rivers and oceans; the promotion of drinking tap water; and creating safe and clean drinking water in rural areas. It is an illustrative case of a popular and fast-growing social enterprise operating predominantly in the Netherlands but also abroad in other European countries, and in the US and Nepal.

10.1.4 *Reading Guide*

This chapter continues as follows: Section 10.2 explains the space in society for social entrepreneurship to resolving societal issues. Section 10.3 provides extant definitions concerning the concept of social entrepreneurship, and an argument is made that social entrepreneurship can contribute to solving societal crises while complementing the EU's social market economy objectives and the protection of the environment. Section 10.4 discusses the options under Dutch law, or rather the lack of a tailor-made legal form for social enterprises, for a start-up social enterprise such as Dopper. This gap has resulted in the development of innovative legal and governance structures for this social enterprise. Subsequently, Section 10.5 justifies the choice of the authors to develop a case study about Dopper in its early stages, and the methodology employed. In Section 10.6, the case study illustrates the issues exhibited in the legal and governance structure employed by Dopper and the involvement of stakeholders. Finally, conclusions are drawn in Section 10.7.

10.2 A SPACE FOR SOCIAL ENTREPRENEURSHIP IN A CONTEMPORARY EUROPE

10.2.1 *From Welfare States towards Transaction Economies in the EU*

In the second half of the twentieth century, a transition took place in society and traditional governance models.[24] European countries concentrated on

---

[23] See, for example, the publications of the Dutch Environmental Assessment Agency (Planbureau voor de Leefomgeving) and other research organisations, demonstrating, for example, these ecological deteriorations, available at: www.pbl.nl/en/publications.
[24] H. Kievit, 'Dienstbaar organiseren in de regio in sociaal en economisch perspectief – van dienstverlening naar nieuwe dienstbaarheid' (2015) *Christelijke Hogeschool Ede*, 1–38.

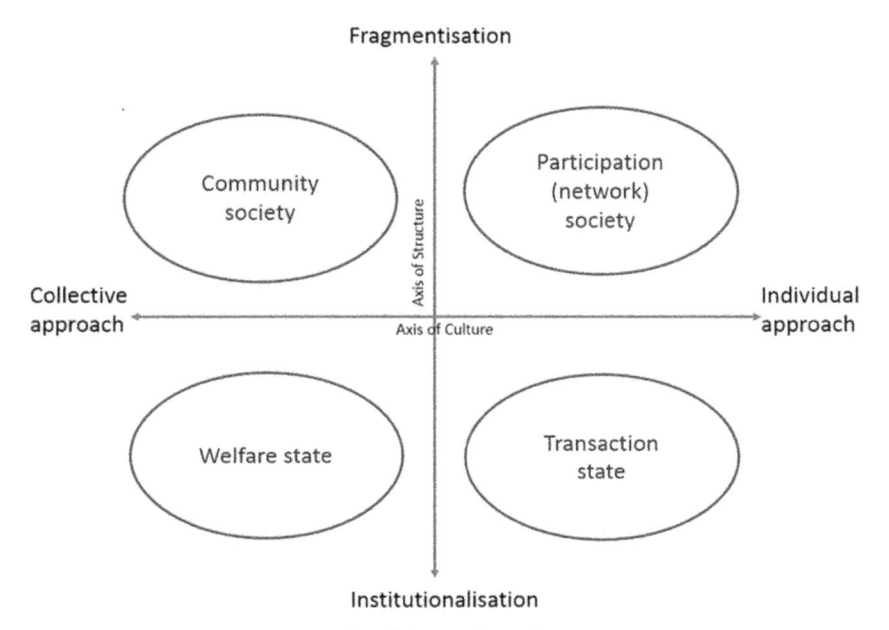

FIGURE 10.1 *Parallel transformation processes*[25]

creating a welfare state, with emphasis on economic prosperity for their citizens.[26] Since the end of the 1980s, next to the emerging trends of digitalisation and globalisation, the intermediating role of the government has increasingly transformed into a facilitating relationship between customer and supplier. Societal challenges were settled collectively or privately.[27] The idea of transaction and exchange, normal in the market domain, including in the area of (quasi-) public services, became an accepted approach for public policies employed by the state aimed at fulfilling societal goals. At an institutional level, the welfare state transformed into a 'transaction state' in which public policies employ market mechanisms.

In this transaction state, the starting point lies in the power of the individual participant. Rationality is emphasised, whereas collective values such as solidarity and social justice fade into the background (Figure 10.1). At the horizontal 'axis of culture', at the level of culture, values and beliefs in society, collective approaches move towards individual approaches. At the vertical 'axis of

[25]   Ibid.
[26]   R. M. Titmuss, 'What is Social Policy?' (1974), in S. Leibfried and S. Mau (eds.), *Welfare States: Construction, Deconstruction, Reconstruction, Vol. I, Analytical Approaches* (Cheltenham: Edward Elgar Publishing, 2008), pp. 138–147.
[27]   G. Esping-Andersen, *The Three Worlds of Welfare Capitalism* (Cambridge: Polity Press, 1990), pp. 1–244.

structure', at the level of structure and institutions, a transformation occurs from a high level of institutionalisation towards a situation in which services are available in a more fragmented way. The changes in cultural and structural reality happen at the same time and correspond with each other. De-institutionalisation and the promotion of a self-supporting attitude of citizens effectively reduce the welfare state. This results in an overall move from the welfare state (left quadrant below) to the participation (network) society (right quadrant above).

The participation approach is characterised by a high degree of individuality; the individual citizen has to seek support from other citizens, and only in hardship cases can s/he ask for assistance from public institutions.

10.2.2 *From a Transaction Economy towards a Participation (Network) Society in the Netherlands*

We saw the transformation phases of European welfare state regimes,[28] in the Netherlands, as going from a transaction state[29] to a participation (network) society.[30] In a participation society there is greater demand for individual solutions to address societal challenges in business and civil society. International public institutions, governments and civil society pushed business to take on more social and ecological responsibility, including responsibility for international supply chains and waste production.[31] Corporate social responsibility (CSR) was embraced as a solution for managing many societal challenges, from human rights violations in the mines in Africa and Indonesia, to engaging in the reduction of CO_2 emissions in order to mitigate adverse impacts on the climate. Emphasis was put on transparency around corporate activities and the negative impacts thereof, and on legislators and courts to hold companies accountable for externalities.

However, in the same period, it became more difficult for non-governmental organisations (NGOs) to receive funds from governments. They had to develop a business model aimed at receiving funds or donations from the public, for

[28] K. Josifidis, J. B. Hall, N. Supic and E. Beker Pucar, 'The European Welfare State Regimes: Questioning the Typology during the Crisis' (2015) 21 *Technological and Economic Development of Economy*, 577–595.

[29] D. J. Wolfson, *Transactie als bestuurlijke vernieuwing; op zoek naar samenhang in beleid en uitvoering* (The Hague/Amsterdam: WRR/Amsterdam University Press, 2005), pp. 1–142.

[30] A. Hemerijck, 'Two or Three Waves of Welfare State Transition' and J. Jenson, 'Redesigning Citizenship Regimes after Neoliberalism: Moving Towards Social Investment', in N. Morel, B. Palier and J. Palme (eds.), *Toward a Social Investment Welfare State? Ideas, Policies, and Challenges* (Bristol: The Policy Press, 2012), pp. 33–60 and 61–88.

[31] T. E. Lambooy, *Corporate Social Responsibility. Legal and Semi-Legal Frameworks Supporting CSR* (Deventer: Kluwer Law International, 2010), pp. 1–767.

example by crowd-funding, and/or they had to find private investors. The business model could comprise selling services and products to companies, government institutions and citizens. To this end, several NGOs transformed themselves into social enterprises. Hence, value-based network organisations emerged,[32] for which public and private goals became intertwined.

10.2.3 *Participation of Stakeholders in Decision-Making Processes*

The shift towards de-institutionalisation is important because it requires a reorientation as to who needs to participate in decision-making processes. This question applies to government agencies, regular companies, social enterprises, NGOs and other types of organisations. Strong emphasis is thereby placed on processes, and especially on the 'process' of interaction in the network society. Pertinent questions are: 'With whom do we work?' and 'How do we create collaboration between the public and private sphere?'.[33] This governance perspective of 'process interaction' and the 'relational perspective', at least on the scale at which it currently occurs, is very important and quite new.

In this context, Glastra van Loon indicates that society can be viewed as one large ocean of public space in which many private spaces and islands are present:[34] public spaces are characterised by openness that is owed to all citizens and is moreover governed by the law – thus a higher level of institutionalisation. The public space offers possibilities for joint decision-making, freedom of expression, development and organisation.[35] Privately organised spaces, however, are closed and only accessible to stakeholders. Nonetheless, as also in the past, actors of the public and private space sometimes work together, in 'public–private partnerships', for example. Lessons learnt include that this type of cooperation can generate tensions and frictions in cultural transmission or in the establishment of the governance over jointly held projects.

In a different way, Pestoff distinguishes between the public and the private space; the for-profit and the non-profit space; and the formally regulated and the informally regulated space (see Figure 10.2).[36] His framework is based

[32] L. Sepulveda, 'Social Enterprise – A New Phenomenon in the Field of Economic and Social Welfare?' (2015) 49(7) *Social Policy & Administration*, 842–861.

[33] R. van Tulder and A. van der Zwart, *International Business-Society Management: Linking Corporate Responsibility and Globalization* (London: Routledge Publishing, 2006), pp. 1–440.

[34] J. Glastra van Loon, 'De ruimte waarin wij leven', in C. de Vries and K. Schuyt (eds.), *De open samenleving en haar vrienden – in discussie met Jan Glastra van Loon* (Amsterdam: uitgeverij Boom, 1995), pp. 9–48.

[35] Ibid., p. 10.

[36] V. Pestoff, *Reforming Social Services in Central and Eastern Europe – An Eleven Nation Overview* (Cracow: Academy of Economics, 1995), pp. 29–117.

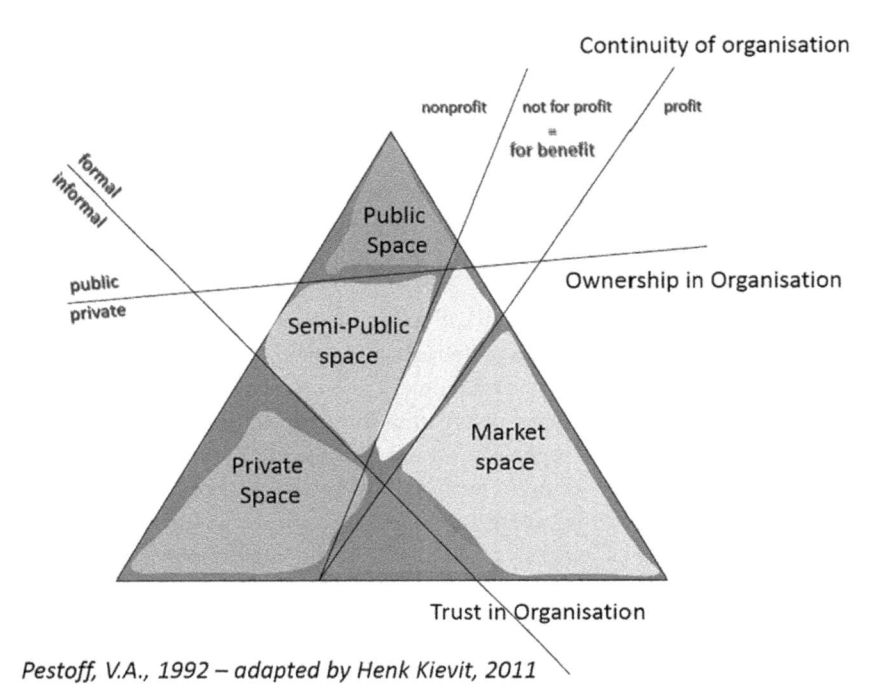

Pestoff, V.A., 1992 – adapted by Henk Kievit, 2011

FIGURE 10.2 *Pestoff's analysis of society*[37]

on the 'basic social order' as developed by Streeck and Schmitter,[38] which included the community, the market, the government and organisations.

In terms of participating in the decision-making processes, each of Pestoff's domains has its own leading principles, dominant actors, motives and results. Within the public space, a government organisation focuses, in principle, on the general interest of the citizens. This is to maintain the current laws and to be able to institute new laws. Citizens have the ability, mainly through political representation, to exert influence. They can appeal to their parliamentary representatives and government organisations, as well as vote, to 'discipline' the government. Within the market space, gaining profit is an important goal. Current mainstream economic thinking pushes for profit-maximisation.[39]

---

[37] Pestoff, *Reforming Social Services in Central and Eastern Europe*, pp. 29–117.

[38] W. Streeck and P. C. Schmitter, 'Community, Market, State-and Associations? The Prospective Contribution of Interest Governance to Social Order' (1985) 1(2) *European Sociological Review*, 119–138.

[39] Concerning the discussion on the EU social market economy (SME) model versus a liberal market economy (LME) model and how the Treaty of Lisbon has rearranged only in theory its priorities, see Scharpf, 'The Asymmetry of European Integration', 212.

The market operates on the basis of the price mechanism. When those who buy the products or services are disappointed, they will choose a competitor, and in this way consumers discipline – through their choice-mechanisms – producers or service providers. In private household spaces, family loyalty, love or altruism and the incentive to live together prevail over legal and economic interests.

Pestoff focused explicitly on civil society space in which NGOs operate by voicing opinions, influencing developments in society and balancing private and public concerns. In particular, civil society organisations represent not necessarily the public (or societal) interest, but rather special interests, voicing different views on the public interest from government agencies. Around the special interests, values and ideals of civil society organisations, people have been voluntarily connected.

The indicators that Pestoff uses for classifying organisations can be combined with specific values in society. His formal/informal division represents the value of trust. The profit/non-profit division marks the value of the products and services that are exchanged. The division between public/private marks the ownership of the organisation in general. By public, we refer to the governmental sphere. These values are depicted in Figure 10.2 by the lines that cut the triangle in multiple spaces. Since approximately the period 2000–2005, a new space has come into existence. This space is indicated in Figure 10.2 as 'not-for-profit' and 'for benefit'. It lies between the traditional spaces – market, government, civil society and private households. It is occupied by hybrid organisations that operate on a not-for-profit and for benefit base, such as social enterprises, but also NGOs that have developed a business model, and other types of community organisations that aim to produce benefits for the community.

10.2.4 *Positioning Social Entrepreneurship in Modern Society*

The Pestoff model provides an indication of how the participatory style and the answers provided by social entrepreneurship to societal questions and problems differ from those in the traditional spaces. Social entrepreneurship has introduced market-like relationships for solving societal problems, but this time by thinking and acting in a more business-wise approach. This manner deviates from the traditional ways in which citizens were involved in solving societal problems only by giving donations to charity organisations and NGOs. With the social enterprise model, the value of trust plays a role (creating value in the public domain) as does the value of exchange (economic transactions). Embedding a participatory governance model is also a feature of these hybrid organisations.

10.3 EXTANT LITERATURE OF SOCIAL ENTREPRENEURSHIP

10.3.1 *Categorising Social Entrepreneurship in the Context of Entrepreneurship*

International academic literature provides a variety of social entrepreneurship definitions.[40] The term 'social entrepreneurship' is an articulation of a combination of two concepts that are not directly a natural fit.[41] Social entrepreneurship merges rational economic calculation with a socially, environmentally and ecologically inspired vision.[42] Social entrepreneurs do not prioritise pursuing profits and maximising shareholder value above their societal goals, but instead they prioritise contributing to finding solutions to societal challenges. Such entrepreneurs seek to combine economic prosperity with societal progress for the benefit of society.[43] In a seminal article, Dees indicates that social entrepreneurs operate in conditions of market failure.[44]

Wei-Skillern and colleagues define social entrepreneurship as 'an innovative, social value creating activity that can occur within or across the non-profit, business, or government sector'.[45] Nevertheless, not all social entrepreneurship activities need to be innovative. Some solutions to societal problems are in themselves simple, but they require a lot of personal commitment, particularly when the cause of the problem is persistent. Social entrepreneurship is a process that catalyses social change and addresses societal needs in such a way that it is not dominated by immediate financial advantage for the social entrepreneurs.[46] Social entrepreneurship manifests innovation,

---

[40] A. Nicholls, *Social Entrepreneurship: New Models of Sustainable Social Change* (Oxford: Oxford University Press, 2006); A. Nicholls, 'We Do Good Things Don't We?: Blended Value Accounting In Social Entrepreneurship' (2009) 34(6–7) *Accounting, Organisations and Society*, 755–769 at 755.

[41] M. Bull, 'Challenging Tensions: Critical, Theoretical and Empirical Perspectives on Social Enterprise' (2008) 14(5) *International Journal of Entrepreneurial Behavior & Research*, 268–275 at 271.

[42] G. E. Shockley, R. Stough, K.E. Haynes and P.M. Frank, 'Toward a Theory of Public Sector Entrepreneurship' (2006) 6(3) *International Journal of Entrepreneurship and Innovation Management*, 205–223 at 208.

[43] J. Thompson, G. Alvy and A. Lees, 'Social Entrepreneurship: A New Look at the People and the Potential' (2000) 38(5) *Management Decision*, 328–338 at 330.

[44] J. G. Dees, 'The Meaning of "Social Entrepreneurship"' (1998) *Kauffman Foundation*, 3.

[45] J. Wei-Skillern, J. E. Austin, H. Leonard and H. Stevenson, *Entrepreneurship in the Social Sector* (Los Angeles: SAGE Publishing, 2007), p. 4.

[46] J. Mair, J. Robinson and K. Hockerts (eds.), *Social Entrepreneurship* (London: Palgrave Macmillan, 2006); see also Nicholls above note 40.

market orientation and social orientation.[47] Its various definitions differ in substance and direction. Some scholars focus on the process of establishing a social enterprise,[48] whereas others tend to emphasise the innovative character of the entrepreneurial activities to fix societal problems,[49] or produce social value.[50] Also, some scholars categorise an 'environmental issue' as a 'social issue',[51] while others consider 'environmental entrepreneurship' as a process of economic opportunities to explore, surface, evaluate and exploit market failures, ultimately to stop environmental degradation.[52]

10.3.2 *A New Generation of Entrepreneurs*

Social problems (people) and environmental/ecological problems (planet) give rise to opportunities for social entrepreneurs if they can respond to the problems with innovation, technology, employment and prosperity that are necessary for systemic change.[53] An illustration of this is the comment from Drayton of the Ashoka Foundation, that social entrepreneurs are not content with catching fish or teaching people to fish; they will not rest until they have revolutionised the entire fishing industry in order to make its activities sustainable (usually from an environmental and a social perspective).[54]

Social entrepreneurship plays the role of a change agent to create and maintain social and/or environmental value besides financial value, without being limited to resources that are not currently available.[55] Schumpeter described the entrepreneur as someone who brings innovations to the marketplace, in

---

[47] A. Nicholls and A. H. Cho, 'Social Entrepreneurship: The Structuration of a Field', in A. Nicholls (ed.), *Social Entrepreneurship: New Models of Sustainable Social Change*, (Oxford: Oxford University Press, 2006), pp. 99–118.

[48] Dees, 'The Meaning of "Social Entrepreneurship"', 4.

[49] A. Fowler, 'NGDOs as a Moment in History: Beyond Aid to Social Entrepreneurship or Civic Innovation?' (2000) 21(4) *Third World Quarterly*, 637–654 at 647–648.

[50] J. Austin, H. Stevenson and J. Wei-Skillern, 'Social and Commercial Entrepreneurship: Same, Different, or Both?' (2006) 30(1) *Entrepreneurship Theory and Practice*, 1–22.

[51] Mair, Robinson and Hockerts, *Social Entrepreneurship* above note 46; H. Neck, C. Brush and E. Allen, 'The Landscape of Social Entrepreneurship' (2009) 52(1) *Business Horizons*, 13–19 at 14.

[52] T. J. Dean and J. S. McMullen, 'Toward a Theory of Sustainable Entrepreneurship: Reducing Environmental Degradation through Entrepreneurial Action' (2007) 22(1) *Journal of Business Venturing*, 50–76; Neck, Brush and Allen, 'The Landscape of Social Entrepreneurship', 14.

[53] Neck, Brush and Allen, 'The Landscape of Social Entrepreneurship', 13–19. M. E. Porter and M. R. Kramer, 'Creating Shared Value' (2011) 89 *Harvard Business Review* 1–2, 62–77.

[54] W. Drayton, 'The Citizen Sector: Becoming as Entrepreneurial and Competitive as Business' (2002) 44(3) *Californian Management Review*, 120–132.

[55] M. Sharir, and M. Lerner, 'Gauging the Success of Social Ventures Initiated by Individual Social Entrepreneurs' (2006) 41(1) *Journal of World Business*, 6–20 at 7.

which s/he creates changes in the economy.[56] Indeed, what is important to the social entrepreneur is achieving sustainable economic development and qualitative change in society. Austin and colleagues distinguish between commercial entrepreneurship and social entrepreneurship, which they assess in particular on the criteria of addressing market failures, mission of the organisation, performance measurement and the mobilisation of resources by the parties concerned.[57] It seems that the process of exploring opportunities is similar for commercial entrepreneurship and social entrepreneurship.[58] Accordingly, social entrepreneurs have to assess how to make economic choices to invest in their approach. For this, one makes risk assessments on the basis of intuition within an environment of uncertainty.[59] This judgement regarding the assessment of risks in investing in the entrepreneurial approach is called 'a venturesome approach'.[60] Zahra and colleagues use the ideas of Hayek, Schumpeter and Kirzner to identify three types of social entrepreneurs.[61] First, Zahra and colleagues elaborate on the 'social bricoleur' who searches for 'opportunities' within local social needs.[62] Secondly, there is a 'social constructionist' who analyses market failure conditions and undertakes therein mediation efforts for disadvantaged groups to improve their well-being.[63] Thirdly, they point to the 'social engineer',[64] who takes a systemic problem within the existing social structures, and proposes a revolutionary solution in a radical way. The social entrepreneur continues to act even when the often-limited funds available are depleted. The main goal is to create benefit with a societal or institutional impact, as beneficiaries often lack the resources (and vision) to emerge above their institutional constraints.

---

[56] S. Bostaph, 'Driving the Market Process: "Alertness" Versus Innovation and "Creative Destruction"' (2013) 16(4) *The Quarterly Journal of Austrian Economics*, 421–458; J. A. Schumpeter, *The Theory of Economic Development: An Inquiry into Profits, Capital, Credit, Interest, and the Business Cycle* (Cambridge, MA: Harvard University Press 1934), pp. 1–320.

[57] See further Austin, Stevenson and Wei-Skillern, 'Social and Commercial Entrepreneurship', 1–22.

[58] P. J. Murphy and S. M. Coombes, 'A Model of Social Entrepreneurial Discovery' (2009) 87(3) *Journal of Business Ethics*, 325–336.

[59] B. D. Blume and J. G. Covin, 'Attributions to Intuition in the Venture Founding Process: Do Entrepreneurs Actually Use Intuition or Just Say that They Do?' (2011) 26(1) *Journal of Business Venturing*, 137–151; S. A. Zahra, 'Entrepreneurial Risk Taking in Family Firms' (2005) 18(1) *Family Business Review*, 23–40.

[60] I. Bassi and J. Grant, *Structuring European Private Equity* (London: Euromoney Institutional Investor, 2006), pp. 1–175.

[61] S. A. Zahra, E. Gedajlovic, D. O. Neubaum and J. M. Shulman, 'A Typology of Social Entrepreneurs: Motives, Search Processes and Ethical Challenges' (2009) 24(5) *Journal of Business Venturing*, 519–532 at 523.

[62] Ibid., 523–524.

[63] Ibid., 524–525.

[64] Ibid., 526–527.

10.3.3 *How Involving Stakeholders Can Support in Realising Societal Goals*

Considering the extant literature on social entrepreneurship, the question often arises how building relationships between a social enterprise and its stakeholders can strengthen the enterprise's achievements of fulfilling its societal goal.[65] As such, further research on social entrepreneurship and the stakeholder participation in the governance structure is needed.[66] Legal and non-legal studies that elaborate on stakeholder participation in social enterprises in various European countries, such as Belgium, the UK and Greece, have been developed.[67] These countries offer in their laws tailor-made legal

[65] For the following distinction see the doctoral dissertation of H. Kievit, *Social venturing entrepreneurship: een plaatsbepaling* (Assen: Koninklijke Van Gorcum, 2012) available only in Dutch at: www.nyenrode.nl/docs/default-source/pdf%27s/pdf%27s---faculteit-research/dissertations/dr-ir-henk-kievit--proefschrift-%27social-venturing-entrepeneurship%27.pdf?sfvrsn=375bc314_2. The literature on social entrepreneurship can broadly be divided into three periods: (1) from 1998 to 2004, scholarship mainly contains descriptions of social entrepreneurial practice and studies that focus on the social entrepreneur; (2) from 2005 to 2008, the first (scientific) books on social entrepreneurship appear, focusing on the definitional debate of what social entrepreneurship actually is, what it entails and how the social entrepreneurial activities can be classified into a typology; (3) from 2008 onwards, scholarship addresses the substance of what social entrepreneurs do, how the processes are set up and what solutions are implemented, what are the results and the differences of social entrepreneurship with traditional/commercial entrepreneurship, how to understand 'opportunity recognition' in social entrepreneurship and what the 'entrepreneurial characteristics' are. S. H. Alvord, L. D. Brown and C. W. Letts, 'Social Entrepreneurship and Societal Transformation' (2004) 40(3) *The Journal of Applied Behavioral Science*, 260–282. S. Johnson, 'Social Entrepreneurship Literature Review' (Paper produced for the Canadian Center for Social Entrepreneurship, University of Alberta: Edmonton Thompson, 2002). R. Jones, J. Latham and M. Betta, 'Narrative Construction of the Social Entrepreneurial Identity' (2008) 14(5) *International Journal of Entrepreneurial Behavior & Research*, 330–345. Nicholls, 'We Do Good Things Don't We?'; see also J. C. Short, T. W. Moss and G. T. Lumpkin, 'Research in social entrepreneurship: past contributions and future opportunities' (2009) 3(2) *Strategic Entrepreneurship Journal*, 161–194.

[66] Doherty, Haugh and Lyon, 'Social Enterprises as Hybrid Organizations: A Review and Research Agenda', 417–436; Argyrou, *Social Enterprises in the EU*, pp. 1–314.

[67] See the studies conducted by the authors Lambooy and Argyrou, 'Improving the Legal Environment', 71–76; See Argyrou, *Social Enterprises in the EU*. A. Argyrou, T. Lambooy, R. J. Blomme and H. Kievit, 'An Empirical Investigation of Supportive Legal Frameworks for Social Enterprises in Belgium: A Cross-Sectoral Comparison of Case Studies for Social Enterprises from the Social Housing, Finance and Energy Sector Perspective', in V. Mauerhofer (ed.), *Legal Aspects of Sustainable Development: Horizontal and Sectorial Policy Issues* (Cham: Springer International Publishing, 2016); A. Argyrou, T. Lambooy, R. J. Blomme and H. Kievit, 'An Understanding How Social Enterprises Can Benefit from Supportive Legal Frameworks: A Case Study Report on Social Entrepreneurial Models in Greece' (2016) 16(4) *International Journal of Business and Globalisation*, 491–511; Argyrou et al., 'Unravelling the Participation of Stakeholders in the Governance Models of Social Enterprises in Greece', 661–677; A. Colenbrander, A. Argyrou, T. Lambooy and R. J. Blomme, 'Inclusive Governance

forms for social enterprises. Such forms typically require that the social enterprise includes stakeholder participation in its organisational form. However,
the Netherlands is a country *without* a supportive tailor-made legal framework
for social enterprises and, as such, there is a gap in the literature concerning
the questions whether and how Dutch social enterprises also follow a participatory organisational structure in pursuit of their social objectives.

10.4 SOCIAL ENTERPRISES IN THE NETHERLANDS

10.4.1 *Legal forms of Dutch Social Enterprises*

In the Netherlands, there are 3,000–4,000 enterprises identifying as social
enterprises.[68] According to a survey-based empirical study conducted in 2020
with 242 social enterprises, many of them (48 per cent) are incorporated as
ordinary private limited liability companies (*besloten vennootschap*).[69] Fewer
(29 per cent) make use of the Dutch foundation, whereas some of them use
the combination of a private limited liability company and a foundation.[70]
Other – rarely chosen – legal models are the cooperative, a one-man business
and a (general) partnership.[71]

  Book 2 of the Dutch Civil Code (i.e. the Dutch Company Law, hereafter
DCC) did not provide for a tailor-made social enterprise form at the time the
case study for this chapter was conducted, nor when this chapter was finished
(March 2021).[72] Hence, Dutch social enterprises tend to be custom-made legal
organisations through which they can operationalise their activities. One way

---

in Social Enterprises in the Netherlands: A Case Study' (2017) 88(4) *Annals of Public and
  Cooperative Economics*, 543–566.
[68] M. Hillen, S. Panhuijsen and W. Verloop, 'Iedereen winst. Samen met de overheid naar
  een bloeiende social enterprise sector' (2014), available at: www.social-enterprise.nl/beleid/
  publicaties/intern/iedereen-winst-overheid-social-enterprise-sector-539.
[69] T. Lambooy, A. Argyrou and A. Bolhuis, 'A Tailor-Made Legal Form for Social Enterprises in
  the Netherlands is on Its Way' (2021) 18(1) *European Company Law Journal*, 22–25. See also
  A. Argyrou, P. A. Anthoni and T. Lambooy, 'Legal Forms for Social Enterprises in the Dutch
  Legal Framework: An Empirical Analysis of Social Entrepreneurs' Attitudes on the Needs of
  Social Enterprises in the Netherlands' (2017) 12(3) *International and Comparative Corporate
  Law Journal*, 1–46 at 19.
[70] Ibid.; see also T. Lambooy, P. A. Anthoni and A. Argyrou, 'Aren't We All Pursuing Societal
  Goals in our Businesses? Defining 'Societal Purpose' as Pursued by Social Enterprises' (2020)
  28(3) *Sustainable Development*, 485–494.
[71] Ibid; see also Hillen, Panhuijsen and Verloop, 'Iedereen winst. Samen met de overheid naar
  een bloeiende social enterprise sector'.
[72] Book 2 of the Dutch Civil Code (Burgerlijk Wetboek). On the contrary, many EU countries
  have already developed legislation that is tailor-made to social enterprises, for example Italy,
  Belgium, Greece and the UK. See Argyrou, *Social Enterprises in the EU*, 32–35.

of conducting a business that can pursue a societal objective is to deploy a combination of two types of Dutch legal entities: a for-profit legal form and a non-profit legal form. This is also the case with the social enterprise Dopper (see Section 10.5). In this chapter, Dopper is examined in its initial stages of its development (in 2014–2017). The social enterprise comprised the following combination of legal forms, which is a common combination for Dutch social enterprises:[73]

1. A *besloten vennootschap*, a Dutch privately held limited liability company (Article 2:175 DCC and onwards, hereafter BV) for running the entrepreneurial activities. The BV holds the part of the social enterprise that offers the goods and/or services.
2. A *stichting*, a foundation (Article 2:285 DCC and onwards), for setting funds apart that are destined to contribute to fulfilling the societal purpose of the social enterprise.[74]

10.4.2 *Characteristics of the Dutch BV and the Foundation*

Since January 2013, there has no longer been any minimum capital requirement for privately held limited liability companies; a company can have a shareholder with just one share of €0.01, for example. Consequently, incorporating a BV is not a difficult option for a young and starting social enterprise. Moreover, at any time, a BV has the possibility to raise (additional) capital by issuing shares. The shares in a BV can have voting rights or profit rights, or both, depending on which option has been selected and included in the Articles of Incorporation. This is also stated in the BV's Articles of Association. Shareholders are considered stakeholders in the Dutch legal context. Instead of raising capital by issuing shares, a bank loan is also a possibility for a social enterprise.

A Dutch foundation has no share capital but can receive donations and subsidies. If a foundation qualifies as an *algemeen nut beogende instelling* (public benefit organisation), it can benefit from tax advantages with regard to receiving gifts, donations and inheritance, and energy taxes.[75] This option is

---

[73] Argyrou, Anthoni and Lambooy, 'Legal Forms for Social Enterprises in the Dutch Legal Framework: An Empirical Analysis of Social Entrepreneurs', 8–9.
[74] W. Verloop and M. Hillen, *Verbeter de wereld, begin een bedrijf. Hoe social enterprises winst voor iedereen creëren*, (Amsterdam: Uitgeverij Business Contact 2013), pp. 141–142.
[75] Argyrou, Anthoni and Lambooy, 'Legal Forms for Social Enterprises in the Dutch Legal Framework', 9. For example, the inheritance tax exemption is provided in article 32(1)(3) of the Dutch Inheritance Tax Law 1956. The gift tax exemption can be found in article 33(4) and (10) of the Dutch Inheritance Tax Law 1956 (Successiewet 1956). See T. J. Van der

considered important by social enterprises using the combination model of a BV and a foundation, because many of them donate part of their turnover or profits earned by the BV to the foundation, which can spend those funds to support the societal purpose of the social enterprise. Dopper also followed this path, as we will see in Section 10.5.

Another important aspect of foundations is that funds may not be distributed to any member of the board (or other body of the foundation) or the foundation's incorporators (Article 2:285(3) DCC). Financial distributions can only be made to third parties for charitable or social purposes and in accordance with the purpose stipulated in its Articles of Association.[76]

10.4.3 Governance Structure of the Dutch BV and the Foundation

The governance structure of a Dutch social enterprise that combines a BV with a foundation involves various actors and governing bodies. The foundation has an obligatory governing body, the board, which is responsible for managing the foundation. There is no legal minimum with respect to the number of members; one is sufficient. On the other hand, the BV comprises two obligatory bodies, the board and the general meeting of shareholders. In Article 2:189a DCC, other optional bodies are summed up, such as a supervisory board (or instead: a one-tier board).[77] Finally, the employees of the foundation and the BV are regarded as stakeholders. Although the DCC does not see the employees collectively as a 'body' in the sense of the DCC, a separate law, the Dutch Works Council Act (DWCA), sets out the powers of the employees as a group.[78] Any enterprise in which normally at least fifty persons are working is obliged to establish a Works Council, regardless of the legal form adopted for the enterprise. When an enterprise has ten to fifty employees, such as the case study company Dopper in its early stages, the entrepreneur is obliged to meet with the employees twice per calendar year (Article 35b DWCA). The entrepreneur is also obliged to provide general information on the activities and the financial results of the enterprise. In addition, the entrepreneur has to give the employees the opportunity to render advice with

Ploeg, 'Nonprofit Organizations in the Netherlands', in K. J. Hopt and T. Von Hippel (eds.), *Comparative Corporate Governance of Non-Profit Organizations* (Cambridge: Cambridge University Press 2010), pp. 228–264 at pp. 235–236.

[76] Examples are provided in Hillen, Panhuijsen and Verloop, 'Iedereen winst. Samen met de overheid naar een bloeiende social enterprise sector', 12–17.

[77] In case of large private limited liability companies a supervisory board – or a one tier board – is obligatory. See art. 264 et seq. of Book 2 of the Dutch Civil Code (Burgerlijk Wetboek).

[78] Works Council Act 1971 (Wet op de Ondernemingsraden 1971).

regard to certain issues that concern employment, employment conditions or employment circumstances.[79]

10.4.4 *Do Social Enterprises Merit a Tailor-Made Legal Form? The Discourse in the Netherlands*

In order to support and recognise social enterprises as hybrid organisations, the majority of European countries had introduced new tailor-made legal forms for social enterprises by 2014.[80] In the Netherlands, up until the time of finalising this chapter (March 2021), no separate legal regime has been adopted for social enterprises.[81] There was an attempt to introduce a legal model in 2009. A bill introducing a new legal form for the *maatschappelijke onderneming* (societal or public purpose enterprise) was drafted by the government, but it never became law.[82] In 2013, the bill was officially withdrawn.[83] Originally, the idea behind the bill was to introduce a legal regime solely for one category of enterprises: those active in the semi-public sector that originated in the 'privatisation wave' described in Section 10.2.[84] In the Netherlands, the discourse on social – or societal – enterprises has been divided into two categories: the enterprises in the quasi-public sector – especially institutions that deal with the public tasks of healthcare, education and housing, usually large organisations and basically funded with public money – and all other social enterprises, often small and young enterprises, typically funded with private money. Considering Pestoff's model (Figure 10.2), they operate for benefit and sometimes also for profit in the market sector.

In January 2014, the acknowledged platform organisation in the Netherlands, Social Enterprise NL, published a policy agenda stimulating the discourse

---

[79] In enterprises with ten to fifty persons, it is also possible to set up an employee representative body. At the request of the majority of the persons working in the enterprise, the entrepreneur is obliged to do so (Article 35c DWAC). In that case, the employee representative body has a right of approval with regard to decisions that concern certain working conditions. In Dopper, no such request had been made and thus no employee representative body exist. Enterprises with a staff of fewer than ten persons are not obliged to set up an employee representative body (Article 35d DWAC).

[80] Lambooy and Argyrou, 'Improving the Legal Environment', 71–76.

[81] Ibid.

[82] Wetsvoorstel [legislative proposal] 32003–2, introduced by the Dutch cabinet on 3 July 2009, available at: www.eerstekamer.nl/behandeling/20130123/brief_regering_brief_houdende_3.

[83] Ibid.

[84] Formation of the cabinet 2006, 30891–4, 29 and 33, available at: https://zoek.officielebekendmakingen.nl/zoeken/parlementaire_documenten. See also the report ordered by the Dutch Minister of Justice, 'Rapport van de projectgroep rechtsvorm maatschappelijke onderneming' (September 2006) at 7–8, available at: www.rijksoverheid.nl/documenten/rapporten/2006/09/18/rapport-projectgroep-rechtsvorm-maatschappelijke-onderneming.

regarding social entrepreneurship in the Netherlands. Suggestions were made to the Dutch government with regard to the development of the social enterprise sector.[85] These included two legislative suggestions: to create a separate legal company form for social enterprises based on the BV legal form, and to stimulate social enterprises fiscally. The former Dutch Minister of Economic Affairs and Climate Policy (Minister EA&CP) responded by summing up activities that are already being done by the government to stimulate the social enterprise sector. Subsequently, the government requested the Dutch Social and Economic Council (Sociaal-Economische Raad, SER) for advice on social entrepreneurship:[86] what social enterprises are, what their added value is, what obstacles they face and what still needs to be done and by whom. The main question entailed what the government's role should be in view of these developments.[87] The former Minister EA&CP declared in a statement that there are no plans for developing and adopting a separate legal structure for social enterprises, because – in the minister's view – the existing legal structures offered enough flexibility for social enterprises.[88] However, advocates for a legal model provided several reasons why introducing a separate legal model would be a good idea.[89] Furthermore, introducing a separate

---

[85] Hillen, Panhuijsen and Verloop, 'Iedereen winst. Samen met de overheid naar een bloeiende social enterprise sector'.

[86] Letter from the former Dutch Minister EA&CP to Parliament (24 February 2014), available at: www.rijksoverheid.nl/documenten/kamerstukken/2014/02/24/kamerbrief-met-reactie-op-rapport-stichting-social-enterprise-nl. The official request for advice took place on 30 June 2014, and the advice was published in June 2015. For the official request, see www.ser.nl (search for 'Sociaal Ondernemerschap'; only available in Dutch). The SER advised the Dutch government 'to facilitate social enterprises – for example by removing unnecessary obstacles, increasing knowledge, and offering support in impact measurement – and to look critically at its own role in procurement'. For the advice, see Sociaal-Economische Raad (SER), *'Summary of Council Advisory Report on Social Enterprises'* (June 2015), available at: www.ser.nl/~/media/files/internet/talen/engels/2015/2015-social-enterprises.ashx [the SER Advice]; SER, 'Sociale ondernemingen: een verkennend advies' (Uitgebracht aan de Minister van Sociale Zaken en Werkgelegenheid, NR.3, Advies 15/3, May 2015), available at: www.ser.nl/nl/publicaties/adviezen/2010-2019/2015/sociale-ondernemingen.aspx.

[87] See fn. 86. See also the: Lists of questions by the House of Representatives and answers by the Minister for Economic Affairs, 2013–2014, available at: https://zoek.officielebekendmakingen.nl/zoeken/parlementaire_documenten (search for 'Dossiernummer' 33750–XIII' and 'Ordernummer' 124; only available in Dutch).

[88] Ibid. See the list of questions by the House of Representatives and answers by the Minister EA&CP, 2013–2014, 33750 XIII, no. 124, at 7.

[89] Timmerman, De Jongh and Schild., 'The Rise of the Social Enterprise', p. 313; J. M. de Jongh, A. J. P. Schild and L. Timmerman, 'Naar Maatschappelijke Varianten van de Rechtsvormen in Boek 2 BW?', in A. J. Eijsbouts et al., *Maatschappelijk verantwoord ondernemen* (Deventer: Kluwer 2010) pp. 205–206; Argyrou, Anthoni and Lambooy, 'Legal Forms for Social Enterprises in the Dutch Legal Framework', 1–46.

legal model for the social enterprise is the trend in EU Member States and supported by the EU Commission and the European Parliament.[90]

The fact that the Dutch government asked the SER to define social enterprises shows that there is still no clear understanding of the social enterprise concept in the Netherlands. In the 2009 bill regarding the *maatschappelijke onderneming*, discussed earlier, the government used a broad definition of social enterprise, including enterprises that belong to the quasi-public sector as outlined in Section 10.2. However, the international term 'social enterprise' was never referred to in the bill. In addition, contributing to the national definitional discourse regarding the term, the platform Social Enterprise NL introduced a narrower definition. In this, institutions, organisations or subsidised organisations that are highly dependent on public money are excluded.[91] One definition provided by the former Minister EA&CP is: 'Social enterprises are enterprises that have one or more social goals as main goal(s), and in case they make profit, they reinvest it in their social goal(s).'[92] He further added that he would abstain from providing a specific definition, in fear of excluding certain enterprises that could contribute to society. The description that was provided by the SER in its 2015 advice concerning social enterprises was broader, however: 'Social enterprises have in common that they are independent enterprises providing a product or rendering a service primarily and explicitly in pursuit of a social objective – in other words, with a view to solving a social problem.'[93]

10.4.5 *Impact First! A Social Enterprise Code in the Netherlands*

Lambooy and Diepeveen explain that the idea of adopting a new legal form for social enterprises was contemplated and presented in the political agendas of various political parties in the Netherlands, in view of the national elections

---

[90] T. E. Lambooy and R. A. Diepeveen, 'Actuele ontwikkelingen betreffende sociale enterprises: een sectorale gedragscode' Juridisch up to date, available at: www.futd.nl/document/jutd/jutd20170096/.

[91] According to Social Enterprise NL, a social enterprise should earn at least around 75 per cent of its income itself. Hillen, Panhuijsen and Verloop, 'Iedereen winst. Samen met de overheid naar een bloeiende social enterprise sector'.

[92] Lists of questions by the House of Representatives and answers by the Minister for Economic Affairs, 2013–2014, 33750 XIII, nr. 124, 1.

[93] Sociaal-Economische Raad (SER), 'Summary of Council Advisory Report on Social Enterprises' (June 2015), available at: www.ser.nl/~/media/files/internet/talen/engels/2015/2015-social-enterprises.ashx [the SER Advice]; SER, 'Sociale ondernemingen: een verkennend advise' (Uitgebracht aan de Minister van Sociale Zaken en Werkgelegenheid, NR.3, Advies 15/3, May 2015), available at: www.ser.nl/nl/publicaties/adviezen/2010-2019/2015/sociale-ondernemingen.aspx.

in March 2017.[94] Subsequently, a proposal for a bill to that end was indeed presented by the Christen Unie (Christian Union) party members of the Dutch Parliament by the end of 2017. However, as it would take years before a new legal form or legal label was introduced and/or entered into force in the Dutch legislation, Social Enterprise NL decided to take action.[95] It considered that social entrepreneurs in practice still struggle daily with the challenge of convincing their clients, customers and financiers that they are truly social entrepreneurs.[96] In 2016, Social Enterprises NL established an independent expert committee, the Social Enterprise Code Committee (Commissie Code Sociaal Ondernemen), with the objective of developing a self-regulatory code, designed to create a reliable quality mark for social entrepreneurs. In 2017, the Social Enterprise Code (Code Sociaal Ondernemen, hereafter the Code) was conceived following the involvement of various stakeholder groups and consultation rounds.[97]

Lambooy and Diepeveen analyse the purpose of the Code – to confer recognition on social enterprise in the market and in wider society.[98] The Code contains a number of basic principles that a social entrepreneur must comply with in order to be admitted to the Registry of Social Enterprises. This is administered by an independent board consisting of members 'who are recognisable and reliable for social enterprise stakeholders'.[99] The principles are: Mission; Stakeholders' Participation; Financing; Implementation; and Transparency. These contain elements similar to those provided in the Commission's Communication of 2011 concerning the Social Business Initiative (SBI) and were inspired by the SBI definition.[100] In the Code,

---

[94] T. E. Lambooy and R. A. Diepeveen, 'Actuele ontwikkelingen betreffende sociale enterprises: een sectorale gedragscode' Juridisch up to date, available at: www.futd.nl/document/jutd/jutd20170096/. See also: Social Enterprise NL, 'Sociaal ondernemerschap op de agenda Verkiezingen' (2 February 2017), available at: www.social-enterprise.nl/actueel/blogs/sociaal-ondernemerschap-op-de-agenda-verkiezingen-753.

[95] Lambooy and Diepeveen, 'Actuele ontwikkelingen betreffende sociale enterprises'. Ibid.

[96] Ibid.

[97] Ibid. See also Social Enterprise NL, 'Commissie Code Sociale Ondernemingen is van start!' and 'Consultatie Code Sociale Ondernemingen geopend!' (7 March 2017), available at: www.social-enterprise.nl/actueel/nieuws/commissie-code-sociale-ondernemingen-is-van-start-699 and www.social-enterprise.nl/actueel/nieuws/consultatie-code-sociale-ondernemingen-geopend-763.

[98] Lambooy and Diepeveen, 'Actuele ontwikkelingen betreffende sociale enterprises'.

[99] Code Sociale Ondernemingen, 'Welcome to the Code Social Enterprises' (27 August 2019), available at: www.codesocialeondernemingen.nl/english. See also Social Enterprise NL, 'Register, Toepasselijkheid en Evaluatie', available at: www.social-enterprise.nl/nieuws-en-evenementen/actueel/nieuws/register-toepasselijkheid-en-evaluatie-761. See the principles of the 'Code Sociale Ondernemingen' only available in Dutch, available at: www.social-enterprise.nl/files/5614/9855/5734/Vastgestelde_versie_Code_Sociale_Ondernemingen.pdf.

[100] Lambooy and Diepeveen, 'Actuele ontwikkelingen betreffende sociale enterprises'. Lambooy and Diepeveen clarify that some additional characteristics featured in the Recommendation of the European Parliament's Committee on Legal Affairs for a possible future EU legal statute for

stakeholder dialogue is among the central obligations for social enterprises, partly in order to avoid mission drift (i.e. when a social enterprise changes its societal mission into a profit-driven one). This means, amongst other things, that the social enterprise should be in a constant dialogue and communication with its stakeholders and should seek broad social support.

10.4.5.1 Principle 2. Relevant Stakeholders: Determination and Dialogue

The company determines who the relevant stakeholders are in the light of the mission. The company organises dialogue with these stakeholders in a strategy that embodies the mission.

Additionally, in order to promote the smoother implementation of the Code, manuals help social entrepreneurs to implement its principles. They provide good practices, for example concerning stakeholder dialogue. According to the peer review system, prescribed in the Code, registered social enterprises should on a regular basis show that they comply with the Code's principles. This is tested by two fellow social entrepreneurs, who can provide recommendations for better implementation. The intention is that such a system of peer review will lead to a 'community of good practice' among social enterprises that participate in this network. In addition, the registered social enterprises should publicly account for their activities and impact on their website. By 2019, the Code and the Register were up and running.

By the end of 2019, the Minister EA&CP was still contemplating whether it should prepare a legislative proposal introducing a legal form or a legal label for social enterprises. In 2019, based on policy reports and consultation with social entrepreneurs,[101] the cabinet demonstrated its support for social enterprises by acknowledging the lack of recognition for social enterprises in society.[102] Subsequently, in 2020, the Minister EA&CP commissioned a study that examined the need and support for – as well as issues of

---

social enterprises were not considered by the Code's preparatory Committee as they were not yet published at the time of drafting the Code. However, the Code is largely in line with those criteria. See Fici, 'A European Statute for Social and Solidarity-Based Enterprise'.

[101] OECD, 'Boosting social entrepreneurship and social enterprise development in the Netherlands' (2019), available at: www.rijksoverheid.nl/documenten/rapporten/2019/02/18/boosting-social-entrepreneurship-and-social-enterprise-development-in-the-netherlands and Utrecht University, 'Versnelling en Verbreding van Sociaal Ondernemerschap – Een Onderzoek Naar de Wenselijkheid van Nieuwe Juridische Kaders' (Onderzoek in Opdracht van het Ministerie van Economische Zaken en Klimaat, Utrecht, 6 Februari 2019), available at: www.rijksoverheid.nl/documenten/rapporten/2019/02/18/versnelling-en-verbreding-van-sociaal-ondernemerschap.

[102] Kamerstuk 32 637, no. 354, available at: https://zoek.officielebekendmakingen.nl/kst-32637-354.html.

enforceability, feasibility and the costs and benefits of – a potential legal form for social enterprises: the BVm, which is a limited liability company with a societal purpose.[103] The study results were in favour of introducing this new legal form in the Dutch legal system.[104] This result was adopted by the Cabinet and reported to the Parliament in 2020. Subsequently, the Minister EA&CP accordingly made plans to launch a bill for public consultation in 2021, and its initiation was announced in March 2021.[105]

10.5 INTRODUCTION TO THE DOPPER CASE STUDY AND THE EMPLOYED METHODOLOGY

10.5.1 *Dopper: Institutional Environment with Respect to Stakeholder Participation*

The (Dutch) social enterprise sector can be considered to be a sector that is piloting the implementation and integration of sustainability in companies' organisations and structures. In the following section, a case study is developed to investigate the inner function of the legal and governance structure of the Dutch social enterprise Dopper in its initial phase as a young and growing organisation as well as the role of stakeholders in that enterprise. The presentation of the case study aims to demonstrate the importance and the relevance of a supportive legal and institutional environment, especially with respect to stakeholder participation in the initial phase of a social enterprise.

A stakeholder-oriented approach is adopted with regard to the concept of governance, treating stakeholders as important actors in the corporate governance system, which is also the approach adopted in Dutch company law. Accordingly, the case study examines the characteristics of the legal and governance structure of one illustrative Dutch social enterprise in its initial and starting phase. The data collected for the case study were obtained through interviews in the period 2014–2017, which have to the greatest extent possible

---

[103] KPMG–Nyenrode, 'Stimuleren van (H)erkenning van Sociale Ondernemingen' (2020), available at: www.rijksoverheid.nl/documenten/rapporten/2020/03/01/stimuleren-van–herkening–van-sociale-ondernemingen.

[104] Ibid. About the study and the results, see T. Lambooy, A. Argyrou and A. Bolhuis, 'A Tailor-Made Legal Form for Social Enterprises in the Netherlands is on its Way' (2021) 18(1) *European Company Law Journal*, 22–25, above note 69.

[105] Letter from the Cabinet to the Parliament of 10 July 2020, available at: www.ornet.nl/wp-content/uploads/2020/07/kamerbrief-over-kabinetsinzet-sociaal-ondernemen.pdf. Rijksoverheid, '*Consultatie maatschappelijke BV (BVm) volgende stap in erkenning sociale ondernemers*' (2021), available at: www.rijksoverheid.nl/actueel/nieuws/2021/03/05/consultatie-maatschappelijke-bv-bvm-volgende-stap-in-erkenning-sociale-ondernemers.

been updated through information and documents collected through the internet (i.e. provided on the Dopper website and annual accounts). This social enterprise, in its initial phase, incorporated its activities in a legal structure comprising a BV (i.e. Dopper BV) and a Dutch foundation (i.e. Dopper Foundation). As the focus of this chapter is the emergence of the social economy, the examined Dutch social enterprise will not be compared with structures and practices of other companies that do not constitute social enterprises. The research question to be examined by this case study is whether, and to what extent, a Dutch social enterprise in its initial and starting phase has organised its legal and governance structure in such a way that it involves its stakeholders in the promotion of its societal objectives.

The examination of Dopper's legal and governance structure in its early stages will assist us to evaluate how this serves its societal objectives and how it is tightly related to the earlier discussion concerning the accomplishment of the EU's social economy market objectives and policies regarding the establishment of new business structures that promote sustainable consumption patterns and the prevention of environmental pollution. The case study also examines the various ways in which various types of stakeholders can influence or participate in the decision-making process of a young Dutch social enterprise looking for best practices and innovative ways. Earlier, in Section 10.1, the significance of stakeholders' inclusion and participation in contributing to the societal objectives of social enterprises was pinpointed.[106] However, owing to the lack of a particular legal framework for social enterprises in the Netherlands, stakeholders' statutory entitlements to participate in their governance are missing. Privately established means of stakeholder participation are possible, though. As such, the case study particularly concerns the investigation of a broader classification of stakeholder mechanisms developed by Dopper with the objective of facilitating stakeholder participation at governance level. Accordingly, these stakeholder mechanisms can be formal (based on legislation or on the Articles of Association) or informal, (organised in another way) direct (allowing stakeholders to directly or physically participate in the decision-making processes) or indirect (allowing the representation of stakeholders in the decision-making process), structural (occurring on a regular basis) or ad hoc (occurring on certain occasions).[107]

[106] See in that respect Argyrou, *Social Enterprises in the EU*, pp. 307–314. See also A. G. Colenbrander and T. E. Lambooy, 'Actuele ontwikkelingen betreffende het organiseren van een gestructureerde stakeholdersdialoog' (2017) *Juridisch up to Date* 2017–0115, available at: www.futd.nl/document/jutd/jutd20170115/.

[107] See the published work by Argyrou, *Social Enterprises in the EU*.

10.5.2 *Data Collection*

In order to develop the case study, relevant information and documents were obtained from Dopper and from online sources, including Dopper's website, whereas additional data were retrieved from semi-structured interviews with key actors from the examined organisation. The relevant documents comprised the Articles of Association of Dopper BV and Dopper Foundation, Dopper BV's Annual Reports from 2014 to 2020, regulations and policies employed by the social enterprise, employee manuals, annual impact reports, Chamber of Commerce extracts, certificates, the 'Dopper Brandbook', and a contract between Dopper Foundation and the Dutch foundation Simavi (a sustainable development organisation). The relevant data provided extensive information that illustrated several aspects of the internal structure of Dopper in its initial and starting phase, the hybrid aspects of the organisation, the social purpose and other company objectives.

The semi-structured interviews were conducted with a board member, the sole shareholder (twice: the focus of the second interview was on updating the collected information), an employee and two external stakeholder(s) (one respondent from Simavi and the other from Dopper Foundation). Valuable information regarding the decision-making processes and the role of stakeholders in governance was collected in this way. The interviews took place in the period from October 2014 to December 2014, and the information was updated in October 2017. The interviews were processed into verbatim transcriptions that were sent to the interviewees for confirmation and feedback. The interviewees were asked to provide feedback and give approval of the interviews. The content of the interviews was later used for the development of the case study.

10.5.3 *Dopper's Societal Goal*

Dopper is a Dutch social enterprise located in Haarlem, which advocates for the circular economy and environmental sustainability in the use and consumption of water.[108] According to its statutory purpose, Dopper aims to stimulate the drinking of tap water in the Netherlands and abroad, thereby reducing plastic waste globally by selling specially designed reusable drinking bottles and related products for storing tap water to companies and individuals. Dopper claims that the more bottles it sells, the fewer disposable water bottles will be used.

---

[108] Dopper is a member of the platform organisation Social Enterprise NL – available at: www.social-enterprise.nl/wie-doen-het/dopper/ – and a certified B-Corporation – www .bcorporation.net/community/dopper-bv. The company has also acquired the Cradle-to-Cradle certification for the Dopper original bottle according to the Dopper Annual Impact Report 2020, available at: https://dopper.com/annual-report-2020-productandservices.

The company sells Dutch-design reusable drinking bottles in multiple countries in Europe and abroad, such as Belgium, Germany, the US and Brazil.

Dopper's mission is 'to create awareness regarding the impact of single-use plastic waste' caused by the continuous use and disposal of plastic water bottles and to 'inspire people to initiate a change' in the use of sustainably designed bottles while 'increasing access to safe drinking water for people' globally.[109] Anyone purchasing or receiving a Dopper bottle is considered 'an ambassador' of 'Dopper's message' to the world, as Dopper's message and societal objective are embodied in the bottle itself: the bottle is the message. At the time of the interviews, Dopper was still a young and growing organisation, which employed twelve persons in total. Since then it has grown exponentially: it had an annual revenue of €9,694,888 in 2017, which increased to €14 million by the end of 2018.[110] In 2020, Dopper had over fifty employees. The company's societal impact has seemingly increased: according to an external party assessment (in 2017), people used forty fewer single-use plastic bottles a year in the first five years of using a Dopper bottle.[111]

Figure 10.3 demonstrates how sales of the specially designed, reusable Dopper bottle support the allocation of the social enterprise's resources to three mission-based destinations:

1. The Dopper Foundation, which was established to realise the societal mission and objectives of the social enterprise by raising awareness and funds. As such, 5 per cent of the net sales of the Dopper are directed to Dopper Foundation, and the latter attracts additional funds from sponsors and donors (e.g. through the Dopper-Run), who aim to contribute to Dopper's societal purpose. In 2016, Dopper BV contributed €354,248 to Dopper Foundation, whereas in 2017, it contributed €465,492, and in 2018, the contribution amounted to €713.559.[112] All amounts were equal to the 5 per cent of net sales of Dopper in 2015, 2016 and 2017.[113]
2. The Water and Waste Academy is an institute introduced by Dopper to raise awareness concerning the impact of plastic waste and the

[109] Dopper Mission, available at: https://dopper.com/mission/.
[110] Dopper's Annual Report 2017, available at: https://dopper.com/annual-report-2017/#03; Dopper's Annual Report 2018, available at: https://dopper.com/annual-report-2018.
[111] Dopper's Annual Impact Report 2020; available at: https://dopper.com/about/our-team.
[112] Dopper's Annual Report 2016, available at: https://dopper.com/annual-report/#01; Annual Report 2017, available at: https://dopper.com/annual-report-2017/#03; Annual Report 2018, available at: https://dopper.com/annual-report-2018.
[113] Dopper's Annual Report 2016, available at: https://dopper.com/annual-report/#01; Annual Report 2017, available at: https://dopper.com/annual-report-2017/#03; Annual Report 2018, available at: https://dopper.com/annual-report-2018.

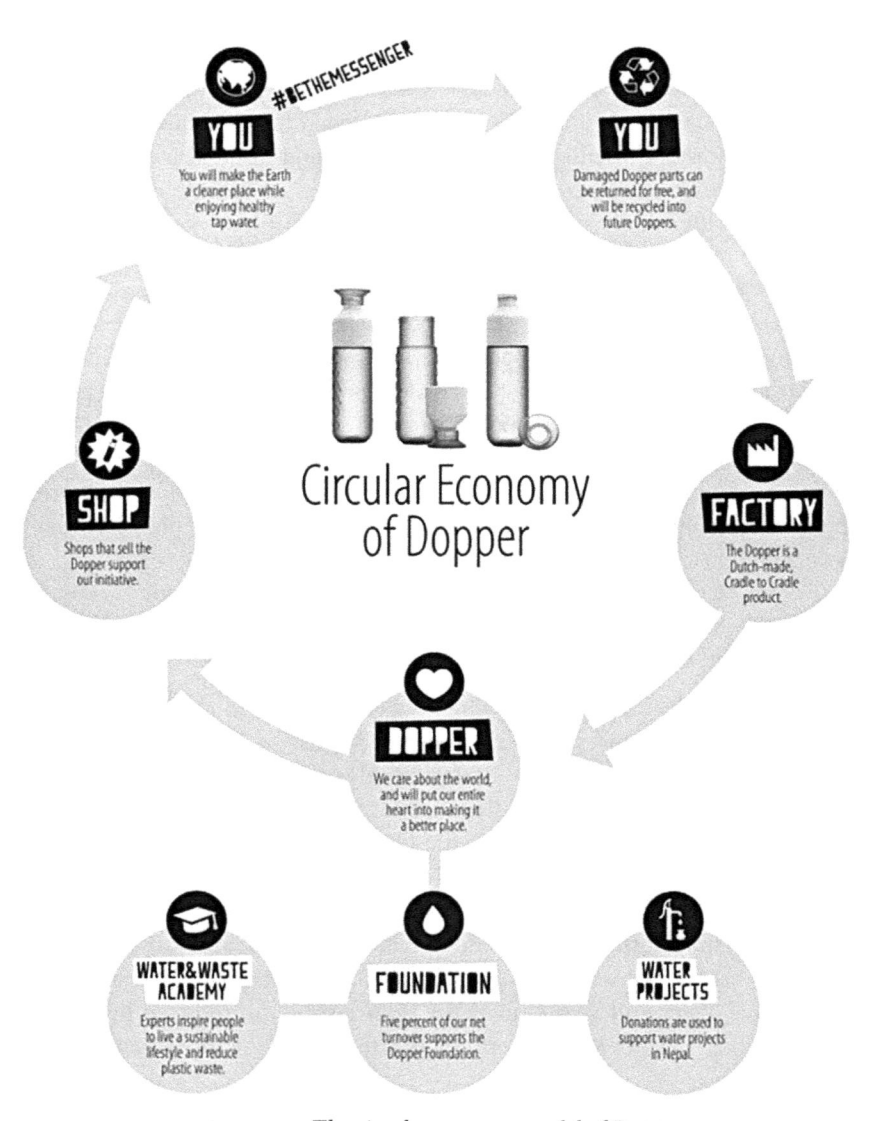

FIGURE 10.3 *The circular economy model of Dopper*

sustainable consumption of tap water. In its initial phase, the Water and Waste Academy offered lectures, seminars and workshops to all levels of education and to business organisations, including primary schools, high schools, colleges, universities and companies. In 2018, an amount exceeding €75,000 was spent by Dopper on educational programmes.[114] These either motivated university students to conduct research concerning access to water, innovation and the reduction of plastic waste, or raised the awareness of school students concerning the problem of 'plastic soup', that is the existence of plastic in the ocean which is above and below the surface of the sea but also in the sea bed.

3. The development of Water Projects in Nepal, which aim to improve access to safe and clean water and sanitation for people in rural areas. Since its incorporation, 2018, Dopper has sponsored various projects that were executed by its partner organisation, the foundation Simavi,[115] in collaboration with the Nepalese NGO Nepal Water for Health (NEWAH).[116] Dopper reported that in 2016 and in 2017, the Dopper Foundation donated up to €150,000 to Simavi's projects in Nepal to support the development of water projects.[117]

10.6 DOPPER'S LEGAL AND GOVERNANCE STRUCTURE AS A START-UP

10.6.1 *Dopper's Legal Structure*

As explained in Section 10.4, Dopper's initial legal structure demonstrated a hybrid form characteristic of young Dutch social enterprises. Figure 10.4 shows that this social enterprise consisted of Dopper BV and Dopper Foundation. The BV was founded in 2010 and the shares were held by its incorporator and only shareholder. Dopper Foundation was founded later in 2013. Dopper BV has pursued objectives that are predominantly commercial but also social, whereas Dopper Foundation has pursued clearly societal objectives: the promotion of tap water in the context of public awareness to reduce plastic waste, the provision of support to drinking-water projects and the reduction of plastic soup in the oceans. However, according to Dopper, the combination of the BV and the foundation constitutes an inefficient legal structure to maintain and to develop its business as a social enterprise.[118]

---

[114] Annual Report of the Stichting Dopper Foundation of 2018, available at: https://anbi.nl/wp-content/uploads/stichting-dopper-foundation/Jaarrekening%202018.pdf.

[115] Interview with Simavi. Also Simavi, available at: https://simavi.nl/partners-en-bedrijven/dopper/. See also Dopper's Annual Report 2017, available at: https://dopper.com/annual-report-2017/#03.

[116] Nepal Water for Health, available at: http://newah.org.np/about-us/.

[117] A similar amount was spent in 2017–2018 (€151,154) for the development of projects in Nepal. See Dopper's Annual Report 2016, available at: https://dopper.com/annual-report/#01 and the Annual Report of the Stichting Dopper Foundation of 2018, available at: https://anbi.nl/wp-content/uploads/stichting-dopper-foundation/Jaarrekening%202018.pdf.

[118] ME Interview, 8 October 2014.

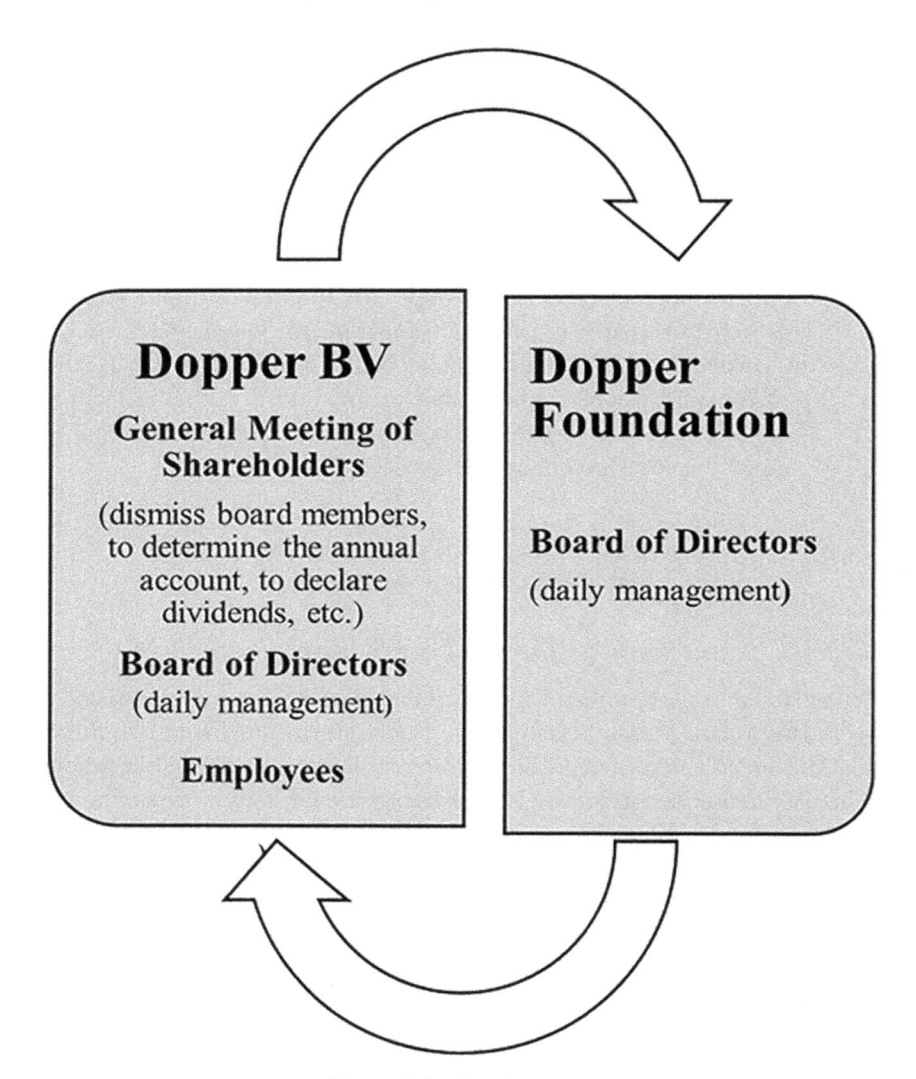

FIGURE 10.4 *Dopper's legal and governance structure*

10.6.2 *Dopper's Governance Structure*

Figure 10.4 also portrays that Dopper's daily governance, the decision-making process, was exercised by the formal Board of Directors of Dopper BV in consultation with two appointed 'general managers': one was appointed to run Dopper BV and the second was in charge of the activities of Dopper Foundation.[119] The Board of Directors of the BV consisted of one member

[119] ME Interview, 11 October 2017.

who was also the sole shareholder in the General Meeting. The latter has the power to appoint board members, to determine the annual accounts, to declare dividends and so on. Dopper BV employed the employees who conducted the activities of the social enterprise. Dopper Foundation maintained a separate Board of Directors that consisted of three members who were in charge of making decisions concerning the activities of Dopper Foundation. Additionally, although it is possible to set up one or more formal advisory committees to advise Dopper BV and/or Dopper Foundation as per 2017, there were no such advisory committees established.[120] The governance structure included the ad hoc advice of specialised advisers in the field of business management and business education.[121]

10.6.2.1 Dopper's Stakeholder Engagement and Stakeholder Participation

The interviews revealed that the core stakeholders of Dopper included its employees, Simavi, Dopper's consumers, volunteers, Dopper's suppliers and retailers, the villages in Nepal that benefitted from Dopper's Water Projects operated by Simavi and NEWAH but financially supported by Dopper, the Municipality of Haarlem where Dopper is located and network, certificate and platform organisations, such as Social Enterprise NL, Cradle to Cradle and B Corp, of which Dopper is a member (Figure 10.5).[122] Dopper's stakeholders were located in multiple countries – its home country, other countries where Dopper sells products, such as Germany, Belgium, Denmark, Brazil and the US, and those in which it operationalises projects, for example in Nepal. In all these countries, by 2021, Dopper still had stakeholders.

In the Dopper Brandbook, which contains the core values of Dopper, the value of connectedness is mentioned. Two phrases illustrate what is meant by 'connected': 'We are thoughtful towards people. We love to connect people and initiatives.' This was a starting point that indicated that Dopper considers its relationship with employees and external stakeholders important. However, the Articles of Association of Dopper BV and Dopper Foundation did not contain any provisions that prescribed the participation of employees or external stakeholders in the formal decision-making processes, through the Board of Directors or General Meeting of Dopper BV or the Board of Directors of Dopper

---

[120] ME Interview, 11 October 2017; Articles of Association of Dopper BV and Dopper Foundation.
[121] ME Interview, 11 October 2017.
[122] Dopper Annual Report 2020, available at: https://dopper.com/annual-report-2020-productandservices.

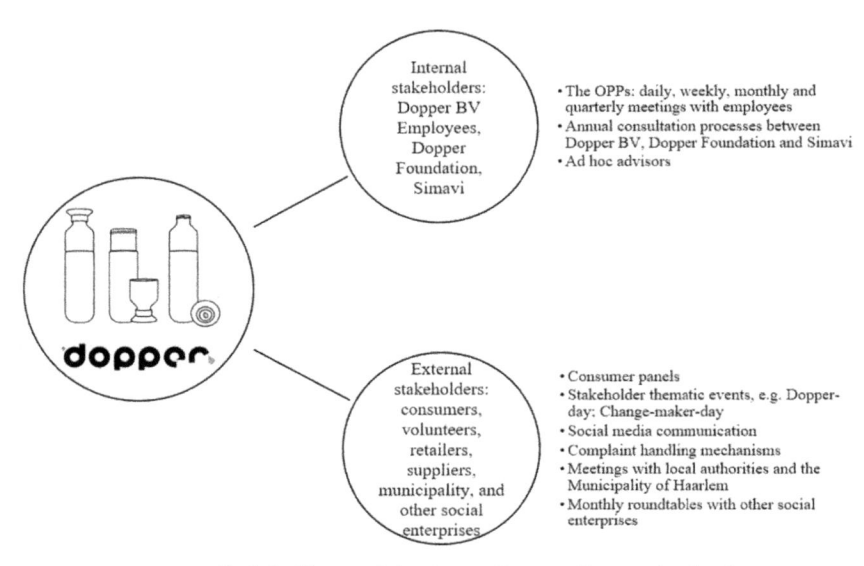

FIGURE 10.5 *Stakeholder participation at Dopper. Source: Authors' own.*

Foundation. Nor were there any additional internal regulations or bylaws that dealt with this topic. As one interviewee mentioned, the employees 'do not need always to sit at the table [...], if we run projects or if important decisions are made then that is the model: there are parties and disciplines involved'.[123] Another interviewee confirmed: 'there are multiple layers – it would not be the case that we all sit at the table of course, and that we all go for decisions [...] but really everyone is there with his/her expertise'.[124] Accordingly, from the content of the interviews and the Dopper Brandbook, it was deduced that Dopper employed numerous informal and internally organised mechanisms to engage and collect the feedback of various stakeholders, and that all involved consider stakeholder engagement and participation very important for the development of the social enterprise and the quality of the activities employed by it. However, the examination of the documents revealed that no formal participatory stakeholder mechanisms were embedded in the legal structure.

10.6.3 *Engagement and Consultation with Internal Stakeholders*

As already mentioned in Section 10.4, Dopper did not establish a formal employee representative body as referred to in the Dutch Works Councils Act, nor was the young enterprise legally obliged to set up a works council

---

[123] BV Interview, 22 October 2014.
[124] JdR Interview, 8 October 2014.

as the total number of employees was below fifty. Additionally, research in the employee manual of Dopper indicated that there were no rules or principles referring to employees' participation in decision-making. An alternative way for employees and external stakeholders to participate formally in the decision-making processes could be by acquiring Dopper's shares and co-deciding as shareholders in the BV's general meeting. Such an idea was contemplated and discussed, but finally rejected when Dopper was shaping its initial legal structure. The Board and the general managers considered co-ownership unpractical owing to the risk of providing shares to 'volatile' employees, those who might decide to quit or change their employment after only a short period of involvement.[125]

Nevertheless, an internal policy developed by Dopper, the One Page Plan (OPP), showed that Dopper involved its employees in the process of decision-making. The employees were involved informally but regularly. The OPPs were principles developed in the organisational functioning of Dopper based on Verne Harnish's book concerning the Rockefeller Habits.[126] These comprised ten exemplary management strategies and routine practices used by J. D. Rockefeller to align team working, to streamline a rhythm of communication between employees and managers and to develop the employees' passion and eagerness to work with purpose.[127] The interviews revealed that following the OPPs, Dopper employees met with the general managers and the statutory director on a daily, monthly and quarterly basis.[128] The OPP meetings had

---

[125] ME Interview, 8 October 2014; BV Interview, 22 October 2014; follow-up ME interview, 11 October 2017.

[126] V. Harnish, *Mastering the Rockfeller Habits 2.0: Scaling Up. How a Few Companies Make it … and Why the Rest Don't* (Ashburn, VA: Gazelles Inc., 2014).

[127] Ibid., pp. 175–190.

[128] Daily communication in the form of brief meetings took place among employees and the general managers to discuss and share priorities concerning daily affairs. As such, employees had insights into each other's tasks and responsibilities. An interviewee mentioned, 'If we didn't have the daily communication, we would have less cohesion' (BV Interview, 22 October 2014). Monthly meetings were also organised between the general managers and the employees. One interviewee mentioned that everyone shares 'his/her successes – or one success moment of the week' (ME Interview, 8 October 2014), 'positive news' (JdR Interview, 8 October 2014) and 'major affairs on an individual level' (BV Interview, 22 October 2014). Common topics in these monthly meetings were: (1) 'how Dopper can go to the next level' (ME Interview, 8 October 2014; JdR Interview, 8 October 2014; BV Interview, 22 October 2014); (2) the handling of questions from customers and the access of customers to questions concerning the Dopper products (ME Interview, 8 October 2014); and (3) new developments in the field in which Dopper operated (ME Interview, 8 October 2014; JdR Interview, 8 October 2014; BV Interview, 22 October 2014). Those meetings were followed-up by four quarterly extensive (one-day) meetings that were dedicated to 'looking back on what has been done' and 'how to make the process better' (JdR Interview, 8 October 2014) on the basis of four themes that shaped the quarterly strategic agenda.

various themes listed on the agenda. First were the OPPs themselves, in other words the behaviour towards each other in the organisation and Dopper's 'behaviour' towards the public. For instance, the theme of handling questions from customers and so on was discussed on a monthly basis. In this respect, it was Dopper's aspiration to promote and maintain a high level of accessibility for customers. According to one interviewee, the extent of access meant that the company is 'easily accessible by phone or by mail' any time of the day and has 'a clear answer' to any questions from Dutch or foreign customers.[129] Other themes discussed during the OPP meetings concerned financial issues; sales and marketing.

Similar arrangements concerning the communication and the collaboration of Dopper, Dopper Foundation and Simavi could be found in the contract between the Dopper Foundation and Simavi. However, there were no rules concerning the participation of Simavi in the formal decision-making process of Dopper BV or of Dopper Foundation. An interviewee mentioned that joint decisions between Dopper and Simavi were always made:

> [in] consultation [...] [and] at the table and they are sometimes successful and/or sometimes they are failing; Dopper is in the lead and we follow [...] so yes, usually it is so that we sit down together at the beginning of the year or at the end of the year – depends on when we will have time [...] we look where we can reinforce each other and where we can help each other together.[130]

10.6.4 *Engagement and Consultation with External Stakeholders*

Various round tables were organised on a monthly basis by Dopper: the 'Benefit for the World talks'.[131] Those were organised either nationally, in the Netherlands, or internationally, in Belgium, Germany, the US and Brazil.[132] In such round tables, Dopper explored opportunities for collaboration with peers and exchanged experiences and good practices in consultation with Dutch and international popular social enterprises.[133] Those round tables constituted Dopper's pursuit to 'join them [other social enterprises] on the social enterprise path' and maintain 'interaction' with this type of stakeholders as well as clearly demonstrated to the stakeholders 'that you can live in a sustainable world with all these good social enterprises around you'.[134]

---

[129] ME Interview, 8 October 2014 and follow-up interview 11 October 2017.
[130] TLR Interview, 17 December 2014.
[131] ME Interview, 11 October 2017.
[132] ME Interview, 11 October 2017.
[133] ME Interview, 8 October 2014; ME Interview, 11 October 2017.
[134] ME Interview, 8 October 2014; ME Interview, 11 October 2017.

The interviews also revealed additional stakeholder mechanisms developed by Dopper to collect feedback and to engage Dopper's customers, retailers and suppliers in the organisational processes. Dopper established on a regular basis consumer panels comprising users of the Dopper bottle and the company's loyal fans who were identified through an established fan-base active on social media.[135] Social media were constantly used by Dopper to attract volunteers from all over the world who pledged their commitment to Dopper's environmental message.[136] Dopper collected and considered their feedback regularly. An interviewee mentioned: 'We have a very large fan base in social media. These are all important stakeholders'.[137] Dopper also developed thematic events to engage with stakeholders, including retailers, customers and the Dopper fans. These thematic events differed annually in their name and form; for example, a 'Dopper-day' was organised in 2014 and a 'Change-maker-day' was organised in 2017.[138] One interviewee mentioned that these events traditionally included 'business-related' customers who were interested in the Dopper story .[139] However, in the course of time, those events were transformed into informal festivals that could be joined by all different kinds of customers and fans. The suppliers were also considered very important stakeholders in Dopper.[140] They provided information concerning the substances that were used in the production process of the Dopper bottle and were contained in the product itself. Obtaining correct and complete information was of great importance to Dopper, because the information was needed to maintain and safeguard its Cradle-to-Cradle certification.[141] The attitude of the retailers was also scrutinised closely by Dopper. Dopper was particularly concerned with potential disruption in the transmission of its message throughout the supply chain – for example, when retailers purchased the Dopper bottles and resold them in the market. In one interview, this was mentioned: 'So there is noise on the line as far as telling the message about what we stand for; that makes the resellers for us a tricky party, because we expect that they do it only for the money'.[142] As such, the Dopper message was constantly emphasised to the suppliers and retailers during the stakeholder thematic events. An interviewee said:

---

[135] BV Interview, 22 October 2014.
[136] JdR Interview, 8 October 2014.
[137] BV Interview, 22 October 2014.
[138] ME Interview, 11 October 2017.
[139] ME Interview, 11 October 2017.
[140] BV Interview, 22 October 2014.
[141] Dopper, Cradle-to-Cradle, available at: https://dopper.com/updates/dopper-cradle-to-cradle-gecertificeerd/.
[142] BV Interview, 22 October 2014.

TABLE 10.1 A *matrix for the classification of participatory governance mechanisms employed by Dopper*

	Formal	Informal	Direct	Indirect	Regular	Ad hoc
The OPPs: daily, weekly, monthly and quarterly meetings with employees		X	X		X	
Consultation processes with Dopper Foundation and Simavi		X	X			X
Round tables with other social enterprises		X	X			X
Consumer panels		X	X			X
Stakeholder thematic events –Dopper-day, Change-maker-day		X	X			X
Social media communication		X	X		X	
Complaint handling mechanisms		X		X		X
Engagement with local authorities and the Municipality of Haarlem		X	X			X
Assisting advisors in decision-making		X	X			X

[W]e are going to invite everyone to the Dopper-day. We consider how we can involve them, how can we give them something special, so that they stay hooked up in what we stand for. [In the events] there are speakers invited. Not only the CEO not only themselves but also other interesting speakers, in the field of social enterprise, will give speeches regarding certification and we will discuss the problems with which we struggle. It will be a special day, but in this way we want to keep our stakeholders on the hook.[143]

Dopper's engagement with the local authorities of the Municipality of Haarlem was also mentioned in the conducted interviews. The Councillor of Haarlem (*alderman*) was invited to Dopper to discuss how the social purpose that Dopper advocates could be spread around the local community.

[143] BV Interview, 22 October 2014.

The importance of engaging with the local and municipal authorities was indicated by an interviewee who mentioned 'we have an appointment soon, with the Councillor of Haarlem. This is an important future stakeholder for us because upon her [the Councillor's] request, she will visit us to watch a presentation regarding Dopper. That is for me a signal that we are heard and seen at the level of policy makers' (BV Interview, 22 October 2014).

10.6.5 A Classification of Informal Stakeholder Participatory Mechanisms Used by Dopper

In the examined case study, Dopper's governance demonstrated that stake-holders did not formally participate in the statutory decision-making processes of Dopper. However, informal participation mechanisms were established in Dopper's organisational governance. These are classified in Table 10.1.

10.7 CONCLUSIONS

This chapter has discussed the emerging role of social enterprises in a Europe in crisis. The introductory parts of this chapter demonstrate that a new sector for social enterprises is developing and increasing all over the EU. In 2021, we can observe that the social enterprise sector has grown substantially over the last decade. Social enterprises have developed responses to the societal gaps that emerged as a result of governments' strategies to withdraw from many areas and activities, and to leave them open for market actors. As indicated in Figure 10.2, social enterprises moved into the new space referred to as 'not-for-profit' and 'for benefit', which lies between the traditional spaces of market, government, civil society and private households. Among them are also NGOs that have developed a business model, and other types of community organisations that aim to produce benefits for the community.

The scholarly interest in defining and establishing the contours of the social enterprise concept is acknowledged. This chapter shows that the emergence of the social enterprise concept has acquired ample support from scholars, legis-lators and policy makers at both national and EU level. European institutions, such as the Commission, clearly advocate the role of social enterprises in addressing societal problems and they promote the establishment of a favour-able (legal) environment for social enterprises. At a national level, most EU countries have developed tailor-made legislation and policies for social enter-prises., whereas only a few other countries have followed a different direction.

Such a country is the Netherlands. At the beginning of 2021, the Netherlands does not provide a tailor-made legal framework to social enterprises, neither there is a tailor-made legal form. Dutch social entrepreneurs incorporate their business activities mainly using a combination of the Dutch BV and the Dutch foundation. Owing to the increase in popularity of the social enterprise sector, public support for such businesses is increasing. In the Netherlands, attention has been paid to the social enterprise sector's call for legislation by important institutions, such as the SER and the Minister EA&CP, and political parties. By the end of 2019, the Minister EA&CP facilitated research into the question whether tailor-made regulation is required and, if so, the form that should be adopted. Simultaneously, private regulation in the form of the Code Sociaal Ondernemen was introduced in 2017 by the sector itself, establishing basic and fundamental principles with which Dutch social entrepreneurs must comply in order to obtain a registration in the Dutch Register Sociale Ondernemingen.

In the Dutch Social Enterprise Code, as is the case in many tailor-made legal regimes for social enterprises in other European jurisdictions, the principle concerning the participation of stakeholders is a central one. Accordingly, this chapter has examined a case study to assess the relevance of the institutional and legal environment to the inner (legal and participatory governance) structure of a young Dutch social enterprise in its initial and starting phase. We found that there were no formalised participation mechanisms in Dopper's governance structure for internal stakeholders (the employees of Dopper BV, Dopper Foundation and the foundation Simavi) or for external stakeholders (peers, consumers, suppliers, retailers and local authorities). However, Dopper introduced innovative informal means and consultation processes to involve stakeholders in its decision-making processes, such as the OPPs, consumer panels and thematic events. Neither the employees of Dopper nor the external stakeholders had acquired shares or membership, and thus they were not entitled to participate in formal decision-making processes, such as the Board of Directors and in the General Meeting of Shareholders. Nonetheless, adequate information was provided to them constantly. Both the internal and the external stakeholders had the power to influence the decisions made by Dopper. They provided ample support and participation.

Dopper is an example of an organisation that engages its stakeholders in a participatory way in order to fulfil its social purpose. Consumers who have obtained a Dopper bottle are still regarded as 'ambassadors': 'the bottle is the message'. The social enterprise underlines that its stakeholders are important in the process of spreading the message. Dopper's message has come through loud and clear, as is demonstrated by the successes published by the company in its Annual Impact Reports.

As there was no tailor-made legal form for social enterprises available when Dopper started its operations, Dopper had to search for other paths to make its societal mission visible in the Dutch market. Other market forces, and particularly the commitment of the consumers, employees and other stakeholders, were employed by Dopper in order to spread its societal message. Dopper developed innovative and informal ways of engaging with stakeholders. However, as these methods have been informal, it becomes clear that such an organisation may suffer from 'mission drift' at some point in the future, owing to changes in ownership, management, economic situation and so on. If the organisation changes its original 'for purpose' mission into a regular 'for profit' mission, all informal stakeholder participation mechanisms will likewise be changed or removed. Only formal structures will guarantee future stakeholder participation and assist in protecting the 'for purpose' mission of the social enterprise. Tailor-made legislation can play that role and accommodate such formalised structures, as is the case in many other European jurisdictions that offer special legal forms to social enterprises (including instructions on stakeholder participation).

This chapter has also demonstrated that there is a potential and a space for the development of further formal means for supporting the legal and governance structure of social enterprises in the Netherlands, thereby contributing to both the development of the social enterprise sector and the mitigation of the environmental and ecological crisis in Europe. By 2021, indeed, the Dutch government is in the process of developing a special legal form for this sector.

Additionally, this chapter has revealed many informal approaches that have been developed and employed by Dopper to involve stakeholders. These insights offer new opportunities to other young social enterprises in the Netherlands and elsewhere in Europe to improve their stakeholder participation.

In conclusion, this chapter demonstrates that social enterprises, which stand at the intersection of the private and public sector, can simultaneously contribute to economic development and to efficient solutions for societal (social, environmental or ecological) problems that constitute small parts of broader societal (social and environmental) challenges.

The Role of Women in Stimulating New Types of Value Creation

Charlotte Villiers and Roseanne Russell

11.1 INTRODUCTION

The global financial crisis resulted in high levels of unemployment (especially amongst young people), businesses failures, gender inequality and social unrest. These problems arose in varying degrees throughout Europe. Greece was notably badly affected.[1] In this chapter, we explore the experience of Greece in the aftermath of the Eurozone crisis as a lens through which to view the problems women encountered, particularly in southern Europe, but also in different ways in other parts of Europe. While it is clear that some corporate practices, including a focus on unsustainable and short-term value creation, were implicated in the financial crisis, it is also clear that business has an important role to play in solving these issues.

We consider how companies might work towards the creation of sustainable value. We also reflect on current European trends for regulating and managing corporations, and the significance this has for corporations' legal status and their operations, as well as for corporations' behaviour towards society and the world. As we seek to recover from the COVID-19 pandemic lockdowns, this chapter explores, more particularly, the role that women might have in the progress towards economic recovery. Women were presented in much of the media as a potential source of recovery and redemption from the financial crisis;[2] so too have female political leaders been shown to have handled the COVID-19 pandemic more effectively for their citizens.[3] However,

---

1 S. Ozturk and A. Sozdemir, 'Effects of Global Financial Crisis on Greece Economy' (2015) 23 *Procedia Economics and Finance*, 568–575. See also S. Abboushi, 'Analysis and Outlook of the Greek Financial Crisis' (2011) 7(1) *Journal of Global Business Management*, 1–8.
2 For a discussion see I. van Staveren, 'The Lehman Sisters Hypothesis' (2014) 38(5) *Cambridge Journal of Economics*, 995–1014.
3 S. Freizer, 'COVID-19 and Women's Leadership: From an Effective Response to Building Back Better' (2020) 18 *Policy Brief, UN Women Policy Brief Series* 3.

we have also observed regressions in terms of gender equality and women's position at work and in society following both the financial crisis,[4] and also the pandemic.[5]

In Greece and across Europe, including in the UK, women appear to have suffered the effects of the recession and austerity measures in different ways than men, and they have found themselves in positions of greater dependency and hardship.[6] This situation has been exacerbated by the pandemic.[7] This experience casts doubt on the European-level policy developments towards increasing the presence and influence of women in company boardrooms and in other business and political decision-making areas. These policies aim to realise the potential of women in stimulating economic growth.[8] We support this recognition of the contribution that women can and do make in the economy, but we also show in this chapter that, not only were some of those policies stalled, but also the business case for including women is limited. We advocate a more solid foundation that addresses empowerment and development of women in society and not just as economic actors. This matters for sustainable value creation for which the Sustainable Agenda 2030 requires women's equal representation to influence corporations' achievement of sustainable value creation and improve their sustainability performance.[9]

In Section 11.2, we look at the situation women faced in Greece after the financial crisis and the suggestions made to include women in economic activity. In Section 11.3, we outline the boardroom diversity debate. We show that similar arguments have been used to appoint women as company

[4] See UN Women Watch, 'The gender perspectives of the financial crisis', 2009, available at: www.un.org/womenwatch/feature/financialcrisis/.

[5] Freizer, 'COVID-19 and Women's Leadership', 4.

[6] D'Ippoliti, Carlo, Bettio, Francesca, Corsi, Marcella, Verashchagina, Alina, Lyberaki, Antigone, Samek Lodovici, Manuel, 'The Impact of the Economic Crisis on the Situation of Women and Men and on Gender Equality Policies, Synthesis Report', (European Commission, December 2012); see also UN Office of the High Commissioner for Human Rights (OHCHR), Gender and Development Network, 'Submission to the Independent Expert on foreign debt and human rights on the links and the impact of economic reforms and austerity measures on women's human rights' (March 2018), available at: www.ohchr.org/Documents/Issues/Development/IEDebt/WomenAusterity/GenderDevelopmentNetwork.pdf.

[7] EIGE, 'Covid 19 derails gender equality gains', European Institute for Gender Equality, 5 March 2021, available at: https://eige.europa.eu/news/covid-19-derails-gender-equality-gains.

[8] See, for example, EIGE, 'Economic benefits of gender equality in the European Union: overall economic impacts of gender equality', European Institute for Gender, Equality, 8 March 2017, available at: https://eige.europa.eu/publications/economic-benefits-gender-equality-european-union-overall-economic-impacts-gender-equality.

[9] M. Romano, A. Cirillo, C. Favino, & A. Netti, 'ESG (Environmental, Social and Governance) Performance and Board Gender Diversity: The Moderating Role of CEO Duality' (2020) *Sustainability* 12:9298.

directors, namely business arguments. In Section 11.4, we describe the business arguments being put forward, why these arguments dominate and what the results are of the business case approach. We note also the unravelling of progress made, largely as a result of the COVID-19 pandemic, highlighting the limitations of relying on the business case. In Section 11.5, we suggest an alternative justification for gender parity in the boardroom and greater gender equality throughout business organisations. We conclude with a plea to focus on women's empowerment and emancipation so that they may reach their potential and fulfilment rather than be seen as tools for economic growth. From this perspective, our discussion of the role women play and the impact of policies on women brings the gender aspects of value creation under the spotlight, and is in keeping with the discourse on sustainability and development internationally, gender equality featuring, for example, as one of the UN Sustainable Development Goals (SDGs) established in 2015.[10]

11.2 THE POSITION OF WOMEN IN GREECE IN THE AFTERMATH OF THE FINANCIAL CRISIS

The Greek financial crisis was a devastating experience on many levels, bringing high unemployment and poverty. Politically, the crisis rocked the Eurozone area as Greece faced a threat of exit from the zone. Marco Veremis wrote in the *Financial Times* on 5 May 2015 that 'the prolonged crisis has cost us a quarter of our GDP, the state is rapidly running out of money and Greece's isolation grows by the day. Greece is perilously close to losing its European path.'[11] A Greek exit could have led to the possibility of another global financial meltdown, similar to that triggered by the 2008 collapse of Lehman Brothers, because of the unquantifiable legal and financial risks involved.[12]

Within Greece and the Eurozone, where the recession occurred, followed by harsh austerity measures, women found themselves to be at the rough end of the crisis. As is suggested by Vaiou, 'there are effects of austerity policies that are unevenly distributed, inscribed as they are on existing inequalities: inequalities among places, between women and men, locals and migrants, big

---

[10] See, for example, SDG 5 on gender equality. See also B. Littig, 'Good Work? Sustainable Work and Sustainable Development: A Critical Gender Perspective from the Global North' (2018) 15(4) *Globalizations*, 565–579.

[11] M. Veremis, 'The reality of trying to build a business in Greece today', *Financial Times*, 5 May 2015, available at: https://ft.com/content/440ce4a6-ef3f-11e4-87dc-00144feab7de.

[12] G. Tett, 'US fears a European sequel to Lehman Brothers', *Financial Times*, 23 April 2015, available at: https://ft.com/content/4b2001ca-e999-11e4-a687-00144feab7de.

and small employers, secure and precarious workers and, most importantly, intersections of these'.[13] Vaiou notes that women saw their personal life projects overturned by the crisis, and they experienced unemployment and poverty as well as fear and insecurity.[14] How did women fare in the Greek business and labour markets? Karamessini notes that modern Greece has retained the 'male breadwinner' family model, in contrast to other European Union (EU) states, which have moved towards a dual earner model.[15] While there is evidence of continued unequal treatment of women even in those labour markets that have adopted a dual earner model (the long-standing gender pay gap in the UK and clustering of women in low-paid, part-time work attests to this), for Matsaganis, the male breadwinner model in Greece 'was rather a socially conservative pattern: it stifled mobility, forced many women to remain housewives, and prevented many young adults from leaving the parental home before an unusually late age'.[16] Greece also has low rates of employment for younger and older women.[17] Overall, the effect of the recession in Greece was that the male employment rate dropped more significantly, reflecting the segregated nature of employment and '[a]lthough women's employment loss is less, these effects reversed the long-term upward trend in female employment rates and pushed up female unemployment rates'.[18]

The Greek experience has been mirrored elsewhere. In the UK, for example, McKay and colleagues document how the UK spending cuts in welfare and public services have had an unequal impact on women because they are more likely to claim welfare benefits, particularly as lone parents, and women tend to work in the public sector and make greater use of public services.[19] An economic downturn can also have the effect of downgrading equality, which is perceived as an unaffordable luxury at a time of public spending restraints.[20]

---

13 D. Vaiou, 'Tracing aspects of the Greek crisis in Athens: Putting women in the picture' (2016) 23(3) *European Urban and Regional Studies*, 220–230 at 221.

14 Ibid., 8.

15 M. Karamessini, 'Introduction – Women's Vulnerability to Recession and Austerity: A Different Crisis, a Different Context', in M. Karamessini and J. Rubery (eds.), *Women and Austerity: The Economic Crisis and the Future for Gender Equality* (London: Routledge, 2014), pp. 3–16 at 7.

16 M. Matsaganis, 'Social Policy in Hard Times: The Case of Greece' (2012) 32(3) *Critical Social Policy* 406–421, 409.

17 M. Karamessini and J. Rubery, 'The Challenge of Austerity for Equality: A Consideration of Eight European Countries in the Crisis' 2014/2(133) *Revue de l'OFCE* 15–39, 18.

18 Ibid., 21.

19 A. McKay, J. Campbell, E. Thomson and S. Ross, 'Economic Recession and Recovery in the UK: What's Gender Got to Do with It?' (2013) 19(3) *Feminist Economics* 108–123, 119.

20 Ibid., 115.

The dominance of the family in the lives of many Greek women is also evident when they enter the paid labour market. Many women work in family businesses, especially seasonal work in tourism and agriculture. They are poorly represented at the highest levels of corporations. In October 2012 women occupied only 7.9 per cent of directorships in the largest publicly listed companies in Greece, significantly behind the then EU average of 15.8 per cent,[21] and, according to data published by the European Commission, in 2018 women in Greece still held less than 10 per cent of boardroom seats compared with the European average of 26.7 per cent.[22] Furthermore, even when women are placed on boards in Greek companies, frequently such companies are family owned and the female family members are offered seats without real decision-making power.[23] Of the eighteen largest public companies in Greece in 2011,[24] 26 per cent of managers were female, but all companies were headed by men and only 6 per cent of board members were female. Women's participation in management is thus nominal or non-existent.[25] A report by PwC on women in work ranked Greece at twenty-sixth out of twenty-seven Organisation for Economic Co-operation and Development (OECD) countries for 2013, and also twenty-fifth for the percentage of women in boardrooms in 2014.[26] A more positive report by Grant Thornton in 2015 ranked Greek women in top management positions in tenth place in the world, holding 19 per cent of executive positions, whilst in the Eurozone the average was 18 per cent and internationally the average was 16 per cent, though many such positions are in human resources, marketing and sales.[27] In the state sector, Greece had already introduced mandatory quotas. Thus in 2000, Greece introduced legislation for a mandatory quota of one-third for each gender on boards. More recently, in 2020, Greece introduced an amendment into its bill to implement the Shareholder Rights

[21] European Commission, 'National Factsheet Gender Balance in Boards: Greece' (January 2013), 1.

[22] European Commission, DG Justice and Consumers, 2019 *Report on Equality Between Men and Women in the EU* (EU, 2019).

[23] N. Papalexandris, 'Women in Management in Greece', in R Burke and A Richardsen (eds.), *Women in Management Worldwide: Signs of Progress*, 3rd edition (London: Routledge, 2017), chapter 3, p. 38 at 45.

[24] A. Petraki-Kottis and Z. Ventoura-Neokosmidi, 'Women in Management in Greece', in M. Davidson and R. J. Burke (eds.), *Women in Management Worldwide: Progress and Prospects*, 2nd edition (Farnham: Gower, 2011), chapter 3.

[25] Ibid.

[26] PwC International Women's Day, *Women in Work Index*, 1 March 2015.

[27] G. Thornton, 'Women in Business: The Path to Leadership', Grand Thornton International Business Report (2015).

Directive II, with a provision mandating Greek companies to meet a 25 per cent quota for female boardroom membership.[28]

Despite this rather gloomy outlook for women in the Greek paid labour market, there is a growing perception that female entrepreneurship is an important source of economic growth, employment and innovation, and women are also engaging more actively in business.[29] Women are perceived as more creative and the economic crisis gave rise to more women entrepreneurs.[30] As women have gained higher levels of education, they are becoming more self-confident, active and optimistic,[31] though they appear to remain more risk averse,[32] and express fears about the Greek economy.[33] Given the higher levels of education for Greek women, it is anticipated that targets for increasing their numbers in decision-making positions are feasible.[34] There are, however, considerable obstacles in establishing a business, including finding start up and operational capital, lack of experience, lack of business connections and negative male preconceptions and attitudes. In Greece many women entrepreneurs work alone. Their enterprises are frequently very small with low turnover and profits, they are service oriented, they face fierce competition and have limited growth potential. However, more recently, prior to the COVID-19 pandemic, there were government initiatives to encourage women's participation, with subsidies and technical expertise for business start-ups.[35] The Greek Association of Women Entrepreneurs (SEGE), has also supported the need for networking and access to information for women, and the organisation offers counselling, training, mentoring, coaching, networking, organisation and business-to-business transactional support, as well as offering information on business issues.[36]

---

[28] Law 4706/2020, Nr of the Gazette 136/A/17-7-2020, 17 July 2020, Article 3. See also Minerva Analytics, 9 July 2020.

[29] K. Sarri, S. Laspita and A. Panopoulos, 'Drivers and Barriers of Entrepreneurial Intentions in Times of Economic Crisis: The Gender Dimension' (2019) 16(2) *South-Eastern Europe Journal of Economics*, 147–170, at 149.

[30] N. Mylonas, L. Kyrgidou and E. Petridou, 'Examining the Impact of Creativity on Entrepreneurship Intentions: The Case of Potential Female Entrepreneurs' (2017) 13(1) *World Review of Entrepreneurship, Management and Sustainable Development*, 84–105.

[31] Ibid.

[32] Ibid.

[33] Militos survey on the Greek Woman entrepreneur, conducted face to face between November 2012 and January 2013: Militos survey results, Spring 2013, available at: www.militos.org.

[34] Papalexandris, 'Women in Management in Greece', p. 49.

[35] See General Secretariat for Gender Equality, Ministry of Interior, Project: Encouraging entrepreneurship among women, expired 2013, available at: www.eyeisotita.gr/en/Pages/ProclamationsFS.aspx?item=1135.

[36] See SEGE website, available at: www.sege.gr/en/sege/.

The Greek crisis was a result of numerous factors including the banking crisis, which affected Europe and the US, and faulty Greek economic policies.[37] Fears of a Greek exit from the Eurozone and long-term consequences of a continued economic crisis and paralysis gave rise to numerous discussions about how the Greek economy might be fixed, and how a sustained recovery throughout Europe and the US might be achieved.[38] Women have been identified as central to any such economic recovery.[39] Vaiou also reveals some optimism, so that while 'the uncertainties that the crisis creates seem to lead to more conservative behaviour and deepening gender divisions of labour; they may also open room for empowerment and negotiation of gender identities'.[40] Furthermore, 'individual practices often move beyond the boundaries of private space and family arrangements and link with collective initiatives, local or otherwise'.[41]

In the UK and the US, following corporate governance scandals and crises during the early 2000s and later, following the banking crises, a major criticism was directed at the poor quality of the work carried out by (predominantly male) directors and non-executive or independent directors.[42] A search was begun to find better qualified, more able boardroom members, and attention turned to women. At a lower level within workplace hierarchies, the potential contribution by women to the economy was also highlighted. Thus, what we have seen during the last decade is a push towards including women more fully in economic activity.

In this chapter, we seek to present a cautionary tale about the business case inspiration for bringing more women into the business arena. Whilst we applaud the fact that women are being recognised for their potential contribution to the economy, we warn that the business case on its own is not a sound

---

[37] A. Katsanidou and Z. Lefkofridi, 'A Decade of Crisis in the European Union: Lessons from Greece' (2020) 58(S1) *JCMS*, 160–172.

[38] J. Frieden and S. Walter, 'Understanding the Political Economy of the Eurozone Crisis' (2017) 20 *Annual Review of Political Science*, 371–390.

[39] See, for example, T. K Thorsdottir, 'Iceland: From Feminist Governance to Gender Blind Austerity?' (2015) 1(2) *Gender, Sexuality and Feminism*, 17–27, noting an emphasis on presumed feminine risk aversion to reverse the damage caused by masculine competitiveness and risk-taking during the years of economic boom in the banking industry.

[40] Vaiou, 'Tracing Aspects of the Greek Crisis in Athens', 8.

[41] Ibid., 9.

[42] See Lord Davies Report, Women on Board 2011, available at: https://assets.publishing.service .gov.uk/government/uploads/system/uploads/attachment_data/file/31480/11-745-women-on-boards.pdf. See also, for example, Financial Reporting Council (2014), available at: www .frc.org.uk/OurWork/Publications/Corporate-Governance/Guidance-on-Audit-Committees-September2014.aspx.

basis upon which women should be encouraged to participate. The business case instrumentalises women and does not necessarily lead to a long-term or meaningful level of participation, but risks instead tokenism and potentially a short-term approach that leaves women vulnerable to precarity and exploitation. Ironically, this mirrors the very unsustainable model of value creation that fuelled the conditions in which the previous decade's financial crisis was allowed to develop. We prefer to pursue arguments that are centred upon women's rights and which recognise the intrinsic worth of women as human beings deserving equal respect and dignity with their male colleagues. We also argue that rather than adhering to arguments that identify gender-based characteristics founded upon stereotyped views of men and women, corporate governance and business actors should take into account feminist theories of business, organisation and economics.

Much of the talk around getting women to participate more fully in the economy in Greece mirrors similar arguments espoused across Europe for encouraging greater boardroom diversity. The emphasis is on the benefits such demographic changes might bring for business rather than on the ethical and human rights-based arguments that some women's groups and feminist organisations have underlined. We will highlight how the arguments have been presented in the boardroom diversity debate. We will then explore the arguments for the business case more fully, and we will show more particularly that this approach is limited and reflects normative choices on the part of business and policy makers to privilege financial capital. We consider that the emphasis on the business case belittles women, undermines their viewpoint and forces their 'voice' to the margins. If companies are sincere about creating long-term sustainable value that allows for business growth without compromising or eroding further the possibilities of securing a sustainable future, it is regressive to treat women as a further source to be mined in the pursuit of even greater value creation. More important for the purposes of sustainable value creation and achieving the SDGs is the need to advance gender equality and to ensure women's economic empowerment across the world.[43]

11.3 THE BOARDROOM DIVERSITY DEBATE IN EUROPE

Boardroom diversity is now a well-established concept in corporate governance. Since Norway legislated for 40 per cent of directorships of public

---

[43] S. Dhar, 'Gender and Sustainable Development Goals (SDGs)' (2018) 25(1) *Indian Journal of Gender Studies*, 47–78.

companies to be drawn from each gender, other nations have followed its example.[44] Measures aiming to increase the number of female board members have predominantly included soft law and voluntary initiatives,[45] and at the European level a proposed directive is still being discussed in the European Council.[46] In June 2014, the Council's Progress Report on the Directive noted a 'broad consensus in favour of the proposal's objective; nevertheless opinions continue to differ sharply regarding the best way of achieving it'.[47] Norway led the way in mandating for boardroom reform through legislative quotas, and, on balance, Norwegian companies have incurred no major harm and may even have witnessed improved corporate governance.[48] Other countries, however, have been reluctant to step that far. The UK, for example, chose instead to adopt soft law measures by introducing requirements for the appointments processes for directors of listed companies to have due regard to the need for diversity and by adopting percentage targets.[49]

Debates in the UK and at EU level have focused on two main arguments around the issue: the business case (including the need for diversity) and, much less frequently, arguments based on the need for substantive equality that challenges existing inequalities of power and resources. Both arguments revolve around the normative consideration of whether, in principle, more women should feature in company boardrooms and, if so, how this goal should be achieved, by legislative requirements or by encouragement and voluntary action.

When examining the EU proposal, the UK House of Lords EU Committee Report expressed support for bringing more women into corporate boardrooms

---

44 B. Sjåfjell, 'Gender Diversity in the Boardroom and its Impacts: Is the Example of Norway a Way Forward?' (2015) 20(1) *Deakin Law Review*, 25–51. See, for example, France: Law 2011–103 (January 27, 2011) entitled 'On the equal representation of men and women on boards of directors and supervisory boards and professional equality'.

45 Relevant countries include Austria, Belgium, France, Spain, Italy and recently Germany, with its new 'Frauenquote' law.

46 European Commission (2012) 'Proposal for a directive of the European Parliament and of the Council on improving the gender balance among non-executive directors of companies listed on stock exchanges and related measures'. For a discussion on this see I. Lynch-Fannon, '"A Toad We Have to Swallow": Perceptions and Participation of Women in Business and the Implications for Sustainability', in B. Sjåfjell and I. Lynch-Fannon, *Creating Corporate Sustainability: Gender as an Agent for Change* (Cambridge: Cambridge University Press, 2018).

47 Council of the European Union, *Press Release: 3323rd Council Meeting Employment, Social Policy, Health & Consumer Affairs* (Council of the EU; Brussels, 19–20 June 2014), available at: www.consilium.europa.eu/uedocs/cms_data/docs/pressdata/en/lsa/143271.pdf.

48 Sjåfjell, 'Gender Diversity in Boardroom and its Impacts' (2015) 20(1) *Deakin Law Review* 25–51.

49 See, for example, UK Corporate Governance Code 2018, Principles J and L.

but preferred to do so through a 'comply or explain' approach that would give companies room to develop their own measures for increasing the female presence.[50] The dominant basis for this approach was the business case: that more women in the boardroom might enhance business and economic performance and that companies should not be forced into legislative targets to achieve these goals. By contrast, equality arguments have been overridden in favour of initiatives that appear grounded in a more instrumental use of women and the idea of diversity in order to give companies a competitive edge. Far from attempting to design corporate boardrooms that take seriously the aim of sustainable value creation, the boardroom diversity debate is emblematic of a neo-liberal co-option of a corporate input – in this case women and diversity – in the pursuit of short-term and unsustainable profit.

11.4 ANALYSIS OF THE BUSINESS CASE

The chief features of the business case in the context of boardroom diversity include: involving senior management in human resource planning; enhancing the organisation's ability to recruit from a diverse general population; increasing the range and depth of the skills of the workforce; and improving staff retention. In addition, the business case presents boardroom diversity as a way of increasing the appeal of the organisation to a wider customer base through offering a more nuanced or differentiated service and product and enhancing the organisation's reputation in the community, as well as enhancing the organisation's ability to predict and respond to customers from diverse backgrounds. Boardroom diversity is said to enable companies to challenge group-think, to take advantage of any innate skills women possess (such as the view that they are less aggressive or risk-taking) and to protect themselves from discrimination allegations.[51] Other claims include that equal opportunities policies more generally may improve business productivity and/or profits through improved recruitment, improved staff utilisation, improved staff morale and employee commitment, greater employee diversity, customer approval and increased share price.[52] Yet the effects will be conditional on the characteristics and environment of each organisation and so the net benefits are not guaranteed.[53] Hamdani and Buckley point out that direct economic benefits

---

[50] House of Lords European Union Select Committee, Women on Boards, 2012, available at: https://publications.parliament.uk/pa/ld201213/ldselect/ldeucom/58/5810.htm.

[51] L. Perriton, '"We Don't Want Complaining Women!" A Critical Analysis of the Business Case for Diversity' (2009) 23 *Management Communication Quarterly*, 218–243, 222.

[52] R. Riley, H. Metcalf and J. Forth, 'The Business Case for Equal Opportunities' (2013) 44(3) *Industrial Relations Journal*, 216, 217.

[53] Ibid.

are not necessarily the primary objective of organisations when they aim to comply with demands from a variety of institutional stakeholders such as law makers, the public and interest groups. Rather, the goal is to seek approval of these various stakeholders so as to earn legitimacy and ensure survival. Thus, economic gains are not the only indicators that capture the potential benefits of diversity; legitimacy, firm reputation and goodwill are also important goals. Some businesses may employ a more diverse workforce as a result of being more successful, so the larger, more visible, more profitable businesses that get scrutinised may have stronger incentives to meet demands of various pressure groups to be fair and equitable.[54]

The business case has provided a basis for some progress, with the effect that boardrooms have been rebalanced to a degree.[55] However, this approach has its limits. A major criticism of the business case for diversity is that it does not challenge existing power relations and the established order, which is vital if we are to achieve sustainable value creation.[56] It is centred on individuals, whereas what is needed is rather an equal outcomes approach, focused on social groups. For Dickens, '[t]here is little indication that the depoliticised business-case approach to equality will generate action on what Cockburn calls the 'long agenda; a transformation in access to power and the nature of it'.[57] This is confirmed by Lanning and colleagues in a report for the Institute for Public Policy Research on gender equality. They find individualistic responses dominate in the experience of women in top jobs, and this does not encourage women to seek changes to working cultures that will benefit other women. Instead, they take on the culture and norms of the organisation that promoted them.[58]

---

[54] M. R. Hamdani and M. R. Buckley, 'Diversity Goals: Reframing the Debate and Enabling a Fair Evaluation' (2011) 54 *Business Horizons*, 33, 37.

[55] In 2010 the percentage of women directors on the boards of the FTSE 100 was 12.5 per cent: see Lord Davies of Abersoch, *Women on Boards* (2011) Department for Business, Innovation and Skills; London, 3. Women in the UK, by 2020 held only 13.2 per cent FTSE 100 boardroom executive directorships and 11.3 per cent of such executive director positions in the FTSE 250, and only 63% of companies in the FTSE 100 and 53% of companies in the FTSE 250 have reached the target of 33 per cent of boardroom positions: see Cranfield University, The Female FTSE Board Report 2020, September 2020, available at: HYPERLINK "http://www.cranfield.ac.uk/som/research-centres/gender-leadership-and-inclusion-centre/female-ftseboard-report" www.cranfield.ac.uk/som/research-centres/gender-leadership-and-inclusion-centre/female-ftseboard-report.

[56] F. Tomlinson and C. Schwabenland, 'Reconciling Competing Discourses of Diversity? The UK Non-Profit Sector Between Social Justice and the Business Case' (2010) 12 *Organization*, 101–121, 104.

[57] L. Dickens, 'The Business Case for Women's Equality: Is the Carrot Better than the Stick?' (1994) 16(8) *Employee Relations*, 5–18, 15 citing C. Cockburn, 'Equal Opportunities: The Short and Long Agenda' (1989) 20(3) *Industrial Relations Journal*, 213–225, 220.

[58] T. Lanning, L. Bradley, R. Darlington and G. Gottfried, 'Great Expectations: Exploring the Promises of Gender Equality' (2013) *IPPR*, 27–28.

Whilst the argument for diversity has the potential for challenging the nature of organisations as currently construed, in the UK, according to Dickens, the business case arguments for equal opportunities are 'more narrowly focused, often pointing out the advantages of particular initiatives ... in terms of competing in the labour market, enhancing organisational performance and competing in the product market'.[59] The narrow focus of the business case is likely to give rise to a selective approach to equal opportunities, and so may 'serve to confine that action, since it involves a targeting of initiatives to reflect the needs of the employer rather than those of the disadvantaged groups'.[60]

In fact, the business case has the effect of subordinating the equality issue to the market. As Perriton argues, 'once a financial justification is used as a means of deciding whether to follow a course of action or not, the social issue in question becomes subordinated to the market. The business case discourse takes up all the discursive space available around the debate and drowns out attempts to qualify it.'[61] In this respect, Elias witnesses 'an apolitical appropriation of gender issues that is distinctly postfeminist in its rejection of the language of feminism and its failure to recognise women's collective political struggles'.[62]

Why is the business case dominant? Three key reasons are suggested. Perriton notes that the dominance of the business case justification can be attributed to the fact that these justifications are heard more often in our society, are given more opportunities to present themselves, monopolise communications and 'make use of strategies of control to ensure their eminence'.[63] This certainly appears to have been true in the boardroom diversity debates in which the voice of business has been more strongly represented because the corporate actors were most vocal in the consultations. For example, in the influential report by Lord Davies, *Women on Boards*, the evidence for relying on the business case was largely based on an earlier report by McKinsey and Co. entitled *Women Matter: Gender Diversity, a Corporate Governance Driver*, published in 2007.

Secondly, in a neo-liberal context, the business case and diversity are preferred over equality. Barmes and Ashtiany suggest that the language of equality and equal opportunities is commonly associated with regulatory interventions and so it is eschewed. As the economic considerations are prioritised, the moral justifications are viewed as serendipitous.[64] The Equality and Human

---

[59] Dickens, 'The Business Case for Women's Equality', 9.

[60] Ibid., 14.

[61] Perriton, '"We Don't Want Complaining Women!"', 239.

[62] J. Elias, 'Davos Woman to the Rescue of Global Capitalism: Postfeminist Politics and Competitiveness Promotion at the World Economic Forum' (2013) 7 *International Political Sociology*, 152–169, 165.

[63] Perriton, '"We Don't Want Complaining Women!"', 240.

[64] L. Barmes and S. Ashtiany, 'The Diversity Approach to Achieving Equality: Problems and Pitfalls' (2003) 32(4) *Industrial Law Journal*, 274–296, 278.

Rights Commission, relying on these two publications, considered the business case for increased diversity at the boardroom level and at executive level to be 'substantiated and unequivocal'.[65] Business case arguments are 'based in a normalized Mega-Discourse that enshrines the achievement of organizational economic goals as the ultimate guiding principle and explanatory device for people in organizations'.[66] This approach is seen as necessary for obtaining resources and cooperation from top management.[67]

The third and more subtle reason is that there is a reluctance to hear women's voices on these issues, which is systematic of a cultural indifference to women's interests. The equality arguments seem to have taken second place despite clear evidence of the insufficiency of existing equality legislation. A frequent rejection of feminism as a broad concept may point to women's issues being regarded as unimportant and to the general subordination of women culturally,[68] with the result that, at best, women are instrumentalised in the context of the women on boards debate. Whilst this third reason is not expressly stated, it is evident that women's viewpoints are regularly undermined. For example, in the modern workplace, despite employment protection legislation purporting to protect women, gender pay equality has yet to be achieved and the 'maternal wall',[69] as it is known, appears still to be a major barrier to women's participation and progression.[70] This affects women with children and without, because of the negative perceptions associated with motherhood in the business context.

---

[65] Response of the Equality and Human Rights Commission to a Consultation Document issued by the Financial Reporting Council, Gender Diversity on Boards, 2011, 3.

[66] D. Litvin, 'Diversity: Making Space for a Better Case', in A Konrad, P. Prasad and J. Pringle (eds.) *Handbook on Workplace Diversity* (London: Sage, 2006), pp. 75–94, cited by Tomlinson and Schwabenland, 'Reconciling Competing Discourses of Diversity?', 104.

[67] Barmes and Ashtiany, 'The Diversity Approach to Achieving Equality', 278.

[68] K. Banyard, *The Equality Illusion: The Truth about Women and Men Today* (London: Faber & Faber, 2010).

[69] J. C. Williams, 'Beyond the Glass Ceiling: The Maternal Wall as a Barrier to Gender Equality' (2003) 26 *Thomas Jefferson Law Review*, 1–14.

[70] The former Equal Opportunities Commission found that the equivalent of 30,000 women each year lost their jobs owing to pregnancy or maternity, with around 2 per cent being dismissed or made redundant: *Greater Expectations: Final Report of the EOC's Investigation into Discrimination against New and Expectant Mothers in the Workplace* (EOC; Manchester, June 2005) at 6. Details of the Equality and Human Rights Commission's ongoing research on 'Pregnancy, maternity and mothers: research on the experiences of employers and mothers in the 21st century' are available at: www.equalityhumanrights.com/about-us/our-work/key-projects/pregnancy-maternity-and-mothers-research-experiences-employers-and-mothers-21st-century. See further, M. B. Ferrante, 'Before Breaking The Glass Ceiling, Women Must Climb The Maternal Wall' *Forbes*, 31 October 2018.

Perriton observes that 'the widespread use of the business case discourse has crowded out a range of other ways of thinking about and responding to problems'.[71] The business case has raised important questions about how women, diversity and even feminist movements have been colonised in the pursuit of financial gain. This can be seen outside the boardroom with the growth in women's investment campaigns and in initiatives to develop women's enterprises. Non-governmental organisations and women's groups have often joined with companies in the quest for corporate gain in what Roberts calls 'transnational business feminism', 'by which is meant an increasingly large coalition of feminist organizations, capitalist states, regional and international funding institutions, non-governmental organizations (NGOs) and transnational corporations (MNCs) that converge on the need to promote women's equality, particularly in the Global South'.[72]

Thus, in addition to being too timid, the business case colludes with corporate power to co-opt women for its own purpose. This so called smart economic approach is as much about 'fixing women' as it is about facilitating development on the cheap and promoting further economic liberalisation to the detriment of sincere attempts at sustainable value creation.[73] Again, we see the myth of the prudent woman emerging in response to depictions of the financial and corporate sectors as being out of control, driven by greed, domination and the dominance of a particular conception of masculinity.[74] Constructing women as an untapped resource embeds the current neo-liberal capitalist order within the corporate sphere.[75] Women are

---

[71] Perriton, '"We Don't Want Complaining Women!"', 240.

[72] A. Roberts, 'Financial Crisis, Financial Firms … and Financial Feminism? The Rise of 'Transnational Business Feminism' and the Necessity of Marxist-Feminist IPE' (2012) 8(2) *Socialist Studies*, 85–108, 87.

[73] See, for example, S. Chant and C. Sweetman, 'Fixing Women or Fixing the World? "Smart Economics", Efficiency Approaches, and Gender Equality in Development' (2012) 20(3) *Gender and Development*, 517–529, 521; A. Roberts and S. Soederberg, 'Gender Equality as Smart Economics? A Critique of the 2012 World Development Report' (2012) 33(5) *Third World Quarterly*, 949–968; M. Bexell, 'Global Governance, Gains and Gender' (2012) 14:3 *International Feminist Journal of Politics*, 389–407; E. Prügl, 'Neoliberalising Feminism' (2015) 20(4) *New Political Economy*, 614–631; C. O'Sullivan, 'The Gendered Corporation: The Role of Masculinities in Shaping Corporate Culture', in Sjåfjell and Lynch Fannon (eds.), *Creating Corporate Sustainability*, .Ch 12, 258-281.

[74] L. McDowell, *Capital Culture: Gender at Work in the City* (Oxford: Blackwell, 1997); L. McDowell 'Capital Culture Revisited: Sex, Testosterone and the City' (2010) 34(3) *International Journal of Urban and Regional Research*, 652–658.

[75] Goldman Sachs, *The Power of the Purse: Gender Equality and Middle-Class Spending* (Goldman Sachs Global Markets Institute, 5 August 2009) especially at 21 at which it is stated that 'Economic growth and gender equality form a virtuous cycle …', available at: www.goldmansachs.com/korea/ideas/demographic-change/power-of-purse-doc.pdf

merely co-opted as another resource to be mined rather than using gender as a lens to reveal the deep-seated structural inequalities generated by the current economic and political order. For Roberts, '[i]t is partly this unproblematic linking of women's interests, development and corporate profitability that makes the business case for gender equality so appealing to such a wide range of social forces'.[76] Eisenstein identifies the issue more starkly when she talks of the 'dangerous liaison' between feminism and capitalism,[77] perhaps most clearly revealed in Sandberg's 'Lean In' campaign and Anne-Marie Slaughter's paper 'Why Women Still Can't Have it All' in the *Atlantic* in 2012.[78] Efficiency in the corporate context is not a neutral term, and it can have a negative impact on women as it is about cost-saving and profit-seeking. It leads to a focus on shareholders, the majority of whom are men. Women bear the worst cost of this approach in the context of workplaces designed around the male body and the male experience. Moreover, outside the workplace they are further excluded from participation in the company because they are less likely to be the holders of financial capital.[79] One might object to this approach by questioning why women should have to 'earn' equality. This is not equality at all.[80]

Overall, at least within the context of boardroom diversity, the business case has resulted in some change but at a disappointing level, even on its own terms. With women in the UK by 2020 taking up only 13.2 per cent FTSE 100 boardroom executive directorships and 11.3 per cent of such executive director positions in the FTSE 250,[81] this is hardly making best use of the talent pool as is claimed in the business case approach. Indeed, the target of 33 per cent of boardroom positions overall has been met in the UK by only 63 per cent of FTSE 100 and 53 per cent of FTSE 250 companies.[82] In Greece, by 2018–2019 women took up only 10 per cent of boardroom positions, and across Europe by April 2019 women in the largest listed companies held 28 per cent

[76] Roberts, 'Financial Crisis, Financial Firms … and Financial Feminism?', 92.

[77] H. Eisenstein, 'A Dangerous Liaison? Feminism and Corporate Globalization' (2005) 69(3) *Science & Society*, 487–518, 498.

[78] See also C. Rottenberg, 'The Rise of Neoliberal Feminism' (2014) 28(3) *Cultural Studies*, 418–437.

[79] J. Sarra, 'The Gender Implications of Corporate Governance Change' (2002) 1(2) *Seattle Journal for Social Justice*, 457–502, 472.

[80] See M. M. T. Holzhammer, 'The Proposed Gender Equality Directive: Legality, Legitimacy, and Efficacy of Mandated Gender Equality in Business Leadership' (2014) *Yearbook of European Laws*, 433–465.

[81] Cranfield University, The Female FTSE Board Report 2020, September 2020, available at: www.cranfield.ac.uk/som/research-centres/gender-leadership-and-inclusion-centre/female-ftse-board-report.

[82] Ibid.

of boardroom positions.[83] The danger of continued reliance on the business case is that women become commodified as a group, as another 'emerging market'.[84] As Elias observes, 'gender issues are instrumentalized in order to link women's empowerment and gender equality straightforwardly to economic growth and competitiveness'.[85] This can be a precarious approach to gender equality, which fluctuates with changing economic conditions.

It is notable that the proposed European Directive has remained dormant after it was introduced, having been stalled in the European institutions, particularly being still blocked in the Council in 2022 as a result of reservations around subsidiarity expressed by some member states.[86] The proposal's dormancy appears also to have coincided with other crises within the EU, including the ongoing migrant crisis,[87] and Brexit negotiations,[88] which may have occupied the minds of EU leaders more urgently than the question of boardroom quotas. The drift downwards in the European agenda of the proposed Directive arguably highlights the ultimate weakness of the neo-liberal arguments around women's positions in boardrooms and workplaces generally.[89] Interestingly, the European Commission announced plans to revive the proposed Directive as part of its five-year gender strategy, published in March 2020,[90] and in the European Parliament

---

[83] European Institute for Gender Equality, Gender Statistics Database, 28 June 2019, available at: https://eige.europa.eu/gender-statistics/dgs/data-talks/legislative-quotas-can-be-strong-drivers-gender-balance-boardrooms.

[84] See, for example, N. Major, 'Women: The Next Emerging Market – Supporting Women to Fulfil their Potential' (London: EY, 2013), and see also G. Pellegrino, S. D'Amato and A. Weiseberg, 'The Gender Dividend: Making the Business Case for Investing in Women' (Deloitte, 2011).

[85] Elias, 'Davos Woman to the Rescue of Global Capitalism', 166.

[86] www.consilium.europa.eu/en/policies/gender-balance-corporate-boards/.

[87] BBC, 'Migrant crisis: Migration to Europe explained in seven charts', *BBC News*, 4 March 2016, available at: www.bbc.co.uk/news/world-europe-34131911, and UNICEF, 'Humanitarian action for children, refugee and migrant crisis in Europe, 2021', available at: www.unicef.org/media/87571/file/2021-HAC-Refugee-and-migrant-crisis-Europe.pdf.

[88] European Commission, Relations with the United Kingdom, available at: https://ec.europa.eu/info/relations-united-kingdom_en.

[89] A. L. Humbert, E. K. Kelan and K. Clayton-Hathway, 'A Rights-Based Approach to Board Quotas and How Hard Sanctions Work for Gender Equality' (2019) *European Journal of Women's Studies*, 447–468; A. Elomäki, 'The Ambivalent Neoliberalism of the EU Directive on Gender Balance on Corporate Boards' (June 2015), in *4th European Conference on Politics and Gender, Uppsala, Sweden, June* (pp. 11–13), and A. Elomäki, 'Gender Quotas for Corporate Boards: Depoliticizing Gender and the Economy' (2018) 26(1) *NORA-Nordic Journal of Feminist and Gender Research* 53–68.

[90] Communication From The Commission To The European Parliament, The Council, The European Economic And Social Committee And The Committee Of The Regions A *Union Of Equality: Gender Equality Strategy 2020–2025*, Com/2020/152 Final 5 March 2020, at p. 13.

in October 2020, a plenary debate took place with calls to unblock the Directive from its stalled progress.[91] Finally, agreement on the proposal was reached in the European Parliament in June 2022 after being blocked in the Council for more than a decade and the Directive will enter into force later in 2022.[92] The Commission, until this time, has relied on the business case, referring to the:

> positive link between improved performance and gender balance, strengthening the case for gender balance. By making full use of the under-utilised talent pool of qualified, competent and motivated women, companies can better understand their customers and stakeholders and bring diversity of thought to the boardroom and to other management positions, thus strengthening the company's competitive advantage.[93]

The European Commission notes also the relevance of the COVID-19 pandemic, and observes that women have been under-represented in this context in which 'gender equality and inclusive leadership matter more than ever'.[94] Indeed, the pandemic has been damaging for gender equality across the world, and has had a regressive impact on women's progress:[95] the World Economic Forum reports that the pandemic has pushed back progress on gender parity by a generation.[96] Clearly, the business case for gender equality and women's economic and political participation is not strong enough to withstand social or economic crises.

An alternative approach is to start by hearing women's voices within companies and through the whole corporate structure, and this is what we discuss in Section 11.5.

---

[91] L. Hutchinson, 'Women on boards directive must be unblocked in Council, MEPs argue', *The Parliament Magazine*, 6 October 2020, available at: www.theparliamentmagazine.eu/news/article/women-on-boards-directive-must-be-unblocked-in-council-meps-argue.

[92] See Press Release, 'Women on Boards: Deal to boost gender balance in companies, European Parliament', 7 June 2022, available at: www.europarl.europa.eu/news/en/press-room/20220603IPR32195/women-on-boards-deal-to-boost-gender-balance-in-companies.

[93] European Commission, DG Justice and Consumer, 2021 *Report on Gender Equality in the EU* (2021), 38.

[94] Ibid.

[95] McKinsey Global Institute, 'COVID-19 and gender equality: countering the regressive effects', July 15, 2020, available at: www.mckinsey.com/featured-insights/future-of-work/covid-19-and-gender-equality-countering-the-regressive-effects#, and European Institute for Gender Equality, 'Covid 19 derails gender equality gains', 5 March 2021, available at: https://eige.europa.eu/news/covid-19-derails-gender-equality-gains.

[96] World Economic Forum, 'Global gender gap report 2021', March 2021, available at: www3.weforum.org/docs/WEF_GGGR_2021.pdf.

11.5 AN ALTERNATIVE APPROACH

In our view, gender parity and inclusive participation in the economy is required for a true democracy and for a more sustainable approach to value creation within the economy. This entails that women not only vote and have a chance to run for political office but that they visibly participate in the public institutions of the state.[97] Thus, according to Szydlo, 'Because gender parity is necessary to legitimise governance, and because corporations play an important role in economic governance, gender parity must be implemented not only in state institutions, but also in companies (and in other private sector organisations) that participate, together with public authorities, in modern economic governance at the EU and national levels.'[98] The argument should then be that 'gender balance on the boards of companies democratically legitimises economic governance and its public and private participants'.[99] This would also require fair and equal treatment for women throughout the whole of a company and across the economy.

Gender balance is a starting point, and there are many shared commonalities between women and their experiences, but we also need to strive towards more representative boardrooms across other areas. As Harris has argued, focusing on womanhood alone masks the complex and varying experiences of women when gender interacts with other characteristics such as race, age, class and disability.[100] For this reason, we would advocate for boardrooms that represent the range of male and female experiences with appointees being capable of asserting genuine influence such as has been reported following the introduction of the quotas in Norway:

> The women directors report their own behaviour as assertive and active, they have influence on decisions and participate in informal socialising outside the boardroom. Further, they do not experience out-group attitudes towards themselves as a group. They feel they are being respected and listened to, and they are included in information sharing and social interaction with other members of the board.[101]

---

[97] M. Szydlo, 'Gender Equality on the Boards of EU Companies: Between Economic Efficiency, Fundamental Rights and Democratic Legitimisation of Economic Governance' (2015) 21(1) *European Law Journal*, 97–115.

[98] Ibid., 109.

[99] Ibid., 110.

[100] A. Harris, 'Race and Essentialism in Feminist Legal Theory' (1990) 42 *Stanford Law Review*, 581–616.

[101] G. Ladegard, 'Legitimacy, Inclusion and Influence: Investigating Women Directors' Board Experiences', in S. Machold et al. (eds.) *Getting Women on to Corporate Boards: A Snowball Starting in Norway* (Cheltenham: Edward Elgar, 2013), pp. 147–154 at 150.

Elstad and Ladegard also note that an increased ratio of women on the board is likely to impact positively on their experienced participation and influence.[102]

Companies exercise powerful social influence and their decisions affect everyone in society, so we need gender balance in the processes through which corporate decisions are reached, otherwise such companies are not legitimate.[103] Boardrooms have critical social influence, and so their leadership is beyond being a private problem of the individual company, but is really a problem of democratic magnitude.[104] Therefore, women deserve equal representation at all levels, including the very highest of corporate governance.[105]

Putting women at the top might lead to changes throughout the organisation, so it becomes a virtuous circle as top women become role models for women at all levels. Indeed, those women who reach the top face expectations that they will influence structural changes that will help other women to succeed and be empowered, albeit that framing women's empowerment in distinctly economic terms has drawn widespread criticism.[106]

'Whole-istic feminism', as defined by Cynthia Cockburn,[107] is concerned with the need to tackle patriarchy on a number of fronts. From this perspective, the debate on boardroom gender quotas might be considered as too narrow. In reality, as we noted earlier, women have borne the brunt of austerity and now the COVID-19 pandemic with higher job losses, as a result of more women being in the public sectors and in jobs most affected by the risks of the pandemic, while they also frequently suffer worse terms and conditions at work. Thus, as we have already stated, the debate about women in the boardroom needs to go beyond focusing just on women who may or may not reach the boardroom level; it is a debate that should be concerned also with power representation across the corporate enterprise and outside it. Women in boardrooms do not just become role models for other women aspiring to those positions, but they should also see within their role the protection of all women, including those unlikely to rise beyond the lowest levels within the

---

[102] B. Elstad and G. Ladegard, 'Women on Corporate Boards: Key Influencers or Tokens?' (2012) 16(4) *Journal of Management & Governance*, 595–615.

[103] Holzhammer, 'The Proposed Gender Equality Directive', 5.

[104] Ibid., 23–23.

[105] Ibid., 5.

[106] J. Elias. 'Davos Woman to the Rescue of Global Capitalism: Postfeminist Politics and Competitiveness Promotion at the World Economic Forum' (2013) 7 *International Political Sociology*, 152–169.

[107] C. Cockburn, 'Challenging patriarchy and other power relations', *Open Democracy*, 4 November 2014, available at: www.opendemocracy.net/5050/cynthia-cockburn/challenging-patriarchy-and-other-power-relations.

workplace hierarchy. From this perspective, many of the pro quota advocates observe a need for a gender diversity ecosystem within a company as quotas alone will not change the company's culture. Quotas will be part of that ecosystem, but they will need to be supported by other mechanisms such as reporting requirements, mentoring and networking support for women as they climb the career ladder. Along these lines, we support the suggestions made by the European Trades Union Congress for:

> a series of substantial and integrated implementation policies aimed at tackling the current obstacles for women to reach top positions: persistent unequal access to economic, social and cultural resources between women and men, inequalities in the share of paid and unpaid work, discriminations and persistent undervaluation of women's work, lack of respect and or adequate supports for social dialogue to play its role in closing the gender pay gap and ensuring representation of women in decision making.[108]

Perriton argues that 'human beings, even ones that occupy senior positions in business organisations, need to be reacquainted with the "moral case" for change'.[109] She shows that appeal to extrinsic motivation such as financial benefits diminishes our motivation to obey moral rules despite the individual and societal benefits that those would result in. To further develop a strong counter-movement against unsustainable value creation by business, there is arguably a need for feminist movements to collectivise with other social movements to embed ideals of sustainability inside and outside business. Unions might be the best hope as they seek to protect all workers, men and women of all classes. Lanning and others note that women fared better when unionised.[110] However, there is a need for, not just empowerment, but also resistance that will run counter to the neo-liberal model, and that will demand redistribution of resources, challenge the operation of markets and organise against state repression, and associate with forms of collective action that involve possibilities of social transformation.[111] This will involve citizens and consumers participating in such transformation through measures such as changing the manner in which we eat, consume and ultimately live. Indeed, the interlinkages of gender equality and sustainability have been recognised by organisations such as the OECD who acknowledge

[108] ETUC, Resolution, 'Enhancing gender balance in company boardrooms', 23 September 2020, available at: www.etuc.org/sites/default/files/document/file/2020-09/EN-Adopted%20 Resolution%20Enhancing%20gender%20balance%20in%20company%20boardrooms.pdf at 5.
[109] Perriton, '"We Don't Want Complaining Women!"', 240.
[110] Lanning et al., 'Great Expectations', 20.
[111] A. Cornwall, J. Gideon and K. Wilson, 'Introduction: Reclaiming Feminism: Gender and Neoliberalism' (2008) 39(6) *Institute of Development Studies Bulletin*, 1, 8.

that gender equality is an antecedent of sustainability,[112] and therefore also of sustainable value creation.

Coming back to the situation in Greece, we have witnessed that all Greek citizens suffered under the financial crisis and the austerity measures but women and young people were especially hit hard. Similarly, they have suffered badly in the COVID-19 pandemic.[113] From this position. we applaud measures that have been taken in Greece to try to get women into the workplace and to participate in the economy, such as conferences aimed at getting more women entrepreneurs into technology,[114] and the establishment of organisations such as the Greek Association of Women Entrepreneurs. Such measures are a good start, but it is also necessary to focus on women's empowerment and emancipation, at least by starting to improve on gender equality.

Research indicates the relevance of context for the success of entrepreneurial activity.[115] As Tonia Warnecke notes, economic behaviour is 'embedded in concrete, ongoing systems of social relations',[116] and 'institutions make certain forms of interaction harder or easier'.[117] She adds that 'institutions shape the linkage between entrepreneurial activity, the fulfilment of human capabilities, and the quantity, quality, and distribution of economic growth'.[118] Women cannot build the economy without institutional background support. In Sweden, women have been encouraged to participate in the labour market by measures taken to deal with their home life. Thus married couples were no longer taxed jointly but individually, parental leave replaced maternity leave and childcare facilities were expanded.[119] In Greece, women entrepreneurs report

---

[112] OECD, *Policy Coherence for Sustainable Development and Gender Equality – Fostering and Integrated Policy Agenda* (Paris: OECD, 2018).

[113] See, for example, Chioni-Chatouman, 'Domestic violence and discrimination in Greece during the Covid-19 pandemic' *European Law and Gender*, 14 April 2020, available at: https://elan.jus .unipi.it/blog/domestic-violence-and-discrimination-in-greece-during-the-covid-19-pandemic/.

[114] See commentary in I. Kamberidou 'Women entrepreneurs: we cannot have change unless we have men in the room' (2013) 2(6) *Journal of Innovation and Entrepreneurship*, 1–18, available at: www.innovation-entrepreneurship.com/content/2/1/6, observing a conference in Athens in November 2012 entitled 'More Technologies? More Women Entrepreneurs!' See also Militos survey.

[115] F. Welter, C. Brush and A. de Bruin, 'The Gendering of Entrepreneurship Context' 01/14 *Working Paper*, Institut für Mittelstandforschung, Bonn, available at: www.ifm-bonn.org.

[116] T. Warnecke, 'Entrepreneurship and Gender: An Institutional Perspective' (2013) 47(2) *Journal of Economic Issues*, 455–463, 460, quoting M. Granovetter, 'Economic Action and Social Structure: The Problem of Embeddedness' (1985) 91(3) *American Journal of Sociology*, 481–510, 487.

[117] Ibid.

[118] Ibid.

[119] L. Achtenhagen and M. Tillmar, 'Studies on Women's Entrepreneurship for Nordic Countries and Beyond' (2013) 5(1) *International Journal of Gender and Entrepreneurship*, 4–16.

that Greek society does not approve of them as much as it should, and that they feel guilty about the lack of time they are devoting to their family.[120] Nevertheless, the same survey shows that those who are in business are satisfied with their decision to start in business, that they are highly educated, and that they feel successful. There is a seed of hope in the results of this survey. Greek women, arguably, are located somewhere between necessity entrepreneurs ('creating self-employment in response to job loss or when their options for work or participation in the economy are either absent or unsatisfactory') and opportunity entrepreneurs ('able to identify available opportunities and exploit them').[121] Necessity entrepreneurs tend to be 'not highly educated, without prior managerial experience, access to capital or formal business networks'.[122] Opportunity entrepreneurs are often 'highly educated, possess prior managerial experience and usually have solid job alternatives with good salaries'.[123] It is important to build on the experience of those who are successful by publicising the value of women and showing that they are equal. This must start with education and giving to women genuine opportunities to develop and flourish, not just as economic participants but as social equals too.[124] This is a lesson from which the rest of Europe may learn.

11.6 CONCLUSION

The Greek case has mirrored many of the issues arising more broadly within the EU and also within the boardroom diversity debates. The business case has been pushed more strongly than the equality arguments in European policy. This may be viewed as a positive start in that it recognises the need to help women in economic terms. Similarly, from a business perspective, there has been acceptance of the need for more women to participate in boardrooms, and there has been an increase in the number of female directors. However, there are limitations in the business case. Thus, for example, the increase in number of women directors has not been as great as it could be and nor has progress on the legislative developments at European level. This slow progress on boardroom diversity shows that although the business case has been

---

[120] Militos survey on the Greek Woman entrepreneur, conducted face to face between November 2012 and January 2013: Militos survey results, Spring 2013, available at: www.militos.org.
[121] Warnecke, 'Entrepreneurship and Gender', 459.
[122] Ibid.
[123] Ibid.
[124] See Z. Ventoura, A. Neokosmidi , A. Theofilou , and P. Ioannidis, 'Women Equality in Labour Market, a Myth or a Reality? The Case of Women PR Managers' (2007) 2(4) *Journal of Diversity Management*, 61–68.

important as a catalyst for change and it is an argument that business leaders will recognise, it also has the potential to damage the full democratic capacity of women in the business and political domains. Not only does this business-oriented approach instrumentalise women for the purpose of corporate profits and the shareholders' benefit, but it also commodifies women as a group. The business case risks drowning out equality and social justice-based arguments. Changes that arise from the business arguments might also be temporary rather than permanent, and so they could be considered as more precarious. More worryingly, we see the preference for the business case as reflecting a more general undermining of women's interests that pervades societies across the globe. Women's voices seem to have gained little recognition over different areas, and this dominance of the business case perpetuates the struggle for women's interests to be taken seriously.

A more solid foundation for women's inclusion in business is required, with decision-making that focuses more directly on their empowerment and development as social actors and not just as economic actors.[125] This approach would also be consistent with the increasingly important sustainable value creation agenda promoted throughout this book.

---

[125] H. Al-Dajani and S. Marlow, 'Empowerment and Entrepreneurship: A Theoretical Framework' (2013) 19(5) *International Journal of Entrepreneurial Behaviour and Research*, 503–524. See also UN Global Compact.

PART IV

THINKING AHEAD

Pathways to Sustainable Value Creation

Charlotte Villiers, Beate Sjåfjell and Georgina Tsagas

12.1 CONTINUING ECONOMIC, SOCIAL, POLITICAL AND ENVIRONMENTAL CHALLENGES ACROSS EUROPE

Europe has faced many challenges since the global financial crisis of 2007–2008, which was highly damaging across the world. Countries in the European Economic Area – the European Union (EU) and the three European Free Trade Association states of the European Economic Areas Agreement – did not escape the severe economic impacts. The austerity policies that many countries implemented brought with them further problems, putting the euro under strain, and many European countries, especially in Southern Europe, saw unemployment levels rise whilst they fell into crippling debt.[1] The experience of Greece, for example, was profoundly destabilising, and the political and economic state of the country and the high debt levels had painful outcomes for many Greek citizens. The response of the EU to Greece's ordeal did little to alleviate the pain. This book was inspired by the Greek debt crisis, and the chapter contributions together demonstrate that the financial crisis and its aftermath was one of many challenges to threaten the stability of the EU. The financial crisis left scars that have still not fully healed and that leave the EU vulnerable to further financial and economic disturbances. Greece continues its recovery process with no guarantee of a lasting positive outcome.

More recently, Brexit has now been completed with the UK's transition to departure ending on 31 December 2021. The UK is no longer a member of the EU. The process leading up to the exit date was exhausting and politically

---

[1] K. Busch, C. Hermann, K. Hinrichs and T. Schulten, *Euro Crisis, Austerity Policy and the European Social Model: How Crisis Policies in Southern Europe Threaten the EU's Social Dimension* (Berlin: Friedrich Ebert Stiftung, 2013).

difficult for the UK and EU negotiators, resulting in a compromise in the Trade and Cooperation Agreement that forms the basis of subsequent negotiations for trade agreements that are likely to be just as, if not more, difficult. Indeed, the first quarter of 2021 was fraught with bureaucratic costs and barriers for imports and exports between the UK and the EU. In January 2021, for example, the UK experienced a 40.7 per cent (£5.6 billion) fall in exports of goods to the EU and a 28.8 per cent (£6.6 billion) fall in imports of goods from the EU.[2] Brexit has led to tensions for the Northern Ireland Peace settlement, with border controls leading to growing threats to the peace that was reached by the Good Friday Agreement in 1998.[3] Brexit has potential repercussions beyond the relationship between the UK and the EU. At best, Brexit has left the EU potentially less stable than before,[4] and the EU will require strenuous efforts among the remaining twenty-seven states to maintain unity and solidarity in the face of further challenges.

On top of these economic and political challenges, the world was plunged into an enormous health crisis at the very end of 2019 that fully took hold early in 2020. Zetsche and Consiglio have highlighted starkly in Chapter 2 the immense tragedy of the world-wide COVID 19 pandemic.[5] The number of lives lost and the monstrous strain placed upon healthcare systems and the enormous disruption were monumental across the globe. The economic challenges have, of course, been increased by the pandemic, and some of these challenges have spilled over into socio-political tensions connected to vaccine supplies and roll-outs with some nationalistic and protectionist signals becoming apparent.[6] The pandemic laid bare the severe global inequalities

---

[2]   Office for National Statistics, 'UK Trade: January 2021' (12 March 2021), available at: www.ons
      .gov.uk/economy/nationalaccounts/balanceofpayments/bulletins/uktrade/january2021.
[3]   Directorate General for Internal Policies, Policy Department for Citizens' Rights and
      Constitutional Affairs, UK Withdrawal ('Brexit') and the Good Friday Agreement,
      European Parliament, PE 596.826, November 2017; A. Fleming, 'Analysis: What is Brexit
      doing to Northern Ireland?', BBC, (9 April 2021), available at: www.bbc.co.uk/news/uk-
      politics-56678489; R. Gramer and A. McKinnon, 'Brexit Fallout Could 'Collapse' the Good
      Friday Agreement', Foreign Policy Insider Access (24 September 2021), available at: https://
      foreignpolicy.com/2021/09/24/northern-ireland-coveney-brexit-protocol-good-friday/.
[4]   G. Baldini, and N. Chelotti, 'The Brexit Effect: Political Implications of the Exit of the United
      Kingdom from the European Union' (2022) 43(3) *International Political Science Review*,
      319–328. For a different view see M. Gastinger, 'Introducing the EU exit index measuring
      each member state's propensity to leave the European Union' (2021), 22(3) *European Union
      Politics*, 566–585.
[5]   D. Zetsche and R. Consiglio, 'Ten Million or One Hundred Million Casualties? COVID-19
      Crisis and Europe's Sustainability Agenda', Chapter 2 in this volume.
[6]   BBC, 'Covid: What is happening with the EU vaccine rollout?' (25 April 2021), available at:
      www.bbc.co.uk/news/explainers-52380823.

that were already in existence before the virus struck, and it showed that vulnerable groups and minorities were especially susceptible to the malign impacts of disease and economic fragility. Villiers and Russell have shown in Chapter 11 how women had already borne the brunt of the economic downturn following the financial crisis and in the Greek debt crisis.[7] Research has also shown that across the world, women also suffered noticeably from COVID-19, not so much physically but economically, and progress in terms of gender equality was stalled.[8]

Alongside these difficult political issues, the world is witnessing increasingly alarming evidence of global climate change. The Indonesian floods and Californian and Australian bushfires of 2020 were just as much a matter of concern for the EU as for the rest of the planet. The refugee/migrant crisis that has affected Europe since 2015, whilst predominantly arising from situations of conflict, could also be connected to climate change, which may have contributed to instability such as the four-year drought that preceded the 2011 uprising against the Assad regime in Syria.[9]

The EU regulatory and political structures exacerbate some of the inequalities that the Greek example brought out in the midst of the global financial downturn and that the COVID-19 pandemic also highlighted. Some of those inequalities also arise as a result of the behaviours of corporate leaders and their investors. Corporations, and the laws and social norms under which they operate, continue to be influenced by the shareholder primacy approach, which imposes significant limitations on the potential of business to be a force for good. However, there is a growing interest in the concept of corporate purpose,[10] and the possibilities for corporations to be designed to operate for social benefit through integrating the concept of sustainable value creation. There are examples presented within the book that provide some optimism. Lynch Fannon and Boland, for example, write in Chapter 3 about the possibilities for corporations to make a substantial contribution towards the EU social market

7   C. Villiers and R. Russell, 'The Role of Women in Stimulating New Types of Value Creation', Chapter 11 in this volume.

8   United Nations, 'Policy Brief: The Impact of Covid 19 on Women' (9 April 2020); and European Commission, '2021 Report on Gender Equality in the EU' (10 August 2021).

9   UK Climate Change and Migration Coalition, 'Briefing Q&A: climate change and the refugee crisis' (September 2015), available at: https://climatemigration.org.uk/ briefing-qa-climate-change-and-the-refugee-crisis/.

10 See, for example, World Economic Forum, 'It's time to redefine the purpose of business. Here's a roadmap', available at: www.weforum.org/agenda/2020/01/its-time-for-a-radical-rethink-of-corporate-purpose/#:~:text=So%2C%20let%20me%20be%20clear,fair%20%E2%80%93%20not%20fake%20%E2%80%93%20profits.

economy,[11] and Lambooy and colleagues highlight in Chapter 10 the positive example of the Dutch social enterprise Dopper.[12] These examples might be extended by ensuring that business in general is operated along more ethical lines and contributes to global societal goals of sustainability. This includes but is not limited to supporting the United Nations Sustainable Development Goals,[13] and by upholding principles of equality, including gender equality, as is suggested by Villiers and Russell in Chapter 11.[14]

A number of the contributions in this book have noted the continuing influence of neo-liberal ideologies within the Eurozone. Johnston and Pugh, for example, demonstrate, in Chapter 4 how these ideological drivers have led to the pursuit of the spending cuts and austerity measures that sought to protect the Eurozone from further outside shocks, but their effect was to increase the inequality that was already made worse by the quantitative easing that was used to mitigate the effects of the financial crisis.[15] The economic measures that were introduced resulted in reducing labour income and power, which only weakened the different economies further, creating a risk of both economic and political instability. Such neo-liberal policies are unlikely to make improvements. Some international institutions such as the International Monetary Fund and the Organisation for Economic Co-operation and Development (OECD) have now recognised the mistaken responses and have suggested that neo-liberalism may in fact have been 'oversold'.[16]

Despite the continuing challenges and threats, the EU has shown a real willingness to strive towards a more sustainable future and has set in motion a number of plans and projects to bring about the required changes. Sustainability is now on the agenda of many EU policies, as underlined in the EU's Green Deal, its Sustainable Finance initiative, its Sustainable Corporate

[11] I. Lynch Fannon and M. J. Boland, 'The Corporation and the EU Social Market Economy: A Renewed Commitment', Chapter 3 in this volume.

[12] T. E. Lambooy et al., 'The Contribution of Social Enterprises to Value Creation in Europe', Chapter 10 in this volume.

[13] United Nations, United Nations General Assembly resolution 70/1, *Transforming Our World: The 2030 Agenda for Sustainable Development*, A/RES/70/1 (25 September 2015), available at: www.un.org/en/development/desa/population/migration/generalassembly/docs/globalcompact/A_RES_70_1_E.pdf.

[14] Villiers and Russell, Chapter 11 in this volume.

[15] A. Johnston and T. Pugh, 'Fiscal Austerity and Monetary Largesse: The EU's Constitutional and Ideological Straitjacket', Chapter 4 in this volume.

[16] See, for example, J. D. Ostry, P. Loungani and D. Furceri, 'Neoliberalism Oversold?' (June 2016) 53(2) *Finance and Development*, 38–41, available at: www.imf.org/external/pubs/ft/fandd/2016/06/ostry.htm; P. Pierris and P. Wegmann, 'The OECD: new wings or still the same old club?', OECD Observer (7 April 2017), available at: www.oecd-ilibrary.org/sites/4f89f03f-en/index.html?itemId=/content/paper/4f89f03f-en.

Governance initiative and its plan for a way out of the global pandemic and into a 'greener, more digital and more socially just Europe'.[17] What could be suggested as possible pathways towards a future in which sustainable value creation can be achieved?

12.2 ALTERNATIVES TO AUSTERITY – INSTITUTIONAL STRENGTH, REBALANCED STRUCTURES AND FISCAL RISK SHARING

Chapter 6, from Liargovas and Kratimenou, which provides an account of the impact of fiscal austerity imposed on Greece, shows that the austerity and rescue package did not work and created further inequalities among the different EU Member States.[18] Liargovas and Kratimenou put forward an argument that, to be successful, austerity measures should be sensitive to the peculiarities and weakness of the economies that they are targeting. Greece, for example, not only had a weak export base but also had governance problems that included policies that impeded growth, corruption and rent seeking. Yet the austerity package imposed on Greece did not take account of these features. Greece requires instead a larger export base and stronger institutions. More specifically, Greece should have developed a minimum income guarantee to boost spending power of its citizens, a land use plan, greater fiscal transparency and a more stable tax system. The austerity programme did not introduce these measures and so was not effective for Greece. The Greek experience has taught us that in countries of weak economic base, institutional capacities and policy effectiveness, austerity leads to worse economic outcomes and no gains in terms of gross domestic product growth. As well as expanding its export base, Greece should make effort to improve its institutions as a protection against

---

[17] The European Commission, Communication from the Commission to the European Parliament, the European Council, the Council, the European Economic and Social Committee and the Committee of the Regions: The European Green Deal, 11.12.2019, COM (2019) 640 final; European Commission, Communication from the Commission to the European Parliament, the European Council, the Council, the European Central Bank, the European Economic and Social Committee and the Committee of the Regions, 'Action Plan: Financing Sustainable Growth', 08.03.2018, COM(2018) 97 final; the Sustainable Corporate Governance initiative as put forward in the European Green Deal section 2.2.1, see the European Commission's public consultation on the topic at: www.ec.europa.eu/ info/law/better-regulation/have-your-say/initiatives/12548-Sustainable-corporate-governance_ en; the European Commission, 'Tackling the COVID-19 pandemic and starting Europe's recovery', in *Von der Leyen Commission: Two Years On*, available at: www.ec.europa.eu/info/ about-european-commission/what-european-commission-does/delivering-political-priorities/ von-der-leyen-commission-two-years_en.

[18] P. Liargovas and V. Kratimenou, 'The Economic Adjustment Programmes of Greece (2010–2018): Why Failure?', Chapter 6 in this volume.

further crises or shocks. Greek policy makers should also seek to change its policy mix from tax-based austerity to an expenditure-based programme.

More broadly, across the EU, a similar shift away from a debt-fuelled growth model that has acted as a political and social substitute for productivity-enhancing reforms is required, but not by means of a neo-liberal prescription of weakened and cheapened labour or reduced social protection. Increased fiscal risk-sharing and a banking union within the Eurozone to address the structural imbalances may be part of the answer. Further, tax and transfer policies may have a positive role if they are well designed and implemented, alongside support for lifelong skills development and learning. Additionally, some levelling up of economies by means of income transfers between Member States and a supranational social security system could be of assistance, but for all these measures to be possible there will be legal and political structures to overcome. Indeed, as Johnston and Pugh observe in Chapter 4, without constitutional change, whether loosening the constraints on public debt or providing for fiscal transfers between Member States, and without an ideological shift away from neo-liberalism, sustainable growth within the EU will remain elusive.

12.3 STRIVING TOWARDS SUSTAINABILITY

In Chapter 5, Kyriakides explores the meaning of the concept of sustainability in the context of the new Eurozone after the global financial crisis.[19] Sustainability has been an important theme throughout this book, and hopefully this contributes somewhat to the literature that has sought to make sense of the word. Kyriakides concludes that there are three key elements within sustainability: the temporal, multi-generational requirement that demands consideration by the current generation for the needs of future generations; the need to include socio-political and ecological factors in the evaluation of sustainability, and not be confined in economic indicators; and the ability of a system to adequately respond to external shocks, especially the existence of a capital stock that could provide a buffer for coping with unforeseen circumstances. Kyriakides confirms that overall, sustainability still remains unachieved. Whilst there is now widespread concern for sustainability, that concern still focuses too closely upon financial issues,[20] but does not consider the broader socio-political and ecological perspectives. This narrow

---

[19] A. Kyriakides, 'Sustainability and Eurozone 2.0: Still Impossible?', Chapter 5 in this volume.
[20] See, for example, S. Hiss, 'The Politics of the Financialization of Sustainability' (2013) 17(3) *Competition & Change*, 234–247.

approach did not give rise to wholly effective responses to European-wide crises. As Kyriakides demonstrated, the pre-crisis EU and Eurozone operating framework had strong ordoliberal foundations, weak technocratic institutions, and few references to sustainability. This overall framework was characterised by extensive imbalances, and there were significant inequalities among the Member States, particularly those within the Eurozone. Despite these inequalities, the response to the financial crisis resulted in 'even more rules of even stricter budgetary discipline, with enhanced sanctions upon non-compliance'.[21] The effect was to impose difficult and damaging economic challenges upon those Member States that were already suffering debt problems. The financial assistance offered to those countries was accompanied by austerity policies that created obstacles to any sustainability possibilities.

From a sustainability perspective, there were measures assumed during the Eurozone crisis that could have furthered sustainable development within the Eurozone, including the creation of a Eurozone-targeted financial assistance mechanism, the evaluation of the macro-economic effect of policies through the European Innovation Partnership and the enhanced coordination of pension systems through the European Insurance and Occupational Pensions Authority. However, the economic paradigm that still underlies these measures leads to them having a negative rather than a positive effect. Kyriakides concludes that in order to improve sustainability within the Eurozone, additional steps are required. First the crisis measures and their implementation need to be divorced from a neo-liberal stance, and secondly the institutions need to be more democratic and perhaps less technocratic. This can be achieved by simplifying the operating framework of all the different institutions and actors involved in the policy-making process, as well as their legal and regulatory frameworks in order to make their impact quicker and stronger and more democratic.[22]

The suggestions made by Cullen, Mähönen and Rapp Nilsen in Chapter 8, which aim to elevate the focus on sustainability and the risks of unsustainability in the arena of financial regulation and European Central Bank policy development, shows how the financial system can be geared towards making a significant contribution towards ensuring sustainable value creation.[23] The European Central Bank, for example, has capacity to use its mandate to support the financing of sustainable investments where this does not conflict with

[21] Kyriakides, Chapter 5 in this volume.

[22] Ibid.

[23] J. Cullen, J. Mähönen and H. Rapp Nilsen, 'Financing Sustainable Value Creation', Chapter 8 in this volume.

its primary objective of maintaining price stability. The European Central Bank could incorporate risks to sustainability into its strategy and operations via the use of monetary policy through collateral asset eligibility, and via the margins charged on collateral when accepted in exchange for reserves.

Noting that many of the work programmes at EU level around sustainability have been limited to the climate change aspects, Cullen, Mähönen and Rapp Nilsen propose a more comprehensive parameter through which to assess sustainability impacts. They view an incentive-generative 'green supporting factor' as inadequate and suggest instead the introduction of a comprehensive set of harmful activities factors. By raising the capital requirements on certain unsustainable assets, banks would have to fund such assets with a greater proportion of capital (shareholder funds), thereby raising banks' cost of funding. In addition, the chapter includes a proposal of strict duties of due diligence, requiring a positive compliance obligation to assess and demonstrate how financial institutions have mitigated or prevented sustainability risks from materialising. The chapter argues overall for a fundamental recalibration of the role and duties of financial system participants to prevent funding of unsustainable activities causing damage to the ecosystem and to the social foundation of humanity.[24]

12.4 LEGAL FRAMEWORK SUPPORT

As well as the political and financial institutions within the Eurozone and the EU as a whole, it is clear that business institutions also have a role to play. A number of chapters within the book have explored the role of business actors. Businesses have potential to help drive us along the journey towards sustainability and a stronger economy but they are also part of the problems faced. The legal framework surrounding the corporate activities is of significance and this is highlighted in Chapter 7, contributed by Mähönen, which calls for hard law to be created that will assist the sustainability activists within the business community.[25] Mähönen argues that the key problem of corporate law is whether the institutional investor and asset manager engagement contributes to long-term sustainability of public companies, or just increases their attractiveness for short-term profit maximising. Ultimately, however, corporate governance is about value choices, whether it is more efficient to use the corporate added value to provide shareholders with dividends and share buy-backs or to make investments and future added value. In response to this corporate governance dilemma, Mähönen suggests that hard law is required

---

[24] Ibid.
[25] J. Mähönen, 'Shareholder Activism: Driver or Obstacle for Sustainable Value Creation?', Chapter 7 in this volume.

to enable the activists to face up to the powerful short-term investors who currently benefit from a shareholder primacy paradigm that pervades the decisions and behaviours of the corporate leaders. The short-term investors have ability to use derivatives and other financial innovations to decouple their voting power from their economic interest. Other institutional investors, such as pension funds, can offer little help, since they are vulnerable to being used as a vehicle for advancing political/social goals unrelated to shareholder interests generally. The state as a market actor has greater potential to support a sustainability agenda since the state is governed not only by market rationality and corporate law but also by public law considerations. The state investor's governance structure is regulated by constitutional and administrative law, and its actions governed by judicial review. Strong state market actors such as Norway, either directly as a shareholder in state-owned enterprises or indirectly through sovereign wealth funds, has been shown in this way to be an important driver for sustainability.[26]

12.5 SAY GOODBYE TO SHAREHOLDER PRIMACY

The problem with advancing a shareholder primacy business model is that it allows money managers and their advocates to demand additional rights that limit the ability of corporations to pursue the most profitable courses of action for the end-user investors and to pursue a sustainable business course. The boards bow to the pressure and frequently resort to pursuing distributable profits under a short-term orientation rather than pursuing a longer term agenda of increasing the company's going concern value, keeping a solid balance sheet, capital investments, research and development, and preserving jobs.

A first step towards countering this pervasive shareholder power is to improve the transparency of shareholder activism. The Transparency Directive goes some way towards this, alongside other measures such as making derivative arrangements transparent; requiring institutional investors to make their investment policies public; and tightening 'act in concert' regulation. Another step is to alter the fiduciary duties of the boards of both the productive companies and the institutional investors to act in the best interest of their end-investors and ultimate beneficiaries, as suggested by the High Level Expert Group on Sustainable Finance in its Final Report in January 2018,[27] and endorsed by the European Commission in its Action Plan on sustainable finance in March 2018.

---

[26] Ibid.
[27] EU High-level Expert Group on Sustainable Finance, 'Financing a sustainable European economy: final report 2018' (31 January 2018), available at: www.ec.europa.eu/info/sites/default/files/180131-sustainable-finance-final-report_en.pdf.

Such a step should include the Commission's suggested Actions 7 and 10, fostering sustainable corporate governance and attenuating short-termism in capital markets and clarifying institutional investors' and asset managers' duties.[28] Ultimately, in answer to the question of what is the board's possibility to ensure a sustainable business model, Mähönen concludes in Chapter 7 that hard law on the corporate purpose and board duties might be the only efficient way to ensure sustainability, rather than relying on the shareholders.[29]

More broadly, in Chapter 3, Lynch Fannon and Boland identify the real challenge as establishing how to reconcile economics and ethics and how to articulate a legal theory which will support an ethical corporation and the actors within that corporation.[30] In the European context they see some potential in communitarian theory, including Catholic social theory, which resonates with the values of 'social Europe' (perhaps not surprising as the EU is largely made up of European states with Catholic traditions). The pope decries an economic system that 'tends to devour everything which stands in the way of increased profits, whatever is fragile, like the environment, is defenceless before the interests of a deified market, which becomes the only rule'.[31] To what extent these theories will have influence over the long term remains to be seen in the future but, for now, we can look to some more positive practices that provide examples of the possibilities already evident.

In Chapter 9, Sjafjell and Tsagas highlight the importance of incorporating sustainable value creation into company law and corporate governance.[32] They underline the need to move away from the misleading emphasis upon shareholder primacy towards a more sustainability-oriented and participative approach to regulating the corporation. Building on the emerging concept of sustainable value creation in corporate governance, they position their discussion of how to integrate sustainable value fully into corporate governance on the research-based concept of sustainability that forms the framework for this volume.[33] Drawing on the results of the EU-funded project Sustainable Market Actors for Responsible Trade (SMART, 2016–2020), of which all

---

[28] European Commission, 'Action Plan: Financing Sustainable Growth', sections 3.2 and 4.2.

[29] Mähönen, Chapter 7 in this volume.

[30] Lynch Fannon and Boland, Chapter 3 in this volume.

[31] *Apostolic Exhortation Evangelii Gaudium of the Holy Father Francis to the Bishops, Clergy, Consecrated Persons and the Lay Faithful on the Proclamation of the Gospel in Today's World* (Vatican City: Vatican Press, 2013), para. 56, p. 47, cited in Lynch Fannon and Boland, Chapter 3 in this volume.

[32] B. Sjåfjell and G. Tsagas, 'Integrating Sustainable Value Creation in Corporate Governance: Company Law, Corporate Governance and the Constitution of the Company', Chapter 9 in this volume.

[33] As outlined in C. Villiers, B. Sjåfjell and G. Tsagas, 'Stimulating Value Creation in a Europe in Crisis', Chapter 1 in this volume.

editors and several of the contributors were members, they outline how sustainable value creation within planetary boundaries could be integrated in corporate governance through an EU company law reform, with sustainability due diligence across global value chains as a key tool. This engages with and contributes to the debate on the ongoing work of the EU with its Sustainable Corporate Governance Initiative.

Corporate Governance Codes, which very much have been proponents for shareholder primacy, have begun to shift towards sustainable value creation. However, as Sjåfjell and Tsagas identify, this shift is not consistent across the EU, nor is it clear in its understanding of what 'sustainable value' means even in Codes where this language is used. The authors therefore suggest that further revisions of Corporate Governance Codes should be undertaken, with a more systematic inclusion of a research-based concept of sustainable value creation, as suggested in the law reform proposal.

The individual company will need to integrate sustainability into its governance, whether that is a result of effective legislative reform in Europe, or of compliance with corporate governance codes that are revised to promote sustainability, or in the absence of either and rather in recognition of the business and financial risks of continued unsustainability. To set the tone from the top, crucial to integrate sustainability into the governance of a company, Sjåfjell and Tsagas suggest a model for how to integrate sustainable value creation into the constitution of the individual company – and how policymakers across Europe could do so in model constitutions as well.

12.6 SOCIAL ENTERPRISE AND INNOVATION IN BUSINESS

In Chapter 10, Lambooy and colleagues have demonstrated the potential contribution of social enterprises, a fast-growing sector developing across the EU.[34] These social enterprises have developed responses to the societal gaps that emerged as a result of governments' strategies to withdraw from many areas and activities, and to leave them open for market actors. The social enterprises operate alongside those corporations and actors in the traditional spaces, these being market, government, civil society and private households. The growing significance of social enterprises has encouraged various EU countries to develop their own tailor-made legislation.

Other countries, such as the Netherlands, have not taken that step, leaving for social entrepreneurs the option to incorporate their business activities by using mainly a combination of the Dutch BV and the Dutch foundation, and it

[34] Lambooy et al., Chapter 10 in this volume.

seems likely that steps will be taken in the future to introduce more tailor-made legislation. A notable feature of the social enterprise and the regulations to support it across the European jurisdictions is the principle concerning the participation of stakeholders. The chapter presents a case study of Dopper BV, assessing the relevance of the institutional and legal environment with the inner (legal and participatory governance) structure of the enterprise. Whilst there are no formalised participation mechanisms in Dopper's governance structure for internal stakeholders, nor for external stakeholders, Dopper has introduced innovative informal means and consultation processes to involve the stakeholders in the decision-making process, such as the One Page Plans, consumer panels, thematic events and so on. Although neither the employees nor the external stakeholders have acquired shares or membership and thus they are not entitled to participate in formal decision-making processes, they receive adequate information enabling them to influence the decisions.

Dopper is an example of a participatory way of contributing to fulfilling the social purpose: but without formal supportive legislation there is a risk of 'mission drift' at some point in the future, owing to change in ownership, management, economic situation and so on. For example, if the organisation were to change its original 'for purpose' mission into a regular 'for profit' mission, all informal stakeholder participation mechanisms would likewise be changed or removed. Only formalised structures guarantee stakeholder participation in the future, and can assist in protecting the 'for purpose' mission of the social enterprise. Tailor-made legislation can play that role and accommodate such formalised structures. The chapter showed that social enterprises have the potential to contribute to growth and simultaneously to development of a sustainable path towards the future. Supporting legislation could strengthen the contribution of this sector.

12.7 GENDER EQUALITY AND ENCOURAGING FEMALE PARTICIPATION IN BUSINESS

In Chapter 11, Villiers and Russell highlight the important contribution that women have made to the global economy and that it is important to include them in policy decisions and in business activities.[35] They show how the Greek experience mirrors many of the issues arising more broadly within the EU and also within the boardroom diversity debates. They also highlight how women suffer more seriously the impacts of economic stress and other crises such as the COVID-19 pandemic. They also note the contribution of women

---

[35] Villiers and Russell, Chapter 11 in this volume.

to value creation as well as supporting their economies and their social and family communities in times of crisis. Villiers and Russell suggest that whilst the business case has its place, it would be a mistake to rely solely on that approach to encourage female participation and gender equality in business. The risk is that this approach would merely instrumentalise their role to enhance profits rather than address the particular challenges that women have faced in the European economy. Whilst the business case has been important as a catalyst for change and it is an argument that business leaders will recognise, it also has the potential to damage the full democratic capacity of women in the business and political domains. The business case risks drowning out equality and social justice-based arguments. An urgent requirement is a more solid foundation for women's inclusion in business and decision-making that focuses more directly on their empowerment and development as social actors and not just as economic actors.

12.8 CONCLUDING REFLECTIONS

This book has flagged up some pressing concerns as regards the development and future of the EU and offers suggestions on how to move forward in addressing the challenges ahead. The EU needs to continue its emergent shift away from a neo-liberal agenda and fully onto a path towards a genuine sustainability agenda that is underpinned by solid and strong theories, promoting and reinforcing possibilities for positive futures.

Neo-liberalism and shareholder primacy have had their time. They have not produced a prosperous, sustainable economy or society for Europe or for any other regions of the globe. More stable, resilient and democratic institutional structures are necessary that can support more equal distributions between states and between people. Business actors have a role to play because their actions impact upon the possibilities. The COVID-19 pandemic has highlighted the risks and the potential of relying on business to help in providing solutions and supporting the recovery efforts. The more progressive business forms, including some social enterprises, are providing some useful examples, as are many of the active political and entrepreneurial women.

At the same time, sustainable value creation must not be seen as a niche approach for certain segments of the business world. Reform of mainstream business and finance is therefore crucial. Our volume has engaged with some of the fundamentally important fields in this context. We do not, however, present these as the only elements of reform. From a perspective of policy coherence for sustainability and very much in line with the EU's overarching Treaty goals, legal duties and legal bases, all areas of law and policy should

314 Charlotte Villiers, Beate Sjåfjell and Georgina Tsagas

be assessed and reformed as and to the extent necessary, to integrate sustainability into the operations and activities of the EU.[36] From a business perspective, important fields, besides those dealt with in our volume, include product regulation, notably the Circular Economy Packages,[37] public procurement with its potential for channelling public investments towards sustainability,[38] and competition law and state aid law, which also shape and may constrain business cooperation and business-state collaboration to promote sustainability.[39] In the field of international law and policy, the EU should strengthen its role as a global actor with a sustainability-oriented perspective, and work to mitigate and reverse the unsustainabilities of the current trade and investment regimes,[40] including the area of intellectual property rights.[41]

A common thread through all legislative and policy reforms of and relevant to business and finance should be sustainable value creation within planetary boundaries as an overarching purpose for business, with mandatory rules to ensure that sustainability is integrated into the governance of business across global value chains. These are key features that will provide a context that can make a more sustainable economy truly possible.

[36] C. Gammage, 'The EU's Evolving Commitment to Promoting Sustainability in its External Actions: Policy (In)Coherence for Development?' (2020) SMART working paper on file with current authors, University of Oslo; C. Gammage, S. E. Stave, H. Ahlström and B. Sjåfjell, 'SMART Guidelines: Making Policy Coherence for Development Fit for Purpose' (8 May 2020), 2020–13 *University of Oslo Faculty of Law Research Paper*, 20–11 *Nordic & European Company Law Working Paper*, available at SSRN: https://ssrn.com/abstract=3596036.

[37] The European Commission, 'EU Circular Economy Action Plan', available at: www.ec.europa.eu/environment/circular-economy/; E. Maitre-Ekern, 'Re-Thinking Producer Responsibility for a Sustainable Circular Economy: From Extended Producer Responsibility to Pre-market Producer Responsibility' (2021) 286 *Journal of Cleaner Production*, 125454.

[38] The European Commission, 'Green and Sustainable Public Procurement', available at: www.ec.europa.eu/environment/gpp/versus_en.htm; M. Andhov, R. Caranta, T. Stoffel, J. Grandia, W. A. Janssen, R. Vornicu, J. J. Czarnezki, A. Gromnica, K. Tallbo, O. Martin-Ortega, L. Mélon, Å. Edman, P. Göthberg, P. Nohrstedt and A. Wiesbrock, 'Sustainability through public procurement: the way forward – reform proposals' (23 March 2020), available at SSRN: https://ssrn.com/abstract=3559393.

[39] J. Nowag, *Environmental Integration in Competition and Free-Movement Laws* (Oxford: Oxford University Press, 2016).

[40] T. Novitz, 'Supply Chains and Temporary Migrant Labour: The Relevance of Trade and Sustainability Frameworks', in D. Ashiagbor (ed.), *Re-imagining Labour Law for Development: Informal Work in the Global North and South*, (Oxford: Hart Publishing, 2019), pp. 191–211; B. Sjåfjell, J. T. Mähönen, M. B. Taylor, E. Maitre-Ekern, M. van der Velden, T. A. Novitz, C. Gammage, J. Cullen, M. Andhov and R. Caranta, 'Supporting the Transition to Sustainability: SMART Reform Proposals' (13 December 13 2019) 2019–63 *University of Oslo Faculty of Law Research Paper*, 20–05 *Nordic & European Company Law Working Paper*, available at SSRN: https://ssrn.com/abstract=3503310.

[41] O. A. Rognstad and I. B. Ørstavik (eds.), *Intellectual Property and Sustainable Markets* (Cheltenham: Edward Elgar Publishing, 2021).

Index